Steck-Vaughn

GED

SCIENCE

PROGRAM CONSULTANTS

Liz Anderson, Director of Adult Education/Skills Training
Northwest Shoals Community College
Muscle Shoals, Alabama

Mary Ann Corley, Ph.D., Director
Lindy Boggs National Center for Community Literacy
Loyola University New Orleans
New Orleans, Louisiana

Nancy Dunlap, Adult Education Coordinator
Northside Independent School District
San Antonio, Texas

Roger M. Hansard, Director of Adult Education
CCARE Learning Center
Tazewell, Tennessee

Nancy Lawrence, M.A.
Education and Curriculum Consultant
Butler, Pennsylvania

Pat L. Taylor, STARS Consultant for GEDTS
Adult Education/GED Programs
Mesa, Arizona

STECK-VAUGHN
ELEMENTARY · SECONDARY · ADULT · LIBRARY

A Harcourt Company

www.steck-vaughn.com

Acknowledgments

Executive Editor: Ellen Northcutt

Supervising Editor: Julie Higgins

Associate Director of Design: Cynthia Ellis

Designers: Rusty Kaim
Katie Nott

Media Researcher: Sarah Fraser

Editorial Development: Learning Unlimited, Oak Park, Illinois

Production Development: LaurelTech

Cartographer: maps.com

Photography: Cover: (lightning) ©Kent Wood/Photo Researchers, Inc.; (prism) ©James L. Amos/Peter Arnold, Inc.; (red eyed tree frog) ©Tim Davis/ Photo Researchers, Inc.; (space station) Courtesy NASA; p.i ©Kent Wood/Photo Researchers, Inc.; p.32a ©Eyewire; p.32b ©David Gifford/Science Photo Library/ Photo Researchers, Inc.; pp.108a, 108b ©SYGMA; p.156a ©Larry Mulvehill/ Science Source/Photo Researchers, Inc.

ISBN 0-7398-2833-9

Printed in the United States of America.

21 22 23 0877 14 13

4500443199

Contents

What Are the GED Tests?

You have taken a big step in your life by deciding to take the GED Tests. By the time that you have opened this book, you have made a second important decision: to put in the time and effort to prepare for the tests. You may feel nervous about what is ahead, which is only natural. Relax and read the following pages to find out more about the GED Tests in general and the Science Test in particular.

The GED Tests are the five tests of General Educational Development. The GED Testing Service of the American Council on Education makes them available to adults who did not graduate from high school. When you pass the GED Tests, you will receive a certificate that is regarded as equivalent to a high school diploma. Employers in private industry and government, as well as admissions officers in colleges and universities, accept the GED certificate as they would a high school diploma.

The GED Tests cover the same subjects that people study in high school. The five subject areas include: Language Arts, Writing and Language Arts, Reading (which, together, are equivalent to high school English), Social Studies, Science, and Mathematics. You will not be required to know all the information that is usually taught in high school. However, across the five tests you will be tested on your ability to read and process information, solve problems, and communicate effectively. Some of the states in the U.S. also require a test on the U.S. Constitution or on state government. Check with your local adult education center to see if your state requires such a test.

Each year more than 800,000 people take the GED Tests. Of those completing the test battery, 70 percent earn their GED certificates. The *Steck-Vaughn GED Series* will help you pass the GED Tests by providing instruction and practice in the skill areas needed to pass, practice with test items like those found on the GED Test, test-taking tips, timed-test practice, and evaluation charts to help track your progress.

There are five separate GED Tests. The chart on page 2 gives you information on the content, number of items, and time limit for each test. Because states have different requirements for how many tests you take in a day or testing period, you need to check with your local adult education center for the requirements in your state, province, or territory.

The Tests of General Educational Development

Test	Content Areas	Items	Time Limit
Language Arts, Writing, Part I	Organization 15% Sentence Structure 30% Usage 30% Mechanics 25%	50 questions	75 minutes
Language Arts, Writing, Part II	Essay		45 minutes
Social Studies	U.S. History 25% World History 15% Civics and Government 25% Geography 15% Economics 20%	50 questions	70 minutes
Science	Life Science 45% Earth and Space Science 20% Physical Science 35%	50 questions	80 minutes
Language Arts, Reading	Nonfiction Texts 25% Literary Texts 75% • Prose Fiction • Poetry • Drama	40 questions	65 minutes

Mathematics	Number Operations
	  and Number Sense 25%
	Measurement and
	  Geometry 25%
	Data Analysis, Statistics,
	  and Probability 25%
	Algebra 25%
		Part I: 25 questions
		with a calculator
		Part II: 25 questions
			90 minutes

In addition to these content areas, you will be asked to answer items based on work- and consumer-related texts across all five tests. These do not require any specialized knowledge, but will ask you draw upon your own observations and life experiences.

The Language Arts, Reading, Social Studies, and Science Tests will ask you to answer questions by interpreting reading passages, diagrams, charts and graphs, maps, cartoons, and practical and historical documents.

The Language Arts, Writing Test will ask you to detect and correct common errors in Edited American English as well as decide on the most effective organization of text. The Essay portion of the Writing Test will ask you to write an essay offering your opinion or an explanation on a single topic of general knowledge.

The Mathematics Test will ask you to solve a variety of word problems, many with graphics, using basic computation, analytical, and reasoning skills.

GED Scores

After you complete each GED Test, you will receive a score for that test. Once you have completed all five GED Tests, you will receive a total score. The total score is an average of all the other scores. The highest score possible on a single test is 800. The scores needed to pass the GED vary depending on where you live. Contact your local adult education center for the minimum passing scores for your state, province, or territory.

Where Can You Go to Take the GED Tests?

The GED Tests are offered year-round throughout the United States and its possessions, on U.S. military bases worldwide, and in Canada. To find out when and where tests are held near you, contact the GED Hot Line at 1-800-62-MY-GED (1-800-626-9433) or one of these institutions in your area:

- An adult education center
- A continuing education center
- A local community college
- A public library
- A private business school or technical school
- The public board of education

In addition, the GED Hot Line and the institutions can give you information regarding necessary identification, testing fees, and writing implements, and on the scientific calculator to be used on the GED Mathematics Test. Also, check on the testing schedule at each institution; some testing centers are open several days a week, and others are open only on weekends.

Other GED Resources

- www.acenet.edu This is the official site for the GED Testing Service. Just follow the GED links throughout the site for information on the test.

- www.steckvaughn.com Follow the Adult Learners link to learn more about available GED preparation materials and www.gedpractice.com. This site also provides other resources for adult learners.

- www.nifl.gov/nifl/ The National Institute for Literacy's site provides information on instruction, federal policies, and national initiatives that affect adult education.

- www.doleta.gov U.S. Department of Labor's Employment and Training Administration site offers information on adult training programs.

Why Should You Take the GED Tests?

A GED certificate is widely recognized as the equivalent of a high school diploma and can help you in the following ways:

Employment

People with GED certificates have proven their determination to succeed by following through with their education. They generally have less difficulty changing jobs or moving up in their present companies. In many cases, employers will not hire someone who does not have a high school diploma or the equivalent.

Education

Many technical schools, vocational schools, or other training programs may require a high school diploma or the equivalent in order to enroll in their programs. However, to enter a college or university, you must have a high school diploma or the equivalent.

Personal Development

The most important thing is how you feel about yourself. You now have the unique opportunity to accomplish an important goal. With some effort, you can attain a GED certificate that will help you in the future and make you feel proud of yourself now.

How to Prepare for the GED Tests

Classes for GED preparation are available to anyone who wants to prepare to take the GED Tests.

Most GED preparation programs offer individualized instruction and tutors who can help you identify areas in which you may need help. Many adult education centers offer free day or night classes. The classes are usually informal and allow you to work at your own pace and with other adults who also are studying for the GED Tests.

If you prefer to study by yourself, the *Steck-Vaughn GED Series* has been developed to guide your study through skill instruction and practice exercises. *Steck-Vaughn GED Exercise* books and gedpractice.com are also available to provide you with additional practice for each test.

In addition to working on specific skills, you will be able to take practice GED Tests (like those in this book) in order to check your progress. For information about classes available near you, contact one of the resources in the list on page 3.

What You Need to Know to Pass the Science Test

The GED Science Test examines your ability to understand and interpret science information. You will be asked to think about what you read. You will not be tested on any outside knowledge about science. You will have 80 minutes to answer 50 questions that are based on science text or graphics such as maps, charts, graphs, or diagrams. The test questions are based on material in the areas of Life Science, Earth and Space Science, and Physical Science.

Content Areas

Life Science

About forty-five percent of the items in the test are based on such topics as cells, heredity, health, functions such as respiration and photosynthesis, and the behavior and interdependence of organisms.

Earth and Space Science

About twenty percent of the items are based on such topics as Earth's structure, including landforms and water; earthquakes and volcanoes; weather and climate; and the origin and development of Earth, solar system, and universe.

Physical Science

About thirty-five percent of the test is based on such physical science topics as atoms, elements, compounds, molecules, bonding, radioactivity, matter, energy, waves, and magnetism.

The context for many test items in these content areas also reflects the following areas as described in the National Science Education Standards.

Science as Inquiry

This topic reflects the ability to understand the principles behind scientific methods, reasoning, and processes.

Science and Technology

This topic reflects the use of technology in scientific processes and findings.

Unifying Concepts and Processes

This topic involves an understanding of major concepts, such as "constancy and change" that cut across science content areas.

Science in Personal and Social Perspectives

This topic relates to understanding and action on contemporary issues, such as personal and community health.

History and Nature of Science

This relates to the pursuit of scientific knowledge and historical perspectives on it.

Thinking Skills

The items on the GED Science Test require you to think about science ideas or graphics in several ways. To answer the questions, you will be using four types of thinking skills that you will study in this book.

Comprehension

Comprehension questions require a basic understanding of the meaning and intent of written and graphic materials. They measure the ability to recognize a restatement, paraphrasing, or summary or to identify what is implied in the text. Twenty percent of the questions test comprehension.

Application

Application questions require the ability to apply information that you are given or remember from one situation to a new situation or context. These questions require the ability to identify an illustration of a generalization, principle, or strategy and to apply the appropriate abstraction to a new problem. Twenty percent of the questions test application skills.

Analysis

Analysis questions require the ability to break down information and to see relationships between ideas in order to draw a conclusion, make an inference, distinguish fact from opinion and conclusions from supporting detail, identify cause-and-effect relationships, compare and contrast information, and recognize unstated assumptions. Forty percent of the questions test analysis skills.

Evaluation

Evaluation questions require the ability to assess the validity or accuracy of both written and graphic information, make judgements, draw conclusions, recognize faulty logic, and identify values and beliefs. These also require recognition of the role that values, beliefs, and convictions play in decision-making. Twenty percent of the questions test evaluation skills.

On the following two pages, you will find a sample paragraph and four items. These are similar to actual GED Science Test items and illustrate the four basic thinking skills evaluated on the test. Some of the items on the test are similar to the sample paragraph with several questions based on it. However, many of the items on the test are single items—a short amount of reading material or a graphic—followed by one question. Although it is important to have a familiarity with the science concepts in this book, you will not be asked any questions that require you to simply remember a scientific fact.

Sample Passage and Items

The following is a sample paragraph and test items. Although the paragraph is much shorter than those on the GED Test, the items that follow are similar to those on the test. Following each item is an explanation of the skill area that the item tests as well as an explanation of the correct answer.

Some Amazonian Indians have learned to manage farm plots so that over the years the land changes gradually from cleared farmland back to tropical rain forest. The plots go through stages. In the first stage, the plot is cleared and regular crops are grown. In the second stage, certain wild trees and plants are allowed to return gradually. These wild species provide a variety of products, such as medicines and pesticides. In the third stage, the rain forest eventually reclaims the plot. Meanwhile, other plots are in different stages of use. As a result, the soil and the forest constantly renew themselves while supporting the Indians. In contrast, settlers in the Amazon have cleared millions of acres for crops or timber. After a few years of cultivation, the land wears out.

1. What happens to the farm plot during the second stage?

   (1) The land is cleared.
   (2) Only regular crops grow.
   (3) A mix of crops and wild plants grow.
   (4) Only wild plants grow.
   (5) The rain forest takes over the plot.

Answer: **(3) A mix of crops and wild plants grow.**

Explanation: This item tests comprehension skills. You can find the information in the fourth sentence of the passage, which states that during the second stage, certain wild plants are allowed to return gradually. From this, you can make the inference that both farm crops and wild plants are grown at this stage.

2. The Indians' method of managing farmland in the Amazon is most similar to which of the following?

   (1) grazing cattle in fields
   (2) rotating crops to renew the soil
   (3) using chemical pesticides
   (4) growing a single crop on a large farm
   (5) using fertilizer

Answer: **(2) rotating crops to renew the soil**

Explanation: This item tests your ability to apply the information that you are given to another situation. First, you must understand that some Amazonian Indians manage their farmland so that the soil and the forest can renew themselves. This idea is similar to crop rotation, in which a different crop is planted each season. The other options do not involve the natural renewal of the land.

3. If the Indians kept the wild plants from returning to the farm plot, what would be the result over a few seasons?

   (1) More crops would be grown.
   (2) The wild plants would die out.
   (3) The quality of the crops would improve.
   (4) The crops would wear out the soil.
   (5) The rain forest would take it over.

Answer: **(4) The crops would wear out the soil.**

Explanation: The item tests your ability to analyze information. In this case you are being asked to predict the result of an action. If the Indians continue to grow crops, it is likely that the same thing that happened to millions of acres that were cleared for crops and timber would happen to the small farm plots also. The land would wear out.

4. Which of the following conclusions is supported by information in the passage?

   (1) Large-scale clearing for farming is the best long-term use of the rain forest.
   (2) Acres of rain forest should not be used for growing crops.
   (3) The rain forest is being destroyed at a rate of millions of acres per year.
   (4) Dairy farming would be a better use of the rain forest.
   (5) Some farmers can use the rain forest without destroying it.

Answer: **(5) Some farmers can use the rain forest without destroying it.**

Explanation: This item requires you to evaluate information. First, you must understand the passage. Then, you must choose the conclusion that logically follows from the ideas in the passage. In this case, the conclusion supported by the passage is that a resource, such as a rain forest, can be used without being destroyed. Options (1) and (2) are clearly contradicted by the passage. Option (3) may be true, but nothing in the passage proves it. Option (4) is not mentioned in the passage and there is nothing to support it.

     To help you develop your reading and thinking skills, the answer key for each item in this book has an explanation of why the correct answer is right and why the incorrect answer is wrong. By studying these explanations, you will learn strategies for understanding and thinking about science.

Test-Taking Skills

The GED Science Test will test your ability to apply reading and critical thinking skills to text. This book will help you prepare for this test. In addition, there are some specific ways that you can improve your performance on the test.

Answering the Test Items

- Never skim the directions. Read them carefully so that you know exactly what to do. If you are unsure, ask the test-giver if the directions can be explained.

- Read each question carefully to make sure that you know what it is asking.

- Read all of the answer options carefully, even if you think you know the right answer. Some of the answers may not seem wrong at first glance, but only one answer will be the correct one.

- Before you answer a question, be sure that there is evidence in the passage to support your choice. Don't rely on what you know outside the context of the passage.

- Answer all the items. If you cannot find the correct answer, reduce the number of possible answers by eliminating all the answers you know are wrong. Then go back to the passage to figure out the correct answer. If you still cannot decide, make your best guess.

- Fill in your answer sheet carefully. To record your answers, mark one numbered space on the answer sheet beside the number that corresponds to the item. Mark only one answer space for each item; multiple answers will be scored as incorrect.

- Remember that the GED is a timed test. When the test begins, write down the time you have to finish. Then keep an eye on the time. Do not take a long time on any one item. Answer each item as best you can and go on. If you are spending a lot of time on one item, skip it, making a very light mark next to the item number on the sheet. If you finish before time is up, go back to the items you skipped or were unsure of and give them more thought. (Be sure to erase any extraneous marks you have made.)

- Don't change an answer unless you are certain your answer was wrong. Usually the first answer you choose is the correct one.

- If you feel that you are getting nervous, stop working for a moment. Take a few deep breaths and relax. Then begin working again.

Study Skills

Study Regularly

- If you can, set aside an hour to study every day. If you do not have time every day, set up a schedule of the days you can study. Be sure to pick times when you will be the most relaxed and least likely to be bothered by outside distractions.

- Let others know your study time. Ask them to leave you alone for that period. It helps if you explain to others why this is important.

- You should be relaxed when you study, so find an area that is comfortable for you. If you cannot study at home, go to the library. Most public libraries have areas for reading and studying. If there is a college or university near you, find out if you can use its library. All libraries have dictionaries, encyclopedias, and other resources you can use if you need more information while you're studying.

Organize Your Study Materials

- Be sure to have pens, sharp pencils, and paper for any notes you might want to take.

- Keep all of your books together. If you are taking an adult education class, you probably will be able to borrow some books or other study material.

- Make a notebook or folder for each subject you are studying. Folders with pockets are useful for storing loose papers.

- Keep all of your materials in one place so you do not waste time looking for it each time you study.

Read Regularly

- Read the newspaper, read magazines, read books. Read whatever appeals to you—but read! Regular, daily reading is the best way to improve your reading skills.

- Use the library to find material you like to read. Check the magazine section for publications of interest to you. Most libraries subscribe to hundreds of magazines ranging in interest from news to cars to music to sewing to sports. If you are not familiar with the library, ask a librarian for help. Get a library card so that you can check out material to use at home.

Take Notes

- Take notes on things that interest you or things that you think might be useful.

- When you take notes, do not copy the words directly from the book. Restate the information in your own words.

- Take notes any way you want. You do not have to write in full sentences as long as you can understand your notes later.

- Use outlines, charts, or diagrams to help you organize information and make it easier to learn.

- You may want to take notes in a question-and-answer form, such as: *What is the main idea? The main idea is . . .*

Improve Your Vocabulary

- As you read, do not skip a word you do not know. Instead, try to figure out what the word means. First, omit it from the sentence. Read the sentence without the word and try to put another word in its place. Is the meaning of the sentence the same?

- Make a list of unfamiliar words, look them up in the dictionary, and write down the meanings.

- Since a word may have several meanings, it is best to look up the word while you have the passage with you. Then you can try out the different meanings in the context.

- When you read the definition of a word, restate it in your own words. Use the word in a sentence or two.

- Use the Glossary at the end of this book to review the meanings of the key terms. All of the words you see in **boldface** type are defined in the Glossary. In addition, definitions of other important words are included. Use this list to review important vocabulary for the content areas you are studying.

Make a List of Subject Areas that Give You Trouble

As you go through this book, make a note whenever you do not understand something. Then ask your teacher or another person for help. Later go back and review the topic.

Taking the Test

Before the Test

- If you have never been to the test center, go there the day before you take the test. If you drive, find out where to park.

- Prepare the things you need for the test: your admission ticket (if necessary), acceptable identification, some sharpened No. 2 pencils with erasers, a watch, glasses, a jacket or sweater (in case the room is cold), and a snack to eat during breaks.

- Eat a meal and get a good night's sleep. If the test is early in the morning, set the alarm.

The Day of the Test

- Eat a good breakfast. Wear comfortable clothing. Make sure that you have all of the materials you need.

- Try to arrive at the test center about twenty minutes early. This allows time if, for example, there is a last-minute change of room.

- If you are going to be at the test center all day, you might pack a lunch. If you have to find a restaurant or if you wait a long time to be served, you may be late for the rest of the test.

Using this Book

- Start with the Pretest. It is identical to the real test in format and length. It will give you an idea of what the GED Science Test is like. Then use the Pretest Performance Analysis Chart at the end of the test to figure out your areas of strength and the areas you need to review. The chart will refer you to units and page numbers to study. You also can use the Study Planner on page 31 to plan your work after you take the Pretest and again, after the Posttest.

- As you study, use the Cumulative Review and the Performance Analysis Chart at the end of each unit to find out if you need to review any lessons before continuing

- After you complete your review, use the Posttest to decide if you are ready for the real GED Test. The Performance Analysis Chart will tell you if you need additional review. Then use the Simulated Test and its Performance Analysis Chart as a final check of your test-readiness.

SCIENCE

Directions

The Science Pretest consists of multiple-choice questions intended to measure your understanding of general concepts in science. The questions are based on short readings or on graphs, charts, or diagrams. Study the information given, and then answer the questions that follow. Refer to the information as often as necessary in answering the questions.

You should spend no more than 80 minutes answering the 50 questions on the Science Pretest. Work carefully, but do not spend too much time on any one question. Do not skip any items. Make a reasonable guess when you are not sure of an answer. You will not be penalized for incorrect answers.

When time is up, mark the last item you finished. This will tell you whether you can finish the real GED Test in the time allowed. Then complete the test.

Record your answers to the questions on a copy of the answer sheet on page 340. Be sure that all required information is properly recorded on the answer sheet.

To record your answers, mark the numbered space on the answer sheet that corresponds to the answer you choose for each question on the test.

Example:

Which of the following is the smallest unit in a living thing?

(1) tissue
(2) organ
(3) cell
(4) muscle
(5) capillary   ① ② ● ④ ⑤

The correct answer is "cell"; therefore, answer space 3 should be marked on the answer sheet.

Do not rest the point of your pencil on the answer sheet while you are considering your answer. Make no stray or unnecessary marks. If you change an answer, erase your first mark completely. Mark only one answer space for each question; multiple answers will be scored as incorrect. Do not fold or crease your answer sheet.

When you finish the test, use the Performance Analysis Chart on page 30 to determine whether you are ready to take the real GED Test, and, if not, which skill areas need additional review.

Adapted with permission of the American Council on Education.

Directions: Choose the one best answer to each question.

Questions 1 and 2 refer to the following graph.

Question 3 refers to the following diagram.

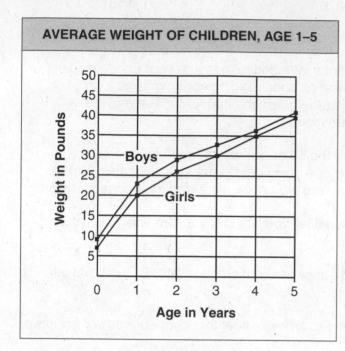

AVERAGE WEIGHT OF CHILDREN, AGE 1–5

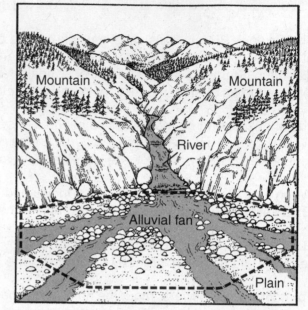

ALLUVIAL FAN IN THE MOUNTAINS

1. During which age range, between 0 and 5 years, do both boys and girls gain the most weight?

   (1) 0–1 year
   (2) 1–2 years
   (3) 2–3 years
   (4) 3–4 years
   (5) 4–5 years

2. Billy is a 4-year-old boy who weighs 39 pounds. How does Billy's weight compare with that of other children?

   (1) Billy's weight is average for his age and sex.
   (2) Billy's weight is above average for his age and sex.
   (3) Billy weighs more than the average 5-year-old boy.
   (4) Billy weighs less than the average 4-year-old girl.
   (5) Billy weighs less than the average 3-year-old boy.

3. Which of the following is an assumption you need to make to interpret this diagram correctly?

   (1) A river flows from a higher elevation to a lower elevation.
   (2) The slopes of mountains are partially covered with trees.
   (3) An alluvial fan forms where a mountain river flows out onto a plain.
   (4) An alluvial fan consists of soil and rocks.
   (5) An alluvial fan forms only near a volcano.

Question 4 refers to the following information and graph.

For most traits, organisms of a single species show continuous variation, that is, small degrees of difference over a more or less continuous range. For example, the weight of a fruit is a trait that shows continuous variation. In the following bar graph, the weight of 72 tomatoes of the same genetic stock is plotted.

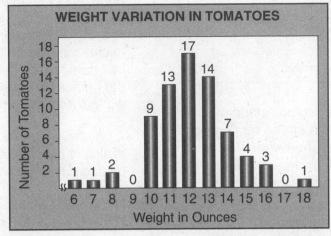

Source: *Concepts of Genetics*, William S. Klug and Michael R. Cummings, Prentice-Hall, 2000

4. Which of the following is a conclusion rather than a supporting detail?

   (1) Two tomatoes weighed 8 ounces.
   (2) None of the tomatoes weighed less than 6 ounces.
   (3) None of the tomatoes weighed 9 or 17 ounces.
   (4) The most common weight was 12 ounces.
   (5) The majority of tomatoes fell in the middle of the weight range.

5. According to Boyle's law, if temperature remains constant, the volume of a gas changes when the pressure on it changes. For example, doubling the pressure on a gas will decrease its volume by one half. If all other conditions stay the same, the volume of a gas becomes smaller as the pressure becomes greater.

   Why is oxygen gas usually stored under pressure in metal cylinders?

   (1) to prevent it from mixing with nitrogen and other gases in air
   (2) to heat up the oxygen
   (3) to illustrate Boyle's law
   (4) to store a great deal of oxygen in a small space
   (5) to turn oxygen into a gas

6. In 1665, Englishman Robert Hooke was the first to describe cork cells, which he saw through a simple microscope. Hooke was amazed that there were about twelve hundred million cells in a cubic inch of cork. About the same time, Dutch scientist Anton Leeuwenhoek examined pond water through a microscope. He was surprised to find one-celled organisms, which he called animalcules. By the 1820s, improvements in microscope lenses brought cells into sharper focus. In 1838, two German scientists, Matthias Schleiden and Theodor Schwann, were the first to explain that cells are the basic units of life and that all organisms are made of one or more cells. These generalizations form the basis of the cell theory.

   Which of the following would be the best title for this information?

   (1) Microscopes over the Centuries
   (2) A Close-up View of Cells
   (3) The First Life Scientists
   (4) Robert Hooke, Biologist
   (5) The Development of the Cell Theory

Question 7 refers to the following diagram.

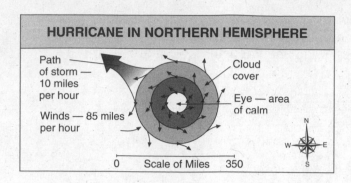

HURRICANE IN NORTHERN HEMISPHERE

Path of storm — 10 miles per hour

Winds — 85 miles per hour

Cloud cover

Eye — area of calm

0   Scale of Miles   350

7. A family on the East Coast took steps to protect their house from a strong hurricane. For more than ten hours, heavy rain fell and hurricane-force winds blew from the east. Then the storm quieted, and the sky grew lighter.

What should the family do next?

(1) Remove the storm protection measures from the house because the hurricane is over.
(2) Remove the storm protection measures from the house because the rest of the hurricane will be mild.
(3) Leave the storm protection measures in place because the rain and winds will start again soon.
(4) Leave the storm protection measures in place because there may be another hurricane tomorrow.
(5) Take a walk down to the shore to see whether the hurricane has done much damage.

8. Corrosion, or rusting, is a process in which iron reacts with air and water to form rust. Rust is brittle and flakes off, so fresh surfaces of the iron continue to be exposed to corrosion.

Which of the following is a practical method of treating cast-iron cookware to prevent rusting?

(1) wash it in detergent and water
(2) do not expose it to liquids
(3) do not expose it to air
(4) coat it lightly with oil so that air and water will not reach the surface
(5) heat it slowly over a low flame before cooking

9. To make compost, a gardener makes a pile of material that was once living. Some kitchen wastes, including vegetable parings and egg shells, work well in a compost pile. (High-protein wastes are usually omitted because they give off a strong smell and often attract animals.) Yard wastes, such as grass clippings, are also often added to a compost pile. In the compost pile, microscopic organisms change this waste into humus. The gardener can then spread the humus on the soil to fertilize plants without adding humanmade chemicals.

A gardener wants to start a compost pile. Which of the following materials would be best to put in the pile?

(1) fertilizer and soil
(2) fruit peels and coffee grounds
(3) old eggs and egg shells
(4) dead branches and meat bones
(5) microscopic organisms

Question 10 refers to the following chart.

BOILING POINTS OF SOME LIQUIDS	
Liquid	Boiling Point at Sea Level (°C)
Chloroform ($CHCl_3$)	61.7
Ethanol (C_2H_5OH)	78.5
Water (H_2O)	100.0
Octane (C_8H_{18})	126.0

10. At sea level, which of the following substances would boil first if they were all heated at the same rate?

(1) chloroform
(2) ethanol
(3) water
(4) octane
(5) They would all start boiling at the same time.

Questions 11 through 13 refer to the following information.

Mammals are a class of animals whose females give birth to live young and produce milk to feed their young. Mammals are divided into several groups. Five of the groups are described below.

Carnivores are meat-eaters that have teeth adapted for gripping and tearing flesh.

Cetaceans have very large heads and tapering bodies; they live in the water, usually the ocean.

Marsupials are mammals whose females have pouches in which the young develop after birth.

Rodents are small mammals with two pairs of incisors—upper and lower front teeth that are used for gnawing; they primarily eat plants.

Primates are mammals with complex brains, specialized limbs used for grasping, and eyes that can perceive depth.

11. The domestic cat is often valued as a mouse catcher. Of which group of mammals is the domestic cat a member?

   (1) carnivores
   (2) cetaceans
   (3) marsupials
   (4) rodents
   (5) primates

12. Kangaroos are mammals with powerful hind legs, long feet, and front paws used for grasping. The young kangaroo is born in an undeveloped state. It spends about six months in its mother's pouch, where it feeds on the milk she produces. Which of the following characteristics is key to classifying kangaroos as marsupials?

   (1) powerful hind legs
   (2) long feet
   (3) front paws used for grasping
   (4) a pouch where the young stay after birth
   (5) production of milk by the mother

13. Which of the following groups of mammals would most likely be of interest to a physical anthropologist, a scientist who studies the evolution of humans?

   (1) carnivores
   (2) cetaceans
   (3) marsupials
   (4) rodents
   (5) primates

Question 14 refers to the following diagram.

BUOYANCY

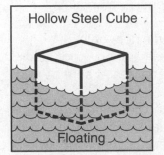
Hollow Steel Cube
Floating

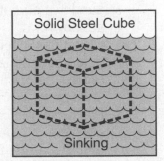
Solid Steel Cube
Sinking

An object floats if its density is less than that of water.

An object sinks if its density is greater than that of water.

14. A solid steel cube will sink when placed in water, but a steel ship will float. Based on the diagram, which of the following is the best explanation for why a steel ship floats?

   (1) When a steel ship's hull is intact and it isn't overloaded, it will not sink.
   (2) Steel is denser than water.
   (3) Steel is less dense than water.
   (4) The steel and air in a ship are less dense than water.
   (5) The steel and air in a ship are denser than water.

15. Passive solar devices collect heat energy from the sun without themselves requiring extra energy to work. To provide extra heat for a house, the passive solar device absorbs heat energy during the day and radiates it when the temperature falls at night. Which of the following experiments would best help determine which material radiates heat most slowly, thus making it suitable for a passive solar device?

    (1) Place identical containers holding different materials in a sunny spot, and record their temperatures just at sundown and at regular intervals after sundown.
    (2) Place identical containers holding different materials in a sunny spot, and record their temperatures at sunrise and sundown.
    (3) Place different sized containers holding one type of material in a sunny spot, and record their temperatures at sundown and at regular intervals after sundown.
    (4) Place different kinds of containers holding different materials in a sunny spot, and feel them before sundown and at regular intervals after sundown to see how warm they are.
    (5) Place identical containers holding different materials in a shaded spot, and record their temperatures just at sundown and at regular intervals after sundown.

16. Every magnet has a north pole and a south pole. The north pole of one magnet is attracted to the south pole of another magnet.

    Suppose a bar magnet is cut in half across the middle. What poles will each one of the resulting magnets have?

    (1) two north poles only
    (2) two south poles only
    (3) one north pole only
    (4) one south pole only
    (5) one north pole and one south pole

17. Ants are social animals that live together in a colony. Each ant plays a part in helping the group survive. Usually, a colony has one queen, who lays eggs. There are winged males, which develop from unfertilized eggs, and die soon after leaving the nest to mate with other queens. However, most of the ants are workers. These are females that cannot lay fertilized eggs. Their job is to find food and sometimes to fight to protect the colony. Based on this information, which of the following statements best explains why there are fewer males than worker ants in an ant colony?

    (1) Males do not live long, and only a few are required to fertilize a queen.
    (2) Workers are so numerous that they crowd off the males.
    (3) The formation of wings requires a specialized environment.
    (4) Winged males develop from unfertilized eggs.
    (5) Winged males must sometimes fight to protect the colony.

18. For decades, scientists thought that people were born with all the brain cells they would ever have and that deteriorated or damaged brain cells were not repaired or replaced. However, recent research suggests that people may add billions of new brain cells from infancy through adolescence. Even adults may maintain brain function by adding new cells. Many scientists have had difficulty believing the new findings because these findings did not agree with longstanding ideas about the brain.

    Which is an unstated assumption related to this paragraph?

    (1) Scientists thought people were born with all the brain cells they would ever have.
    (2) Scientists, like other people, sometimes have trouble changing long-held beliefs.
    (3) When brain cells are injured, they cannot repair or replace themselves.
    (4) Recent research on brain cells is not very surprising.
    (5) Even adults may be able to add new brain cells.

19. Researchers have used electricity to help remove a common industrial solvent from contaminated soil. They sank electrodes up to 45 feet deep and ran an electric current through them. The electrodes attracted water laced with the solvent to the treatment zone. There, clay mixed with iron filings broke the solvent down. Electrical cleanup can be done on site, rather than by shipping contaminated soil elsewhere. Thus, according to researchers, this method is likely to prove less expensive to use than traditional decontamination techniques.

Which of the following is an opinion rather than a fact about using electricity to clean up contaminated soil?

(1) Electricity is being used in a new method of decontaminating soil at industrial sites polluted with certain solvents.
(2) Electrodes are sunk up to 45 feet deep in contaminated soil.
(3) Electric current attracts water laced with the contaminating solvent to the electrodes.
(4) Clay mixed with iron filings breaks down the solvent.
(5) Using electricity to clean up industrial solvents should be cheaper than using traditional methods.

20. Cellular respiration is a series of chemical reactions in which complex fat, protein, and carbohydrate molecules are broken down, giving off energy in living organisms.

What is the purpose of cellular respiration?

(1) to break down fat molecules
(2) to build protein molecules
(3) to release energy
(4) to take in food molecules
(5) to use up carbohydrate molecules

Question 21 refers to the following paragraph and chart.

Friction is a force that prevents or slows movement. It occurs between any surfaces that are in contact. The chart describes the three main types of friction.

Type of Friction	Description
Static Friction	Occurs when nonmoving surfaces are in contact and must be overcome for either surface to move; produces neither heat nor wear
Sliding Friction	Occurs when one surface slides over another; produces high amounts of heat and wear
Rolling Friction	Occurs when a wheel or other round objects moves over another surface; produces lower amounts of heat and wear than sliding friction does

21. An office worker is assigned to rearrange the furniture in the office. To make space, she needs to move a file cabinet across the office. Her coworkers start pushing the file cabinet, but she stops them and loads the file cabinet onto a dolly.

In moving the file cabinet, which of the kinds of friction have the people in the office encountered?

(1) static friction
(2) rolling friction
(3) static and rolling friction
(4) rolling and sliding friction
(5) static, rolling, and sliding friction

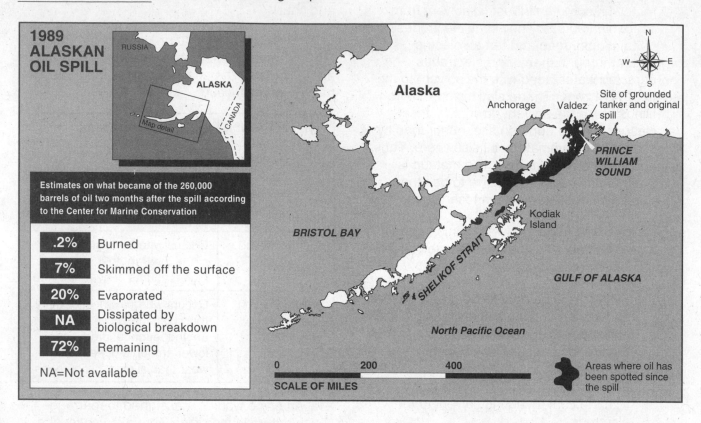

22. The map was compiled two months after the original oil spill. Which conclusion does the information on the map best support?

    (1) Most of the oil was cleaned up in the first two months.
    (2) The oil will probably spread farther south and west.
    (3) The oil will probably be completely cleaned up in the next two months.
    (4) The ocean will probably absorb most of the remaining oil.
    (5) The remaining oil will probably evaporate in the next two months.

23. The oil spill caused millions of dollars of damage to the Alaskan salmon and herring fisheries and to the marine ecosystem. Afterward, Congress passed federal safety requirements for oil tankers and placed the major burden of paying for cleaning up spills on the oil companies. Based on this information, what is a major incentive for oil companies to prevent similar spills from occurring again?

    (1) concern for the physical marine environment
    (2) concern for the welfare of coastal marine wildlife
    (3) concern for the Alaskan salmon and herring fisheries
    (4) reluctance to spend profits on cleaning up accidents
    (5) dedication to keeping employee morale high

Question 24 refers to the following information and diagram.

Atoms can bond, or join together, in many ways. In covalent bonding, atoms combine by sharing electrons. For example, two fluorine atoms can bond by sharing a pair of electrons in their outer electron shells, forming a fluorine gas molecule. The bond can be represented by electron dot symbols.

COVALENT BONDING OF FLUORINE

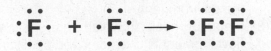

24. How many electrons does a single, unbonded atom of fluorine have in its outer electron shell?

    (1) one
    (2) two
    (3) seven
    (4) eight
    (5) nine

25. Potential energy is an object's ability to do work because of a change in its shape or position.

    Based on the information above, which of the following objects has potential energy?

    (1) a stretched rubber band
    (2) a large boulder
    (3) a cement sidewalk
    (4) a building
    (5) a train track

Question 26 refers to the following information and diagrams.

Radar was first used in combat during World War II. Radio waves from a radar transmitter radiate out in a cone shape, bounce off a distant object, and return to a receiver, providing information about the object's shape and location.

THE TECHNOLOGY OF RADAR

When incoming signals were equal, the target was straight ahead.

Unbalanced returned signals meant the target was off to one side or above or below the fighter plane.

26. Suppose the target plane in the top diagram dove a hundred feet. What would be the effect on the returning radar signals?

    The return signals would

    (1) remain balanced
    (2) become unbalanced
    (3) fade out gradually
    (4) stop suddenly
    (5) not be picked up by the fighter plane

Question 27 refers to the following information and graph.

Predators are animals that get their food by hunting and killing other animals, their prey. The population of predators and prey in a community rises and falls in a cycle.

PREDATOR AND PREY POPULATIONS

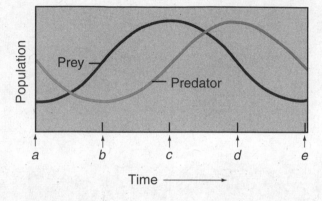

27. Which of the following most likely caused the increase in the predator population between time *b* and time *d*?

    (1) the decrease in the prey population between time *a* and time *b*
    (2) the decrease in the prey population between time *d* and time *e*
    (3) the increase in the prey population between time *a* and time *c*
    (4) the increase in the prey population between time *d* and time *e*
    (5) the lag time between increases in the prey and predator populations

28. During photosynthesis, green plants use energy from the sun and water and carbon dioxide from the air to produce food and oxygen.

    In which of the following situations does photosynthesis play a major part?

    (1) the nitrogen cycle, in which bacteria take nitrogen from the air and change it into forms that organisms can use
    (2) the carbon-oxygen cycle, in which carbon and oxygen are cycled through the environment
    (3) metamorphosis, in which an organism's development is characterized by distinct changes in form or structure
    (4) the cell cycle, in which cells grow, replicate their DNA, and divide
    (5) the solar cycle, a periodic fluctuation in the number of sunspots

29. Two or more organisms may compete for resources such as living space, food, or mates. Competition may exist between members of the same species or between different species.

    Which of the following statements supports the conclusion that competition between members of the same species is usually more intense than competition between members of different species?

    (1) Organisms may compete for living space.
    (2) Organisms may compete for food.
    (3) Members of different species compete for the same mates.
    (4) Members of the same species need the same resources.
    (5) Members of different species need the same resources.

Questions 30 through 32 refer to the following information.

A continuous path along which electric current flows is called an electric circuit. Each circuit must have a source of electromotive force (EMF) to drive the current. In the circuit below, a battery provides the electromotive force. The drawing and the schematic diagram show the same circuit.

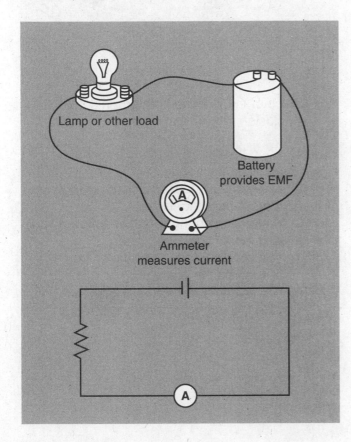

30. What is a good title for this information?

(1) Using an Ammeter
(2) Electricity
(3) An Electric Circuit
(4) The Electromotive Force
(5) How a Light Bulb Works

31. In the circuit shown on top, what would happen if the wire connecting the battery and the ammeter were cut?

(1) The chemicals in the battery would immediately be used up
(2) The ammeter would register an increase in current.
(3) The current would continue to flow, but the ammeter would not work.
(4) The current would continue to flow, but the light bulb would not light up.
(5) The current would stop flowing, and the light bulb would not light up.

32. In which of the following situations would a schematic diagram be most useful?

(1) checking a house for electrical safety hazards
(2) writing directions for consumers on how to use a washing machine
(3) installing the wiring for a new apartment building
(4) deciding what size battery you need for a flashlight
(5) measuring the actual amount of current in a circuit

GEYSER

Boiling water and steam

Hot rocks

Water boiled by heat from rocks

CAPILLARY AND TISSUE CELLS

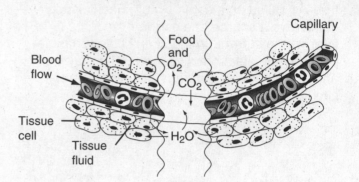

Capillary

Blood flow

Food and O_2

CO_2

Tissue cell

Tissue fluid

H_2O

33. Which of the following best summarizes what is shown in the diagram?

   (1) A geyser consists mostly of boiling water.
   (2) A geyser forms when lake or river water is heated to boiling.
   (3) A geyser erupts when hot underground rocks heat water to boiling.
   (4) A geyser is caused by underground movement of heated rocks.
   (5) A geyser like Old Faithful erupts at regular intervals.

34. What is the most practical way people could use the water from geysers?

   (1) for drinking water
   (2) in a hot-water heating system
   (3) for showers at campsites
   (4) in a water park
   (5) for irrigating crops

35. Which of the following statements is a conclusion rather than a supporting detail?

   (1) Food passes from blood into the surrounding tissue.
   (2) Oxygen (O_2) passes from the blood into the surrounding tissue.
   (3) Water is exchanged between the blood and the surrounding tissue.
   (4) Carbon dioxide (CO_2) passes from the tissue into the blood.
   (5) Capillaries transport substances in the blood to and from the body's tissues.

Questions 36 and 37 refer to the following map.

MAJOR U.S. WATERSHEDS

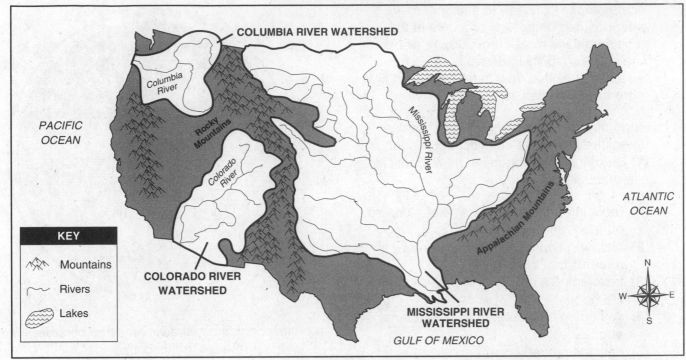

36. The area of land drained by a river is known as a watershed. Why does water in most watersheds eventually drain into an ocean?

   (1) The oceans are the largest bodies of water on Earth.
   (2) Each land mass is surrounded by an ocean.
   (3) In the United States, water flows south toward the equator.
   (4) Water flows from high elevations, such as mountains, to sea level.
   (5) Too much water flows into the ocean too quickly.

37. Lewis and Clark were American explorers who traveled up the Mississippi watershed toward the Northwest. As they crossed the Rocky Mountains, they started looking for a water passage to the Pacific. How could they confirm that their Indian guides were leading them in the correct direction?

   (1) They conserved water for the journey over the Rocky Mountains.
   (2) They saw that the Columbia River was flowing to the west.
   (3) They found the source of the Columbia River.
   (4) They encountered flooding in the Columbia River watershed.
   (5) They determined that the Columbia River was too high to make it a major watershed.

38. Fire beetles lay their eggs in smoldering trees. To find trees that are on fire, the beetles have infrared detectors that can locate sources of heat. In addition, their antennas can detect tiny amounts of the substances in smoke from burning wood. The beetles' ability to detect burning trees is so sensitive that they can home in on fires more than 30 miles away.

Understanding precisely how the beetles detect fire may have practical applications. Which of the following might be a practical use of this knowledge?

(1) reducing the amount of smoke given off during fires
(2) planning controlled burns of forest underbrush
(3) developing a new type of insecticide for fire beetles
(4) designing new antennas for cellular phones
(5) developing early warning detectors for forest fires

39. Phthalates (pronounced THAL-ates) are chemicals added to plastic to make it flexible. The plastic is often used in tubes for blood transfusions, intravenous feeding, and other life support systems. Small amounts of the chemicals can leach into the bloodstream. According to some scientists, phthalates may be dangerous to humans because they have caused cancer and organ damage in animals.

Based on the information above, which use of phthalates is most likely to cause harm to people?

(1) in plastic items used in laboratories for testing medical specimens
(2) in plastic wrap used to protect food from contamination or moisture
(3) in plastic bags used for items that have been dry cleaned
(4) in the plastic packaging that protects toys, games, and other boxed items in stores
(5) in the plastic used to make certain kinds of modeling clay for art projects

Question 40 refers to the following graph.

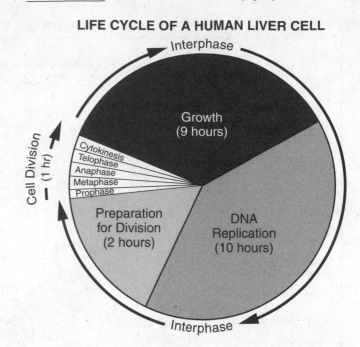

LIFE CYCLE OF A HUMAN LIVER CELL

40. How does the cell division stage contrast with interphase in this cell?

(1) Cell division takes about one-twentieth the time that interphase takes.
(2) Cell division takes half the time that interphase takes.
(3) Cell division takes twice the time that interphase takes.
(4) Cell division is divided into five phases, and interphase is divided into eight phases.
(5) Human liver cells undergo cell division but not interphase.

Question 41 refers to the following chart.

SOME MEDICAL SPECIALISTS	
Type of Doctor	Concerned With
Cardiologist	Heart and arteries
Endocrinologist	Hormones
Hematologist	Blood
Oncologist	Growths, tumors, and cancer
Orthopedist	Bones, joints, and muscles

41. A patient has been complaining of chest pain, and a blood test shows a very high cholesterol level. To which specialist is his family doctor likely to refer him?

    (1) a cardiologist
    (2) an endocrinologist
    (3) a hematologist
    (4) an oncologist
    (5) an orthopedist

42. In nuclear reactors, nuclear fission reactions produce energy and radioactive waste. Disposal of the waste is a problem, because it remains radioactive, and thus harmful to living things, for many years. When a nuclear waste site is proposed for a location, people who live nearby generally organize to oppose it.

Of the following, which do people opposing a nuclear waste disposal site in their neighborhood probably value the most?

    (1) individualism
    (2) ambition
    (3) money
    (4) good health
    (5) neighborliness

Question 43 refers to the following information and diagram.

You can model a wave by holding one end of a rope and giving it a quick up-and-down shake. Each point on the rope transfers energy to the next point as the wave travels.

WAVE MOTION

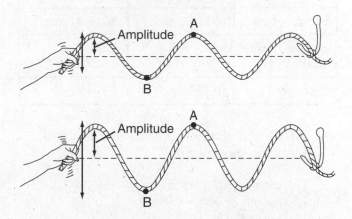

43. Which of the following statements is supported by the information given about the model of the wave?

    (1) Most of the energy from the hand movement is transferred to the air.
    (2) One up-and-down shake will produce waves indefinitely.
    (3) A more energetic shake will produce a wave of greater amplitude.
    (4) The amplitude of a wave is the distance between two peaks.
    (5) Point B on the rope will always be below point A.

Question 44 refers to the following chart.

COMPARING EARTH AND MARS		
Characteristic	Earth	Mars
Distance from sun	150,000,000 km	228,000,000 km
Length of year	365 days	687 days
Length of day	23 hr, 56 min	24 hr, 37 min
Surface gravity (Earth = 1)	1	0.38
Diameter	12,756 km	6,794 km

44. Which of the characteristics of Earth and Mars are most similar?

    (1) distance from sun
    (2) length of year
    (3) length of day
    (4) surface gravity
    (5) diameter

45. Many organisms have developed camouflage. For example, fish are often darker colored on their backs and lighter on their bellies. When viewed from above, the fish blend in with the dark water. When viewed from below, the fish blend in with the bright sky.

    Which of the following is an unstated assumption important for understanding the paragraph?

    (1) Many organisms have developed camouflage.
    (2) Camouflage protects organisms by making them difficult to detect.
    (3) Many fish are darker colored above and lighter colored below.
    (4) When viewed from above, a dark colored fish is hard to see.
    (5) When viewed from below, a light colored fish blends in with the bright sky.

Question 46 refers to the following information and diagram.

A wedge is a type of simple machine. The diagram shows that when a wedge is moved, it creates a sideward force that acts at right angles to the direction of movement.

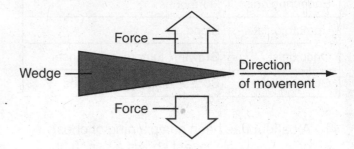

46. Which of the following involves the use of a wedge?

    (1) a steering wheel used to turn a car
    (2) a balance scale used to weigh objects
    (3) a handcart used to move a heavy load
    (4) a faucet handle used to turn on the water
    (5) an ax used to split wood

47. Scientists conducted a study to see whether the fat content of a controlled calorie diet affected the weight of the subjects. The fat content of the diets ranged from 0 to 70 percent. Results indicated that the amount of fat in the diet was not a factor in weight loss or gain. Instead, the number of calories, from whatever source, affected weight gain or loss.

    Based on the outcome of this study, which of the following actions would be most likely to result in weight loss?

    (1) decrease calorie intake
    (2) increase calorie intake
    (3) decrease fat intake
    (4) increase fat intake
    (5) decrease fat but increase calories from other sources

48. In sexual reproduction, two different sex cells, containing genetic material from two parent organisms, combine to create an offspring. In asexual reproduction, an individual organism duplicates its genetic material for its offspring.

Which of the following is implied by this information?

(1) Sexual reproduction exists only among animals.
(2) Asexual reproduction exists only among plants.
(3) Offspring of sexual reproduction differ genetically from each parent.
(4) Offspring of asexual reproduction combine genetic material from the parents.
(5) More organisms reproduce asexually than reproduce sexually.

49. Natural motor oils begin to cloud at about 15°F, when some of the molecules freeze into crystals. Manufacturers mix organic additives with natural motor oil to lower the freezing point to −30° or −35°F. Synthetic motor oil has an even lower freezing point. It doesn't solidify until the temperature falls below −40°F.

Which of the following statements supports the conclusion that people living in colder climates should use synthetic motor oil in their vehicles?

(1) Some molecules in natural motor oil freeze at 15°F.
(2) Organic additives are mixed with natural motor oil.
(3) Organic additives lower the freezing point of natural motor oil.
(4) Synthetic motor oil has a lower freezing point than natural motor oil.
(5) Once it freezes, motor oil stops functioning as an engine lubricant.

Question 50 refers to the following diagram.

THE WATER CYCLE

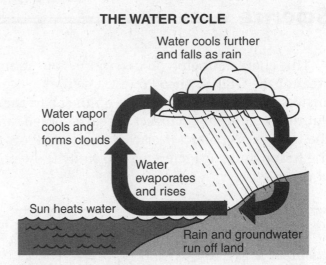

Water cools further and falls as rain

Water vapor cools and forms clouds

Water evaporates and rises

Sun heats water

Rain and groundwater run off land

50. Which of the following best summarizes what is shown in the diagram?

(1) Clouds form as water vapor cools and collects.
(2) Groundwater and rain run off the land into the ocean.
(3) The sun provides the heat energy to evaporate water.
(4) Water evaporates and rises into the air, where it cools, forming clouds and then rain.
(5) Rain falls when the water vapor in clouds cools.

Answers start on page 260.

Pretest Performance Analysis Chart
Science

This chart can help you determine your strengths and weaknesses on the content and skill areas of the GED Science Pretest. Use the Answers and Explanations on page 260 to check your answers to the test. Then circle on the chart the numbers of the test items you answered correctly. Put the total number correct for each content area and skill area in each row and column. Look at the total items correct in each column and row and decide which areas are difficult for you. Use the lesson and page references to study those areas. Use the Study Planner on page 31 to guide your studying.

Thinking Skill / Content Area	Comprehension (Lessons 1, 2, 6, 9, 13)	Application (Lessons 8, 15)	Analysis (Lessons 3, 4, 7, 10, 14, 17, 19)	Evaluation (Lessons 5, 11, 12, 16, 18, 20)	Total Correct
Life Science (Pages 32–107)	**1**, 6, 20, 48	9, 11, 13, 28, 38, 39, **41**	**2**, **4**, 18, **27**, **35**, **40**, 45, 47	12, 17, **23**, 29	_____/23
Earth and Space Science (Pages 108–155)	**33**, **50**	**7**, **34**, **37**	**3**, **36**, **44**	15, **22**	_____/10
Physical Science (Pages 156–218)	16, **24**, **30**	8, **21**, 25, **32**, **46**	5, **10**, 19, **26**, **31**	**14**, 42, **43**, 49	_____/17
Total Correct	_____/9	_____/15	_____/16	_____/10	_____/50

1–40 → Use the Study Planner on page 31 to organize your work in this book.
41–50 → Use the tests in this book to practice for the GED.

Boldfaced numbers indicate questions based on charts, graphs, diagrams, and drawings.

For additional help, see the *Steck-Vaughn GED Science Exercise Book.*

Science Study Planner

These charts will help you organize your study after you take the Science Pretest and Posttest. After each test, use your results from the Total Correct column on the corresponding Performance Analysis Chart to complete the study planner. Place a check mark next to the areas in which you need more practice. Review your study habits by keeping track of the start and finish dates for each practice. These charts will help you to see your progress as you practice to improve your skills and prepare for the GED Science Test.

Pretest (pages 13–29): Use results from your **Performance Analysis Chart** (page 30).

Content	Correct/Total	✓	Page Numbers	Date Started	Date Finished
Life Science	_____/23		32–107		
Earth and Space Science	_____/10		108–155		
Physical Science	_____/17		156–218		
Thinking Skills			**Lesson Numbers**	**Date Started**	**Date Finished**
Comprehension	_____/9		1, 2, 6, 9, 13		
Application	_____/15		8, 15		
Analysis	_____/16		3, 4, 7, 10, 14, 17, 19		
Evaluation	_____/10		5, 11, 12, 16, 18, 20		

Posttest (pages 219–237): Use results from your **Performance Analysis Chart** (page 238).

Content	Correct/Total	✓	Page Numbers	Date Started	Date Finished
Life Science	_____/23		32–107		
Earth and Space Science	_____/10		108–155		
Physical Science	_____/17		156–218		
Thinking Skills			**Lesson Numbers**	**Date Started**	**Date Finished**
Comprehension	_____/9		1, 2, 6, 9, 13		
Application	_____/15		8, 15		
Analysis	_____/16		3, 4, 7, 10, 14, 17, 19		
Evaluation	_____/10		5, 11, 12, 16, 18, 20		

Life Science

Although we may not always realize it, life science information helps us make daily decisions about health and fitness. On a personal level, life science can help us learn how to improve our health and quality of life. For example, implementing an effective exercise program involves a working knowledge about the muscles, respiratory system, and heart.

On a larger scale, life science helps us to understand how humans and other organisms function and interact with their surroundings and how we can enhance the quality of this interaction. Life scientists are concerned with everything about life systems from the cellular make-up of organisms to the variations among like organisms to the ecosystems found on Earth.

Understanding life science is also very important for success on the GED Science Test. Life science topics are the basis for about 50 percent of the questions on the test.

A fitness instructor needs to be familiar with how the human body, including the heart, works.

The lessons in this unit include:

Lesson 1: **Cell Structures and Functions**
You will learn about the structures of cells—the microscopic units from which all living things are made.

Lesson 2: **Cells and Energy**
You will discover how green plants get energy from the sun and how all organisms store and release energy.

Lesson 3: **Genetics**
You will learn how traits are passed from parents to offspring.

Lesson 4: **Human Body Systems**
You will learn about the major systems of the human body, including the digestive system and the circulatory system.

Lesson 5: **The Nervous System and Behavior**
You will learn about the structure and function of the nervous system and how it relates to human behavior.

Lesson 6: **Evolution**
You will learn about the theory of evolution by natural selection, which explains how organisms change over time.

Lesson 7: **Energy Flow in Ecosystems**
You will find out about food webs, the means by which energy passes from the sun to plants and to animals.

Lesson 8: **Cycles in Ecosystems**
You will discover how substances are cycled between living organisms, their nonliving surroundings, and back again.

THINKING SKILLS

○ Identifying the main idea

○ Restating information

○ Distinguishing fact from opinion

○ Recognizing unstated assumptions

○ Identifying faulty logic

○ Summarizing ideas

○ Distinguishing conclusions from supporting details

○ Applying ideas in new contexts

GED SKILL Identifying the Main Idea

main idea
the central topic of a
paragraph or passage

When you take the GED Test, you will read science passages and graphics for understanding. This means that as you read, you must look for **main ideas** and details that support the main ideas. How can you find the main ideas of a passage? First look over the passage quickly, counting the paragraphs. If there are three paragraphs, you should find three main ideas. Together, the main ideas of the paragraphs form the main idea of the passage.

Each paragraph is a group of sentences about a single topic—the main idea. The main idea of a paragraph is usually stated in the topic sentence. Often the topic sentence is the first or last sentence of the paragraph, but sometimes it is in the middle of the paragraph. Wherever it is, the sentence with the main idea has a meaning general enough to cover all the points in the paragraph.

Sometimes the main idea of a paragraph is not stated clearly in one sentence. In that case, you must read and think about the whole paragraph to understand the main idea. Look for supporting details that will help you. These may be facts, examples, explanations, or proofs that illustrate or tell more about the main idea.

Read the paragraph and answer the question below.

Cloning is the process of artificially producing an exact genetic copy of an existing individual **organism.** In recent years, scientists have done many cloning experiments with mammals. Such experiments start with the **egg cell** of one animal. Scientists remove the **nucleus,** which is the control center, of the egg cell and replace it with the nucleus of a **cell** from a second, fully mature adult animal. Then, they implant the altered egg cell into the uterus of a third animal. The animal that is born is a copy of the adult whose cell nucleus was placed in the egg cell.

To identify the main idea, look for the general idea of the passage. To identify supporting details, watch for names, numbers, dates, and examples. Look for key words including *like, such as,* and *for example.*

Write *M* next to the sentence that best expresses the main idea of the paragraph.

_____ a. Cloning is the process of artificially producing an exact copy of an existing individual organism.

_____ b. Cloning experiments start with the egg cell of one animal.

You were correct if you chose *option a.* The main idea is stated in the first sentence of this paragraph. *Option b* is a detail that supports the main idea.

Use the passage and the diagram to answer the questions below.

Your skin forms a protective surface for your body. Skin is made up of epithelial **tissue,** which is flat and broad. The cells of epithelial tissue are close together. As a result, this tissue tightly controls which substances pass through it. Epithelial tissue also forms a protective lining for organs such as the stomach.

Another type of tissue is connective tissue. This tissue supports and holds together parts of the body. Cells in connective tissue are not close together. Nonliving materials, such as calcium, fill the space between cells. These materials give all connective tissues strength. Bone and cartilage are types of connective tissue.

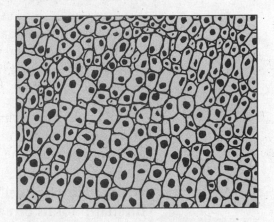

1. Write *M* next to the sentence that tells the main idea of the first paragraph.

    _____ a. The cells of epithelial tissue are close together.

    _____ b. Epithelial tissue forms protective surfaces for the body.

2. Write one detail that supports the main idea of the first paragraph.

    _____

3. Write *M* next to the sentence that tells the main idea of the second paragraph.

    _____ a. The cells of connective tissue are not close together.

    _____ b. Connective tissue supports and holds together parts of the body.

4. Write one detail that supports the main idea of the second paragraph.

    _____

5. Put a check mark next to the part of the body in which you would expect to find the cells shown in the diagram.

    _____ a. the skin

    _____ b. the bones

6. Put a check mark next to the characteristic of the cells in the diagram that helps epithelial tissue control whether a substance passes through it.

    _____ a. The cells are very close together.

    _____ b. The cells have nuclei that are stained a dark color.

Answers start on page 266.

All organisms are made up of microscopic units called cells. Some organisms consist only of a single cell. Other organisms are made up of many cells. All cells, whether they form a single-celled organism or a multicellular organism, carry out life processes. For example, all cells take in food. They all break down food to get energy, and they all give off waste products. Most cells grow and reproduce. All cells eventually die.

Most cells have the structures shown in the diagram. The nucleus is one of the most complex cell structures. The nucleus is the control center of the cell. The **nuclear membrane** protects the nucleus and controls what goes into and out of it. The nucleus contains **chromatin**—the cell's genetic material. When the cell divides, the chromatin forms **chromosomes,** which pass on the hereditary information for the cell. The nucleus also contains nucleoli, which produce **protein**-making structures called **ribosomes.**

Outside the nucleus is a soup-like fluid called **cytoplasm.** The cytoplasm contains a number of cell structures called **organelles.** The organelles work together to help the cell break down food for energy, growth, and reproduction. The cytoplasm and organelles are surrounded by a **cell membrane,** which controls what goes into and out of the cell. Use the diagram to learn about each of the different organelles, the nucleus, and the cell membrane.

A TYPICAL CELL

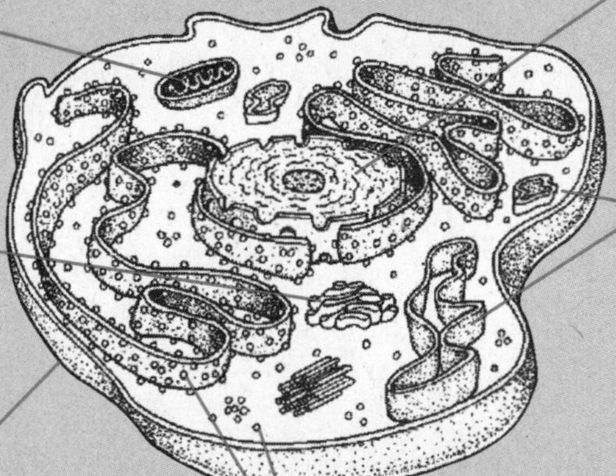

Mitochondrion
Releases energy stored in food. Most cells have many mitochondria.

Golgi Apparatus
Set of sacs in which proteins and lipids are packaged and sent to different places inside or outside the cell.

Cell Membrane
This double layer membrane surrounds and protects the cell, regulating the materials that enter and leave the cell.

Nucleus
Controls the activity of the cell.

Endoplasmic Reticulum
Also called the ER, this system of membranes makes and transports substances throughout the cell. Proteins are made on rough ER, which contains ribosomes. Lipids (fats) are made on smooth ER, which has no ribosomes.

Ribosomes
These tiny structures help make proteins. Some float freely in the cytoplasm or nucleus. Others may be attached to rough endoplasmic reticulum.

Directions: Choose the one best answer to each question.

Questions 1 through 6 refer to the information and diagram on page 36.

1. What is the main idea of the first paragraph?

   (1) All organisms are made up of many cells that eventually die.
   (2) All organisms are made up of cells, which carry out the basic life processes.
   (3) All cells are tiny and can be seen only with a microscope.
   (4) All cells take in food for energy and give off wastes.
   (5) Although most cells grow and reproduce, they all eventually die.

2. What is the main idea of the second paragraph?

   (1) Cells have many different kinds of structures in the cytoplasm.
   (2) The cells of multicellular organisms have a nucleus.
   (3) The nucleus is surrounded by the nuclear membrane.
   (4) The nucleus is often located near the center of the cell.
   (5) The nucleus is one of the cell's most complex structures.

3. Which detail best supports the main idea of the second paragraph?

   (1) The cytoplasm is outside the nucleus.
   (2) The organelles are outside the nucleus.
   (3) Most cells include the structures described in the diagram.
   (4) The nucleus is the control center of the cell.
   (5) There are ribosomes in both the nucleus and the cytoplasm.

4. What is the main purpose of the diagram?

   (1) to show and describe the nucleus
   (2) to show and describe various cell structures
   (3) to describe the functions of ribosomes
   (4) to show the difference between cytoplasm and the nucleus
   (5) to explain how materials pass through the cell membrane

5. According to the diagram, how do different organelles work together to carry out cell processes related to proteins?

   (1) Ribosomes make proteins, the endoplasmic reticulum transports them, and the Golgi apparatus sends them where they are needed.
   (2) Ribosomes make proteins, the Golgi apparatus transports them, and the mitochondria send them where they are needed.
   (3) The mitochondria release energy and the smooth endoplasmic reticulum sends proteins throughout the cell.
   (4) The mitochondria release energy and the Golgi apparatus makes lipids and proteins.
   (5) The mitochondria release energy, the endoplasmic reticulum makes proteins, and the Golgi apparatus makes lipids.

6. What is the main idea of the passage and diagram together?

   (1) Organisms are made of cells that have specialized structures to carry out life processes.
   (2) Some organisms consist of just one cell, and others consist of many different types of cells.
   (3) The life processes of cells include taking in food for energy, growing, and reproducing.
   (4) Cells are microscopic units with many types of structures having different functions.
   (5) The cytoplasm contains organelles needed to carry out the cell's functions.

Answers start on page 266.

GED Practice • Lesson 1

Directions: Choose the <u>one best answer</u> to each question.

<u>Questions 1 through 3</u> refer to the following passage and diagram.

Plant cells have certain structures that animal cells do not have. For example, plant cells have a cell wall surrounding the cell membrane. Cell walls are made of bundles of cellulose and serve to support the plant.

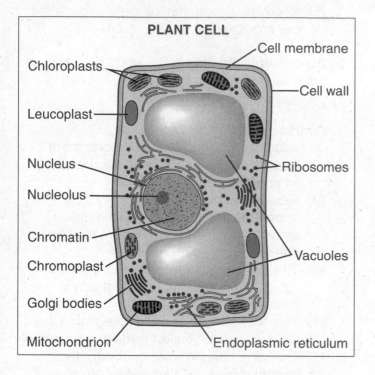

PLANT CELL

Chloroplasts
Cell membrane
Cell wall
Leucoplast
Nucleus
Ribosomes
Nucleolus
Chromatin
Vacuoles
Chromoplast
Golgi bodies
Mitochondrion
Endoplasmic reticulum

Plant cells also gain support from large, water-filled sacs called vacuoles. In a mature plant cell, one or two vacuoles may take up most of the space inside the cell. Animal cells rarely contain vacuoles, and when they are present, they are tiny.

Also unique to plant cells are organelles called plastids. Chloroplasts are one kind of plastid. Chloroplasts contain the green pigment chlorophyll. Plants need chlorophyll to carry out the sugar-making process of photosynthesis. Chromoplasts are another type of plastid containing pigment. Yellow, orange, and red pigments are stored in a plant's chromoplasts. Leucoplasts are a third type of plastid. They make starches and oils for the plant.

1. Which is the best title for the passage and diagram together?

   (1) Plant Cell Structures and Their Functions
   (2) How a Plant Cell Reproduces
   (3) How Plant and Animal Cells Are Alike
   (4) How Plastids Function in Plant Cells
   (5) Parts of a Green Plant

2. Based on the information in the passage, which type of structure gives daffodil and rose petals their color?

   (1) cell membrane
   (2) cell wall
   (3) mitochondria
   (4) chromoplasts
   (5) leucoplasts

3. Lisa did not water her plants for three weeks, and they wilted. Why did the plants wilt?

   (1) The cellulose in the cell walls disintegrated.
   (2) The vacuoles shrank as their water was used up.
   (3) The leucoplasts made too many starches.
   (4) The chloroplasts lost all their chlorophyll and stopped functioning.
   (5) The chromoplasts produced too much pigment.

4. A protein in the mucus in your nasal passages can break down the cell walls of bacteria, many of which cause disease. Which of the following is the most likely result of this action?

   (1) Bacteria will not be able to enter your nose.
   (2) Bacteria that enter your nose will be killed.
   (3) Bacteria will enter your nose more easily.
   (4) Bacteria in your nose will grow more rapidly.
   (5) Bacteria in your nose will not be able to change shape.

APPLYING CELL BIOLOGY TO HUMAN NEEDS

Questions 5 through 7 refer to the following information and diagram.

People once made fun of the notion that someday cell scientists would grow cells in the lab and fashion them into living body parts. Believe it or not, that day has come. The diagram below describes how new blood vessels can be created cell by cell, outside a human body.

BUILDING BLOOD VESSELS, CELL BY CELL

1. Scientist coats the inside of a tube of plastic scaffolding with muscle cells.

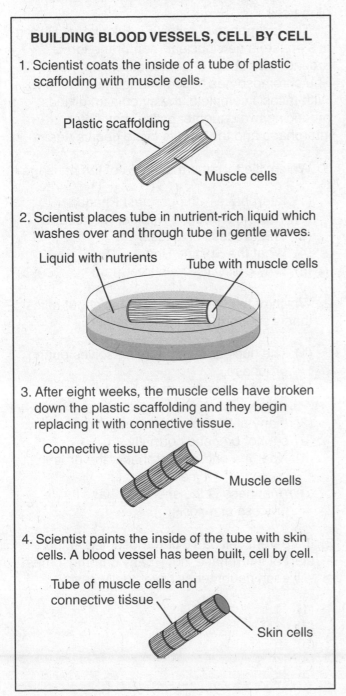

Plastic scaffolding

Muscle cells

2. Scientist places tube in nutrient-rich liquid which washes over and through tube in gentle waves.

Liquid with nutrients

Tube with muscle cells

3. After eight weeks, the muscle cells have broken down the plastic scaffolding and they begin replacing it with connective tissue.

Connective tissue

Muscle cells

4. Scientist paints the inside of the tube with skin cells. A blood vessel has been built, cell by cell.

Tube of muscle cells and connective tissue

Skin cells

5. Which sentence best summarizes the main idea of the paragraph and the diagram?

   (1) Cell biologists have worked hard to meet human needs.
   (2) Cell biologists do not think that they can grow living body parts from cells.
   (3) Blood vessels are not the first body parts cell biologists have been able to grow.
   (4) Cell biologists have succeeded in growing blood vessels from living cells.
   (5) The first step in growing blood vessels is to coat plastic scaffolding with muscle cells.

6. What is the unstated assumption behind this information?

   (1) Artificial body parts are superior to body parts formed from living cells.
   (2) Scientists may someday be able to form replacement body parts from living cells.
   (3) It is extremely easy to form body parts from living cells.
   (4) The process of forming body parts from living cells takes too long to be practical.
   (5) Plastic scaffolding must support new body parts formed from living cells.

7. It may soon be possible that when nerves are cut, doctors can place a type of plastic between the cut nerves to help the nerve cells grow back. What is the most likely function of the plastic?

   (1) to reconnect the two cut nerves
   (2) to supply living nerve cells for reconnecting the damaged nerves
   (3) to provide a physical support for the growing nerve cells
   (4) to carry away the waste products of the damaged nerves
   (5) to allow both muscle cells and nerve cells to grow

Answers start on page 267.

GED Mini-Test • Lesson 1

Directions: This is a ten-minute practice test. After ten minutes, mark the last item you finished. Then complete the test and check your answers. If most of your answers were correct, but you didn't finish, try to work faster next time. Choose the <u>one best answer</u> to each question.

Questions 1 through 3 refer to the following passage and diagram.

As living things, all cells have a life cycle. The cell life cycle has five stages: interphase, prophase, metaphase, anaphase, and telophase. During its life cycle, the cell grows, carries out its special jobs, and divides.

The most important part of cell division is **mitosis**—the division of the nucleus. During mitosis, the chromosomes in the **parent cell** duplicate and divide into two identical sets. One set will go to each of two new **daughter cells.**

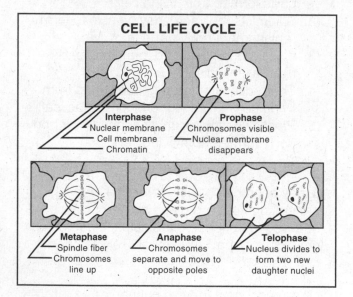

For most cells, interphase is the longest part of the life cycle. During interphase, the cell carries out many different life processes important for its growth and survival. Near the end of interphase, the cell prepares to divide. The chromatin in the nucleus duplicates.

Mitosis begins with prophase. During prophase, the chromatin shortens and thickens to form chromosomes. Each chromosome is made of two identical chromatids, which attach at their centers. A network of fibers called the spindle spans the cell. The nuclear membrane dissolves.

The next phase of mitosis is called metaphase. During metaphase, the chromosomes line up across the middle of the cell. They attach to the spindle fibers.

During anaphase, the chromatids in each chromosome separate. They migrate toward the poles along the spindle fibers. Once separated, the chromatids are called daughter chromosomes. The spindle pulls the two sets of daughter chromosomes to opposite ends of the cell.

The last phase of mitosis is telophase. During this phase, a new nuclear membrane forms around each set of daughter chromosomes. The chromosomes become longer and thinner. With mitosis complete, the cytoplasm divides, producing two daughter cells. They enter interphase and the cell life cycle begins again.

1. Which title tells the main idea of the passage?

   (1) Interphase—the Longest Phase
   (2) The Disappearing Nuclear Membrane
   (3) The Process of Mitosis
   (4) What the Spindle Does
   (5) Why Cell Division Is Important

2. Which of the following is a detail about mitosis that is supported by the diagram?

   (1) The nuclear membrane dissolves during prophase.
   (2) Spindle fiber formation begins in prophase.
   (3) If any of the spindle fibers get cut, mitosis cannot proceed normally.
   (4) Near the end of interphase, the protein content of the cell increases.
   (5) Anaphase is the shortest phase in the process of mitosis.

3. If a parent cell has 6 chromosomes at the start of interphase, how many chromosomes will each daughter cell eventually have?

   (1) 1
   (2) 3
   (3) 6
   (4) 12
   (5) 15

Question 4 refers to the diagram and the paragraph below.

BACTERIAL CELL

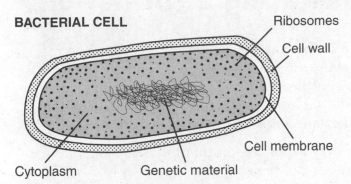

Bacteria are one-celled organisms. Bacterial cells are much smaller than animal and plant cells, and they do not have a nucleus. Like plant cells, bacterial cells have cell walls.

4. Which of the following statements is supported by information in both the diagram and the paragraph?

   (1) Plant and animal cells are smaller than bacterial cells.
   (2) There are no ribosomes in the cytoplasm of a bacterial cell.
   (3) Bacterial cells have a cell membrane but no cell wall.
   (4) Bacterial cells have genetic material but no nucleus.
   (5) Unlike plant and animal cells, bacterial cells do not have cytoplasm.

5. When organisms reproduce sexually, their reproductive cells have half the number of chromosomes found in nonreproductive cells.

   Reproductive cells have a reduced number of chromosomes to allow organisms to reproduce in which of the following ways?

   (1) by splitting in half
   (2) from a single reproductive cell
   (3) by combining its reproductive cell with that of another organism of the same species
   (4) by combining two reproductive cells with two from another organism of the same species
   (5) by combining nonreproductive cells

6. In normal cells, the tips of the chromosomes shrink a tiny bit each time the cell divides. In cancer cells, the tips of the chromosomes are longer than those of normal cells. Cancer is a disease in which cells divide in a rapid, chaotic way.

   What is the unstated main idea of this paragraph?

   (1) When normal cells divide, their chromosomes become shorter.
   (2) The tips of the chromosomes may play a role in the rate of cell division.
   (3) The structure of the chromosome does not influence the rate of cell division.
   (4) Cancer cells multiply very rapidly.
   (5) Normal cells multiply faster than cancer cells.

7. The drawings below show some types of cells in the human body. Which of the following cells is likely to line the passages inside your nose, using hair-like structures called cilia to filter out dust?

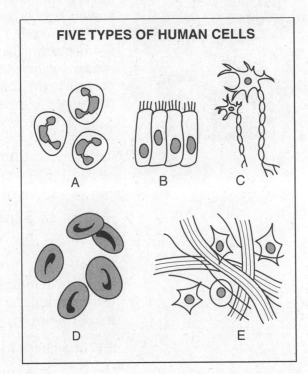

FIVE TYPES OF HUMAN CELLS

   (1) A
   (2) B
   (3) C
   (4) D
   (5) E

Answers start on page 267.

GED SKILL **Restating Information**

restate information
to say something in
another way

When you **restate information,** you say it in another way.
Sometimes you simply use different words. Other times you may
restate information by putting it in the form of a diagram, graph,
chart, or formula. Restating information is a good strategy to use
to make sure you understand important science concepts.

The most common way to restate information is to paraphrase,
or rewrite an idea, sentence, or paragraph in your own words. When
you take notes in class or while reading, you usually paraphrase.

When information is restated, all the facts remain the same.
However, the way the facts are presented changes. For example,
the order of the information may be rearranged. Or information
presented in sentences may be restated in pictorial form.

Read the passage and answer the questions below.

TIP

When restating
information, be
sure all the facts
and ideas stay the
same. Only the words
or the arrangement
of information
should change.

Runners pace themselves during a long race. Their muscle cells need
a steady supply of energy. Cells usually get energy through a chemical
process called **cellular respiration.** In this process, cells use oxygen to
break down sugar which releases energy. When a runner can't breathe
fast enough to keep her muscle cells supplied with oxygen, the cells
switch to another energy-releasing process, called **fermentation.**
Fermentation also breaks down sugar to release energy, but it does not
require oxygen. Lactic acid is a byproduct of fermentation. As lactic acid
collects in the cells, the runner's muscles start to ache. This may cause
the runner to slow down or even stop running.

1. Put a check mark by the restatement of the fermentation process.

_____ a. a chemical process in which energy and lactic acid are
released from the breakdown of sugar in the absence
of oxygen

_____ b. a chemical process in which muscle cells use lactic acid
to release energy

You were correct if you chose *option a.* Fermentation is explained
in the fifth and sixth sentences of the paragraph. *Option a* paraphrases
those sentences. *Option b* is not true; lactic acid is a by-product of
fermentation.

2. Put a check mark by the restatement of the passage's last idea.

_____ a. A runner's legs ache because of a build-up of oxygen.

_____ b. A runner's legs ache because of a build-up of lactic acid.

You were correct if you chose *option b.* It restates the idea in
slightly different words. *Option a* is not true; muscle fatigue results
from too little oxygen.

Use the passage to answer the questions below.

Alcoholic fermentation is a process that occurs naturally in the production of bread. In this type of fermentation, a single-celled microorganism called yeast breaks down sugars to produce alcohol and bubbles of carbon dioxide gas and to release small amounts of energy.

The carbon dioxide gas produced by fermentation causes dough to rise. When yeast grows and produces carbon dioxide in bread dough, the gas bubbles produced by the carbon dioxide become trapped in the dough and create air pockets, and the bread rises. Other fermentation processes not related to baking allow the carbon dioxide to escape.

1. Write *R* next to the sentence that restates the main idea of the passage.

   _____ a. In the process of alcoholic fermentation, yeast breaks down sugars.

   _____ b. Producing bread involves a natural process called alcoholic fermentation.

2. Write a sentence in your own words that restates the first sentence of the second paragraph.

   _____

   _____

3. Write *R* next to the sentence that is a restatement of what happens when dough rises.

   _____ a. Dough rises because of the bubbles that are formed by carbon dioxide gas.

   _____ b. Dough rises because of the carbon dioxide that is allowed to escape.

4. Write *R* next to the sentence that is a restatement of what happens when yeast breaks down sugars.

   _____ a. Alcohol, carbon dioxide bubbles, and small amounts of energy are produced.

   _____ b. Alcohol and bubbles of carbon dioxide produce and capture energy.

Answers start on page 268.

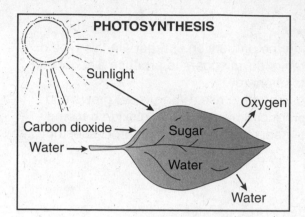

PHOTOSYNTHESIS

Sunlight

Oxygen

Carbon dioxide →

Sugar

Water →

Water

Water

The sun provides almost all the energy used by living things on Earth. Plants use the sun's energy to produce their own food through a process called **photosynthesis.** Animals get energy by eating plants or other animals that eat plants.

In photosynthesis, green plants take water, carbon dioxide, and energy from sunlight to make sugar, oxygen, and water. The sugar is used as food and to build other substances that the plant needs, such as **starches.** When animals eat plants, they get energy from the sugar created in photosynthesis. The water is used by the plant or released into the atmosphere. The oxygen is released into the atmosphere, where it can be used by other organisms.

The first phase of photosynthesis consists of reactions that require light, usually sunlight. Light energy from the sun is trapped by the plant's chlorophyll, or green coloring, located in the chloroplasts. The chlorophyll changes light energy to chemical energy, which is used to split **molecules** of water into hydrogen and oxygen.

The second phase of photosynthesis consists of "dark" reactions, those that do not require light to take place. During this phase, the hydrogen produced from water in the light reactions combines with carbon (from carbon dioxide taken from the air) to form sugar. The rest of the hydrogen combines with oxygen to form water.

Photosynthesis can be shown as a chemical equation. In the equation below, the arrow with the words *light energy* and *chlorophyll* means "yield when these elements are present."

$$6CO_2 + 12H_2O \xrightarrow[\text{chlorophyll}]{\text{light energy}} C_6H_{12}O_6 + 6O_2 + 6H_2O$$

carbon dioxide + water $\longrightarrow$ sugar + oxygen + water

This equation summarizes all the reactions that make up photosynthesis. The ingredients of photosynthesis—six molecules of carbon dioxide and twelve molecules of water—are shown on the left side of the equation. The products of photosynthesis, one molecule of sugar (glucose), six molecules of oxygen, and six molecules of water, are shown on the right side of the equation.

Directions: Choose the one best answer to each question.

Questions 1 through 6 refer to the passage and diagram on page 44.

1. Which of the following restates the main idea of the passage?

   (1) Animals eat plants for food.
   (2) Plants make their own food through photosynthesis.
   (3) Photosynthesis takes place in green plants.
   (4) Photosynthesis replaces the oxygen in the atmosphere that is used by animals.
   (5) Light is needed for photosynthesis to occur.

2. Which substance produced during photosynthesis does the plant use for food?

   (1) sugar
   (2) oxygen
   (3) water
   (4) carbon dioxide
   (5) chlorophyll

3. Which of the following restates the equation for photosynthesis?

   (1) Water plus carbon dioxide, in the presence of sunlight, yields sugar, oxygen, and water.
   (2) Water plus carbon dioxide, in the presence of chlorophyll, yields sugar, oxygen, and water.
   (3) Water plus carbon dioxide, in the presence of light and chlorophyll, yields sugar, hydrogen, and water.
   (4) Water plus oxygen, in the presence of light and chlorophyll, yields sugar, carbon dioxide, and water.
   (5) Water plus carbon dioxide, in the presence of light and chlorophyll, yields sugar, oxygen, and water.

4. Which of the following statements about photosynthesis is correct?

   (1) Both the light reactions and the dark reactions produce oxygen and water as byproducts.
   (2) Water is a product of the light reactions, and carbon dioxide is a product of the dark reactions.
   (3) In the light reactions, chemical energy splits water into hydrogen and oxygen.
   (4) Carbon dioxide absorbed from the atmosphere is used in the light reactions.
   (5) The light reactions yield light products, and the dark reactions yield dark products.

5. According to the diagram and the passage, which of the following is both a necessary ingredient and a product of photosynthesis?

   (1) carbon dioxide
   (2) chemical energy
   (3) light energy
   (4) sugar
   (5) water

6. Which of the following statements is supported by the passage and the diagram?

   (1) Green plants capture the sun's light energy and change it to chemical energy that plants and animals can use.
   (2) The ultimate source of all energy on Earth is the chemical energy in green plants.
   (3) The energy conversions of photosynthesis take place in the plant's stems and roots.
   (4) Without the process of photosynthesis, there would be no water on Earth.
   (5) Photosynthesis takes place only in sunlight, not in artificial light.

Answers start on page 268.

GED Practice • Lesson 2

Directions: Choose the one best answer to each question.

Questions 1 through 4 refer to the following passage and diagram.

Metabolism is the total of all the chemical reactions that take place in a cell. There are two basic metabolic processes: anabolism and catabolism.

In anabolic reactions, raw materials that enter the cell are used to make more complex molecules, such as proteins and fats. These complex molecules are used for cell growth and maintenance. In catabolic reactions, such as cellular respiration, energy is released from the breakdown of organic materials.

ANABOLISM AND CATABOLISM

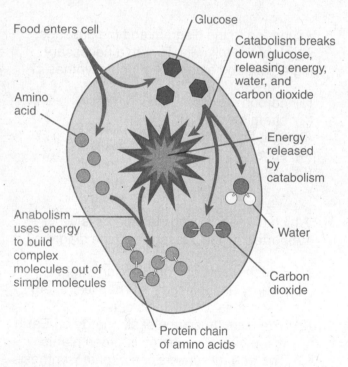

When an organism's anabolism is greater than its catabolism, then the organism grows or gains weight. When catabolism is greater than anabolism, an organism loses weight. When the two processes are balanced, the organism is in a state of equilibrium.

1. What is metabolism?

    (1) the process by which organisms capture energy from sunlight
    (2) the sum of all the chemical processes carried out by a cell
    (3) the process by which energy is released from glucose
    (4) the total amount of energy released by cellular respiration
    (5) the total amount of raw material used by the cell to get energy

2. Which symbol or symbols in the diagram represent the energy released by catabolic reactions?

    (1) arrows
    (2) circles
    (3) chained circles
    (4) hexagons
    (5) sunburst

3. If the amount of glucose entering the cell decreases, which of the following is likely to happen?

    (1) Light energy decreases.
    (2) Fewer amino acids enter the cell.
    (3) More proteins are produced.
    (4) There are fewer catabolic reactions.
    (5) The cell produces more energy.

4. Kayla wants to lose weight by exercising more each day. If she succeeds, what change will she have made in her cell metabolism?

    (1) increased photosynthesis
    (2) increased catabolic reactions
    (3) increased anabolic reactions
    (4) decreased photosynthesis
    (5) decreased catabolic reactions

MEASURING A PRODUCT OF CELLULAR RESPIRATION

Questions 5 through 7 refer to the following passage.

Carbon dioxide is a waste product of cellular respiration. It leaves the body in the air you exhale and can be measured. First, breathe for one minute exhaling through a straw into a flask containing 100 ml of water. The CO_2 in your breath dissolves in the water to form a weak acid. Add five drops of phenolphthalein, an acid-base indicator. Then, add sodium hydroxide, a basic solution, drop by drop. The more drops needed to neutralize the acid and turn the water pink, the more carbon dioxide in the water and in your exhaled breath.

To test whether exercise affects the amount of carbon dioxide in exhaled air, Jason ran in place for five minutes and then tested his breath using the method described above. It took five drops of sodium hydroxide solution to turn the water pink.

5. Jason hypothesized that exercise would result in an increased level of carbon dioxide in his exhaled breath. What was the assumption underlying Jason's hypothesis?

(1) Plants use the carbon dioxide produced during cellular respiration in the process of photosynthesis.
(2) Plants release oxygen into the air as a result of photosynthesis.
(3) Less cellular respiration is needed to produce the energy required by five minutes of exercise.
(4) The rate of cellular respiration goes up during exercise to give additional energy to the body.
(5) The capacity of the lungs to hold air decreases during exercise.

> **TIP** An assumption is not actually stated in a passage. When you are asked what the writer's assumptions are, you must decide what the writer thinks you already know.

6. In addition to the flask, water, straws, phenolphthalein, and sodium hydroxide solution, which of the following items would be useful for this procedure?

(1) a Bunsen burner
(2) a dropper
(3) a measuring spoon
(4) a test tube
(5) a centrifuge

7. What was wrong with the method that Jason used to test whether the level of carbon dioxide in exhaled breath increases as a result of exercise?

(1) Jason ran in place for five minutes, which is not enough time to increase the level of carbon dioxide in exhaled breath.
(2) After running in place for five minutes, Jason should have rested for two minutes before exhaling into the flask.
(3) Jason did not measure the level of carbon dioxide in his breath when at rest, so he did not have enough data to draw a conclusion.
(4) Jason used phenolphthalein rather than sodium hydroxide solution to measure the amount of carbon dioxide in his breath.
(5) Running is not a suitable form of exercise to use when testing carbon dioxide levels in exhaled breath after exercise.

8. The leaf is the plant structure in which most photosynthesis takes place. Which characteristic of most leaves maximizes the amount of light energy that can be captured for photosynthesis?

(1) pores on the underside
(2) broad, flat shape
(3) main stalk
(4) network of veins
(5) root system

Answers start on page 269.

GED Mini-Test • Lesson 2

Directions: This is a ten-minute practice test. After ten minutes, mark the last question you finished. Then complete the test and check your answers. If most of your answers were correct but you didn't finish, try to work faster next time. Choose the <u>one best answer</u> to each question.

<u>Questions 1 through 3</u> refer to the following passage and diagram.

People and other animals get their energy from food. When you eat, your digestive system breaks down the **carbohydrates** in food into simple sugar, called glucose. Glucose enters the cells of the body, where it is broken down to release energy. This complex chemical process is called cellular respiration.

CELLULAR RESPIRATION

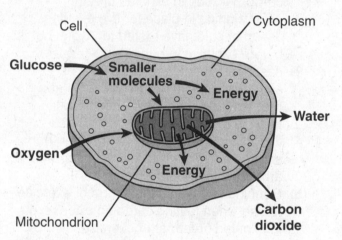

During cellular respiration, oxygen combines with glucose to release chemical energy and the byproducts carbon dioxide and water. Cellular respiration occurs in stages. The stage in which most of the energy is released takes place in the mitochondria.

$$C_6H_{12}O_6 + 6O_2 \longrightarrow 6CO_2 + 6H_2O + energy$$

glucose + oxygen $\longrightarrow$ carbon dioxide + water + energy

1. In which cell structure is most of the energy resulting from cellular respiration released?

   (1) cell membrane
   (2) cytoplasm
   (3) chloroplast
   (4) mitochondrion
   (5) nucleus

2. Which of the following sentences restates the equation for cellular respiration?

   (1) Carbon dioxide and water combine in the presence of light energy and chlorophyll to yield glucose, oxygen, and water.
   (2) Glucose and water combine to yield carbon dioxide, oxygen, and energy.
   (3) Glucose and carbon dioxide combine to yield oxygen, water, and energy.
   (4) Glucose, oxygen, and energy combine to yield carbon dioxide and water.
   (5) Glucose and oxygen combine to yield carbon dioxide, water, and energy.

3. Which of the following is likely to result if the supply of oxygen to the cell is reduced?

   (1) Less energy is released.
   (2) More energy is released.
   (3) Cellular respiration speeds up.
   (4) More carbon dioxide is released.
   (5) Cellular respiration is not affected.

4. Cellular respiration and photosynthesis are opposite processes. In cellular respiration, oxygen is used, and energy and carbon dioxide are released. In photosynthesis, energy and carbon dioxide are used, and oxygen is released. Together, the processes help keep the levels of oxygen and carbon dioxide in the air in balance.

   Which of the following statements does this information support?

   (1) More green plants means less oxygen in the air.
   (2) More green plants means more oxygen in the air.
   (3) Fewer green plants means less carbon dioxide in the air.
   (4) Fewer green plants means more energy is stored in glucose.
   (5) There is more oxygen than carbon dioxide in the air.

Questions 5 and 6 refer to the following information.

Carbohydrates are nutrients that contain only carbon, hydrogen, and oxygen. We obtain carbohydrates by eating plants. Some carbohydrates are in the form of sugars, which are easily digested and converted into glucose and fructose. Syrup, candy, and fruit are sources of sugar. Other carbohydrates are in the form of starches. Potatoes, bread, rice, and pasta are sources of starches. Before they can be used by the body, starches are broken down by enzymes into simple sugars like glucose.

Once carbohydrates have been broken down into simple sugars, such as glucose, they can be further broken down by the process of cellular respiration in order to release energy.

5. Which of the following does the passage imply?

    (1) Carbohydrates are excellent sources of energy.
    (2) More energy is contained in sugars than in starches.
    (3) Carbohydrates are not part of a healthy diet.
    (4) Potatoes contain more starch than rice and pasta.
    (5) Carbohydrates are formed during photosynthesis.

6. An enzyme in saliva begins the process of breaking down starch in the mouth. Which of the following supports this statement?

    (1) Bread is made from flour, which is a source of starch.
    (2) Potatoes and rice contain large amounts of starch.
    (3) Bread begins to taste sweet after it is chewed for several seconds.
    (4) Corn syrup tastes sweet because it is a source of sugar.
    (5) Carbohydrates are nutrients that contain carbon, hydrogen, and oxygen.

7. In the process of photosynthesis, green plants use water, carbon dioxide, and the energy from light to make their own food. At the University of California's Kearney Agricultural Center, researchers have demonstrated that tomato plants grow bigger and produce more tomatoes when the soil is covered with sheets of silver-colored reflective plastic. According to the researchers, when this plastic is used, more photosynthesis takes place and the plants grow larger.

Which property of the plastic is likely to cause the increase in photosynthesis?

    (1) its thickness
    (2) its weight
    (3) its reflectivity
    (4) its length
    (5) its flatness

8. The energy released by cellular respiration is stored in a molecule called adenosine triphosphate (ATP). Cellular respiration requiring oxygen results in 19 times as many ATP molecules as does lactic acid fermentation, a form of cellular respiration that does not require oxygen.

Which of the following statements is supported by this information?

    (1) Lactic acid fermentation yields more ATP molecules than does cellular respiration using oxygen.
    (2) Cellular respiration using oxygen is a more efficient way to release energy than lactic acid fermentation.
    (3) Lactic acid fermentation uses oxygen to break down glucose in order to release energy.
    (4) Once a cell's oxygen is used up, the cell can use the process of lactic acid fermentation to release energy.
    (5) ATP molecules release energy during the process of photosynthesis.

Answers start on page 269.

GED SKILL Distinguishing Fact from Opinion

fact
something that can be proved true

opinion
a belief that may or may not be true

A **fact** is something that has objective reality. A fact can be proved to be true. On the other hand, an **opinion** is what someone thinks is true. An opinion may or may not be true, and it cannot be proved true or false.

You deal with facts and opinions all the time. For example, your friend's hairline forms a widow's peak just like her mother's. It is a fact that her hairline comes to a point in the middle of her forehead. It is a fact that she inherited this **trait,** or the way a characteristic is displayed, from her mother. You may think your friend's hair is pretty. This is your opinion. You cannot prove that your friend's hair is pretty. Others may not agree.

Much of what you read in science is fact. However, you will also read scientists' opinions. Scientists observe things and then form an opinion. They may use their opinion to formulate a hypothesis to explain their observations. Then they experiment to learn if the hypothesis is supported by the data collected.

Read the passage. Then complete the fact and opinion table below.

Scientists have produced a type of squash that is resistant to a deadly virus. They did this by changing some of the squash's genetic material. The new squash was approved by the Department of Agriculture despite controversy over the risks it may pose to the environment. Some scientists think that the genetically engineered squash will breed with wild squash. The offspring may inherit the resistance to the virus. Then wild squash may spread like a "superweed" throughout farmers' fields or in the wild. Other scientists think that the government was right to approve the new squash. They say the environmental risks are exaggerated, and the benefits of the new squash outweigh the risks.

When distinguishing fact from opinion, watch for words and phrases that signal opinions. These include *according to, it is possible, believe, think, feel, suggest, may, might, should, agree,* and *disagree.*

Also look for words that express an evaluation or degree of quality such as *best, worst, prettiest, easier, harder, preferable.*

Fact	Opinion
Scientists genetically engineered squash to make it resistant to a deadly virus.	Some scientists believe approval of the genetically engineered squash is a mistake; others think the government was right to approve it.

Facts from the passage include: *The Department of Agriculture approved the squash. There is controversy over it.* From the fourth sentence to the end, the author presents opinions about the squash. You should have written two of these in the Opinion column.

Use the passage and the diagram to answer the questions below.

Genetics is the study of traits and how they are passed from parent to offspring. The father of genetics is Gregor Mendel, an Austrian monk who began experimenting in 1857. He bred pea plants because they have many traits that are easy to identify from one generation to the next. For example, when he crossed a tall pea plant with a short pea plant, all the resulting plants were either tall or short—none were medium-sized.

Round

In recent years, some people have suggested that some of Mendel's results may have been wrong. Those people think that Mendel's results were statistically too good to be true. They do not claim that Mendel committed fraud. Instead, they say that Mendel may have been biased in judging the characteristics of the pea plant offspring. For example, in deciding whether an offspring plant had wrinkled or round peas, Mendel may have tended to classify based on the outcome he expected.

Wrinkled

1. Write *F* next to the statement that is a fact.

   _____ a. Genetics is the study of traits and how they are passed from parent to offspring.

   _____ b. The study of genetics has proved to be of little value.

2. Explain why the statement you chose in question 1 is a fact.

   _____

   _____

3. Write *O* next to the statement that expresses an opinion.

   _____ a. Gregor Mendel was an Austrian monk who began genetics experiments in 1857.

   _____ b. Gregor Mendel should have used animals rather than plants in his genetics experiments.

4. Explain why the statement you chose in question 3 is an opinion.

   _____

   _____

5. Put a check mark next to each statement that can be proved true. Mark all that apply.

   _____ a. In the diagram, one pea has many more wrinkles than the other pea.

   _____ b. Mendel had to judge whether offspring plants had wrinkled or round peas.

   _____ c. Mendel's results are flawed because he miscategorized his peas.

Answers start on page 270.

GED CONTENT **Genetics**

Mendel began his experiments to find out how traits are passed from parents to offspring by breeding **purebred** pea plants. These plants always produced offspring with the same traits. For example, the offspring were always tall rather than short or always produced wrinkled peas rather than round peas.

Next, Mendel crossed, or bred, plants with opposite traits. For example, he crossed purebred tall plants with purebred short plants. He referred to this parental generation of plants as the P generation. Much to Mendel's surprise, all the plants that resulted were tall. Mendel called this F_1 generation of plants **hybrids.** The hybrids had received the traits for both tallness and shortness even though only the tallness showed.

Then Mendel crossed tall hybrid plants from the F_1 generation. Some plants in the resulting F_2 hybrid generation were tall and some were short. Each time Mendel repeated the experiment, he found that, on average, there were three tall plants for one short plant.

How did Mendel explain the results of this experiment? He reasoned that the offspring inherited traits from both parents in units we now call **genes.** However, some traits were more powerful than others. He called these traits dominant. **Dominant traits** are shown by a capital letter. In the illustration, T represents the dominant trait for tallness. Mendel called the traits that did not show in the F_1 generation recessive. **Recessive traits** are represented by a lowercase letter, in this case t for shortness. In the F_2 generation, the plants that show the recessive trait (the short plants) must be plants that did not inherit the dominant trait for tallness.

Another way to show how dominant and recessive traits are passed from generation to generation is by using a Punnett square. The Punnett square on the left shows the combinations of traits that can result when two hybrid tall plants from the F_1 generation are crossed.

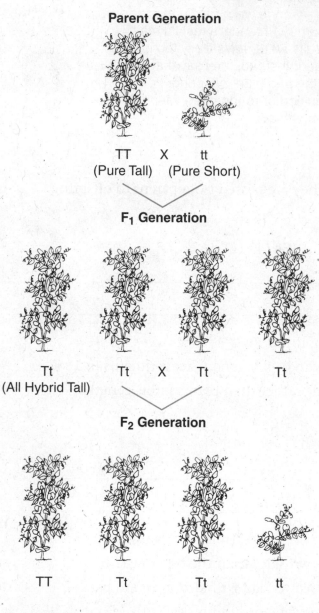

Parent Generation

TT   X   tt
(Pure Tall)   (Pure Short)

F_1 Generation

Tt   Tt   X   Tt   Tt
(All Hybrid Tall)

F_2 Generation

TT   Tt   Tt   tt

PUNNETT SQUARE

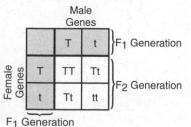

Male Genes

	T	t
T	TT	Tt
t	Tt	tt

Female Genes

F_1 Generation (top) } F_2 Generation

F_1 Generation

Directions: Choose the one best answer to each question.

Questions 1 through 5 refer to the information and the diagram on page 52.

1. In which offspring does a dominant trait appear?

   (1) in all offspring of any parent that shows it
   (2) in only those offspring whose parents both show it
   (3) in all offspring that have a gene for it
   (4) in only those offspring that have received two genes for it
   (5) in all F_1 offspring but no F_2 offspring

2. What evidence supports Mendel's conclusion that the recessive trait was carried by the F_1 generation even though none of these plants showed the recessive trait?

   (1) None of the F_1 generation plants was a hybrid.
   (2) All of the F_1 generation plants showed the dominant characteristic.
   (3) Some of the F_2 generation plants showed the recessive trait.
   (4) Some of the F_2 generation plants showed the dominant trait.
   (5) All of the F_2 generation plants showed the recessive trait.

3. Which of the following is an opinion rather than a fact?

   (1) A Punnett square shows the possible combinations of traits in the offspring of two parents.
   (2) A Punnett square is easier to read than sketches showing traits passing from parents to offspring.
   (3) When a dominant trait is combined with a recessive trait, the recessive trait is hidden.
   (4) Purebred pea plants can be either tall or short.
   (5) On average, three of four offspring of two hybrid tall pea plants will be tall.

4. Mendel made sure that the results of his experiments would be accurate by using which of the following plants as the parent generation?

   (1) purebred plants
   (2) hybrid plants with opposite traits
   (3) plants with several opposite traits
   (4) only short plants
   (5) only tall plants

5. Mendel was the first to suggest that traits are passed from parent to offspring by means of "hereditary elements" we now call genes. Since Mendel could not see genes, how did he know they existed?

   (1) He studied the male and female sex cells and observed the genes in those cells.
   (2) From patterns of inheritance, he reasoned that traits must be transmitted on physical units.
   (3) Because he was experimenting with plants, he knew that traits passed from one generation to the next.
   (4) He used plants with only one trait.
   (5) He used an organism with simple patterns of inheritance so he could breed hybrids.

Question 6 refers to the following diagram.

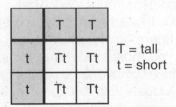

6. What is the chance that an offspring plant shown in this Punnett square will be short?

   (1) no chance
   (2) 1 out of 4
   (3) 2 out of 4
   (4) 3 out of 4
   (5) 4 out of 4

Answers start on page 270.

GED Practice • Lesson 3

Directions: Choose the one best answer to each question.

Questions 1 and 2 refer to the following passage and diagram.

A gene is a portion of the genetic molecule that determines a particular trait. Plants and animals that result from **sexual reproduction** inherit one gene for each trait from each parent. The set of genes that a plant or animal inherits is called its **genotype.**

To depict the traits that will be inherited, scientists use a Punnett square. The Punnett square below shows the possible combination of genes in the offspring of two parents with cleft chins. A cleft chin is one with a vertical groove. It is a dominant trait.

The genotype of the male parent is CC. Letters representing the genes from the father are across the top of the square. The genotype of the female parent is Cc. Letters representing the mother's genes are down the left side of the square. Each child inherits one gene from each parent.

	C	C
C	CC	CC
c	Cc	Cc

C = cleft chin
c = smooth chin

The Punnett square shows the possible genotypes of the offspring, but what appearence does each genotype represent? That is, what would a child with each genotype actually look like? To figure out the **phenotype,** or appearance, you must look at the dominant trait of each individual, shown by a capital letter. For example, individuals with the genotypes CC or Cc have cleft chins. When an individual has the dominant gene for a trait, that trait always shows, even when it is paired with the recessive gene for the trait. Only when an individual has two recessive genes in his or her genotype does the recessive trait actually show.

1. How many phenotypes are shown in the Punnett square?

   (1) 0
   (2) 1
   (3) 2
   (4) 3
   (5) 4

2. If you saw a girl with a cleft chin, what could you tell with the greatest accuracy?

   (1) the phenotype of her chin
   (2) the genotype of her chin
   (3) whether she has a recessive gene for chin type
   (4) whether her mother has a cleft chin
   (5) whether her father has a cleft chin

3. Traits are not always dominant or recessive. Sometimes the inheritance of traits occurs in a pattern called **incomplete dominance.** For example, the four o'clock plant has three genotypes for flower color. The genotype RR results in a red flower; rr results in a white flower; and Rr results in a pink flower.

   If you crossed a white-flowered four o'clock plant with a red-flowered four o'clock plant, what is the chance of producing a plant with pink flowers?

   (1) no chance
   (2) 1 out of 4
   (3) 2 out of 4
   (4) 3 out of 4
   (5) 4 out of 4

TIP Some questions are easier to answer if you draw a sketch, diagram, or chart. Making a Punnett square can help you answer genetics questions correctly.

SEQUENCING THE HUMAN GENOME

Questions 4 through 6 refer to the following passage.

The genetic code of an organism is called its **genome.** It is determined by the sequence in which four chemicals (called nitrogen bases and abbreviated A, T, C, and G) appear in the **DNA** molecules that make up genes. Variations in the sequence of these four nitrogen bases account for the unique genetic code of each organism.

The Human Genome Project began in 1990. This was an effort to identify individual genes, map their locations along the chromosomes, and identify the sequence of nitrogen bases within them. Scientists have approached this project in several steps. First they have worked on mapping the location of genes along large portions of DNA; next they have been sequencing the nitrogen bases that make up each gene. Because the human genome has about 3 billion nitrogen-base pairs, the project was expected to take about 15 years.

However, in 1998, a private company developed a new technology, enabling them to sequence all the nitrogen bases in the entire human genome in a few years, before identifying and mapping the gene locations. Millions of fragments of human DNA were run through high-speed sequencing machines. Then they were reassembled by powerful supercomputers. The company completed the sequencing in 2000. Early in 2000 details were published on the mapping of the human genome.

Some scientists argue that this procedure may have led to errors in reassembling the DNA fragments, so that individual genes cannot be accurately identified and mapped. Supporters say the results will be adequate for use in a variety of research.

4. What has been the main purpose of the recent research on the human genome?

   (1) to analyze the DNA chemicals
   (2) to locate DNA in human body cells
   (3) to map and sequence human DNA
   (4) to develop sequencing technology
   (5) to sell the genetic code to researchers

5. Which of the following is an opinion rather than a fact?

   (1) The U.S. Government's Human Genome Project was expected to take 15 years.
   (2) The human genome consists of about 3 billion nitrogen-base pairs.
   (3) Each organism has a genetic code called a genome.
   (4) A private company developed sequencers that analyzed the human genome in a few years.
   (5) The results of the private company's sequencing and mapping are of poor quality.

6. In which of the following areas should scientists' ability to "read" the human genome be of greatest advantage?

   (1) designing and producing more efficient gene-sequencing machines
   (2) improving the course of study in medical schools
   (3) preventing and treating hereditary diseases
   (4) preventing and treating bacterial diseases
   (5) improving the quality of genetically engineered agricultural products

7. Each person has a unique pattern of DNA that can be analyzed. Because the results of such an analysis are unique to each individual, they are often called a "DNA fingerprint."

Which of the following would be the most useful application of DNA fingerprinting?

   (1) identifying criminals
   (2) typing blood
   (3) analyzing the nutrients in food
   (4) doing laser surgery
   (5) treating disease

Answers start on page 271.

GED Mini-Test • Lesson 3

Directions: This is a ten-minute practice test. After ten minutes, mark the last question you finished. Then complete the test and check your answers. If most of your answers were correct but you didn't finish, try to work faster next time. Choose the <u>one best answer</u> to each question.

<u>Questions 1 through 3</u> refer to the following passage and diagram.

In 1903 American geneticist Walter Sutton, who was studying the egg and sperm cells of grasshoppers, discovered that Mendel's units of heredity—genes—were located on the chromosomes. Chromosomes are composed of a chemical called DNA. The structure of the DNA molecule was not known until 1953, when an American biologist, James D. Watson, and a British biophysicist, Francis Crick, worked it out. They described DNA as a double helix, or spiral, made up of two strands wound around each other and connected by crosspieces. The DNA molecule looks like a twisted ladder.

DNA MOLECULE

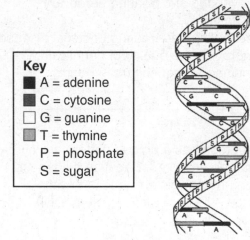

Key
- ■ A = adenine
- ■ C = cytosine
- □ G = guanine
- ▨ T = thymine
- P = phosphate
- S = sugar

The sidepieces of DNA are made of sugar and phosphate. The rungs of the DNA ladder are composed of pairs of four nitrogen bases: adenine, cytosine, guanine, and thymine. On the rungs, adenine always pairs with thymine, and guanine always pairs with cytosine. The sequence of bases along the ladder varies in different organisms (but each cell in a given organism has the same sequence in its copy of DNA). These variations form a genetic code that controls the production of proteins in the organism's cells. The proteins help determine the characteristics and functions of an organism.

1. Which of the following is a function of DNA?

   (1) controlling the production of proteins in the cell
   (2) breaking down proteins in the cell
   (3) producing energy from food molecules inside the cell
   (4) controlling substances that enter and leave the cell
   (5) joining adenine with thymine and cytosine with guanine

2. Suppose the sequence of bases along one side of a particular section of DNA is ATGTCAGC. Which of the following is the correct sequence of bases with which this sequence would be paired?

   (1) CTAGATAT
   (2) CTAGTGCT
   (3) TACACTCG
   (4) TACAGTCG
   (5) ATGTCAGC

3. Which of the following statements is supported by the information shown in the diagram?

   (1) Sugars and phosphates form the crosspieces of DNA molecules.
   (2) Of the two sidepieces of DNA, one is formed of only sugar and the other of only phosphate.
   (3) The base thymine is always attached to a guanine base.
   (4) Only the base adenine can attach to the sidepieces of the DNA.
   (5) The sidepieces of DNA are formed of alternating units of sugar and phosphate.

Questions 4 and 5 refer to the following passage and diagram.

Protein synthesis occurs in the cytoplasm of the cell and uses instructions from the DNA in the cell's nucleus. During the first stage of protein synthesis, the two sides of the DNA strands unzip, exposing a section of the molecule. The exposed bases on the DNA segment act as a template to make messenger RNA. Bases on messenger RNA nucleotides sequence themselves to pair correctly with the bases on the DNA segment. This template for the original DNA segment, called messenger RNA, then passes from the nucleus into the cytoplasm.

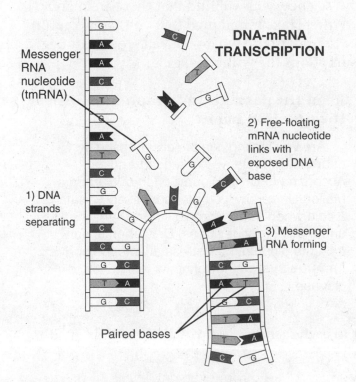

Messenger RNA nucleotide (tmRNA)

DNA-mRNA TRANSCRIPTION

2) Free-floating mRNA nucleotide links with exposed DNA base

1) DNA strands separating

3) Messenger RNA forming

Paired bases

The messenger RNA attaches itself to a ribosome in the cytoplasm, which reads the sequence of bases. Each group of three base pairs, called a codon, specifies a particular amino acid. In the ribosome, the codons are matched with the correct amino acids, the building blocks of proteins. A protein may contain 100 to 500 amino acids linked in a chain.

4. Which of the following would be the best title for the diagram?

(1) Protein Synthesis in the Cytoplasm
(2) The Separation of a DNA Strand
(3) The Formation of Messenger RNA
(4) Codon Specification for Amino Acids
(5) Amino Acid Formation in the Nucleus

5. A mutation occurs when one DNA base is substituted for another in error, causing a change in a codon. What is the most likely result of such a mutation?

(1) a change in the sequence of amino acids in a protein
(2) a change in the cytoplasm of the organism's cells
(3) a change in the nuclei of the organism's cells
(4) a change in the ribosomes of the organism's cells
(5) the death of the organism

Questions 6 and 7 refer to the following passage.

In 1998 the government of Iceland granted a biotechnology company the right to develop a computerized database. The database will contain the DNA profile, genealogical background, and medical history of every person in Iceland. Supporters of the plan argue that the database will produce a wealth of new and useful knowledge. Opponents claim it violates the rights of individuals to their privacy.

6. Which of the following statements is an opinion about the Iceland database project?

(1) A biotechnology firm has been granted the right to develop the database.
(2) The database will contain DNA profiles of every person in Iceland.
(3) Each Icelander's medical history will be part of the database.
(4) Genealogical records will be incorporated into the database.
(5) The DNA database violates Icelanders' right to privacy.

7. For which of the following would the database be most useful?

(1) preventing the spread of HIV/AIDS
(2) identifying bacterial infections
(3) improving the diets of Icelanders
(4) screening for genetic diseases
(5) vaccinating infants

Answers start on page 272.

GED SKILL Recognizing Unstated Assumptions

When people communicate, they often assume that the listener or reader knows certain facts. These facts or ideas are called **unstated assumptions.** You need to be able to identify such facts.

unstated assumption
a fact or idea that is taken for granted and not actually stated

You make unstated assumptions all the time. For example, when you tell a friend that there may be a thunderstorm this afternoon, you assume she knows what a thunderstorm is. Therefore, you do not describe the thunder, lightning, wind, and rain.

When you read about science, you will find that there are many unstated assumptions. Writers take for granted that you know certain common facts. In order to understand what you read, you must be able to identify the assumptions the writer makes.

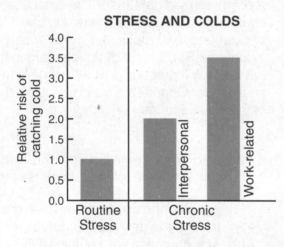

STRESS AND COLDS

Read the passage and graph and answer the question below.

Are you feeling completely stressed by quarrels with relatives or a dead-end job? According to Dr. Sheldon Cohen of Carnegie Mellon University, you are more likely to catch a cold when under chronic stress than when under mild, routine stress. Dr. Cohen is now trying to pinpoint how stress affects the body's **immune system,** lowering its resistance to disease.

Put a check mark next to each fact that the writer takes for granted and does not state in the passage or show in the graph.

_____ a. Mild, routine stress is part of our everyday lives.

_____ b. The immune system fights disease-causing agents.

_____ c. Chronic stress increases your chance of catching cold.

_____ d. People suffering interpersonal chronic stress are twice as likely to catch cold as those suffering routine stress.

_____ e. Chronic stress is severe stress that lasts a long time.

_____ f. Work-related chronic stress has a greater effect on the risk of catching cold than interpersonal chronic stress.

You were correct if you chose *options a, b,* and *e.* These are facts that the writer assumes you know, so they are not actually stated. The other options are explained in the paragraph or shown in the graph.

TIP

Both passages and diagrams may have unstated assumptions. Ask yourself: What does the writer or illustrator think I already know?

Use the passage and the diagram to answer the questions below.

The purpose of the **respiratory system** is to bring oxygen into the body and to release carbon dioxide into the air. Air enters the body through the nose or mouth. It then passes down a tube called the **trachea,** which runs from the back of the mouth to the lungs. The trachea divides into two **bronchi,** one for each lung. Each of these tubes divides, forming branches called **bronchioles.** The bronchioles end in small air sacs called **alveoli.**

The exchange of oxygen and carbon dioxide takes place in the alveoli. They are covered by a network of tiny blood vessels called **capillaries.** Oxygen from the air in the alveoli passes into the bloodstream. Carbon dioxide in the blood passes from the capillaries into the air in the lungs. The carbon dioxide leaves the body with each exhalation.

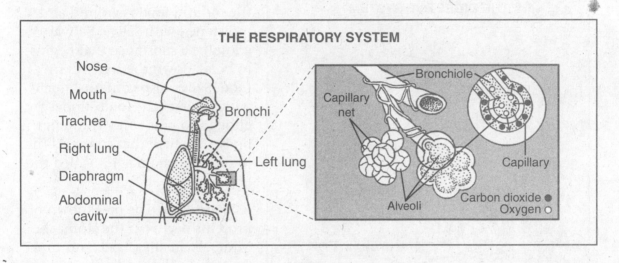

THE RESPIRATORY SYSTEM

1. Put a check mark next to all of the following unstated assumptions from the first paragraph.

   _____ a. Air is pulled into and pushed out of the lungs by the diaphragm.

   _____ b. The trachea branches into two tubes called bronchi.

   _____ c. Carbon dioxide and oxygen are gases in the air.

2. Put a check mark next to an unstated assumption from the second paragraph.

   _____ a. The exchange of gases takes place in the alveoli.

   _____ b. Capillary walls are thin enough to allow gas molecules to pass through.

3. Put a check mark next to all of the following facts that the illustrator assumes you know.

   _____ a. There are two lungs, one on the left, and one on the right.

   _____ b. The alveoli are enlarged to show detail; they are much smaller than the lungs.

   _____ c. The trachea branches into two tubes called bronchi.

Answers start on page 272.

The human body is made up of systems of **organs** that work together to perform a particular function such as gas exchange, blood circulation, or reproduction.

One human body system is the **digestive system,** which breaks down food into substances the body can use. The human digestive system consists of a long tube called the **alimentary canal.** It is made up of the mouth, esophagus, stomach, small intestine, and large intestine. In a human adult, the alimentary canal is about 30 feet long. The liver and pancreas, which also have a role in digestion, are connected to the alimentary canal by small tubes.

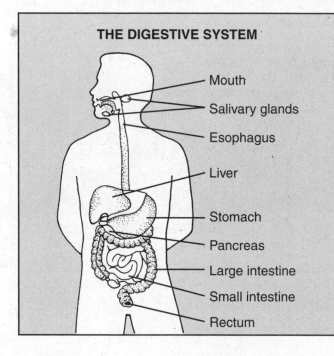

THE DIGESTIVE SYSTEM

- Mouth
- Salivary glands
- Esophagus
- Liver
- Stomach
- Pancreas
- Large intestine
- Small intestine
- Rectum

Mouth and Esophagus. In the mouth, food is ground and moistened with saliva. Saliva contains a substance that begins to break down the starches in food. Saliva also contains mucus, which makes the food slippery enough to pass easily through the body. The tube that connects the mouth and stomach is called the esophagus.

Stomach. The breakdown of proteins begins in the stomach. Minerals are dissolved, and bacteria in the food are killed by acid produced by the stomach. The stomach makes mucus to protect its lining from the acid.

Small Intestine. The small intestine is about $1\frac{1}{2}$ inches wide and 23 feet long. Most of the digestive process takes place here. The food is further broken down into separate **nutrients,** such as proteins, carbohydrates, fats, minerals, and vitamins. These nutrients pass from the small intestine into the bloodstream.

Pancreas and Liver. The pancreas secretes substances that help break down proteins, starches, and fats. Bile from the liver breaks up fats into smaller droplets. Substances from the pancreas and liver enter the small intestine by means of tubes called ducts.

Large Intestine. The undigested material from the small intestine contains a lot of water. One of the main functions of the large intestine is to absorb this water. As a result, the undigested material becomes more solid before it passes out of the body through the rectum.

Directions: Choose the one best answer to each question.

Questions 1 through 7 refer to the passage and the diagram on page 60.

1. What is the purpose of the digestive system?

   (1) to move food from the mouth to the stomach
   (2) to break down food into substances the body can use
   (3) to protect the lining of the organs from harmful substances swallowed with food
   (4) to protect the body against disease
   (5) to absorb oxygen from the air and release carbon dioxide

2. Ducts conduct substances between which organs?

   (1) from the pancreas and the liver to the small intestine
   (2) from the pancreas to the liver
   (3) from the esophagus to the stomach
   (4) from the stomach to the small intestine
   (5) from the small intestine to the large intestine

3. What assumption does the writer make about digestion in the stomach?

   (1) The tube that connects the mouth and the stomach is the esophagus.
   (2) The stomach begins the breakdown of proteins.
   (3) Minerals dissolve in the stomach.
   (4) Mucus protects the stomach lining from acid.
   (5) Stomach acid is strong enough to damage the stomach lining.

TIP When answering a question about a specific detail like the liver, skim the passage or diagram to find the word *liver*. Then find the answer.

4. According to the passage, where does material go after leaving the small intestine?

   (1) to the esophagus
   (2) to the stomach
   (3) to the liver
   (4) to the large intestine
   (5) to the pancreas

5. Which of the following is an unstated assumption that the writer makes about digestion in the mouth?

   (1) Food is ground up in the mouth.
   (2) Food is moistened by saliva.
   (3) Saliva is a liquid.
   (4) Saliva contains mucus.
   (5) Saliva begins to break down starches.

6. How would damage to the liver affect digestion?

   (1) Foods would not be ground up.
   (2) Proteins would not be broken down.
   (3) Starches would be changed to sugars.
   (4) Fats would not be digested properly.
   (5) Too much water would be absorbed by the large intestine.

7. Which of the following is supported by the information in the passage and the diagram?

   (1) The function of the digestive system is to remove liquid waste from the body.
   (2) The salivary glands in the mouth produce saliva, which begins the breakdown of starches.
   (3) Proteins are broken down into smaller substances in the liver.
   (4) Solid waste passes out of the body through the kidneys.
   (5) Bile is a nutrient that is absorbed by the liver.

Answers start on page 272.

Directions: Choose the one best answer to each question.

Questions 1 through 3 refer to the following passage and diagram.

The major organ of the **circulatory system** is the heart, which pumps blood throughout the body. The right and left sides of the heart are divided by a wall called the septum. Each side is divided into two chambers called the **atria** and the **ventricles.**

Oxygen-poor blood from the body enters the right atrium through large **veins** called the venae cavae. When the atrium contracts, it forces the blood into the right ventricle. Next the right ventricle contracts, forcing the blood into the pulmonary **arteries,** which carry it to the lungs. In the lungs the blood picks up oxygen. The oxygen-rich blood then flows through the pulmonary veins and back to the heart where it enters the left atrium. The left atrium contracts and forces the blood into the left ventricle. As the left ventricle contracts, it forces the blood into a large artery called the **aorta.** From the aorta, blood flows into a system of blood vessels that carry it throughout the body.

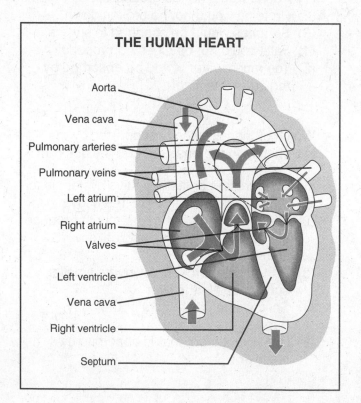

THE HUMAN HEART

Aorta

Vena cava

Pulmonary arteries

Pulmonary veins

Left atrium

Right atrium

Valves

Left ventricle

Vena cava

Right ventricle

Septum

1. Which chamber sends blood from the heart through the body?

    (1) the right ventricle
    (2) the right atrium
    (3) the left ventricle
    (4) the left atrium
    (5) the venae cavae

2. What would be most likely to happen if the aorta were partially blocked?

    (1) Too much blood would enter the left ventricle.
    (2) Not enough oxygen-poor blood would enter the heart.
    (3) Oxygen-poor blood would not be able to reach the lungs.
    (4) The body would not get enough oxygen-rich blood.
    (5) Oxygen-rich blood would enter the venae cavae.

3. Which of the following does the writer assume the reader already knows?

    (1) The arteries and veins are blood vessels, and they are part of the circulatory system.
    (2) The atria are the upper chambers of the heart, and the ventricles are the lower chambers.
    (3) The pulmonary veins carry blood from the lungs to the left atrium of the heart.
    (4) The septum separates the left and right sides of the heart.
    (5) In the heart, blood flows from the atria to the ventricles.

TIP When referring to information on a diagram, think about everything you know that may relate to the topic. Apply your own knowledge as you read the new information.

A VACCINE FOR LYME DISEASE

Questions 4 and 5 refer to the following paragraph and map.

The Food and Drug Administration (FDA) recently approved a **vaccine** against Lyme disease, a bacterial infection transmitted to humans through the bite of a deer tick. The three-dose vaccine is approved only for adults. It works by stimulating the immune system to produce **antibodies** that destroy the bacteria. In studies involving 11,000 people, the vaccine was shown to be about 78 percent effective. Scientists are advising people who work or play in wooded or overgrown areas where Lyme disease and deer ticks are common to get the vaccine.

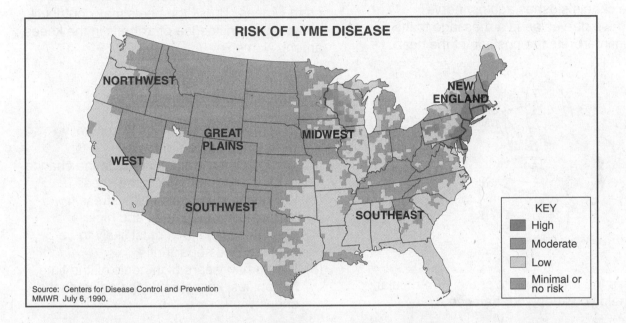

RISK OF LYME DISEASE

KEY
- High
- Moderate
- Low
- Minimal or no risk

Source: Centers for Disease Control and Prevention
MMWR July 6, 1990.

4. Based on the paragraph and the map, which of the following people would probably be advised to get vaccinated against Lyme disease?

   (1) a woman who lives in a wooded area of the Upper Midwest
   (2) a man who lives and works in Chicago
   (3) a woman who lives on a ranch in the Great Plains region
   (4) a man who works on a cargo ship
   (5) a young child who lives in a wooded area of New England

5. Which of the following statements is supported by the information that is given in the paragraph?

   (1) Lyme disease is a viral infection whose incidence is on the increase.
   (2) Everyone who lives in an area with a high risk of Lyme disease should be vaccinated.
   (3) The FDA requires the vaccine be given in four doses.
   (4) People who have received the vaccine are completely safe from contracting Lyme disease.
   (5) The vaccine stimulates the immune system to make bacteria-killing antibodies.

TIP When a question refers to a passage and a diagram, be alert for unstated assumptions in both.

Answers start on page 273.

GED Mini-Test • Lesson 4

Directions: This is a ten-minute practice test. After ten minutes, mark the last question you finished. Then complete the test and check your answers. If most of your answers were correct but you didn't finish, try to work faster next time. Choose the one best answer to each question.

Question 1 refers to the following paragraph and diagram.

The semicircular canals in the ear help the body to keep its balance. When the head moves, liquid in the canals sloshes against nerve endings. These nerves send a message to the brain, which interprets the position of the head.

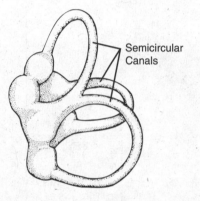

Semicircular Canals

1. How does the arrangement of the semicircular canals help you keep your balance?

   (1) They are aligned in a row so you can detect motion along a straight line.
   (2) They are aligned one on top of the other so you can detect up-and-down motion.
   (3) They are at right angles so head movement in any direction can be detected.
   (4) Each canal is in a different part of the ear so any head movement can be detected.
   (5) Each canal can separate from the others to detect changes in motion.

2. Blood moves throughout the body in tubelike blood vessels called arteries, veins, and capillaries. How would having clogged blood vessels affect the circulatory system?

   (1) More blood would circulate in the body.
   (2) Less blood would circulate in the body.
   (3) Arteries would become capillaries.
   (4) Bleeding would occur.
   (5) The body would produce more blood.

3. Women are twice as likely as men to develop osteoarthritis in their knees. By observing 20 healthy women walking in high heels, researchers at Harvard Medical School showed that the high heels increased stress on the knees. Thus high heels may contribute to the higher incidence of arthritis in the knees among women.

   Which of the following statements is supported by this information?

   (1) The knees of women are structurally weaker than those of men.
   (2) Wearing sneakers may reduce the chance of developing arthritis in the knees.
   (3) Walking in high heels shifts stress from the ankles to the knees and hips.
   (4) The knee is the joint most likely to be crippled by osteoarthritis.
   (5) If a woman wears high heels all the time, her ankles, knees, and hips adjust to the shoes.

4. A transplant is the placing of organs or grafting of tissue from one person or animal into another or from one part of the body to another part. The success of a transplant depends on compatibility between donor and recipient. If the donor organ or tissue is not compatible, the recipient's immune system may reject it.

   Which of the following transplants is most likely to succeed?

   (1) A man receives a heart from a baboon.
   (2) A boy receives a kidney from a cousin.
   (3) A girl receives a lung from an unrelated woman.
   (4) Healthy sections of a man's intestine are used to replace diseased sections.
   (5) A leukemia patient receives a bone marrow transplant from her aunt.

Questions 5 through 8 refer to the following paragraph and chart.

The endocrine system consists of glands that secrete chemicals called hormones. Hormones travel throughout the entire body but affect only some parts of it.

Endocrine Gland	Hormone	Effect
Thyroid	Thyroxine	Controls how quickly food is converted to energy in cells
Parathyroid	Parathormone	Regulates body's use of calcium and phosphorus
Thymus	Thymosin	May affect the formation of antibodies in children
Adrenal	Adrenaline Cortisone	Prepares the body to meet emergencies Maintains salt balance
Pancreas	Insulin	Decreases level of sugar in the blood
Ovaries (female gonads)	Estrogen	Controls the development of secondary sex characteristics
Testes (male gonads)	Testosterone	Controls the development of secondary sex characteristics
Pituitary	Growth hormone Oxytocin ACTH, TSH, FSH, LH	Controls the growth of bones and muscles Causes uterine contractions in labor Regulates the secretions of the other endocrine glands

5. In an emergency, your heart rate and breathing quicken and you have a sudden burst of energy. Which endocrine gland causes this reaction?

(1) adrenal
(2) pituitary
(3) thymus
(4) parathyroid
(5) pancreas

6. Which hormone causes the uterus to contract during childbirth?

(1) glucagon
(2) oxytocin
(3) estrogen
(4) testosterone
(5) adrenaline

7. Which of the following is the unstated method by which hormones are carried throughout the body?

(1) by the digestive system
(2) by the nerves
(3) by the blood
(4) by the saliva
(5) by the skin

8. A person with high levels of sugar in the blood has a disease called diabetes. One type of diabetes is caused by lack of a particular hormone. Which hormone would a person with this type of diabetes lack?

(1) parathormone
(2) adrenaline
(3) insulin
(4) oxytocin
(5) thymosin

Answers start on page 273.

GED SKILL Identifying Faulty Logic

faulty logic
errors in reasoning

oversimplification
reduction of the complexity of a concept or topic so much that the presentation becomes incorrect

either-or error
when only two choices are presented although there are actually other possibilities

TIP

To identify faulty logic, go over the material step-by-step. Look for things that are too simple or too general. Look for things that don't make sense.

Scientific reasoning is logical most of the time. Sometimes, however, scientists' reasoning breaks down, and they use **faulty logic.** You have to read carefully to identify faulty logic.

One type of faulty logic is **oversimplification.** This happens when the complexity of a topic is reduced so much that the discussion is no longer correct. Oversimplification often occurs in statements of cause and effect. For example, you may have heard that a high-fat diet causes heart disease. This is an oversimplification. A high-fat diet may contribute to the development of heart disease in many people.

Sometimes oversimplification takes the form of the **either-or error.** In the either-or error, only two choices are set up when other choices also exist. For example, suppose someone says, "Heart disease is caused by a high-fat diet or by smoking." In truth, both diet and smoking contribute to heart disease, but so do lack of exercise, heredity causes, and other factors.

Read the paragraph and answer the questions that follow.

For years, people have debated whether human behavior is determined by nature (your genetic inheritance) or nurture (your experience in the environment). The ancient Greek Plato thought that personality is inborn. Another ancient Greek, Aristotle, thought that everything in the mind comes in through the senses. The debate continues: Are gender differences due to biology or experience? Is personality shaped by heredity or environment? Today scientists think both nature and nurture influence human behavior.

1. Put a check mark next to the sentence that states what Plato thought about personality.

    _____ a. Personality is influenced by the environment.

    _____ b. Personality is inborn.

You were correct if you chose *option b.* Plato thought biology determines personality.

2. Put a check mark next to the reason Plato's view of personality is an oversimplification.

    _____ a. Personality is determined by many factors, both inborn and environmental.

    _____ b. Personality is really the result of experience.

You were correct if you chose *option a.* Personality is complex and determined by many factors. When you try to attribute personality to one cause, the result may be faulty logic.

Use the passage and the diagram to answer the questions below.

Research shows that the brain's two sides, or hemispheres, are specialized to some extent. The left hemisphere deals mostly with verbal and logical tasks. The right hemisphere processes visual and emotional cues. The two sides of the brain are connected by a wide band of nerve tissue called the **corpus callosum.**

At one time, a popular notion was that the left and right sides of the brain had different functions. Verbal, logical people were sometimes referred to as "left-brained." Artistic, emotional people were called "right-brained."

However, scientists have found that many functions are not located in just one hemisphere or the other. In fact, complex activities require both sides of the brain. Studies show that reading a story involves processing by both hemispheres. The left hemisphere is processing the words while the right hemisphere is processing visual imagery and emotional content.

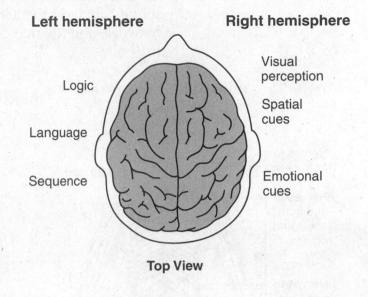

Left hemisphere   **Right hemisphere**

Logic

Language

Sequence

Visual perception

Spatial cues

Emotional cues

Top View

1. Write *L* for *left* next to the functions that are handled primarily by the left side of the brain and *R* for *right* next to those that are handled primarily by the right side of the brain.

    ____ a. language   ____ c. logic   ____ e. spatial cues

    ____ b. visual cues   ____ d. emotions   ____ f. sequence

2. Put a check mark next to the example of faulty logic that resulted from the fact that the two hemispheres of the brain have different functions.

    ____ a. People are either right-brained or left-brained, depending on whether they are logical or artistic.

    ____ b. Complex activities require processing by both sides of the brain.

3. Put a check mark next to each fact that suggests both sides of the brain are involved in complex activities.

    ____ a. Messages can travel between the two hemispheres of the brain across the corpus callosum.

    ____ b. The surface of both the left and right side of the brain is wrinkled and has deep grooves.

    ____ c. When you read a story, the right side of the brain processes visual and emotional cues and the left side processes language.

    ____ d. Spatial tasks, visual perception, and emotional content are processed by the right hemisphere.

Answers start on page 274.

GED CONTENT **The Nervous System and Behavior**

The control and communications network of the human body is the **nervous system.** The nervous system consists of the brain, the spinal cord, and the nerves. The brain and spinal cord control the network, and the nerves link the brain and spinal cord to the rest of the body.

HUMAN NERVOUS SYSTEM

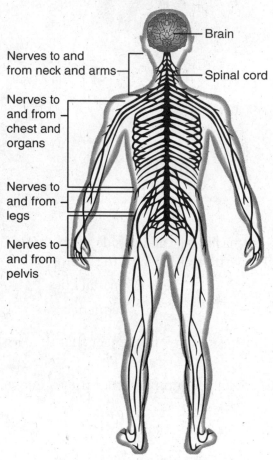

The human nervous system has four basic functions.

1. It receives information about the environment from the **senses.**
2. It organizes that information and integrates it with stored information.
3. It uses the information to send instructions to muscles and glands.
4. It provides us with conscious experience—the thoughts, perceptions, and feelings of our mental life.

The basic unit of the nervous system is the **neuron,** or nerve cell. There are three types of neurons. Sensory neurons carry information from sensory organs like the eyes or skin to the spinal cord and brain. Interneurons carry messages within the brain and spinal cord. They process information and link sensory and motor neurons. Motor neurons carry messages from the brain and spinal cord to muscles and glands throughout the body.

Interneurons have the most complex task. There are about 100 billion interneurons and a few million sensory and motor neurons.

The diagram below shows a motor neuron. The motor neuron receives signals from other neurons through its dendrites and cell body. It then sends its own impulses down the axon, which ends in axon terminals that touch a muscle fiber.

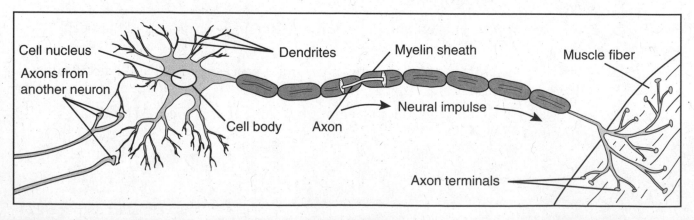

Directions: Choose the one best answer to each question.

Questions 1 through 6 refer to the passage and the diagrams on page 68.

1. According to the passage and the bottom diagram, from what does a motor neuron receive signals?

   (1) the axons of interneurons or other motor neurons
   (2) the axons of sensory neurons
   (3) the dendrites of another motor neuron
   (4) the dendrites of interneurons
   (5) the cell bodies of sensory neurons

2. Many sensory neurons are located in the skin. Which of the following is likely to have the most sensory neurons?

   (1) the forehead
   (2) the tops of feet
   (3) the tops of hands
   (4) the torso
   (5) the fingertips

3. The space between the axon of one neuron and the dendrites of another is called the **synapse.** A signal is carried by electrical impulses from the cell body to the end of the axon. There the signal crosses the synapse by means of a chemical messenger called a **neurotransmitter.** Based on this information and the information on page 68, which of the following statements is true?

   (1) Signals travel from neuron to neuron by electrical impulses.
   (2) Neurotransmitters carry the signal from one neuron to another.
   (3) A neuron has a dendrite or it has an axon.
   (4) Motor neurons pass information to sensory neurons.
   (5) Only motor neurons produce neurotransmitters.

4. What would be the most probable result if the spinal cord were cut around waist level?

   (1) The spinal cord would stop functioning altogether.
   (2) Messages from the brain would not reach the legs and the pelvis.
   (3) Messages from the brain would not reach the chest and the heart.
   (4) Messages from the neck and arms would not reach the brain.
   (5) Messages from the chest and the heart would not reach the brain.

5. Why is the nervous system described as a communications network?

   (1) The brain helps control the muscles and many glands in the body.
   (2) The spinal cord carries nerve bundles up to the brain.
   (3) Information is transmitted to and from all parts of the body via the brain and spinal cord.
   (4) New information is integrated with stored information.
   (5) The brain, spinal cord, and nerves are made up of neurons.

6. "The brain controls the activities of the nervous system." Why is this statement an example of faulty logic?

   (1) The nervous system consists of the brain, spinal cord, and nerves.
   (2) The brain is made up of billions of interneurons.
   (3) The spinal cord controls some activities of the nervous system.
   (4) The nervous system is made of different types of neurons.
   (5) The brain does not receive information from the senses.

Answers start on page 274.

GED Practice • Lesson 5

Directions: Choose the one best answer to each question.

Questions 1 through 3 refer to the following passage and diagram.

Some human behavior, like a simple **reflex,** is inborn. A simple reflex is an automatic response to a **stimulus.** For example, if a flame burns your finger, you automatically withdraw your hand.

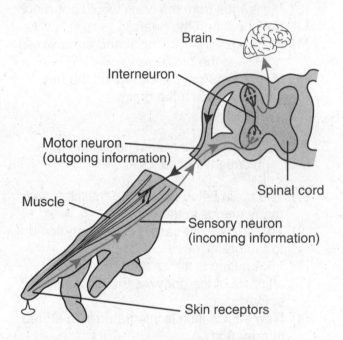

Brain

Interneuron

Motor neuron
(outgoing information)

Muscle

Spinal cord

Sensory neuron
(incoming information)

Skin receptors

A simple reflex works this way: A sensory neuron carries information about a stimulus from your skin to your spinal cord. In your spinal cord, the information is passed to motor neurons that go to muscles in your arm and hand. You pull your hand away quickly. The reflex is so rapid that it takes place before information about the event has time to reach your brain. Once it reaches your brain, you experience pain.

However, much human behavior is not innate. Instead, it is learned. You learn to associate events, such as the smell of cooking with the arrival of dinner. You learn to repeat behavior that brings rewards and avoid behavior that brings punishment. And by observation, you learn from the experiences and examples of others. Unlike simple reflexes, learning involves complex pathways in the brain.

1. "In a simple reflex, information is transmitted from a sensory neuron directly to a motor neuron." According to the diagram, in what way does this statement show faulty logic?

   (1) Only sensory neurons are involved in simple reflexes.
   (2) Only motor neurons are involved in simple reflexes.
   (3) Only interneurons are involved in simple reflexes.
   (4) Simple reflexes are processed by the brain, not the neurons.
   (5) Information is also passed by interneurons in the spinal cord.

2. Which of the following is an example of learning to repeat a behavior because it brings rewards?

   (1) A child cringes when he sees lightning because he knows that thunder will follow.
   (2) A woman learns to drive within the speed limit because she gets a speeding ticket.
   (3) A child learns to say "please" because she then gets what she asked for.
   (4) A man burns his hand on a hot stove and pulls it away quickly.
   (5) A child watches his father perform a trick and then tries it himself.

3. What is a difference between a simple reflex and learned behavior?

   (1) A simple reflex involves the brain, and learned behavior involves the spinal cord.
   (2) A simple reflex involves the spinal cord, and learned behavior involves the brain.
   (3) Both simple reflexes and learned behavior involve the brain.
   (4) A simple reflex involves sensory neurons and learned behavior does not.
   (5) A simple reflex involves motor neurons and learned behavior does not.

Science as Inquiry
PAVLOV'S EXPERIMENTS

Questions 4 through 6 refer to the following passage and chart.

Ivan Pavlov, a Russian scientist who studied the digestive system, knew that when he gave a dog meat, the dog would salivate. Pavlov also noticed that when he kept working with a particular dog, the dog began salivating to stimuli associated with the meat—approaching footsteps, the food dish, and so on.

Pavlov conducted experiments to discover what was happening. He put the dog in a small room and attached a device that would measure its saliva. From the next room, he could present the food after a neutral stimulus, like sounding a tone. After several pairings of the tone and the food, Pavlov presented the tone without the food. The dog began salivating. The dog had learned to associate the tone with being fed. Using the same method, Pavlov taught dogs to salivate to a buzzer, a light, a touch on the leg, and the sight of a circle.

PAVLOV'S EXPERIMENT

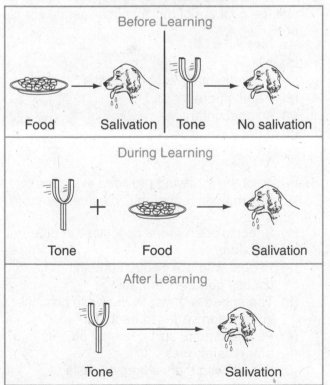

4. After hearing a tone and being fed, why did Pavlov's dog begin to salivate when Pavlov just sounded the tone?

    (1) The dog was extremely hungry.
    (2) The dog's saliva was being measured.
    (3) The dog learned to link the tone with food.
    (4) The dog learned to link the tone with punishment.
    (5) Dogs always salivate at a tone.

5. Suppose that Pavlov continued to present the tone to the dog, but he no longer fed the dog when he sounded the tone. Which of the following would the dog be most likely to do?

    (1) continue to salivate at the sound of the tone
    (2) continue to salivate when the tone and food were paired
    (3) eventually stop salivating at the sound of the tone
    (4) eventually stop salivating when presented with food
    (5) sometimes salivate at the tone and when presented with food

6. Which of the following is most similar to the type of learning shown by Pavlov's dog?

    (1) A dog learns to hide from a child who frequently pulled its tail.
    (2) A student memorizes a long list of vocabulary words to prepare for an exam.
    (3) A pigeon learns to recognize a human face by seeing it repeatedly.
    (4) A child learns that throwing a tantrum is rewarded with attention.
    (5) A chimpanzee learns to use a branch or stone to crack nuts.

Answers start on page 275.

Directions: This is a ten-minute practice test. After ten minutes, mark the last question you finished. Then complete the test and check your answers. If most of your answers were correct but you didn't finish, try to work faster next time. Choose the <u>one best answer</u> to each question.

Questions 1 through 4 refer to the following passage and chart.

One point of view on what constitutes intelligence is the concept of multiple intelligences. According to this theory, there are various forms of intelligence that people possess in varying degrees.

MULTIPLE INTELLIGENCES	
Type of Intelligence	**Description**
Linguistic	Language ability, especially the ability to understand shades of meaning
Logical-Mathematical	The ability to reason
Spatial	The ability to perceive and draw spatial relationships
Musical	Musical ability, including singing, playing an instrument, and composing
Bodily-Kinesthetic	The ability to control muscle movements gracefully
Interpersonal	The ability to understand and get along with others
Intrapersonal	The ability to understand oneself and use that knowledge to guide one's behavior

1. Which of the following can be inferred from the concept of multiple intelligences?

   (1) Intelligence depends on the speed with which the brain processes information.
   (2) Intelligence is a single, general mental ability.
   (3) Multiple intelligences cannot be measured by standard intelligence tests.
   (4) People who have strong bodily-kinesthetic intelligence often lack linguistic intelligence.
   (5) People who have strong spatial intelligence often lack interpersonal intelligence.

2. According to the theory, which forms of intelligence are you using while studying this book?

   (1) linguistic and logical-mathematical
   (2) logical-mathematical and spatial
   (3) spatial and bodily-kinesthetic
   (4) bodily-kinesthetic and interpersonal
   (5) interpersonal and intrapersonal

3. Which of the following people is most likely to use the concept of multiple intelligences in his or her work?

   (1) a lawyer
   (2) an elementary school teacher
   (3) a sales person
   (4) an accountant
   (5) a doctor

4. Which of the following provides evidence to support the concept of multiple intelligences?

   (1) Specific brain areas specialize in different functions.
   (2) People who are good at one thing are usually good at other things.
   (3) The speed with which the brain processes information varies in each person.
   (4) People tend to sort common objects into broad categories.
   (5) People with high scores on tests of short-term memory tend to be intelligent.

Questions 5 through 7 refer to the following passage and diagram.

The human brain has three main parts: the cerebrum, the cerebellum, and the brain stem.

The cerebrum is the largest part of the brain. It is responsible for sensory perception, voluntary movement (motor control), language, memory, and thought. Different areas of the cerebrum control different functions.

The cerebellum controls movements you make automatically, such as those related to posture. It also coordinates information from the eyes, inner ears, and muscles to help you maintain balance.

The brain stem controls heartbeat, breathing, and other vital functions of the body.

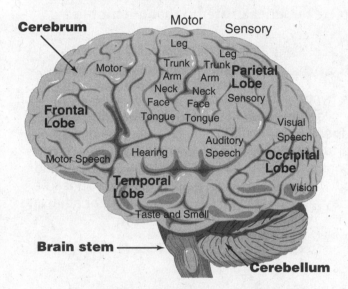

5. "The cerebellum is the part of the brain that controls movement." Which statement corrects the faulty logic of the previous sentence?

(1) The cerebellum controls balance, not movement.
(2) The cerebellum controls vital functions as well as movement.
(3) Both the cerebellum and the cerebrum control movement.
(4) The brain stem controls involuntary movement.
(5) The brain stem controls heartbeat and breathing.

6. Which of the following functions is most likely to be affected by a blow to the back of the head?

(1) taste
(2) vision
(3) heart rate
(4) hearing
(5) leg movement

7. What would be the best title for this passage and diagram?

(1) The Human Nervous System
(2) The Human Brain
(3) The Cerebrum
(4) The Brain
(5) The Nervous System

8. At any given moment, your senses are bombarded by many stimuli. For example, you may hear passing traffic, people talking, and birds chirping; you may see cars whizzing by and neighbors strolling down the sidewalk; you might smell cut grass and brewing coffee; at the same time, you might feel an itch on your foot and taste a bite of your steaming, hot breakfast cereal. Selective attention is the process by which the brain chooses the stimuli to which it will pay attention.

In which situation would you be most likely to employ selective attention?

(1) while watching an exciting movie in a movie theater
(2) when feeling sunlight strike your skin on a hot, humid summer day
(3) when smelling the aroma of a simmering stew when you enter a restaurant
(4) while tasting the sweetness of a sugary soft drink
(5) while listening to one person's voice at a crowded party

Answers start on page 275.

Lesson 6

GED SKILL Summarizing Ideas

summarize
to briefly tell the important points

When you **summarize** something, you cover the main points briefly. For example, if you tell a friend what happened on a TV program, you don't take half an hour to describe each detail. Instead, you take a minute to tell only the most important things.

Summarizing is a skill you use when you read about science. When you summarize a passage, you look for the main ideas. The main idea is often stated in the topic sentence of a paragraph. All main ideas should be in a summary. Very important details should also be in a summary.

You can also summarize a diagram or chart. How? Study the title, labels, or column heads. Ask yourself: What does this diagram or chart show? A complete but brief answer to that question is a summary.

Read the paragraph and answer the questions below.

Some scientists have hypothesized that dinosaurs are the ancestors of birds. As evidence, they cite many shared traits, such as wishbones. In the late 1990s, the first **fossils,** or remains, of ancient birdlike dinosaurs were found, providing further evidence that birds and dinosaurs are related. One such ancient **species** had long tail feathers. The other had feathers on its limbs, body, and tail. However, neither of these dinosaurs could fly. The feathers may have been for insulation, balance, or attracting a mate.

When summarizing, ask yourself, "Is this point important?" If the point is not essential, leave it out.

1. Write *M* next to the sentence that is the main idea of the paragraph.

　　　 a.　Scientists have hypothesized that dinosaurs are the ancestors of birds.

　　　 b.　Dinosaur feathers may have been used for balance.

You were right if you chose *option a*. The main idea is that there may be a relationship between dinosaurs and birds.

2. Write *S* next to the sentence that is a summary of the paragraph.

　　　 a.　Dinosaurs may be the ancestors of birds. Evidence for this includes shared traits, such as wishbones, and fossil evidence, such as feathered, birdlike dinosaurs.

　　　 b.　Fossils of birdlike dinosaurs have been found. Dinosaur feathers may have been used to insulate, provide balance, or attract mates.

You were correct if you chose *option a*. This option tells the main idea and the other important points very briefly.

Use the passage and the diagram to answer the questions below.

Getting rid of head lice used to be easy. You simply used a shampoo or rinse containing an insecticide called permethrin. However, in recent years, head lice have developed resistance to permethrin, so the shampoos and rinses often do not work very well.

How did lice develop resistance to this insecticide? When permethrin was applied to a **population** of lice, most of them died. However, a few lice survived because they were different: they had a **mutation** in their genes that made them resistant to the insecticide. These resistant lice lived to reproduce and pass their resistance on to their offspring. After many generations, most lice are resistant to permethrin.

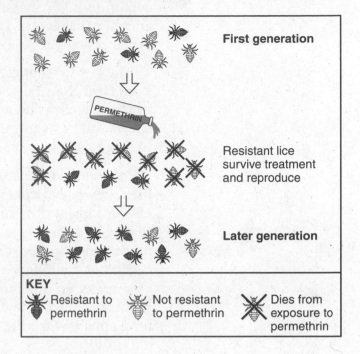

1. Write *M* next to the sentence that is the main idea of the passage.

_____ a. The insecticide permethrin was used to kill head lice.

_____ b. Head lice have developed resistance to the insecticide permethrin.

2. Write *S* next to the sentence that is a summary of the passage.

_____ a. To get rid of head lice, you use a shampoo or rinse containing the insecticide permethrin. Permethrin does not work well anymore, so many lice survive this treatment.

_____ b. Permethrin is no longer effective in treating head lice. A mutation that made the lice resistant to the insecticide has been passed down through generations, and now most lice are resistant.

3. Write *S* next to the sentence that is a summary of the diagram.

_____ a. Head lice that were resistant to permethrin survived treatment. They reproduced and their offspring inherited this resistance.

_____ b. Insecticide shampoos and rinses are no longer effective treatments for head lice. The lice survive treatment, so they must be destroyed by other means.

4. Write *S* next to the sentence that is a summary of the passage <u>and</u> the diagram.

_____ a. Permethrin is no longer effective in treating head lice. A mutation gave some lice resistance, and they passed the resistance to their offspring.

_____ b. All insecticide shampoos and rinses are ineffective in treating head lice. The lice survive treatment, and so do their offspring.

Answers start on page 276.

Evolution involves change over time. In science, the theory of evolution holds that all organisms living today have a common ancestor that evolved from the first living cells. These first cells developed about 3.5 billion years ago.

The key to Charles Darwin's theory of evolution is **natural selection.** Natural selection is the process by which weak or poorly suited organisms do not survive in a population, leaving only the strongest and fittest, that is, those best adapted to the environment, to breed and carry on the species.

An example of natural selection is the peppered moth. At one time, nearly all peppered moths were light-colored. The few dark-colored moths could easily be spotted where they rested on tree trunks, and they were eaten by birds. During the 1800s, the peppered moth's environment in England changed. Smoke from new factories began blackening tree trunks with soot. Soon, light-colored moths were easier for birds to find and eat. The number of light-colored moths declined. The dark moths, now camouflaged against the blackened tree trunks, survived to reproduce and pass on their dark coloring.

The steps involved in natural selection are summarized in the following chart.

THE STEPS IN NATURAL SELECTION	
Step	**Description**
Overproduction	Most organisms have many offspring. However, the environment cannot support as many organisms as are born because resources are limited.
Competition	Too many offspring and limited resources mean that organisms compete for food, water, and other needs.
Variation	Individual organisms of a species vary a great deal in the traits they inherit. In addition, some of them may have variations caused by genetic mutations.
Survival	Some individuals have inherited traits that help them use the resources of the environment or use them more efficiently. These individuals are more likely to survive. As the environment changes, the traits that help an individual survive may also change.
Reproduction	Individuals that survive and mate pass their traits to their offspring.

Directions: Choose the one best answer to each question.

Questions 1 through 6 refer to the passage and the chart on page 76.

1. What is evolution?

   (1) environmental changes that take place quickly
   (2) the passing of traits from parents to offspring over generations
   (3) the process by which certain organisms survive and reproduce
   (4) the survival of the fittest to breed and produce offspring
   (5) the process by which living things change over time

2. How did the soot produced by industrialization favor the survival of dark peppered moths?

   (1) Soot did not do any damage to dark-colored moths.
   (2) Soot killed the trees on which the light-colored moths fed.
   (3) Soot darkened the tree trunks, better camouflaging the dark moths.
   (4) Soot clogged birds' lungs, killing them before they could eat moths.
   (5) Soot poisoned the food supply, killing the light-colored moths.

3. Some peppered moths were light in color; others were dark. Of which step in natural selection is this an example?

   (1) overproduction
   (2) competition
   (3) variation
   (4) survival
   (5) reproduction

4. Cactus plants store large amounts of water and can thrive in the desert during the long periods of dry weather. Of which step in natural selection is this an example?

   (1) overproduction
   (2) competition
   (3) variation
   (4) survival
   (5) reproduction

5. Which of the following best summarizes the process of natural selection?

   (1) Plant and animal species, which have a common ancestor, evolved into their present forms over time.
   (2) In any given environment, certain traits make some individuals more likely to survive than others.
   (3) Weak die, leaving well-adapted individuals to reproduce and pass on their traits.
   (4) The environment cannot support all the offspring that are produced, so they compete among themselves for resources.
   (5) Some variations among individuals of a species are caused by genetic mutations, which may or may not be harmful.

6. How will the passage of a million years affect today's plant and animal species?

   (1) Plant and animal species will continue to evolve.
   (2) Animals will continue to evolve, but plants will remain the same.
   (3) Plants will continue to evolve, but animals will remain the same.
   (4) Plants and animals will cease to be affected by natural selection.
   (5) Plant and animal species will not change over the next million years.

Answers start on page 276.

GED Practice • Lesson 6

Directions: Choose the one best answer to each question.

Questions 1 through 3 refer to the following passage and diagram.

There is much evidence to support the theory of evolution. One type of evidence is the presence of similar structures in different organisms. Called **homologous structures,** these body parts from different organisms have similar structures but perform different functions. For example, the body parts shown below are homologous structures. Each of these limbs is used in a different way.

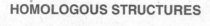

HOMOLOGOUS STRUCTURES

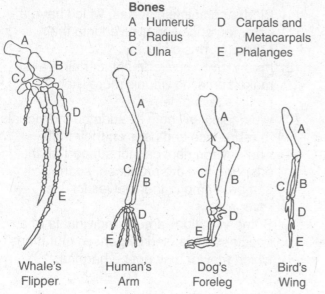

Bones
A Humerus   D Carpals and
B Radius   Metacarpals
C Ulna   E Phalanges

Whale's Flipper   Human's Arm   Dog's Foreleg   Bird's Wing

The bones of each limb are very similar. For this reason, they have the same names. The similarity of their forelimbs suggests that these organisms evolved from a common ancestor. The differences are the result of adaptation over millions of years to different environments.

TIP
When summarizing, look for the main idea. Sometimes it is stated in a topic sentence. If it is not, you must read the details to figure it out.

1. According to the diagram, what is similar about the radius and ulna bones of whales, humans, dogs, and birds?

   (1) They form fingerlike structures.
   (2) They form footlike structures.
   (3) They are positioned side by side below the humerus.
   (4) They are the same shape and perform the same functions.
   (5) They are parts of the organisms' skulls.

2. Which of the following statements summarizes the passage?

   (1) Homologous structures are evidence supporting the theory of evolution.
   (2) Similarity among bones exists in organisms with a common ancestor.
   (3) Birds, whales, humans, and dogs had a common ancestor.
   (4) Wings, flippers, arms, and forelegs are homologous structures.
   (5) Homologous structures have the same functions in related organisms.

3. Which of the following statements is supported by information given in the passage and the diagram?

   (1) Homologous structures are common to all animals.
   (2) Birds are more closely related to humans than dogs are.
   (3) Whales, humans, dogs, and birds had a common ancestor.
   (4) Phalanges are bones in the human wrist and dog's leg.
   (5) All mammals have carpals and metacarpals in their arms.

Unifying Concepts
GENETIC EVIDENCE FOR THE THEORY OF EVOLUTION

Questions 4 through 6 refer to the following passage and diagram.

Darwin formulated the theory of natural selection in the 1850s, before genes and DNA were known. He based his theory on observations of similarities among different animals in body structure and early development. Recently scientists have begun to compare DNA sequences of different species. The more similar the sequences, the closer the evolutionary relationship.

New evidence from comparative DNA sequencing is overturning some long-held theories about relationships among species. Until 1800 all organisms were classified into two kingdoms—plants and animals. During the 1800s, scientists began to realize this division was too simple, and five kingdoms were eventually proposed: bacteria, protists, fungi, plants, and animals. Today, scientists divide organisms into three main groups: bacteria, archaea, and eukaryota. Plants, animals, and fungi are eukaryota.

For many years scientists thought that multicellular plants and animals evolved from single-celled eukarya at about the same time. New DNA evidence suggests that red plants evolved first, followed by brown and green plants about the same time. Later, animals and fungi evolved. These branching trees show old and new theories of how the eukaryota evolved.

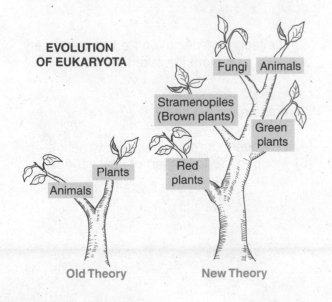

EVOLUTION OF EUKARYOTA

Fungi Animals

Stramenopiles (Brown plants)

Green plants

Red plants

Plants

Animals

Old Theory   New Theory

4. According to the new branching tree, which group of organisms is most closely related to animals?

(1) plants
(2) red plants
(3) brown plants
(4) fungi
(5) green plants

5. For which of the following might comparative DNA sequencing be used?

(1) determining if two people are related
(2) extracting DNA from fossils
(3) determining the age of an organism
(4) discovering the general structure of DNA
(5) estimating the age of Earth

6. Which of the following is the best summary of the passage and the diagram?

(1) DNA sequencing provides evidence for evolutionary relationships, sometimes overturning previously held views.
(2) By comparing the sequences of the DNA of two species, scientists can determine how closely related they are.
(3) It was once thought that plants and animals evolved at about the same time from single-celled organisms.
(4) The five major groups of multicellular organisms are red plants, brown plants, green plants, fungi, and animals.
(5) Darwin formulated the theory of evolution based on observations of similarities between species, before DNA had been discovered.

TIP When summarizing a passage and a diagram, be sure to include the important points from both.

Answers start on page 276.

Directions: This is a ten-minute practice test. After ten minutes, mark the last question you finished. Then complete the test and check your answers. If most of your answers were correct but you didn't finish, try to work faster next time. Choose the one best answer to each question.

Questions 1 through 4 refer to the following passage and diagram.

A species is a group of organisms whose members can mate with one another and produce fertile offspring. The development of a new species from an old one is called speciation. Speciation may occur when environments change or when groups separate, moving to different places. The result of speciation is two or more groups of organisms that can no longer reproduce with each other.

Sometimes many species evolve from one species, a process called adaptive radiation. Adaptive radiation occurs when small groups of individuals become separated from the rest of the population. This often happens on island chains or in areas bounded by mountains. For example, in Hawaii separated groups of honeycreepers became adapted to their different environments. Over time, each isolated group developed a beak shape ideally suited to exploit the local food resources. Such an adaptation, or trait that helps individuals survive, is passed down to the offspring. Eventually the group develops into a new species.

ADAPTATIONS OF HONEYCREEPERS

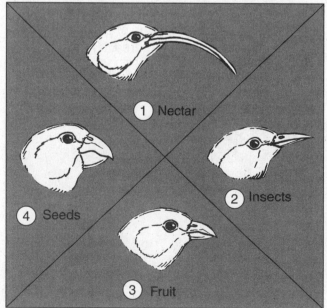

1. Which of the following is the most likely to contribute to speciation?

   (1) environmental changes
   (2) environmental stability
   (3) isolation of an entire species
   (4) no reproductive activity
   (5) plentiful food supply

2. How did the process of adaptive radiation affect honeycreepers?

   (1) They became more alike.
   (2) They reproduced with other species.
   (3) They became less alike.
   (4) There was little or no change.
   (5) There was rapid change within a year.

3. What might happen if an individual honeycreeper with a beak suited to eating nectar strayed into an environment in which nectar was scarce but insects were plentiful?

   (1) It would grow a beak for eating nectar.
   (2) It would grow a beak for eating insects.
   (3) Local birds would provide it with insects.
   (4) Local birds would provide it with nectar.
   (5) It would not be able to eat enough to live.

4. What effect has speciation had on the variety of animal and plant life over time?

   (1) created less variety
   (2) created more variety
   (3) not affected variety
   (4) slowed the formation of new varieties
   (5) stopped the formation of new varieties

Questions 5 and 6 refer to the following paragraph and diagram.

An embryo is an early stage in the development of an organism from a fertilized egg. Similarities in the embryos of fish, birds, and humans suggest that they evolved from a common ancestor. For example, at first, these embryos all have gill slits, but later only fish develop true gills.

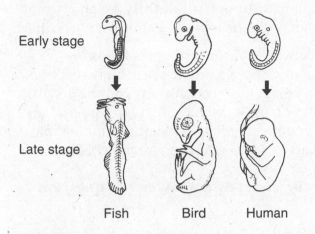

Early stage

Late stage

Fish   Bird   Human

5. Which of the following summarizes the information in the diagram?

   (1) Fish, bird, and human embryos develop from fertilized eggs.
   (2) Fish, bird, and human embryos have gill slits at one stage of development.
   (3) Fish embryos develop scales, and human embryos develop skin.
   (4) Fish, birds, and humans evolved from a common ancestor.
   (5) Fish, bird, and human embryos have similarities at an early stage of development.

6. Which of the following is supported by information in the paragraph and the diagram?

   (1) Humans are more closely related to fish than to birds.
   (2) Birds and fish are more closely related to one another than to humans.
   (3) The similarity among embryos is greatest at the late stage of development.
   (4) As fish, birds, and humans evolved, their embryos looked more similar.
   (5) The common ancestor of fish, birds, and humans was probably a water animal.

7. Convergence occurs when species that are not closely related evolve similar traits independently. These traits are adaptations to a similar environment. For example, sharks and dolphins have similarly shaped bodies and fins, but they are not closely related. Sharks are fish and dolphins are mammals.

Which of the following is another example of convergence?

   (1) Bluebirds and butterflies have wings.
   (2) Dolphins and whales have blowholes.
   (3) Dogs and wolves have sharp canine teeth.
   (4) Chimpanzees and gorillas have thumbs.
   (5) Tigers and leopards have patterned fur.

8. A trait that is favorable to the survival of an organism in one environment may not be favorable in another.

Which of the following would be a favorable trait for an animal living near the North or South Pole?

   (1) white coloring
   (2) dark coloring
   (3) dappled coloring
   (4) sparse fur
   (5) fur on extremities only

9. The fossil record consists of the preserved remains of long-dead organisms that have been studied by scientists. The fossil record provides clues about how and when organisms evolved.

For which of the following would the fossil record be useful?

   (1) predicting which modern species will eventually die out
   (2) plotting the evolutionary relationships among extinct organisms
   (3) determining the life span of an individual member of a modern species
   (4) calculating how long ago Earth first formed
   (5) measuring the number of species on Earth today

Answers start on page 277.

Lesson 7

GED SKILL Distinguishing Conclusions from Supporting Details

Understanding what you read often involves telling the difference between conclusions and supporting statements. A **conclusion** is a logical result or generalization. **Supporting details** are observations, measurements, and other facts that help prove a conclusion is correct.

Telling the difference between conclusions and supporting statements draws on skills you have already learned. Sometimes you must distinguish between a main idea (conclusion) and the details that support it. Sometimes you must decide which facts support an opinion. And sometimes you must follow the logical thinking that leads from a group of details to a generalization, or conclusion.

Read the passage and the chart and answer the question below.

To satisfy consumer demand, the fishing industry has overfished many species, causing sharp declines in some populations. For that reason, environmental groups have begun to offer consumers advice about which fish species are threatened and which are doing well. They hope consumers will change their eating habits to help restore fish populations.

FISH POPULATIONS	
Fish	**Status**
Atlantic cod, haddock, pollock	Years of overfishing caused populations to drop sharply
Wild salmon	Healthy in Alaska, depleted elsewhere
Tuna	Bluefin tuna severely overfished
Striped bass	Restrictions on commercial fishing have brought this endangered species back

Write *SD* if the statement is a supporting detail. Write *C* if it is a conclusion.

_____ a. Striped bass were endangered before fishing was restricted.

_____ b. Atlantic cod and pollock populations are in sharp decline.

_____ c. Consumers can help restore the world's fisheries by changing their eating habits.

You were correct if you marked *option c* as the conclusion. *Options a* and *b* are details (SD) supporting the conclusion that consumers can help restore fish populations by not buying certain fish.

Use the passage and the diagram to answer the questions below.

All living things need energy to carry out life processes. Organisms that get energy from sunlight through photosynthesis are called **producers.** All green plants, such as grasses and seaweeds, are producers.

Organisms that eat other organisms in order to obtain energy are called **consumers.** Primary consumers like rabbits and sea urchins eat producers to obtain energy. Secondary consumers like foxes and seals eat primary consumers to obtain energy. Sometimes there are tertiary (third-level) consumers like owls and killer whales that eat secondary consumers.

A **food chain** shows one way energy can flow from producer to consumers.

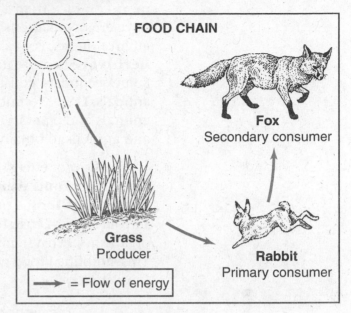

FOOD CHAIN

Fox
Secondary consumer

Grass
Producer

Rabbit
Primary consumer

→ = Flow of energy

1. Write *SD* next to the sentence that is a supporting detail from the first paragraph.

   _____ a. All living things need energy to carry out life processes.

   _____ b. All green plants, such as grasses and seaweeds, are producers.

2. Write two details from the second paragraph.

   _____

   _____

3. Write two details from the diagram.

   _____

   _____

4. Write *C* next to the sentence that is a conclusion supported by the details in the passage and the diagram.

   _____ a. In a food chain, energy flows from the sun to producers and then to consumers.

   _____ b. Consumers can obtain energy directly from sunlight or from producers.

5. Write one detail from either the passage or the diagram that supports the conclusion you selected in question 4.

   _____

   _____

Answers start on page 278.

Energy Flow in Ecosystems

The flow of energy from producers to consumers is generally more complex than a single food chain. Most plants and animals have energy relationships with many other organisms in their environments. For example, a primary consumer is called an **herbivore** because it eats only grasses, berries, or other plant foods. Some secondary consumers are **carnivores** and eat only other animals. Other secondary consumers are **omnivores** and eat both animals and plants. Finally, **decomposers** break down dead plants and animals to obtain energy.

The flow of energy among a group of plants and animals can be shown in a **food web.** A food web shows the energy relationships in an **ecosystem,** a natural community of organisms and its surroundings. Ecosystems like deserts can be sparse, with few organisms. Ecosystems like forests can be rich, with many organisms. This simplified food web shows energy relationships in a woodland ecosystem.

FOOD WEB

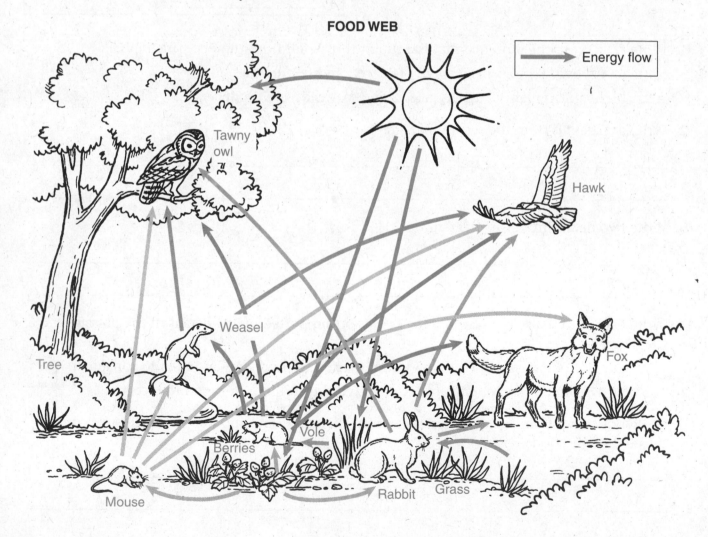

84

Directions: Choose the one best answer to each question.

Questions 1 through 6 refer to the passage and the diagram on page 84.

1. What does a food web show?

    (1) the energy relationships among organisms in an ecosystem
    (2) the energy relationships among animals in an ecosystem
    (3) the relationship between energy and matter
    (4) the food that can be found in wilderness areas
    (5) the food that is no longer available to organisms in an ecosystem

2. Which of the following is one of the consumers shown at the highest level in the food web?

    (1) the grasses
    (2) the rabbit
    (3) the mouse
    (4) the tawny owl
    (5) the vole

3. If all the grasses, berries, and trees in this food web disappeared, the immediate result would be that which of the following would have nothing to eat?

    (1) tawny owls
    (2) hawks
    (3) foxes
    (4) weasels
    (5) rabbits

TIP Supporting statements are usually specific facts, observations, or measurements. When looking for a conclusion, look for more general information.

4. Which of the following is a supporting detail rather than a conclusion?

    (1) Omnivores can be both primary and secondary consumers.
    (2) Without energy from the sun, no life on Earth would be possible.
    (3) In ecosystems, an herbivore is always a primary consumer.
    (4) Weasels get energy by eating mice.
    (5) The energy relationships in ecosystems can be very complex.

5. A backpacker gets lost in the woodland ecosystem. After some time, the food supply he brought with him runs out. As the backpacker looks for food in the woodlands, what role is he likely to take on in the food web of the ecosystem?

    (1) energy source
    (2) producer
    (3) decomposer
    (4) carnivore
    (5) omnivore

6. Which statement is a conclusion rather than a supporting detail?

    (1) Energy is constantly flowing through the woodland ecosystem.
    (2) The sun provides energy for the process of photosynthesis.
    (3) Grasses and berries are producers in the woodland ecosystem.
    (4) Mice, voles, and rabbits are all herbivores common in the woodland ecosystem.
    (5) Foxes and weasels are both carnivores that can be found in the woodlands.

Answers start on page 278.

GED Practice • Lesson 7

Directions: Choose the one best answer to each question.

Questions 1 through 4 refer to the following passage and diagram.

In a food chain, the position occupied by each species is called its **trophic level.** At each trophic level, energy is stored in the **biomass** of living plants or animals. Most of the energy at any given trophic level is used by organisms for life processes or lost to the environment as heat. Thus only about 10 percent of the energy taken in by one trophic level is available to the organisms in the next trophic level.

One way to show the loss of energy at each trophic level of a food chain is to construct an energy pyramid. Each section of the pyramid represents the energy available to the next higher level as well as the amount of biomass. Since only some of the energy at one level is usable by the level above it, each level supports less biomass and fewer organisms.

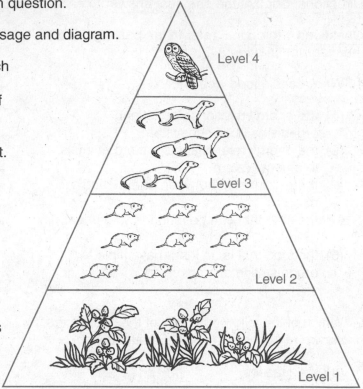

1. How is energy stored in a food chain?

    (1) as trophic levels
    (2) as sunlight
    (3) as heat
    (4) as biomass
    (5) as plants

2. Which of the following is a conclusion rather than a supporting detail?

    (1) Tawny owls occupy the fourth trophic level in this energy pyramid.
    (2) Berries and grasses form the base of the energy pyramid.
    (3) A food chain can support more primary consumers than secondary consumers.
    (4) About 10 percent of the energy in the third level is available to fourth level organisms.
    (5) Weasels provide energy to tawny owls in the food chain.

3. Which of the following statements is supported by the passage and the diagram?

    (1) The higher in the energy pyramid, the more biomass.
    (2) The most biomass is at the base of the energy pyramid.
    (3) There are more weasels than voles in the energy pyramid.
    (4) There are few tawny owls because they have been eaten by weasels.
    (5) As you rise in the energy pyramid, more energy is available.

4. An ocean energy pyramid consists of microscopic organisms called plankton at the base, then mussels, crabs, lobsters, and finally seals. Of which organism would you expect to find the fewest?

    (1) plankton
    (2) mussels
    (3) crabs
    (4) lobsters
    (5) seals

Science in Personal and Social Perspectives

WILY COYOTES TAKE OVER

Questions 5 through 7 refer to the following information.

The spread of human populations has altered natural ecosystems and caused declines in many animal and plant populations throughout the world. However, in North America, even with the huge increase of the human population, coyotes have thrived. Five hundred years ago, they occupied only the western plains. Today they inhabit almost the whole continent.

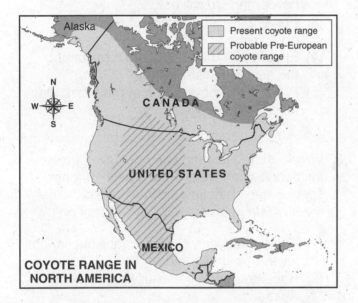

COYOTE RANGE IN NORTH AMERICA

In many areas coyotes are the top **predator,** because humans have eliminated the wolves, the coyotes' natural enemy. In packs, coyotes can bring down large animals like deer. Hunting alone, they feed on small mammals like mice; in the cities and suburbs, they eat cats and small dogs.

Coyotes will eat almost anything. An analysis of coyote waste showed about 100 types of food, from crickets to apples to shoe leather. Landfills and garbage cans provide a plentiful and varied diet.

The human-altered landscape is a good **habitat** for coyotes. They live in the small wooded areas common in suburbia. They have even been seen in Central Park in New York City. Coyotes are often safe from harm because they are frequently mistaken for dogs.

5. Why has the eradication of the wolf helped coyotes to thrive?

(1) In many regions, coyotes now have no natural enemies.
(2) Coyotes can hunt small mammals like mice and cats.
(3) Coyotes live in small wooded areas common in suburbia.
(4) Coyotes forage for food in landfills and garbage cans.
(5) Wolves live in packs, and coyotes live in packs or on their own.

6. Which of the following is a conclusion, not a supporting detail?

(1) People often mistake coyotes for dogs.
(2) Coyotes have been found to feed on dozens of different items.
(3) Hunting alone, coyotes prey upon small mammals.
(4) In packs, coyotes can bring down large animals like deer.
(5) The coyote's adaptability in feeding and other behaviors has helped it enlarge its range.

7. Which statement about the coyotes in North America is supported by information in the map and the passage?

(1) Coyotes prefer to live in urban areas rather than suburban areas.
(2) Coyotes can live in many types of ecosystems and climates.
(3) There are fewer coyotes now than there were five hundred years ago.
(4) Over the years, humans have destroyed coyote habitats.
(5) Coyotes spread from the eastern forests to other areas of North America.

TIP Remember to use the title, key, labels, and compass rose of a map to answer map questions.

Answers start on page 278.

GED Mini-Test • Lesson 7

Directions: This is a ten-minute practice test. After ten minutes, mark the last question you finished. Then complete the test and check your answers. If most of your answers were correct but you didn't finish, try to work faster next time. Choose the one best answer to each question.

Questions 1 through 4 refer to the following information.

There is usually at least one consumer for each plant and animal that serves to check its population growth. That is why numbers of plants and animals usually remain constant from year to year. When you take a species of plant or animal from its natural ecosystem and introduce it into another ecosystem, it might die out quickly. If it survives, the species may reproduce at an incredible rate.

How can a new species succeed so quickly? The food relationships in an ecosystem have evolved slowly, and they change very slowly. Just as many people are reluctant to eat an unfamiliar food, animals are unlikely to eat something they have never seen before. If there is no consumer willing to eat a new species, it will reproduce rapidly. For example, in 1859, 24 rabbits were imported to Australia from Europe. Without predators to keep them in check, the rabbits multiplied. Today, despite pest control measures, Australia has millions of rabbits that cause extensive damage to agricultural lands.

The best solution to overpopulation by an introduced species is to prevent its introduction in the first place. If new organisms do overrun an area, population growth can sometimes be controlled by importing another species that will prey on the first species.

1. Which of the following caused the overpopulation of rabbits in Australia?

   (1) the importing of predators
   (2) the continued importing of rabbits
   (3) an unstable ecosystem
   (4) the overpopulation of predators and slow reproduction of rabbits
   (5) the rapid reproduction of rabbits and lack of predators

2. What is the best way to avoid the problems associated with introducing new organisms into an ecosystem?

   (1) Introduce an animal to prey on the new organism.
   (2) Ensure that there will be something the new organism will eat.
   (3) Prevent the introduction of new organisms.
   (4) Ensure that the ecosystem has nothing the new organism will eat.
   (5) Prevent the introduction of predators that feed on the new organism.

3. Which of the following statements supports the conclusion that overpopulation of a new species can sometimes be controlled by the introduction of an animal that will prey on it?

   (1) The introduction of new organisms cannot always be prevented.
   (2) Rabbits were successfully wiped out in Australia.
   (3) In stable ecosystems, one consumer usually checks another's population growth.
   (4) In time, the population will decrease.
   (5) The overpopulated species cannot find anything to eat.

4. What can you assume about the ecosystem of Australia as it relates to rabbits?

   (1) It has neither food nor predators.
   (2) It has food that rabbits eat.
   (3) It has predators but no food.
   (4) It has many meat-eating animals.
   (5) It is very similar to Europe's ecosystem.

Questions 5 and 6 refer to the following information.

Ecology is the study of organisms and their relationships with one another and with their environments. Ecologists can analyze these relationships at different levels of complexity.

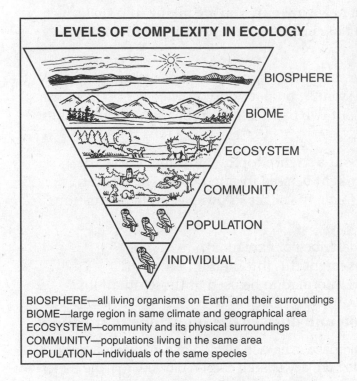

LEVELS OF COMPLEXITY IN ECOLOGY

BIOSPHERE

BIOME

ECOSYSTEM

COMMUNITY

POPULATION

INDIVIDUAL

BIOSPHERE—all living organisms on Earth and their surroundings
BIOME—large region in same climate and geographical area
ECOSYSTEM—community and its physical surroundings
COMMUNITY—populations living in the same area
POPULATION—individuals of the same species

5. G. David Tilman is an ecologist who establishes experimental plots with different plant species, soils, and air quality in order to examine how these factors interact. At what level of complexity is Dr. Tilman working?

    (1) population
    (2) community
    (3) ecosystem
    (4) biome
    (5) biosphere

6. Scientists have attempted to create a large sealed, self-sustaining environment, similar to Earth, with a variety of soils, air, plants, animals, and microclimates. At what level of complexity are they working?

    (1) population
    (2) community
    (3) ecosystem
    (4) biome
    (5) biosphere

Question 7 refers to the following information.

After years of decline, the water bird population of New York Harbor is increasing because of cleaner water. Population trends for two species are shown.

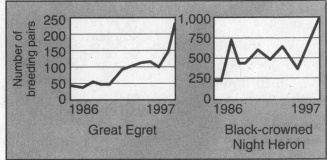

7. Which of the following is supported by the information given?

    (1) Water birds lost harbor island habitats to apartment developments.
    (2) The Clean Air Act of 1970 reduced the release of pollutants from cars.
    (3) There are more herons and egrets because clean water means more fish to eat.
    (4) Water bird populations are increasing because they have no predators.
    (5) Heron and egret females lay only one or two eggs per year.

8. Parasitism is a relationship in which one species benefits at the expense of another. Which of the following is an example of parasitism?

    (1) Cowbirds lay their eggs in the nests of songbirds, which incubate and raise cowbird chicks.
    (2) The remora fish obtains food by picking parasitic organisms off the skin of a shark.
    (3) Plants with nitrogen-fixing bacteria on their roots gain nitrogen compounds while the bacteria gain food.
    (4) The crocodile bird obtains food from the crocodile's teeth while cleaning them.
    (5) Sea anemones get food from hermit crabs while protecting the crabs from predators.

Answers start on page 279.

Lesson 8

GED SKILL Applying Ideas in New Contexts

applying ideas
taking information learned in one situation and using it in another set of circumstances

context
the situation within which something is said or done

When you put your knowledge to use in new situations, you are **applying ideas** to a new **context.** You are taking information you learned in one set of circumstances and using it in another set of circumstances.

For example, in Lesson 1 you learned about cell structures and their functions. In Lesson 2, you put your knowledge of cells to use when you learned about two basic cellular processes, photosynthesis and respiration.

When you read about a science topic, think about how the knowledge you gain might be used in other contexts. You can increase your ability to apply science knowledge to new situations by asking yourself:

- What is being described or explained?
- What situations might this information relate to?
- How would this information be used in those situations?

Read the paragraph and answer the questions that follow.

One cause of the increase in carbon dioxide gas in the **atmosphere** is deforestation. Plants normally absorb carbon dioxide from the air for use in photosynthesis. But when large areas are cleared of trees, there are fewer plants to absorb carbon dioxide. Increased carbon dioxide gas in the atmosphere may cause **global warming** by trapping heat from the sun.

When you apply information to a new situation, ask yourself what you already know about the new situation. Then ask yourself how the information applies to the new context.

1. Put a check mark next to the statement that applies information about photosynthesis to a new situation.

 _____ a. Clearing large areas of trees is called deforestation.

 _____ b. Cutting down trees may contribute to global warming.

You were correct if you chose *option b.* The theory of a reduced level of photosynthesis helps explain how deforestation may contribute to global warming, a larger context.

2. Put a check mark next to a scenario that is similar to deforestation.

 _____ a. The aquatic plants in a goldfish tank die.

 _____ b. Some animals in a zoo have difficulty reproducing.

You are correct if you checked *option a.* Deforestation is similar to the death of plants in an aquarium. In both situations, there are fewer plants and a lower rate of photosynthesis.

Use the passage and the diagram to answer the questions below.

The two main processes involved in the **carbon-oxygen cycle** are respiration and photosynthesis. Each of these processes produces substances used in the other process. Respiration takes place in both plants and animals. During respiration, oxygen is used to break down sugar to release energy and a byproduct, carbon dioxide. During photosynthesis, water, carbon dioxide, and light energy from the sun produce sugar, oxygen, and water. Only plants carry out photosynthesis.

THE CARBON-OXYGEN CYCLE

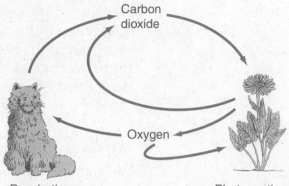

Respiration

Photosynthesis and respiration

1. Put a check mark next to each sentence that is true of respiration.

_____ a. It takes place only in animals.

_____ b. It takes place in animals and plants.

_____ c. Oxygen is used.

_____ d. Carbon dioxide is released.

2. Put a check mark next to the statement of how the respiration of organisms fits into the carbon-oxygen cycle.

_____ a. Respiration uses up oxygen from the air and releases carbon dioxide into the air.

_____ b. Respiration is a cellular process that releases energy from sugar.

3. Put a check mark next to each statement that is true of photosynthesis.

_____ a. It takes place only in plants.

_____ b. It takes place in animals and plants.

_____ c. The sun's energy is needed for it to take place.

_____ d. Carbon dioxide is used.

_____ e. Oxygen is released.

4. Put a check mark next to the statement of how photosynthesis fits into the carbon-oxygen cycle.

_____ a. Photosynthesis uses up carbon dioxide from the air and releases oxygen into the air.

_____ b. Photosynthesis is a process in which sugars are produced using the sun's energy.

Answers start on page 280.

One way to understand ecosystems is to follow the flow of energy in food webs. Another way is to analyze how substances, like carbon, cycle between the living and nonliving parts of ecosystems.

One substance that cycles through ecosystems is nitrogen. Plants and animals must have nitrogen to make proteins. There is plenty of nitrogen in the air, but plants and animals cannot use nitrogen in gas form. Instead, plants get nitrogen from the soil. They rely on bacteria to convert nitrogen gas into forms that they can use. Animals get nitrogen by eating plants or other animals.

Through a process called **nitrogen fixation,** certain kinds of bacteria take nitrogen from the air and combine it with other substances to make nitrates, which plants can use. Nitrogen-fixing bacteria are found in bumps, or nodules, on the roots of legume plants such as soybeans, as well as free-living in the soil.

Lightning causes nitrogen and oxygen to combine to form nitrogen compounds that fall to Earth in rain. Elemental nitrogen also enters the soil when dead plants and animals decay. Nitrifying bacteria in the soil convert nitrogen from these sources to ammonia, nitrites, and nitrates. This process, called **nitrification,** provides more nitrogen for plants.

Plants use nitrogen to make proteins. Animals get nitrogen by eating plants or by eating other animals that have eaten plants. When plants and animals die and decay, some of their nitrogen compounds are nitrified, providing more nitrogen for living plants.

Some of the nitrogen compounds in soil are broken down by denitrifying bacteria, which return nitrogen gas to the air. This process is called **denitrification.**

THE NITROGEN CYCLE

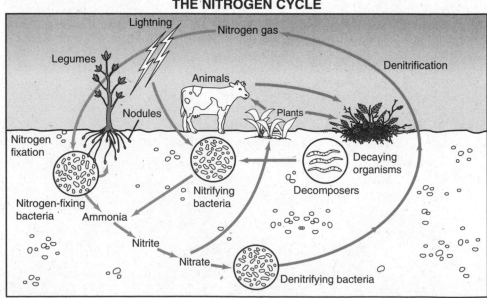

Directions: Choose the one best answer to each question.

Questions 1 through 7 refer to the passage and the diagram on page 92.

1. Where do most plants get their nitrogen?

   (1) from other plants
   (2) directly from the atmosphere
   (3) from animals
   (4) from the soil
   (5) from protein

2. According to the diagram, where does the process of nitrogen fixation take place?

   (1) in decaying organisms only
   (2) in the soil and in the leaves of plants
   (3) in the soil and in the roots of all plants
   (4) in the atmosphere
   (5) in the soil and in the roots of legumes

3. By what process do bacteria break down the protein in decaying organisms into nitrite and nitrate compounds?

   (1) nitrogen fixation
   (2) denitrification
   (3) erosion
   (4) nitrification
   (5) ionization

4. A fire destroys several acres of brush, grasses, and trees. What is the most likely immediate effect on the **nitrogen cycle** in that area?

   (1) The amount of nitrogen processed will decrease.
   (2) The nitrogen cycle will speed up.
   (3) Plants will get nitrogen from the air.
   (4) Animals will get nitrogen from the air.
   (5) The number of legumes will increase.

5. A farmer plants soybeans—a legume—on several acres. Where are the soybeans likely to obtain most of their nitrogen?

   (1) from nitrous oxide after lightning strikes
   (2) from nitrogen-fixing bacteria on their roots
   (3) from nitrogen gas in the atmosphere
   (4) from denitrifying bacteria that return nitrogen to the air
   (5) from decomposing organisms in the soil

6. Goats break out of their pen on the farm and get into the soybean fields. During the time they are loose, where are they likely to obtain most of their nitrogen?

   (1) from legumes
   (2) from lightning strikes
   (3) from grass
   (4) from other animals
   (5) from nitrifying bacteria in the soil

7. If the nitrogen cycle were interrupted, which process of living things would be affected first?

   (1) cell division
   (2) respiration
   (3) photosynthesis
   (4) protein synthesis
   (5) circulation

TIP
To apply information from one context to another, ask yourself what the two contexts have in common. Then apply the information relating to that commonality from one context to the other.

Answers start on page 280.

GED Practice • Lesson 8

Directions: Choose the one best answer to each question.

Questions 1 and 2 refer to the following passage and diagram.

All plants and animals must have water in order to live. Cells are made mostly of water, and most of the chemical reactions in living things must take place in water. However, the amount of Earth's water is limited. It must be used again and again. The constant circulation of Earth's water is called the **water cycle.**

Heat from the sun causes large amounts of water from the oceans and from freshwater sources to **evaporate,** or change to a gas called water vapor. Plants and animals also give off water vapor as a byproduct of cellular respiration. When the air cools, water vapor **condenses,** or turns back into liquid water, forming clouds. Finally, the water droplets in clouds become heavy, and they fall to Earth in the form of rain or snow.

THE WATER CYCLE

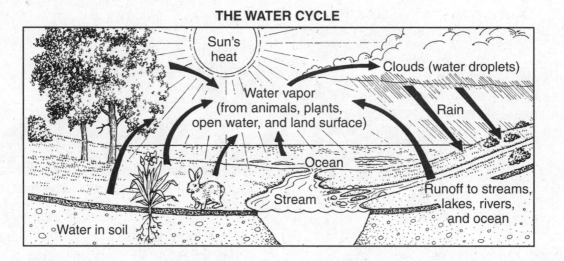

1. Which of the following best explains how clouds form?

    (1) Water vapor in the air condenses into droplets.
    (2) Droplets of water in the air become heavy.
    (3) Droplets of water in the air evaporate.
    (4) Heat from the sun reacts with gases in the air.
    (5) Warm air above Earth combines with cool air on the surface.

2. Which of the following is most similar to Earth's water cycle?

    (1) snow falling to the ground and then melting
    (2) water running down the bathroom walls after someone takes a hot bath
    (3) plants taking in carbon dioxide and releasing oxygen
    (4) drinking a glass of water when you are thirsty
    (5) ice cubes melting on the counter and refreezing in the freezer

REDWOODS CAPTURE WATER FROM FOG

Questions 3 through 6 refer to the following passage.

When fog rolls into a redwood forest on the West Coast, the water droplets suspended in the fog condense on the tree's needles and then drip down the needles, branches, and trunk. Studies have shown that in one foggy night, a redwood tree can collect as much water as would fall during a heavy rainstorm. The redwoods' ability to capture water from fog is crucial to the other plants and animals in its habitat.

Scientists have measured the fog dripping off redwoods in forested areas and also the fog dripping off humanmade fog collectors in deforested areas. In deforested areas, the air warms up and dries out quickly; the water droplets evaporate before becoming heavy enough to fall to the ground. Thus, much less water is captured from fog in the deforested areas than in the redwood forests.

The fact that fog drip contributes to the water supply of an area is used by conservationists as an argument for saving stands of redwoods from logging. People whose wells and springs dwindle during the dry summers are beginning to realize the role redwoods play in maintaining their water supply.

3. How did scientists show that deforested areas collect less fog drip than redwood forests?

   (1) by observing that water drips down a redwood's needles, branches, and trunk
   (2) by comparing the amount of water dripping off redwoods to the amount collected in deforested areas
   (3) by observing whether streams dry up in deforested areas along the West Coast
   (4) by redirecting the fog from forested to deforested areas along the West Coast
   (5) by measuring the height of the redwood trees and comparing their height to the amount of water collected

4. Which of the following is most similar to redwoods capturing water for their habitats?

   (1) removing impurities from rainwater by filtering it
   (2) collecting rainwater and runoff in a large reservoir
   (3) removing salt from ocean water by evaporation and condensation
   (4) using fog collectors in dry coastal regions to collect water
   (5) using a system of gutters and tanks to collect rainwater

5. Which of the following supports the conclusion that redwoods contribute water to their habitat?

   (1) Fog rolls into the redwood forests from the Pacific Ocean.
   (2) Water droplets are suspended in fog and intercepted by redwood trees.
   (3) Water from fog drips down the needles, branches, and trunks of redwoods into the soil.
   (4) Other plants and animals rely on the water supply provided by the redwoods.
   (5) Only about 4 percent of the original redwood forest still stands.

6. Which of the following provides the greatest motivation for the majority of people who live in a region with redwoods to oppose the logging of these trees?

   (1) Over the years, humans have destroyed most of the redwood forests.
   (2) A single redwood tree may contain wood worth hundreds of thousands of dollars.
   (3) Homes made of redwood lumber are long-lasting and easy to care for.
   (4) The lumber industry provides jobs for people in the area.
   (5) Deforestation contributes to the drying up of local wells and springs.

Answers start on page 280.

GED Mini-Test • Lesson 8

Directions: This is a ten-minute practice test. After ten minutes, mark the last question you finished. Then complete the test and check your answers. If most of your answers were correct but you didn't finish, try to work faster next time. Choose the <u>one best answer</u> to each question.

<u>Questions 1 through 3</u> refer to the following passage and diagram.

Factories, power stations, and cars produce waste gases like sulfur dioxide and nitrogen oxides. These gases rise into the air and react with water vapor to form acids. Acid rain then falls, sometimes hundreds of miles away from its origin. Acid rain damages plants and pollutes streams and lakes.

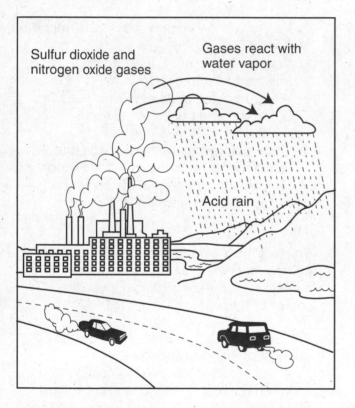

1. What causes acid rain?

   (1) emissions from factories, power plants, and cars
   (2) condensation of water vapor in the air
   (3) pesticide runoff from agricultural areas
   (4) industrial discharges into streams and lakes
   (5) heavy metal residues in lake and stream bottoms

2. State officials wish to reduce the state's acid rain, so they place controls on industrial and vehicle emissions in the state. Why might this plan not reduce acid rain in the state?

   (1) It is difficult to reduce industrial and car emissions enough to reduce acid rain.
   (2) The state will not be able to enforce their controls on industrial and vehicle emissions.
   (3) It is possible to reduce industrial emissions but not vehicle emissions.
   (4) The emissions that cause acid rain in the state probably originate in some other place.
   (5) The amount of acid rain that falls depends mostly on climate, not emissions.

3. What is the likely effect of acid rain pollution of streams and lakes?

   (1) damage to aquatic organisms
   (2) increased industrial emissions
   (3) increased pollution upstream
   (4) reduced industrial emissions
   (5) reduced pollution upstream

4. When an organism dies, its complex organic compounds are broken down into simpler substances. Large decomposers like earthworms break down large pieces of dead matter so that smaller decomposers like fungi and bacteria can complete the process, releasing carbon dioxide, nitrates, phosphates and other substances into the environment.

Decomposition is <u>most similar</u> to which of the following human body processes?

   (1) respiration
   (2) urination
   (3) circulation
   (4) digestion
   (5) locomotion

Questions 5 through 7 refer to the following diagram and passage.

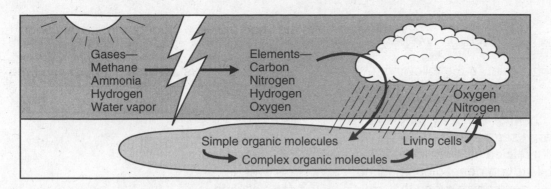

Life is thought to have first appeared on Earth about 3.5 billion years ago. Many scientists believe that the atmosphere was then made up mostly of methane, ammonia, hydrogen, and water vapor. These gases contain the elements carbon, nitrogen, hydrogen, and oxygen, which are found in organic molecules. Organic molecules are the building blocks of all living things on Earth.

According to one theory, energy from lightning or sunlight caused chemical reactions among these molecules. As a result, the elements carbon, nitrogen, hydrogen, and oxygen recombined to form simple organic molecules. Rain washed some of the organic molecules down to Earth's surface. There they combined with each other, eventually forming living cells. As these single-celled organisms evolved and multiplied, they added oxygen and nitrogen to the atmosphere, changing the balance of gases. Eventually, more complex life forms that use oxygen evolved.

5. What is thought to have caused chemical reactions among the gas molecules of the early atmosphere?

(1) water vapor
(2) organic molecules
(3) methane
(4) rain
(5) lightning

6. Organic molecules must have existed before life could form because they performed which of the following functions related to life?

(1) combined to form living things
(2) gave rise to carbon
(3) provided energy
(4) combined to form air
(5) combined to form rain

7. Which of the following can you infer from the information in the passage and the diagram?

(1) The composition of the atmosphere has changed through constant interaction with living things.
(2) Today's atmosphere has less oxygen than the atmosphere of early Earth, which was mostly oxygen.
(3) The first living cells were animal cells that gave off carbon dioxide, water vapor, and nitrogen wastes.
(4) Even when Earth first formed almost 5 billion years ago, life existed both in the atmosphere and the oceans.
(5) The first living things contained methane, ammonia, hydrogen, and water and were very complex.

Answers start on page 281.

Unit 1 Cumulative Review Life Science

<u>Directions</u>: Choose the <u>one best answer</u> to each question.

<u>Questions 1 through 4</u> refer to the following passage.

Herbicides are chemicals that kill plants. When herbicides are used on crops, it is important that the herbicide kill only the weeds and not the crops. Through genetic engineering, scientists have been developing crops that are not affected by specific herbicides. These resistant crops enable farmers to use herbicides to control weeds. For example, scientists have developed a strain of cotton that is resistant to the herbicide bromoxynil. When this herbicide is used, it kills weeds but not the resistant cotton plants. Other crops that have varieties resistant to certain herbicides are soybeans, tobacco, tomatoes, and sugar beets.

Some environmental groups are opposed to the development of herbicide-resistant crops. They say that these crops encourage farmers to continue to use chemicals that pollute the environment for long periods and that may be unsafe. These groups favor methods such as improved cultivation techniques and creative planting plans that make the use of chemicals unnecessary.

1. What is the main idea of the passage?

   (1) The use of herbicide-resistant crops is controversial.
   (2) Herbicide-resistant crops are preferable to creative planting plans.
   (3) Scientists are developing crops that are herbicide-resistant through genetic engineering.
   (4) Herbicides are chemicals used to kill weeds, not crop plants.
   (5) A type of cotton is resistant to the herbicide bromoxynil.

2. A herbicide-resistant crop can withstand the effects of which of the following?

   (1) herbicides
   (2) disease
   (3) insect pests
   (4) weeds
   (5) pollution

3. Based on the passage, which of the following is an opinion rather than a fact?

   (1) Herbicides are used to kill weeds.
   (2) Some varieties of soybean and tobacco plants are resistant to certain herbicides.
   (3) Bromoxynil is a type of herbicide.
   (4) Improved cultivation techniques are preferable to herbicide use.
   (5) Scientists have developed strains of herbicide-resistant crops.

4. Based on the information given, it is assumed that the reader already knows which of the following?

   (1) Use of herbicides is completely safe.
   (2) Crops cannot be grown without herbicides.
   (3) Weeds are a problem in large farming areas.
   (4) All cotton plants are resistant to herbicides.
   (5) Most crops are naturally resistant to herbicides.

TIP
Pay particular attention to definitions of key terms in passages. Often you can use the definition of a term to help you answer a question.

Question 5 refers to the following paragraph and diagram.

Many species have vestigial structures—organs or limbs that are small and lack any recognizable function. Scientists believe that vestigial structures are the remains of structures that were well-developed and functional in the ancestors of present-day organisms.

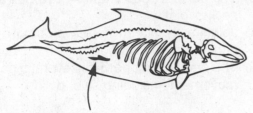

Remains of leg bones in porpoise

5. Which of the following is a conclusion rather than a supporting detail?

   (1) The modern porpoise has small, vestigial leg bones.
   (2) Vestigial structures serve no recognizable purpose.
   (3) Vestigial structures are the remains of well-developed and functional structures.
   (4) Many species, including the porpoise, have structures with no function.
   (5) Vestigial structures like the porpoise's legs are often small.

6. Lipids, which include fats, are one class of the organic compounds that make up living things. Cells store energy in lipids for later use.

   Which of the following is an example of an organism's use of lipids?

   (1) During the winter, a hibernating bear lives on the energy stored as fat.
   (2) In the absence of light energy, a green plant stops photosynthesizing.
   (3) A student eats an apple for some quick energy.
   (4) Enzymes in saliva break down starches into sugars.
   (5) Lipids are made up of the elements carbon, hydrogen, and oxygen.

Questions 7 and 8 refer to the following paragraph and diagram.

In diffusion, molecules move from an area where they are highly concentrated to an area where they are less concentrated, until a balance has been reached. Osmosis is the diffusion of water molecules across a membrane, such as a cell membrane.

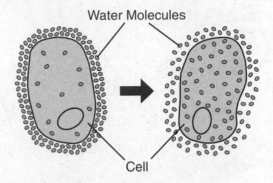

Water Molecules

Cell

7. Which of the following best summarizes the process of osmosis as shown in the diagram?

   (1) Water molecules pass through the cell membrane until a balance between the inside and outside of the cell has been reached.
   (2) Water molecules are constantly passing into the cell, until they are highly concentrated inside the cell.
   (3) Air molecules move into and out of the cell, displacing water molecules.
   (4) It occurs only in plant cells.
   (5) It occurs only in one-celled organisms.

8. Which of the following is an example of osmosis?

   (1) The genetic material of a cell duplicates itself and the cell divides.
   (2) The cells of plant roots absorb water from the surrounding soil.
   (3) Blood cells pick up oxygen in the lungs and get rid of carbon dioxide.
   (4) Water vapor leaves a plant through pores in the leaves.
   (5) Transport proteins let amino acids pass through the cell membrane.

Questions 9 through 11 refer to the following information.

A joint is a place where two or more bones are connected. There are several types of joints in the human body, including those shown below.

EXAMPLES OF JOINTS

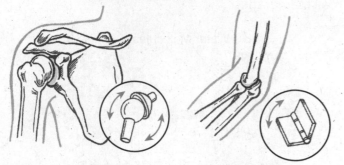

Ball-and-socket joint—
shoulder

Hinge joint—knee and elbow

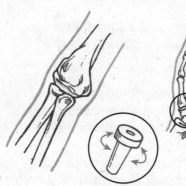

Pivot joint—forearm

Saddle joint—thumb

9. Which of the following best summarizes the diagram?

(1) Different types of joints allow for different types of movement.
(2) Ball-and-socket, hinge, pivot, and saddle joints are all moveable joints.
(3) The skeleton protects and supports the body and allows the body to move.
(4) Joints are places where two or more bones are connected.
(5) Each joint in the skeleton allows all different types of movement.

10. Which of the following does the author of the passage and diagram assume that you know?

(1) Hinge joints allow movement similar to that allowed by the hinge of a door.
(2) One function of the skeleton is to allow the body to move through movement of bones.
(3) The hip is a good example of a ball-and-socket joint.
(4) Joints are places where two or more bones are connected.
(5) The saddle joint permits several types of movement, including side to side.

11. The ball-and-socket joint shown in the diagram is the shoulder. Which of the following is also a ball-and-socket joint?

(1) the hip
(2) the thumb
(3) the elbow
(4) the knuckles
(5) the knee

12. The female cuckoo bird lays her eggs in the nests of other bird species. When the cuckoo chick hatches, it instinctively knocks all the other eggs out of the nest. The cuckoo chick never sees its own parents, but as it grows it behaves as a cuckoo does. It does not learn to behave as its foster parents do.

Based on the information above, which of the following best describes the cuckoo chick's behavior?

(1) It is cruel.
(2) It is superior to that of its foster parents.
(3) It is inferior to that of its foster parents.
(4) It is primarily learned.
(5) It is primarily inborn.

TIP When a diagram shows several examples, be sure to look carefully for both similarities and differences among them.

Questions 13 through 15 refer to the following passage and chart.

The number of people living in a specific area is the population density. Population density is a ratio. It is calculated by dividing the number of people living in an area by the amount of usable land available in that area. If an area's population increases, so does its population density.

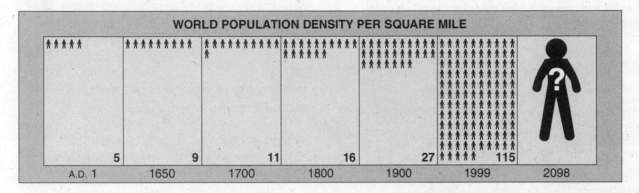

WORLD POPULATION DENSITY PER SQUARE MILE

13. About how many times greater was the world population density in 1999 than in 1700?

    (1) 100
    (2) 50
    (3) 10
    (4) 5
    (5) 3

14. Which of the following is a conclusion rather than a supporting detail?

    (1) Population density in 1999 was very high: 115 people per square mile.
    (2) The world population was least dense in the year A.D. 1.
    (3) Increasing the amount of inhabitable land is one way to reduce population density.
    (4) Population density refers to the number of people living in a given area.
    (5) It took about 1700 years for the human population to double.

TIP A diagram may use images as well as words or numbers. Use the images and words or numbers together to help you understand the information.

15. According to the information in the chart, it is most likely that, if the world population continues to follow the same pattern it has shown over the past 100 years, by 2098 the population density will have done which of the following?

    (1) quadrupled
    (2) doubled
    (3) remained the same
    (4) decreased by one-half
    (5) returned to the 1900 density

16. A virus is a molecule of genetic material covered by a protective protein coat. It shows no sign of life when outside a living cell. To become active, a virus invades a living cell and uses this host cell to duplicate its own genetic material.

    Which is the best restatement of this information?

    (1) A virus is a molecule of genetic material surrounded by a protein coat.
    (2) The protein coat of a virus protects it from threats in the environment.
    (3) A virus is genetic material that appears lifeless until it takes over a cell to reproduce.
    (4) There are about a hundred viruses that cause the common cold.
    (5) Viral diseases are hard to treat because viruses don't respond to antibiotics.

Questions 17 through 19 refer to the following diagram and paragraph.

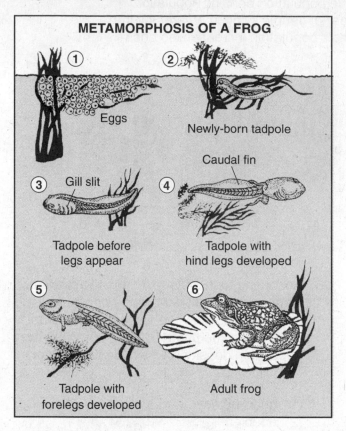

METAMORPHOSIS OF A FROG

① Eggs

② Newly-born tadpole

③ Gill slit — Tadpole before legs appear

④ Caudal fin — Tadpole with hind legs developed

⑤ Tadpole with forelegs developed

⑥ Adult frog

The life cycle of the frog is an example of the process of metamorphosis. Metamorphosis refers to an animal's changing form as it grows. A frog's immature form, called a tadpole, gradually changes into an adult form. The tadpole lives in water and breathes through gills. As it matures, the tadpole loses the gills and develops lungs. The adult frog can live on land because it can breathe through its lungs.

17. What is metamorphosis?

(1) the process of reproduction in frogs and similar organisms
(2) the process by which an immature form changes into a different adult form
(3) the growth of any young organism into an adult
(4) changes in an adult organism caused by becoming older
(5) the process by which tadpoles absorb oxygen from water

18. Which of the following is most similar to the development of a tadpole into a frog?

(1) growth of a puppy into a dog
(2) development of a child into an adult
(3) growth of a lamb into a sheep
(4) development of a caterpillar into a butterfly
(5) development of a chick into a chicken

19. Which of the following statements does the author assume you know?

(1) All animals go through metamorphosis.
(2) All plants go through metamorphosis.
(3) Different body structures are suitable for different environments.
(4) Almost all frog eggs eventually develop into adults.
(5) Metamorphosis occurs in humans.

Question 20 refers to the following line graph.

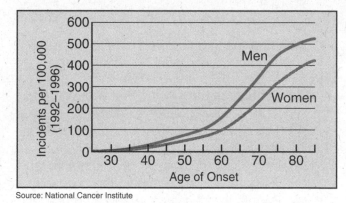

Source: National Cancer Institute

20. "Colon cancer is a man's disease." Based on the graph, why is this statement illogical?

(1) Very few people under age 50 get colon cancer.
(2) There are almost as many women as men with colon cancer.
(3) More women than men get colon cancer.
(4) More young men than old women get cancer.
(5) More men die of lung cancer than of colon cancer.

Questions 21 through 23 refer to the following passage and charts.

There are three different genes—A, B, and O—that determine a person's blood type. Six different genotypes are possible, and they result in four different blood types, as shown in the first chart. For example, a person with blood type A may have genotype AA or AO. The type O gene is recessive, while type A and B genes are both dominant (and so, called codominant). A person who inherits two codominant genes, A and B, has type AB blood.

A person's blood type depends on the two genes inherited from his or her parents. Thus different populations show different frequencies of blood types. The second chart shows how the blood types are distributed in different populations.

Blood Type	Genotype	Can Get Blood From	Can Give Blood To
A	AA, AO	O, A	A, AB
B	BB, BO	O, B	B, AB
AB	AB	A, B, AB, O	AB
O	OO	O	A, B, AB, O

Blood Type	A	B	AB	O
U.S. (White)	41.0%	10.0%	4.0%	45.0%
U.S. (Black)	26.0%	21.0%	3.7%	49.3%
American Indian	7.7%	1.0%	0.0%	91.3%
Swedish	46.7%	10.3%	5.1%	37.9%
Japanese	38.4%	21.8%	8.6%	31.2%
Polynesian	60.8%	2.2%	0.5%	36.5%
Chinese	25.0%	35.0%	10.0%	30.0%

21. People with type O blood are called universal donors because universal donors can do which of the following?

(1) receive blood from anyone
(2) receive only type A blood
(3) receive only type B blood
(4) give blood to anyone
(5) give blood to a person with type O only

22. Which of the following would be the best title for the chart on the right above?

(1) Blood Type Frequency in Selected Populations
(2) Human Blood Types Around the World
(3) Receiving and Giving Blood in Selected Populations
(4) The Genotypes of Each Blood Type
(5) Blood Type Frequency in the United States

23. Which of the following restates the portion of Chinese who have blood type O, as indicated in the chart?

(1) About one-tenth
(2) About one quarter
(3) About three-tenths
(4) About one half
(5) None

TIP

When you come to a passage that has a chart or diagram, preview the chart or diagram first. That way you'll know what the passage is about before you start to read it.

Questions 24 through 26 refer to the following passage and graph.

The ability to learn and remember certain types of things varies with age. This was demonstrated in an experiment in which 1,205 people were asked to learn some names. They watched videotapes on which fourteen people introduced themselves by name and said where they were from. As shown in the line graph, everyone tested recalled more names after the second and third playing of the video, but younger adults consistently outperformed older adults.

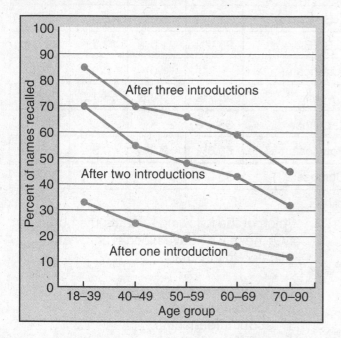

24. Which group remembered the fewest names?

(1) age 18–39 after one introduction
(2) age 50–59 after one introduction
(3) age 50–59 after two introductions
(4) age 70–90 after one introduction
(5) age 70–90 after three introductions

TIP To understand a line graph, you need to read both axes. You also need to study the graph to see what each line represents.

25. "The participants remembered about 66 percent of the names after the third playing of the video." Based on the passage and the graph, why is this statement illogical?

(1) Most participants did not stay for the third playing of the video.
(2) The participants remembered about 50 percent of the names after the third playing.
(3) The 50-59 age group recalled about 66 percent; other age groups did better or worse.
(4) Young people outperformed older people and remembered more names.
(5) The performance gap between the oldest and youngest was greatest after the third playing.

26. Which of the following best summarizes the information in the passage and diagram?

(1) It is difficult to remember people's names when you first meet them.
(2) After seeing the video once, most participants remembered few names.
(3) Adults in the 18 to 39 age group remembered more names than any other group.
(4) People remember the most names after seeing the video once.
(5) The ability to recall names declines with age, but repetition improves recall at all ages.

27. Transpiration is the process by which plants lose water vapor to the air through pores in their leaves. Where are you most likely to observe evidence of transpiration?

(1) in a desert
(2) at the North Pole
(3) in the ocean
(4) in a greenhouse
(5) in a field of vegetables

Questions 28 through 31 refer to the following passage and map.

In the early twentieth century, gray wolves were eradicated throughout the West and in most of the rest of the United States. In 1995 and 1996, gray wolves from Canada were reintroduced to two areas of the West—central Idaho and Yellowstone National Park in Wyoming. Natural immigration of wolves from Canada resulted in a third population in northern Montana.

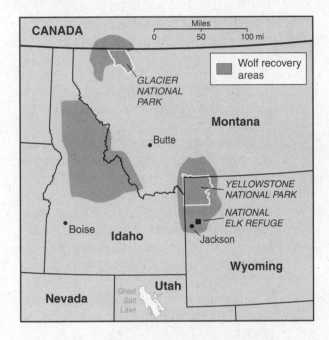

One reason the wolves were imported was to help control the native elk population of Yellowstone, which had grown huge. One wolf pack in Yellowstone has learned how to attack and kill bison as well. They also have killed domesticated animals in their range. During the first three years after their reintroduction in the West, wolves killed 80 cattle, 190 sheep, and 12 dogs. The owners of these animals were compensated for their losses, and the offending wolves were either moved or killed.

Despite the fact that about 10 percent of the wolves die each year, the three populations have increased substantially. There are now several hundred wolves in more than 30 packs. In at least two known instances, wolves from different populations have mated. Eventually there may be a single large population throughout the Rocky Mountain area. Some people argue that the gray wolf should now be removed from the list of endangered species.

28. According to the map, which state has the most scattered areas of wolf population?

(1) Idaho
(2) Montana
(3) Nevada
(4) Utah
(5) Wyoming

29. Which of the following is a title that gives the main idea of the map?

(1) Yellowstone National Park
(2) Idaho, Montana, and Wyoming
(3) National Parks of the Rockies
(4) The Range of the Gray Wolf
(5) Gray Wolves in the National Parks

30. Which of the following is an opinion rather than a fact?

(1) Wolves have learned to hunt bison.
(2) There are over 30 packs of wolves in the U.S. Rockies.
(3) About 10 percent of the wolves in the West die each year.
(4) Owners were paid for livestock killed by wolves.
(5) The gray wolf should no longer be considered endangered.

31. Which of the following is most similar to the reintroduction of gray wolves in the U.S.?

(1) building passways in dams so salmon can migrate upstream
(2) limiting hunting of certain species of game animals to certain times of year
(3) restoring tallgrass varieties to small portions of the Great Plains
(4) introducing a nonnative species to wipe out a pest
(5) preventing nonnative species from entering an area

Questions 32 through 34 refer to the following passage and chart.

People once thought that evil spirits caused disease. In the early 1600s, a new invention—the microscope—allowed scientists to see microorganisms. But scientists needed 200 years to connect microorganisms and disease.

In the 1870s, Robert Koch, a German scientist, discovered that a certain kind of bacterium caused the disease anthrax in sheep, cows, and humans. Koch examined organs of animals that had died of anthrax and found many rod-shaped bacteria in the blood. He transferred some of these into the cut skin of a healthy mouse, which then developed anthrax and died. The same bacteria were in the blood of the dead mouse.

But, Koch wanted to see the bacteria multiply. He set up an experiment to grow the bacteria and infect laboratory animals. His experiments provided significant proof for the idea that microorganisms can cause disease. Koch's procedure for studying disease-causing microorganisms, known as Koch's postulates, is still used today. The steps are shown here.

KOCH'S POSTULATES	
Step	**Description**
1	Isolate the microorganism believed to cause the disease.
2	Grow the microorganism outside the animal in a sterile food medium. A group of microorganisms grown this way is called a culture.
3	Produce the same disease by injecting a healthy animal with microorganisms from the culture.
4	Examine the animal and recover the microorganisms that caused the disease.

32. Which of the following describes a culture?

   (1) a disease-causing microorganism
   (2) bacteria that release toxins
   (3) microorganisms grown in a sterile food medium
   (4) a laboratory in which animal experiments take place
   (5) rod-shaped bacteria that cause anthrax

33. In the mid-1800s the idea that microorganisms cause disease was an opinion. What contributed most directly to this idea being accepted as fact today?

   (1) the development of antibiotics
   (2) the invention of the microscope
   (3) the use of sterile food media to culture bacteria
   (4) Koch's experiments with anthrax bacteria
   (5) the discovery of microorganisms

34. Which of the following statements related to Koch's postulates is an example of faulty logic?

   (1) To prove that a certain bacterium causes a particular disease first isolate that bacteria.
   (2) To prove that bacteria cause a particular disease, inject healthy animals with the suspect bacteria.
   (3) If an animal injected with the suspect bacteria gets a particular disease, that bacteria may cause that disease.
   (4) Using Koch's postulates, scientists have proven that many diseases are caused by bacteria.
   (5) If a disease is not caused by a particular type of bacterium, it must be caused by a virus.

35. The thyroid gland produces a substance containing iodine that helps regulate growth. Goiter is an enlargement of the thyroid gland caused by a lack of iodine in the diet. Goiter is uncommon in coastal areas where people eat seafood that contains a form of iodine. It is more common inland, where people eat food that has been grown in soil lacking iodine.

Which phrase restates the cause of the disease goiter, as given in the passage?

   (1) eating too much fish
   (2) eating too little of foods high in iodine
   (3) exposure to a bacterium found in iodine
   (4) fertilizing the soil with iodine
   (5) inheriting a defective thyroid gene

Answers start on page 282.

Cumulative Review Performance Analysis
Unit 1 • Life Science

Use the Answers and Explanations starting on page 282 to check your answers to the Unit 1 Cumulative Review. Then use the chart to figure out the skill areas in which you need more practice.

On the chart, circle the questions that you answered correctly. Write the number correct for each skill area. Add the number of questions that you got correct on the Cumulative Review. If you feel that you need more practice, go back and review the lessons for the skill areas that were difficult for you.

Questions	Number Correct	Skill Area	Lessons for Review
1, 2, **7**, **9**, 12, **13**, 14, 16, 17, **21**, **22**, **23**, **24**, 26, **28**, 29, 32, 35	____/18	Comprehension	1, 2, 6
3, 4, **5**, **10**, 15, 19, 30, 33	____/8	Analysis	3, 4, 7
6, 8, **11**, 18, 27, 31	____/6	Application	8
20, 25, 34	____/3	Evaluation	5
TOTAL CORRECT	____/35		

Question numbers in **boldface** are based on graphics.

Earth and Space Science

Every day an Earth or space science story makes the news. There may be a story about a devastating earthquake. Perhaps there is a story about lives saved by the evacuation of a coastal town that lies in the path of a predicted hurricane. Or, you may read a story about a probe to Mars or new information about the size of the universe. Even if no natural disaster has occurred and no space story makes the news, there is always one Earth science story—the weather report!

Understanding Earth and space science is very important for success on the GED Science Test. Topics from these areas are the basis for about 20 percent of the questions on the test.

Scientists are working to improve methods of predicting earthquakes and saving lives.

The lessons in this unit include:

Lesson 9:   **The Structure of Earth**
In this lesson, you will learn about the interior of Earth as well as the forces that move continents.

Lesson 10:   **The Changing Earth**
In this lesson, you will discover that the landscape changes quickly, through volcanic eruptions and earthquakes, and slowly, through weathering and erosion.

Lesson 11:   **Weather and Climate**
In this lesson, you will learn about the factors that influence our everyday weather as well as our long-term climate.

Lesson 12:   **Earth's Resources**
In this lesson, you will discover our dependence on resources such as water, fossil fuels, soil, and minerals to sustain human life on Earth.

Lesson 13:   **Earth in Space**
In this lesson, you will find out the latest discoveries about the solar system, stars, and the universe.

> ### THINKING SKILLS
> O Identifying implications
> O Analyzing cause and effect
> O Assessing the adequacy of facts
> O Recognizing values

Lesson 9

GED SKILL Identifying Implications

implication
a fact or idea that is suggested by stated information

imply
to suggest something is true without actually stating it

TIP

To determine if a fact or idea is implied by a passage, ask yourself if the idea is based on something specific in the passage. If it is, the idea or fact is an implication.

When you take what is written and then figure out other things that are probably true, you are identifying **implications**. Implications are not directly expressed in words by the author. Rather, they are suggested by what is written. For example, suppose you read, "A surge in demand for heating oil has driven up the price of this fuel." One implication of this statement is that heating bills are going to rise. Implications are facts or ideas you can be reasonably sure are true because they follow from what is written.

You can increase your ability to identify implications by thinking about consequences. A consequence is an effect or result. If certain conditions exist, what effect does this have? For example, the fact that a tornado passed through a town **implies** the consequence that property was damaged.

Read the passage. Then answer the questions below.

Direct human exploration of Earth's deep interior is impossible. So most of what scientists have learned about Earth's depths comes from studying **seismic waves**—vibrations that travel through Earth. Seismic waves occur naturally as a result of earthquakes and from human-induced nuclear explosions. The travel time of these waves varies, depending on the properties of the matter they encounter. By analyzing differences in seismic waves, scientists have learned a lot about Earth's interior.

1. Put a check mark next to the statement implied by the sentence, "Direct human exploration of Earth's deep interior is impossible."

   _____ a. Earth's interior is dangerous to humans.

   _____ b. Earth's interior is made of iron.

You were correct if you checked *option a*. The fact that human exploration is impossible suggests Earth's interior is dangerous. It does not suggest that Earth is made of iron, as stated in *option b*.

2. Put a check mark next to the statement implied by the references to varying speeds, travel times, and directions of seismic waves.

   _____ a. Seismographic stations are located all over Earth.

   _____ b. The waves speed up, slow down, or change direction as they pass through different types of matter.

You were correct if you checked *option b*. Variations in the speed or direction of seismic waves relate to the material they pass through. *Option a* is true, but not implied by the variations in waves.

Use the passage and diagram to answer the questions below.

From the indirect evidence of seismic waves, scientists have concluded that Earth is made up of four layers: the crust, the mantle, the outer core, and the inner core.

The **crust** is the part of Earth that includes the surface. It is composed of many kinds of rocks. It is about 8 kilometers thick under the oceans and about 40 kilometers thick under the continents.

The **mantle** is composed of rock that contains mainly oxygen, iron, magnesium, and silicon. Some of the rock in the mantle is molten and flows.

The **outer core** is molten iron and nickel. The **inner core,** the center of Earth, is solid iron, which is magnetic, and nickel. The great pressure in the inner core pushes the particles of iron and nickel together so tightly that they remain solid despite the great heat.

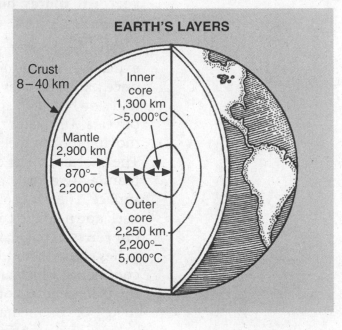

EARTH'S LAYERS

Crust 8–40 km

Inner core 1,300 km >5,000°C

Mantle 2,900 km

870°–2,200°C

Outer core 2,250 km 2,200°–5,000°C

1. Put a check mark next to the statement that is implied by the information in the passage and the diagram.

   _____ a. The crust is the only layer of Earth that people can see.

   _____ b. The crust is the thickest layer of Earth.

2. Put a check mark next to the statement that is implied by the second paragraph of the passage.

   _____ a. The crust beneath Africa is about 8 kilometers thick.

   _____ b. The crust beneath Africa is about 40 kilometers thick.

3. Explain why the statement you chose in question 2 is implied by the information in the passage.

   _____

   _____

4. Put a check mark next to the statement that is implied by the fact that Earth's core is made mostly of iron.

   _____ a. Earth has a magnetic field.

   _____ b. Earth has large quantities of iron in its crust.

5. Explain why the statement you chose in question 4 is implied by the information in the passage.

   _____

   _____

Answers start on page 285.

GED CONTENT The Structure of Earth

The surface of Earth is not one solid piece. Instead, it is made of **tectonic plates,** huge fragments that fit together like the pieces of a puzzle. These plates are formed from the crust and upper mantle.

The theory of plate tectonics explains how the continents were once joined and have separated and slowly drifted apart for millions of years. The plates float on the moving molten rock of the mantle. The enormous heat deep in the mantle drives rock up toward the surface. There it cools and sinks back down. These **convection currents** in the mantle cause the plates above them to move. The continents, which are embedded in the plates, move along with these huge, drifting rock slabs. This is the theory of continental drift.

CONVECTION CURRENTS IN MANTLE

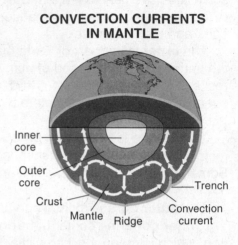

There are about twenty plates that are always moving. Where plates move apart, molten rock wells up from the mantle to form new crust. For example, along the Mid-Atlantic Ridge, the North American and Eurasian and African plates are moving apart, creating new crust. When plates move toward one another, one plate slides under the other, pushing huge mountain ranges up at the boundaries. The Himalayas, for example, arose when the Indo-Australian plate pushed north into the Eurasian plate. Plates can also slide past each other. This occurs along the San Andreas Fault in California, where the Pacific plate is pushing northward past the North American plate, causing frequent earthquakes.

EARTH'S TECTONIC PLATES

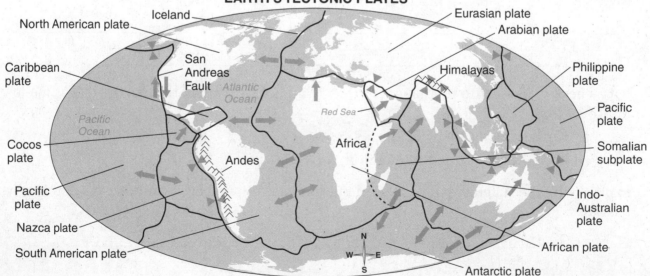

Directions: Choose the one best answer to each question.

Questions 1 through 6 refer to the passage, the diagram, and the map on page 112.

1. Which of the following is implied by the idea of continental drift?

   (1) The continents have been in their present locations for millions of years.
   (2) The locations of the continents in relation to one another are constantly changing.
   (3) Even after millions of years, the movement of continents is barely noticeable.
   (4) Continents float on the molten material of the outer core and mantle.
   (5) The world has always had six main continents.

2. Which of the following is implied by the diagram?

   (1) Materials circulate between the mantle and crust at ridges and trenches.
   (2) Materials from the core move up into the mantle.
   (3) The crust is much thicker than the mantle at the ridges.
   (4) The convection currents of the mantle cover only a few miles.
   (5) Convection currents occur only under the continents.

3. Which of the following statements is supported by the information in the map?

   (1) The Indo-Australian plate is moving toward the Antarctic plate.
   (2) The Antarctic plate was once much farther south.
   (3) The North American plate is moving toward the Eurasian plate.
   (4) Plates are pulling apart mostly under the oceans.
   (5) At most boundaries, plates are sliding past one another.

4. Which of the following is most similar to the formation of the Himalayas?

   (1) the Red Sea, formed as Africa and Arabia move apart
   (2) the San Andreas fault, formed by the sliding of the Pacific and North American plates
   (3) Iceland, formed by the pulling apart of the North American and Eurasian plates
   (4) the Southeast Indian Ridge, formed by the pulling apart of the Indo-Australian and Antarctic plates
   (5) the Andes, formed by the collision of the Nazca and South American plates

5. If after billions of years the interior of Earth cooled down, what might be the result?

   (1) The plates would no longer move and the continents no longer drift.
   (2) The plates would continue to move, but all in the same direction.
   (3) The Mid-Atlantic Ridge would continue to form.
   (4) The Antarctic plate would collide with the North American plate.
   (5) All the continents would be joined in a single large continent.

6. What is the relationship between continental drift and the theory of plate tectonics?

   (1) The theory of continental drift explains how the tectonic plates move.
   (2) The theory of plate tectonics explains how the continents drift.
   (3) Continental drift and plate tectonics both refer only to the movement of continents.
   (4) Continental drift and plate tectonics both refer only to the development of oceans.
   (5) Continental drift and plate tectonics both explain how rocks in the mantle move.

Answers start on page 285.

Directions: Choose the one best answer to each question.

Questions 1 and 2 refer to the following passage and maps.

There are several types of evidence to support the idea that the continents have drifted over hundreds of millions of years. First, some coastlines seem to match. For example, South America and Africa fit together as if they had once been part of the same land mass. Second, rock types and structures found on one continent seem to continue in another. For example, rock types in eastern Brazil match those found in northwestern Africa. In addition, the Appalachian Mountains in eastern North America seem to continue into Greenland and Northern Europe.

Third, fossils of the same types of land plants and animals have been found in South America, Africa, Australia, and Antarctica. This suggests that at one time these continents may have been connected by land.

Fourth, there is evidence that ice sheets covered much of Africa, South America, Australia, and India about 220 or 300 million years ago. If these land masses had formed a supercontinent closer to the South Pole, that would account for the colder climate.

CONTINENTAL DRIFT

1. If you were to draw a map of the world one hundred million years from now, which of the following would the map probably show?

   (1) Earth would look as it does today.
   (2) Earth would be covered by ocean.
   (3) Earth would be covered by continents.
   (4) The Atlantic Ocean would be narrower.
   (5) South America and Africa would be farther apart.

   TIP A series of illustrations that depicts how something developed over time may show a trend that is likely to continue.

2. Before the theory of continental drift was developed, which of the following hypotheses was used to explain the presence of fossils of the same species of land animals on different continents?

   (1) Adjacent rock structures in South America and Africa are the same.
   (2) The animals might have crossed the oceans on driftwood.
   (3) The animals might have swum from one continent to another.
   (4) The fossils may have been carried by ocean currents from one continent to another.
   (5) Ice sheets once covered portions of Africa, South America, Australia, and India.

FROM CONTINENTAL DRIFT TO PLATE TECTONICS

Questions 3 through 5 refer to the following passage.

The idea of continental drift was first set forth by German scientist Alfred Wegener in 1915. Wegener suggested that one supercontinent, which he called Pangaea, once existed. He also proposed that Pangaea began to break into smaller continents about 200 million years ago. These continents then drifted to their present positions. Wegener cited matching coastlines, fossil evidence, similar rock structures across continents, and evidence related to climate to support his idea.

Most of Wegener's contemporaries were very critical of his ideas. They thought that the evidence supporting continental drift was weak. More important, Wegener was unable to explain exactly how the continents moved. He proposed two ideas—either the gravity of the moon gave the continents a westward motion or the continents cut through the ocean floor. Both of these ideas were quickly dismissed as impossible.

For many years, little progress was made to explain how the continents could drift. Then in the 1950s and 1960s advances in technology permitted detailed mapping of the ocean floor. From this mapping came the discovery of a global ridge system under the oceans. In the early 1960s an American scientist, Harry Hess, proposed that the ocean ridges were above upwelling convection currents in the mantle. New crust was formed there, pushing older sea floor crust away and eventually back down into the mantle, forming trenches where the edges slip below other plates. Other evidence has since been found to support the idea of **sea floor spreading.** For the first time, there was a reasonable explanation for how portions of the crust move.

By 1968, the ideas of continental drift and sea floor spreading were united into the broader theory of plate tectonics. This theory is so encompassing that it provides a framework by which to understand most geologic processes.

3. What was the main reason that Wegener's ideas were criticized?

   (1) He cited evidence that was very weak.
   (2) There were other explanations for the evidence he cited.
   (3) There was no evidence for continental drift.
   (4) He did not have a strong explanation for how the continents moved.
   (5) Pangaea was an imaginary supercontinent.

4. Which of the following is a conclusion rather than a supporting statement?

   (1) The coastlines of different continents match up.
   (2) Fossils of the same species have been found on different continents.
   (3) Millions of years ago, the climate was the same in now distant areas.
   (4) Rock structures on adjacent continents match up.
   (5) The continents originally formed one large land mass and then moved apart.

5. Which of the following natural phenomena can best be explained by the theory of plate tectonics?

   (1) the migration of modern land animals from one place to another
   (2) the recycling of water from the atmosphere to the land
   (3) the presence of sediment on large areas of the ocean floor
   (4) the presence of large cities along coastal plate boundaries
   (5) the occurrence of earthquakes along plate boundaries

Answers start on page 285.

GED Mini-Test • Lesson 9

Directions: This is a ten-minute practice test. After ten minutes, mark the last question you finished. Then complete the test and check your answers. If most of your answers were correct but you didn't finish, try to work faster next time. Choose the <u>one best answer</u> to each question.

<u>Questions 1 through 4</u> refer to the following information and diagram.

Sea floor spreading is caused by the upward movement of heated molten rock from the mantle through the crust. Where this material comes to the surface, the sea floor (Earth's crust) cracks, forming a ridge. The new material in the ridge pushes the sea floor on either side away from the ridge in each direction.

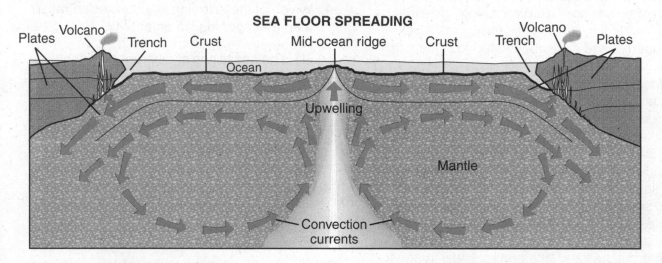

SEA FLOOR SPREADING

1. What causes sea floor spreading?

   (1) heat currents in the crust
   (2) heat currents in the mantle
   (3) the aging of the sea floor
   (4) volcanic activity along the coast
   (5) the drifting of the continents

2. Which of the following is implied by the diagram?

   (1) The farther from the ridge, the younger the sea floor.
   (2) The farther from the ridge, the older the sea floor.
   (3) Sea floor spreading occurs only in the Atlantic Ocean.
   (4) Sea floor spreading occurs only in the Pacific Ocean.
   (5) Sea floor spreading causes the ocean to dry up.

3. What causes the sea floor to descend back into the mantle?

   (1) It collides with a plate and dips below it.
   (2) It is lighter than the continental plates.
   (3) The mantle below it collapses.
   (4) It encounters earthquake action.
   (5) The mantle causes it to rise up.

4. Scientists have calculated that the sea floor in the North Atlantic is spreading about 3.5 centimeters per year. Which of the following conclusions does this evidence support?

   (1) Sea level will rise.
   (2) Sea level will fall.
   (3) The Atlantic Ocean will widen.
   (4) The Atlantic Ocean will narrow.
   (5) The width of the Atlantic Ocean will remain the same.

Questions 5 and 6 refer to the following information and diagram.

Plates meet in three ways forming divergent, convergent, and transform plate boundaries.

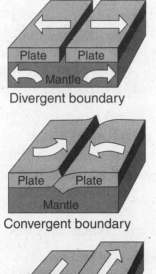
Divergent boundary

Convergent boundary

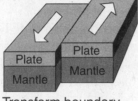
Transform boundary

5. What is the best title for this information?

(1) Plate Tectonics
(2) Types of Faults
(3) Types of Plate Boundaries
(4) Types of Tectonic Plates
(5) Types of Natural Boundaries

6. Which of the following is an example of a convergent boundary?

(1) The Juan de Fuca plate is descending below the North American plate.
(2) The Rift Valley of East Africa is splitting the African plate.
(3) The Arabian plate is moving away from the African plate.
(4) The Pacific and North American plates are sliding past each other in opposite directions.
(5) Two oceanic plates are pulling apart at the Mid-Atlantic Ridge.

7. The theory of plate tectonics originally held that the continental and oceanic plates slide across the moving molten rock of the upper mantle. Research has shown, however, that some continental plates have deep keels of rock that reach more than 300 miles into the upper mantle. The keels extend below the partially molten layer and seem to anchor the continental plates firmly to the upper mantle.

Which of the following conclusions is best supported by this information?

(1) The continental plates and the upper mantle move together rather than independently.
(2) The entire upper mantle is molten rock.
(3) The continental plates slide across the upper mantle, regardless of the existence of the rock keels.
(4) The oceanic plates and the upper mantle move together rather than independently.
(5) The continental plates are shallower than the oceanic plates.

8. Deep V-shaped depressions of the sea floor are called trenches. At the trenches, one plate is descending below another. The deepest trenches, which are in the Pacific, Atlantic, and Indian Oceans, are listed below.

TRENCH DEPTHS		
Ocean	Trench	Depth in Feet
Pacific	Mariana	35,840
	Tonga	35,433
Atlantic	Puerto Rico	28,232
	S. Sandwich	27,313
Indian	Java	23,736
	Ob'	22,553

Which of the following is supported by the information in the table?

(1) The Ob' trench is 27,313 feet deep.
(2) The sea floor spreads apart at a trench.
(3) The deepest trench is the Puerto Rico trench.
(4) The Java trench is deeper than the Tonga trench.
(5) The world's deepest trenches are in the Pacific Ocean.

Answers start on page 286.

GED SKILL Analyzing Cause and Effect

cause
something that makes something else happen

effect
something that happens because something else happened

cause-and-effect relationship
a situation in which one thing (a cause) results in another (an effect)

Cause-and-effect relationships are sometimes signaled by words such as *because, since, thus, effect, affect, result, occurs when, led to,* and *due to.* Look for these words to identify cause-and-effect relationships.

When you feel hungry, you probably eat. Here, hunger is a cause; eating is an effect. A **cause** is something that makes something else happen. An **effect** is what happens as a result of a cause. Causes always occur before effects. Situations in which one thing causes another are called **cause-and-effect relationships.**

Scientists often look for cause-and-effect relationships. They try to discover general laws that can help them predict what will result from specific causes. For example, they try to discover what causes volcanoes to erupt. They also try to discover effects. What happens as a result of a volcanic eruption?

Read the passage and answer the questions below.

From 1943 to 1952, scientists observed the formation of the **volcano** Paricutín. In February 1943, there was much underground activity near the village of Paricutín, Mexico. It caused many small Earth tremors that worried the villagers. On February 20, Dionisio and Paula Pulido noticed smoke rising from a small hole in their cornfield near the village. The hole had been there as long as the farmer and his wife could remember. That night hot rock fragments spewing from the hole looked like fireworks. By morning, the fragments had piled up into a cone about 40 meters high. Within two years it was more than 400 meters high. Ash from the volcano burned and covered the village of Paricutín. **Lava** flows buried another nearby village. After nine years, the volcanic activity stopped.

1. Write *C* next to the cause of the Earth tremors near Paricutín.

   _____ a. underground activity

   _____ b. smoke coming from a hole in the ground

You were correct if you chose *option a.* The underground activity in the area caused the Earth tremors. *Option b* is incorrect; the smoke was a result, not a cause, of the underground activity.

2. Write *E* next to each effect of the eruption of Paricutín. Mark all that apply.

   _____ a. A cone more than 400 meters high was formed.

   _____ b. Ash buried the village of Paricutín.

   _____ c. People resumed their normal lives in the area.

   _____ d. Scientists learned a lot about how volcanoes form.

You were correct if you marked *options a, b,* and *d.* These are all results of the eruption of Paricutín. You can see that one cause may have several effects. Likewise, one effect may have many causes.

Use the passage and the diagram to answer the questions below.

Deep within Earth, rock is a hot liquid called **magma.** In some places, magma works its way toward the surface by melting solid rock or by moving through cracks in Earth's crust. When magma reaches the surface, it is called lava. The place where lava emerges from Earth is called a volcano.

Volcanoes can be classified according to the kind of eruptions that forms them. One type of volcano is called a cinder cone volcano. Cinder cone volcanoes are formed from explosive eruptions. Explosive eruptions are caused when lava in vents, or openings, hardens into rock. Steam and magma build up under the rocks, causing pressure. Eventually the pressure becomes great enough to cause a violent explosion. The volcano is formed out of cinders, ash, and other rock particles that are blown into the air. A cinder cone volcano has a narrow base and steep sides.

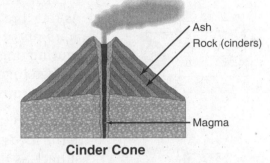

Cinder Cone

1. Write *C* next to the cause of a cinder cone volcano eruption.

      _____ a. Underground ash particles build up, eventually causing an explosion.

      _____ b. Steam and magma create great pressure, eventually causing a forceful eruption.

2. Put a check mark next to the phrase from the second paragraph that helped you answer question 1.

      _____ a. "The volcano is formed out of cinders, ash, and other rock particles . . ."

      _____ b. ". . . the pressure becomes great enough to cause a violent explosion."

3. Write *C* next to the cause of the layering found in a cinder cone volcano.

      _____ a. deposits of two types of materials, ash and cinder

      _____ b. a pool of magma at the base of the volcano

4. Write *R* next to each result of a cinder cone volcano eruption. Mark all that apply.

      _____ a. Cinder and ash explode into the air.

      _____ b. Magma and steam build up underground.

      _____ c. Cinder and ash form a cone-shaped mountain.

      _____ d. Lava flows out very slowly.

      _____ e. Magma works its way through cracks in the slope.

Answers start on page 287.

TYPES OF FAULTS

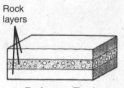

Rock
layers

Before a Fault

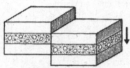

Normal Fault

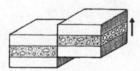

Reverse Fault

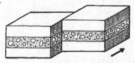

Lateral Fault

An **earthquake** is the shaking and trembling that results from the sudden movement of rock in Earth's crust. Most earthquakes occur along the boundaries of tectonic plates.

The most common cause of earthquakes is faulting. A **fault** is a break in Earth's crust. Rocks on either side of the fault begin to move. As they break and slide past each other, they release enormous amounts of energy. In a normal fault, the rocks are pulled apart, causing one side to slip downward. In a reverse fault, the rocks are pushed together, causing one side to rise up. In a lateral fault, the stresses cause horizontal movement of the rock.

The point beneath Earth's surface where rocks break and move is the focus of the earthquake. Directly above the focus, on Earth's surface, is the epicenter. The most violent shaking occurs at the epicenter.

When rocks in Earth's crust break, vibrations travel out in all directions from the focus. These vibrations are known as **seismic waves.** There are three main types of seismic waves.

The seismic waves that travel the fastest are called primary waves. These waves can travel through solids, liquids, and gases. Primary waves are push-pull waves. They cause pieces of rock to move back and forth in the same direction as the wave is moving.

The seismic waves that travel the next fastest are secondary waves. Secondary waves can travel through solids but not through liquids or gases. Rock pieces disturbed by secondary waves move from side to side at right angles to the direction the wave is traveling.

The slowest seismic waves are surface waves. Surface waves travel from the focus directly up to the epicenter. Surface waves cause the ground to bend and twist, sometimes causing whole buildings to collapse.

The more energy an earthquake releases, the stronger and more destructive it is. The strength of an earthquake is measured on a special scale, the **Richter scale.** The Richter scale measures how much energy an earthquake releases by assigning the earthquake a number from one to ten. Any magnitude of 7 or above on the Richter scale indicates a very strong earthquake. When a strong earthquake hits a populated area, there can be considerable property damage and numerous deaths.

Thousands of earthquakes occur each year, most of them minor. According to the U.S. Geological Survey, an average of 19 earthquakes per year worldwide measure 7 or above on the Richter scale.

Directions: Choose the <u>one best answer</u> to each question.

Questions 1 through 6 refer to the passage and the diagram on page 120.

1. What is the main idea of the second paragraph?

   (1) Earthquakes are movements of Earth's crust.
   (2) Movements along faults cause earthquakes.
   (3) There are three main types of faults.
   (4) In a lateral fault, rocks move horizontally.
   (5) Normal faults are the most common.

2. What is the result of both normal and reverse faults?

   (1) Rocks move sideways.
   (2) A steep face of rock is exposed.
   (3) Rocks are pulled apart.
   (4) Layers of rock are lined up.
   (5) Rocks are pushed together.

3. What is likely to form as a result of normal and reverse faulting over a wide area and long time period?

   (1) rivers
   (2) oceans
   (3) mountains
   (4) level plains
   (5) deserts

TIP In diagrams, there are usually no clue words to signal cause-and-effect relationships. You have to figure out the relationships by asking "What caused this? What effect would this have?"

4. Which of the following conclusions is supported by the information in the passage?

   (1) Surface waves are the most destructive type of seismic wave.
   (2) Primary waves are the most destructive type of seismic wave.
   (3) Secondary waves are the most destructive type of seismic wave.
   (4) All types of seismic waves except surface waves are destructive.
   (5) All types of seismic waves are equally destructive.

5. According to the passage, the strength of an earthquake is directly related to which of the following factors?

   (1) the length of the fault that causes the earthquake
   (2) the speed of the seismic waves produced by the earthquake
   (3) the distance from the focus to the epicenter
   (4) the total amount of rock broken during the earthquake
   (5) the amount of energy released from the focus

6. Why are earthquakes likely to occur in areas along tectonic plate boundaries?

   The boundaries between tectonic plates

   (1) are unstable due to the movements of the tectonic plates.
   (2) are made of solid rock.
   (3) occur along mid-ocean ridges.
   (4) are permanent features.
   (5) usually have many epicenters.

Answers start on page 287.

Directions: Choose the one best answer to each question.

Questions 1 and 2 refer to the following passage.

Earthquakes and volcanoes can quickly change the landscape, but **weathering** usually produces gradual changes. Weathering is the process by which rocks are broken down as a result of exposure to sun, wind, rain, ice, and other elements of the environment.

There are two main types of weathering: mechanical and chemical. In mechanical weathering, rock breaks into bits but its composition remains the same. For example, when water freezes in the cracks of rock, it expands, widening the cracks. Eventually this freeze-thaw weathering can crumble the rock. However this crumbled rock is the same as the original rock. Chemical weathering occurs when substances, such as carbonic acid in rainwater, combine with the rock, dissolving certain minerals and changing the rock's chemical makeup.

Living organisms can cause both mechanical and chemical weathering. Roots from plants can grow into the cracks in a rock, making the cracks bigger. Lichens can grow on a rock, producing chemicals that break down the rock.

1. Which of the following is an example of mechanical weathering?

   (1) A pebble rolls downhill.
   (2) Groundwater dissolves limestone.
   (3) The metal body of a car rusts.
   (4) A jackhammer breaks apart a roadway surface.
   (5) A rock breaks down into clay, salt, and silica.

2. Which of the following is an example of chemical weathering?

   (1) Acid rain wears away marble.
   (2) Potholes form during a cold winter.
   (3) Roots widen the crack in a rock.
   (4) Water freezes and cracks a pool's walls.
   (5) Pipes freeze and burst during a cold spell.

Questions 3 and 4 refer to the following passage and diagram.

In **erosion,** water, ice, or wind wear away rock and soil and transport it elsewhere. Erosion usually produces a gradual change in the land.

The running water of a river has great power to erode rock and soil. The rocks and other debris carried by the river, called load, increase its power to wear away the banks and riverbed. Most erosion takes place at the outside of bends. The banks are undercut, often creating steep cliffs or bluffs down which more soil and rock fall.

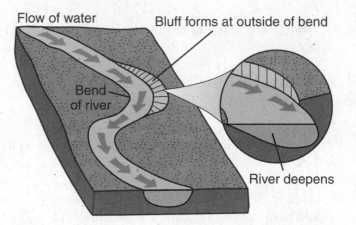

Flow of water   Bluff forms at outside of bend

Bend of river

River deepens

3. Which two processes are involved in erosion?

   (1) wearing away and weathering
   (2) wearing away and transporting
   (3) transporting and depositing
   (4) transporting and loading
   (5) loading and diverging

4. Due to heavy rains upstream, there is a surge of water in a river. What is the likely effect on a bluff at the outside of a river bend?

   (1) The bluff would be exposed to air.
   (2) Erosion would decrease along the bluff.
   (3) Erosion would increase along the bluff.
   (4) The river would carry less load.
   (5) Erosion would temporarily stop.

PREDICTING EARTHQUAKES

Questions 5 through 7 refer to the following information.

There are two main ways of predicting earthquakes. The first is to study the history of large earthquakes in an area. Based on past occurrences, scientists can determine the probability of another earthquake happening. However, these are long-term general forecasts. For example, scientists now forecast that there is a 67 percent chance of an earthquake measuring 6.8 or higher on the Richter scale in the San Francisco area during the next 30 years.

The second method of earthquake prediction relies on measurements of seismic waves and movement along faults. Scientists use seismic instruments to measure wave activity. In recent years, they have been using Global Positioning System (GPS) receivers installed along the San Andreas fault in California and faults in Turkey and Japan. Using signals from GPS satellites, the receivers give precise location data. Thus scientists can now monitor how much movement occurs along a fault. Using this type of information as well as historical data, they can calculate the probability of an earthquake occurring.

Earthquakes tend to occur in clusters that strike a single area in a limited time. There are foreshocks, which occur before the large mainshock. Then there are aftershocks. So far, scientists are better at predicting aftershocks than foreshocks or mainshocks. Still, earthquake predictions in California have helped. For example, in June 1988 the San Francisco area experienced a foreshock measuring 5.1 on the Richter scale. Scientists predicted a mainshock would occur within five days. In response, local government emergency managers ran preparedness drills. Sixty-nine days later, the magnitude 7.1 Loma Prieta mainshock occurred. Local officials claim they were better able to respond than they would have been without the forecast. Still, there were 63 deaths and $6 billion in damage.

5. What are the two main methods of predicting earthquakes?

   (1) analyzing historical data and analyzing climatic data about an area
   (2) installing GPS receivers and measuring movement along faults
   (3) analyzing historical data and measuring seismic activity and movement along faults
   (4) using GPS satellites to directly measure seismic activity and analyzing historical data
   (5) analyzing historical data and waiting for a mainshock to occur

6. Why was the Loma Prieta forecast considered a partial success despite the fact that scientists were wrong about when the mainshock would occur?

   (1) It was the first use of historical data in predicting an earthquake.
   (2) It was the first use of the Global Positioning System in predicting an earthquake.
   (3) It was the first use of seismic activity data in predicting an earthquake.
   (4) Local officials practiced emergency responses and so were better prepared for the earthquake.
   (5) Many people ignored the warning when the shock did not occur in five days.

7. The U.S. government funds much earthquake research. What benefit is the likely reason for such funding being awarded?

   (1) improved seismic instruments to detect wave activity
   (2) improved ability to locate the focus of each earthquake
   (3) better records of historical data on earthquakes
   (4) improved ability to prevent earthquakes
   (5) reduced loss of life and property damage from future earthquakes

Answers start on page 288.

Directions: This is a ten-minute practice test. After ten minutes, mark the last question you finished. Then complete the test and check your answers. If most of your answers were correct but you didn't finish, try to work faster next time. Choose the one best answer to each question.

Questions 1 and 2 refer to the following passage.

A glacier is a thick mass of ice. Most glaciers form in mountains where snow builds up faster than it can melt. As snow falls upon snow year after year, it is compacted into ice. When the ice becomes heavy enough, the pull of gravity causes it to move slowly down the mountain. As the glacier moves, it picks up blocks of rock. As the rocks become frozen into the bottom of the glacier, they carve away more rock. Some of this rock is left behind at the edges of the glacier.

Sometimes a glacier enters a V-shaped river valley that is narrower than the glacier. As the glacier squeezes through the valley, it erodes both the floor and sides of the valley. As a result, the valley changes to a U-shaped valley.

1. Which is the best title for this passage?

   (1) Glaciers Past and Present
   (2) Agents of Erosion
   (3) How Glaciers Form
   (4) How Glaciers Carve Valleys
   (5) Causes and Effects of Glaciers

2. What effect would several unusually long, hot summers have on mountain glaciers?

   (1) Glaciers would move down the mountain more rapidly.
   (2) Glaciers would reach farther down the mountain.
   (3) The edges of the glacier would melt, making it smaller.
   (4) The glaciers would become thicker and more dense.
   (5) The glaciers would carve narrow river valleys into U-shapes.

Questions 3 and 4 refer to the following information and diagram.

A shield volcano results from quiet, often slow, flows of lava. The lava from a shield volcano spreads over a large area, forming a gently sloping dome-shaped mountain.

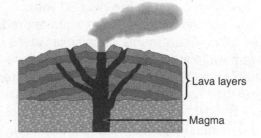

Lava layers
Magma

3. Based on the diagram, which of the following may result from a shield volcano?

   (1) a steep-sided cone
   (2) a cone made of ashes and cinders
   (3) a mountain with a narrow base
   (4) an eruption from a side vent
   (5) a volcano with a small surface area

4. Which of the following volcanoes is a shield volcano?

   (1) Mt. Vesuvius, which erupted violently in A.D. 79, burying Pompeii in three days
   (2) Mt. Fujiyama, a steep-sided, symmetrical cone in Japan
   (3) Mt. Pelee, which erupted with a fiery cloud that destroyed St. Pierre in ten minutes
   (4) Paricutín, a volcano built of lava fragments and ash, which grew to a height of 40 meters overnight
   (5) Kilauea Iki, whose lava spread over Hawaii during several months

Question 5 refers to the following information and diagram.

In deserts, wind-blown sand is one of the main agents of erosion. Continuous "blasting" and battering by sand particles wears away the base of rocks, as shown in the diagram.

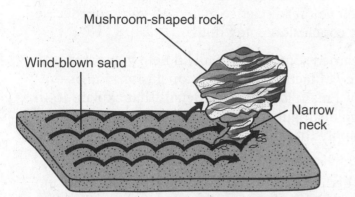

Mushroom-shaped rock

Wind-blown sand

Narrow neck

5. Why does the action of wind and sand affect the base of the rock rather than the top?

(1) Because of its weight, most sand is blown near the ground.
(2) The base of the rock is made of softer material than the top.
(3) Water has already partially eroded the base of the rock.
(4) The top of the rock is protected by rising warm air.
(5) The top of the rock may eventually topple off the base.

6. Igneous rock is a type of rock that forms when magma cools and solidifies. Which of the following conclusions is supported by this information?

(1) Limestone forms from the remains of shells and skeletons.
(2) Limestone turns to marble under great heat and pressure.
(3) Sandstone, formed from cemented sand particles, is an igneous rock.
(4) Rocks formed under great heat and pressure are igneous rocks.
(5) Rocks of volcanic origin are igneous rocks.

Questions 7 and 8 refer to the following map.

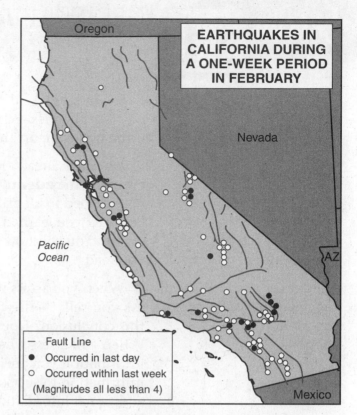

EARTHQUAKES IN CALIFORNIA DURING A ONE-WEEK PERIOD IN FEBRUARY

Oregon

Nevada

Pacific Ocean

AZ

— Fault Line
● Occurred in last day
○ Occurred within last week
(Magnitudes all less than 4)

Mexico

7. Based on the map, which part of California had the most earthquake activity in the last day of the period shown?

(1) the region bordering Oregon
(2) north central California
(3) south central California
(4) the region bordering Nevada
(5) the region bordering Mexico

8. Which of the following conclusions is supported by the information in the map?

(1) Earthquakes rarely occur during the winter in California.
(2) Some California earthquakes had a magnitude of 6 that week.
(3) Many earthquakes were not recorded by seismic stations.
(4) Earthquakes are an everyday occurrence in California.
(5) All the California earthquakes were felt by the general population.

Answers start on page 288.

GED SKILL Assessing the Adequacy of Facts

assess
to determine the importance, adequacy, or significance of something

adequacy
satisfactoriness; being sufficient for the purpose

Scientists present facts, measurements, and observations as support for their theories. When you read science materials, you must decide if the facts support the conclusion being drawn.

You have already learned some skills that will help you **assess,** or evaluate, the **adequacy** of facts to support a conclusion. In Lesson 1 you learned to identify a main idea and the details that explain it. In Lesson 7 you learned to distinguish conclusions from supporting details. You will now apply these skills to evaluating the information you read.

When you assess whether a particular fact supports a conclusion, ask yourself, "Is this fact relevant? Does it have anything to do with this conclusion? Does it contribute logically to this conclusion?" When you assess whether a conclusion is supported by the information you are given, ask yourself, "Is there enough information to support this generalization or conclusion? Is additional information needed to prove this conclusion is correct?"

Read the passage and answer the question below.

El Niño is a disruption in the currents and winds of the tropical Pacific. During El Niño, the ocean along the coast of Peru and Ecuador becomes unusually warm. The winds, which usually blow toward the west, blow toward the east instead. El Niño has many consequences. On the west coast of South America, the high temperature of the ocean disrupts the ecosystem, causing a decline in the commercial fish population. In the southern United States, rainfall increases, sometimes causing flooding.

Put a check mark next to all the facts from the passage that support the conclusion that El Niño depresses the fishing industry on the Pacific Coast of South America.

_____ a. The commercial fish population declines because the ecosystem is disrupted.

_____ b. The anchovy cannot adapt to warmer water.

_____ c. Rainfall increases in the southern United States.

You were correct if you checked *option a*. According to the passage, the commercial fish population declines during an El Niño. That fact supports the conclusion that the fishing industry declines. *Option b* is incorrect because the passage gives no information about anchovies. It may be true, but you cannot evaluate it. *Option c* is true according to the passage, but it does not support the conclusion about the fishing industry.

To assess the adequacy of facts, identify the conclusion and the supporting information in the passage. Then evaluate whether the information specifically supports and logically leads to the conclusion.

Use the passage and the diagram to answer the questions below.

As it **revolves** around the sun, Earth also **rotates** on its axis. Earth's axis is inclined at an angle of about 23.5°. Because Earth revolves and its axis is tilted, different parts of Earth face directly toward the sun at different times of year, resulting in seasons.

On June 21, the northern hemisphere leans directly toward the sun. As a result, this hemisphere gets the most energy from the sun and it experiences the first day of summer. On this day, the northern hemisphere experiences its longest day and its shortest night; temperatures during the summer average higher than they do during the rest of the year. In the southern hemisphere, on June 21, just the opposite happens. The southern hemisphere leans away from the sun. As a result, it gets the least amount of the sun's energy and experiences the first day of winter. On this day, the southern hemisphere experiences its shortest day and its longest night; temperatures average their coolest for the year during the winter season.

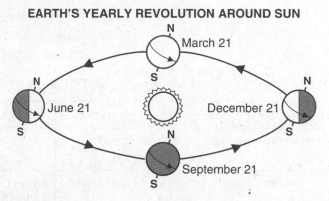

EARTH'S YEARLY REVOLUTION AROUND SUN

On March 21 and September 21, neither hemisphere leans toward the sun; these dates marks the first day of spring in the one hemisphere and the first day of autumn in the other hemisphere.

1. Put a check mark next to the conclusion that is supported by the information in the diagram.

    _____ a. It takes one full year for Earth to revolve around the sun.

    _____ b. The tilt of Earth's axis changes direction as Earth revolves around the sun.

2. Describe the information in the diagram that supports the conclusion you chose in Question 1.

    _____

    _____

3. Put a check mark next to the fact that supports the conclusion, drawn from the passage and the diagram, that a point on Earth will have the same number of hours of daylight on March 21 and September 21.

    _____ a. The southern hemisphere has shorter days and cooler temperatures around June 21.

    _____ b. On March 21 and September 21, neither hemisphere leans toward the sun.

4. Write a sentence telling how the answer you chose supports the conclusion stated in Question 3.

    _____

    _____

Answers start on page 289.

Weather refers to the state of the atmosphere at any given time. Changes in weather are caused by movements of air masses. An **air mass** is a large volume of air with a similar temperature and humidity level throughout. It may cover thousands of square miles.

Air masses are named according to where they form. The four major types of air masses that affect the United States are summarized in the table below. Air masses are called *maritime* if they form over the ocean and *continental* if they form over land.

FOUR TYPES OF AIR MASSES

Type of Air Mass	Type of Air	Where It Forms	Type of Weather in U.S.
Maritime tropical	warm and moist	over ocean near equator	*Summer:* hot and humid *Winter:* often rain or snow
Maritime polar	cool and moist	over cold areas in the Pacific Ocean; in summer, also over the North Atlantic Ocean	*Summer:* fog along the West Coast cold weather in the East *Winter:* cold; heavy snow
Continental tropical	hot and dry	over Mexico during summer	*Summer:* hot, dry weather in the Southwest
Continental polar	cold and dry	over northern Canada	*Winter:* very cold weather

The boundary between two air masses is called a **front.** Typically, the temperature and air pressure differ on the two sides of the front.

A cold front occurs when a cold air mass overtakes a warm air mass. The cold air pushes the warm air up. As the warm air rises, it cools. The result is often condensation, cloud formation, and rain.

In a warm front, a relatively warm air mass overtakes a cold air mass and rises above it. As the air rises, it cools and forms clouds. Eventually, there may be rain.

An occluded front occurs when a warm front is sandwiched between two cold fronts. The warm air between the fronts rises. The result can be a long period of heavy rain.

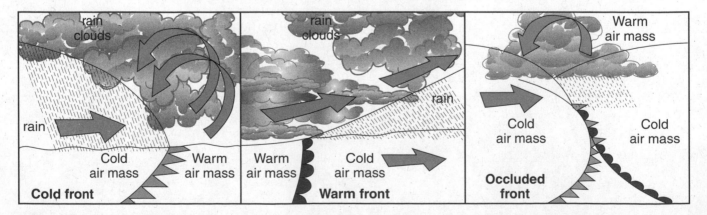

Directions: Choose the one best answer to each question.

Questions 1 through 6 refer to the passage, the chart, and the diagrams on page 128.

1. Which type of air is contained in air masses that form over land?

   (1) cold, moist air
   (2) warm, moist air
   (3) dry air
   (4) moist air
   (5) moist air in winter and dry air in summer

2. Snow in the Northern Pacific states could be caused by which of the following air masses?

   (1) maritime polar
   (2) continental tropical
   (3) continental polar
   (4) maritime polar or continental polar
   (5) continental polar or continental tropical

3. Maritime air masses generally bring damp weather to the United States. Which of the following events supports this generalization?

   (1) A maritime polar air mass brings fog and cool weather to England.
   (2) A maritime polar air mass forms over the Pacific Ocean.
   (3) A maritime tropical air mass brings hot, humid weather to the southern United States.
   (4) A maritime tropical air mass forms over the ocean near the equator.
   (5) A continental polar air mass forms over northern Canada.

TIP
When looking for specific data in a table or chart, check the column heads and entries in the first column (the row headings) to locate the relevant information.

4. A maritime tropical air mass meets a continental polar air mass over the northeastern U.S., forming a warm front. A meteorologist concludes that it will snow. What additional information would you need to determine whether this forecast is likely to be correct?

   (1) time of day
   (2) time of year
   (3) length of the warm front
   (4) size of the continental polar air mass
   (5) size of the maritime tropical air mass

5. If an air mass were to remain in the same place for a few days, what would be the most likely result?

   (1) The air mass would cover thousands of square miles.
   (2) The moisture and temperature of the air mass would change rapidly.
   (3) Alternating periods of clear and rainy weather would occur.
   (4) The weather would be about the same for a few days.
   (5) The weather would become extremely cold or hot.

6. Which of the following conclusions is supported by the information in the passage and the diagrams?

   (1) Rainy weather is associated with continental polar air masses.
   (2) Rainy weather is associated with the passing of a front.
   (3) In the United States, air masses usually move from west to east.
   (4) A warm front brings more rainy weather than a cold front does.
   (5) Cold fronts occur in the winter, and warm fronts occur in the summer.

Answers start on page 289.

Directions: Choose the <u>one best answer</u> to each question.

<u>Questions 1 and 2</u> refer to the passage and the diagram below.

Differences between moist sea air and dry land air cause changes in weather patterns. An example is the sea breeze. During the day, the land heats up more quickly than the ocean. This creates an area of low pressure at ground level as warm air rises up from the land. The cooler, denser sea air flows off the ocean into this area of low pressure. At the same time, the land air flows back out over the ocean at high altitude, creating a convection cell. At night, the situation is reversed.

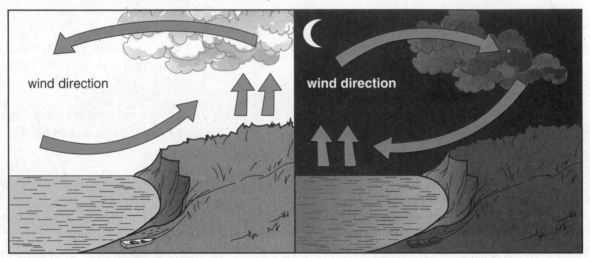

Day—Sea breeze   **Night—Land breeze**

1. What is the main idea of the passage?

   (1) The sea breeze blows off the water during the day.
   (2) Weather patterns result from differences in moist sea air and dry land air.
   (3) Moist air rises over the ocean and sinks over the land.
   (4) Warm and cool air circulate in convection cells.
   (5) The ocean breeze cools off the land each day.

   TIP When looking for a main idea, scan the passage for the topic sentence. The topic sentence gives the main idea. It is often the first or last sentence of a paragraph or passage.

2. At a beach, the wind has been blowing all afternoon, but it dies down around sunset. An hour or two later, the wind resumes blowing, but you observe that it is now blowing from the opposite direction. Based on the diagram, which of the following statements explains why this happens?

   (1) During the day, wind blows off the water onto the land.
   (2) During the night, wind blows off the land onto the water.
   (3) Warm air rises over land because it is lighter than cool air.
   (4) Warm air rises over the land during the day and over the sea during the night.
   (5) The sea breeze forms a convection cell over the shore area.

FORECASTING HURRICANES

Questions 3 through 5 refer to the information below.

A **hurricane** is a large tropical storm with average wind speeds of at least 74 miles per hour, sometimes reaching 150 miles per hour. The winds spiral outward from a calm area of low pressure in the center of the storm. The strong winds are usually accompanied by heavy rainfall and violent surges of ocean water. A hurricane can cause death as well as property damage from wind, rain, and floodwater.

The mission of the Tropical Prediction Center is to save lives and protect property by issuing storm watches, warnings, and forecasts to the general public, armed services, and mariners. It tracks storms over the Atlantic Ocean, Caribbean Sea, Gulf of Mexico, and eastern Pacific Ocean from May through November— prime hurricane season—each year.

Scientists at the center collect data on tropical storms from satellites, reconnaissance aircraft, ocean buoys and vessels, and land-based radar. The data are analyzed by powerful computer models that use current and historical information to project the course that the storm will take. The center issues predictions of the track, or path, of the storm as well as of its intensity.

An early warning of a coming tropical storm or hurricane can help reduce damage and loss of life. However, forecasters face several dilemmas. Should a storm warning be issued to a small area or to a wide area? If the prediction targets the wrong small area, a nearby area will face the storm unprepared. On the other hand, if a warning is issued to a wide area, great amounts of time and money may be spent on preparation that proves unnecessary. In spite of this, the Tropical Prediction Center usually issues a wide-area warning. That is because forecasts are not completely accurate, and forecasters would prefer to err on the side of caution.

3. During which of the following months should you schedule a vacation in the Caribbean if you wish to avoid hurricanes?

    (1) March
    (2) May
    (3) July
    (4) September
    (5) November

4. Suppose that thousands of people are evacuated from their homes as a result of a wide-area hurricane warning that turns out to be wrong. What is a likely effect of such an event?

    (1) widespread property damage
    (2) many deaths
    (3) public skepticism about later hurricane warnings
    (4) a shift to small-area hurricane warnings
    (5) improved data collection techniques

5. Predictions of the path ("track") and intensity of the storm vary in accuracy. Predictions for the next three hours tend to be very accurate, and predictions for the next three days are often wrong. Which statement most adequately explains why short-term storm forecasts are more accurate than long-term forecasts?

    (1) Historical data provide trend patterns on which forecasters model current short-term predictions.
    (2) Historical data are useful, but forecasters cannot rely on these data completely when forecasting tropical storms.
    (3) In short-term forecasts, the current data are very similar to the projected data, increasing accuracy.
    (4) In short-term forecasts, the current data differ substantially from the data projected for three hours out.
    (5) In short-term forecasts, data are collected from a wide variety of land, air, and sea observation instruments.

Answers start on page 290.

GED Mini-Test • Lesson 11

Directions: This is a ten-minute practice test. After ten minutes, mark the last question you finished. Then complete the test and check your answers. If most of your answers were correct but you didn't finish, try to work faster next time. Choose the one best answer to each question.

Questions 1 and 2 refer to the passage and the map below.

Weather changes from day to day, but climate refers to the long-term weather conditions of a region. Temperature and rainfall are the most important factors influencing climate. In addition, the distribution of ocean and land affects climate. Because land heats up and cools off rapidly, landlocked areas have more extreme climates than areas near the ocean. In addition, ocean currents carry heat from the tropics north to colder areas. Thus oceans have a moderating effect on climate.

There are six main climate zones, as shown on the map below.

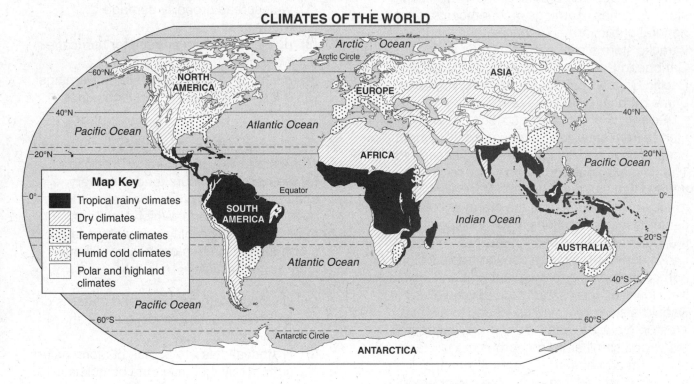

CLIMATES OF THE WORLD

1. What is climate?

   (1) the weather conditions in a particular place at a particular time
   (2) the temperature and rainfall of a particular area
   (3) the weather conditions of a region over a long time
   (4) the average annual rainfall of a region
   (5) the average annual temperature of a region

2. Suppose one of your friends likes living in a climate with four seasons and moderate weather. Which of the following locations would that person probably prefer?

   (1) Central America
   (2) South America
   (3) Europe
   (4) Africa
   (5) Australia

Question 3 refers to the following paragraph and diagram.

The sun's rays strike the area near the equator directly. They are very concentrated. Elsewhere on Earth, the rays strike at an angle. This means they spread out over a much larger area and do not provide as much warmth.

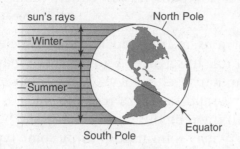

3. Climates near the equator are warmer than climates near the poles. Based on the passage and the diagram, which of the following statements could help explain this observation?

(1) Days are longer near the equator than they are near the poles.
(2) The sun's rays are more concentrated near the equator than near the poles.
(3) There are more sunny days than cloudy days at the equator than at the poles.
(4) There is less ocean water near the equator than near the poles.
(5) There is less wind near the equator than near the poles.

4. From the mid-1970s through most of the 1990s, a pattern of warmer temperatures in the waters of the eastern tropical Pacific Ocean led to more frequent and stronger El Niño events. El Niño caused heavy rains across the southern United States. Since then, the water has cooled in the eastern tropical Pacific.

If this cooling pattern becomes a 20- or 30-year trend, what would be the effect on the weather?

(1) no noticeable change
(2) more heavy rains across the southern United States
(3) more heavy rains across the east coast
(4) more frequent and stronger El Niño events
(5) fewer and weaker El Niño events

Questions 5 and 6 refer to the information below.

Sunspots are dark areas on the sun's surface that are caused by variations in the sun's magnetic field. Changes in sunspots may affect weather on Earth. For example, years of low sunspot activity seem to correlate with periods of drought in North America. It is doubtful, however, that there is a direct cause-and-effect relationship between sunspots and droughts. Perhaps sunspots cause a change in the atmosphere that affects the weather.

5. Based on the passage, which of the following statements is a fact?

(1) The sun always has the same number of sunspots.
(2) There are variations in sunspot activity.
(3) Sunspots cause changes in the weather.
(4) Sunspots affect only North America.
(5) Sunspots cause changes in Earth's atmosphere, affecting weather.

6. In order to demonstrate a cause-and-effect relationship between sunspot activity and drought in North America, what additional information would be needed?

(1) sunspot forecasts for the next few years
(2) position of Earth in relation to sunspots
(3) weather records for North America
(4) the specific way in which sunspots affect weather
(5) surface temperatures of sunspots

7. During an ice age, weather becomes colder, and the ice caps and glaciers spread south and north from the poles. If there were a new ice age, what would people in the northern regions of North America be most likely to do?

(1) move to the Southern Hemisphere
(2) move toward the equator
(3) stay in northern North America
(4) quickly die out because of the ice
(5) enjoy shorter, milder winters

Answers start on page 290.

GED SKILL **Recognizing Values**

value
a belief that is prized
as extremely important

Values are our deepest beliefs about what is important. For example, in the United States, we share certain values: freedom, independence, and individualism. Each of us has our own values. For example, some people value competitiveness. Others value cooperation.

Our values influence our actions, as individuals and as a society. Values also play an important role in science. A government may fund research likely to yield military technology. On the other hand, a government may not readily support areas of research, such as fetal cell research, that conflict with the religious, ethical, or moral beliefs of some of its citizens. A society may refrain from using some types of technology because of the values the society holds.

Read the passage. Then answer the questions below.

Sometimes values are signaled by the same key words as those that signal an opinion, such as *believe, think, feel, accept,* and *embrace.*

In a **nuclear power plant,** a chain reaction of nuclear fission releases tremendous heat, which is used to generate electricity. Such plants are economical to run, but they also pose some risks to safety. There may be an accident that releases radiation, which can kill people close by, contaminate the environment, and cause long-term health problems. Also, no matter how securely radioactive waste is stored, it may leak out.

Some nations, like France, think that the economic benefits of nuclear power outweigh the risks. France gets almost 80 percent of its electricity from nuclear power. In contrast, public concern for safety has closed many nuclear power plants in the United States. The United States gets only 20 percent of its electricity from nuclear power.

1. Write *B* next to each benefit of nuclear power, and *R* next to each risk.

    _____ a. Accidents may harm people and the environment.

    _____ b. Nuclear wastes may release radioactivity.

    _____ c. Nuclear energy produces a lot of electrical power.

You were correct if you wrote *B* for *option c.* Nuclear power produces a lot of electricity. You were correct if you wrote *R* for *options a* and *b.* Nuclear power poses these risks.

2. Put a check mark next to the sentence that explains why the United States doesn't make more use of nuclear power.

    _____ a. U.S. citizens value safety and consider nuclear power risky.

    _____ b. The nation lacks sufficient nuclear fuel.

You were correct if you checked *option a.* In the United States, public concern over safety has limited the use of nuclear power.

Use the passage and the map to answer the questions below.

Scientists and engineers have been looking for alternatives to obtaining energy for human use from oil, coal, and nuclear power. One alternative being explored is ocean thermal energy conversion (OTEC). OTEC is a process by which solar energy stored in the ocean is converted to electric power. In OTEC the temperature difference between surface and deep seawater is used to generate electricity. As long as the temperature difference is 20°C or more, an OTEC system can produce power.

Because traditional sources of energy are still relatively inexpensive, a permanent OTEC plant has not yet been constructed. However, OTEC is a promising source of energy, especially for tropical island nations that now depend on imported fuel. OTEC would enhance the independence of island nations as well as reduce air pollution from burning fuel.

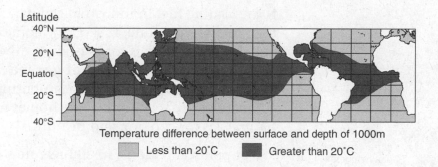

Temperature difference between surface and depth of 1000m

Less than 20°C   Greater than 20°C

1. Put a check mark next to the definition of ocean thermal energy conversion (OTEC).

   _____ a. a process that uses deep seawater to store solar energy

   _____ b. a process that uses solar energy stored in ocean water to produce electricity

2. Put a check mark next to the reason a permanent OTEC plant has not yet been constructed.

   _____ a. Other relatively inexpensive sources of energy are still available.

   _____ b. There are no suitable locations with a temperature difference of at least 20°C.

3. Put a check mark next to the type of nation to which OTEC would be of most value.

   _____ a. island nations near the equator

   _____ b. island nations in far northern and southern oceans

4. Put a check mark next to each value that OTEC would enhance for nations using this source of energy.

   _____ a. political and economic independence

   _____ b. basic human rights

   _____ c. freedom of speech

   _____ d. a cleaner environment

Answers start on page 291.

GED CONTENT Earth's Resources

The things we need to live, such as air, water, soil, minerals, and energy, are called **resources.** As a result of industrialization, we have greatly increased our use of energy resources in the last 150 years.

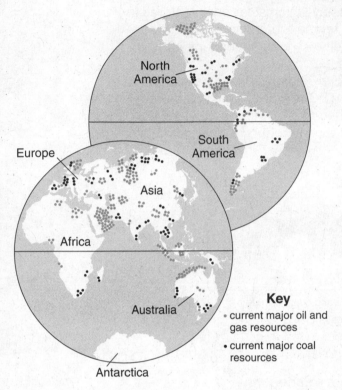

Key
- current major oil and gas resources
- current major coal resources

Most of the energy we use comes from **fossil fuels.** Fossil fuels were formed deep in Earth millions of years ago when the remains of dead plants and animals were compacted beneath layers of mud and other sediments. The chief fossil fuels are coal, petroleum, and natural gas. **Coal** is solid fossil fuel. In the United States, coal is burned mainly to produce electric power. **Petroleum,** or oil, is liquid fossil fuel. Petroleum is the leading fuel in industrialized nations. It is used to make gasoline, fuel oil for home heating, and the raw materials for plastics, synthetic fibers, and cosmetics. **Natural gas** is a fossil fuel in a gaseous state. It is a clean-burning fuel compared to coal and oil. Some homes use natural gas for cooking and heating.

For political reasons, fossil fuels are sometimes in short supply. In the 1970s, for example, the oil-producing nations of the Middle East reduced oil shipments to the United States. During the Gulf War in the 1990s, there was also a shortage of petroleum. However, energy planners and scientists are more concerned about a permanent shortage of oil.

Oil is a **nonrenewable resource,** one that cannot be replaced once it is used up. Scientists disagree about how much oil is left on Earth. Estimating oil reserves is difficult, since new and better technology enables the discovery of new sources. However, some scientists believe we have used between one-tenth and one-fourth of the oil available on Earth.

One place where additional fossil fuel could be mined is Antarctica. However, recovering coal and oil there would severely damage the environment of that continent. Instead, most energy planners believe that we must develop renewable resources, such as energy from the sun, to use in place of oil. A **renewable resource** is one that can be replaced. The most abundant renewable resource is energy from the sun. Scientists have developed solar cells that can convert sunlight into electricity. They have also developed ways to heat homes with solar energy. However, solar energy cannot be produced today at a low enough cost to encourage widespread use or on a large enough scale to meet most of our energy needs.

Directions: Choose the one best answer to each question.

Questions 1 through 6 refer to the passage and the map on page 136.

1. Which of the following phrases describes the origin of fossil fuel?

   (1) produced from chemicals in laboratories
   (2) produced from fossilized materials in laboratories
   (3) formed underground from the remains of plants and animals
   (4) formed underground from molten magma
   (5) produced from crude oil in modern refineries

2. Based on the passage, which of the following best describes the relationship between fossil fuels and industry?

   (1) Fossil fuels were of little importance to industry 100 years ago.
   (2) Fossil fuels were once important to industry but are of little importance now.
   (3) Fossil fuels have only been important to industry for the past 50 years.
   (4) Fossil fuels have been important to industry for more than a century and continue to be of great importance.
   (5) Fossil fuels are of little importance now but will be of great importance in the future.

3. According to the map, which continent has the least coal?

   (1) North America
   (2) South America
   (3) Eurasia
   (4) Africa
   (5) Australia

TIP Maps often combine symbols and colors to represent different things. Always study and understand the key before trying to read the map.

4. Which of the following involves the use of a renewable energy resource in place of a nonrenewable energy resource?

   (1) replacing old windows in a house with modern, double-glazed windows
   (2) using windmills instead of coal-burning power plants to generate electricity
   (3) turning off lights and the television when you leave the room
   (4) replacing an old air conditioner with a newer, more efficient model
   (5) using the drive-up window of a bank or fast-food restaurant rather than parking and walking

5. For a person who values the conservation of natural resources, which of the following would be the least important consideration in a choice about energy use?

   (1) Solar energy is renewable.
   (2) Solar energy is clean.
   (3) Solar energy can heat houses.
   (4) Oil is available and relatively cheap.
   (5) Oil resources are not renewable.

6. If the map of oil and coal resources were to be redrawn in one hundred years, which of the following would be true of the new map?

   (1) Some of the current resources would no longer be indicated, and some new ones would appear on the map.
   (2) There would be more major oil and gas resources on the new map than on the current map.
   (3) There would be more major coal resources on the new map than on the current map.
   (4) Most of the current major resources would no longer be indicated, and there would be no new resources added.
   (5) All of the current resources would no longer be indicated, and no new resources would appear on the map.

Answers start on page 291.

GED Practice • Lesson 12

Directions: Choose the <u>one best answer</u> to each question.

<u>Questions 1 through 3</u> refer to the passage and the diagram below.

The air around Earth is always moving. Moving air is called **wind.** Throughout history, people have used energy from wind to move ships, turn mill wheels, and pump water. In 1890 a windmill that could generate electricity was invented. Wind generators became a common sight on American farms. However, most wind generators fell into disuse in the 1940s, when electricity from electric power plants became available to farmers.

The need to find energy sources other than fossil fuels such as coal, oil, and natural gas sparked new interest in wind energy. Since the 1970s, new materials and designs have been used to make aerodynamic, tough, and efficient wind generators. These machines adjust to changing wind conditions by moving the position of the blades and rotating into the wind. In some places, large wind farms consisting of thousands of linked wind generators can produce as much electricity as a fossil fuel power station. However, wind energy costs more than energy generated from fossil fuels; it accounts for only 0.04 percent of the electricity produced in the United States.

Today, an important use of wind energy is similar to that of the early 1900s—in places not connected to power plants where an independent and self-contained power generation system is needed. In such locations, wind power is economical.

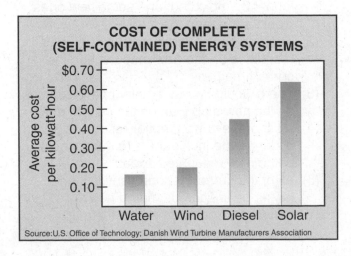

COST OF COMPLETE (SELF-CONTAINED) ENERGY SYSTEMS

Average cost per kilowatt-hour

$0.70
0.60
0.50
0.40
0.30
0.20
0.10

Water   Wind   Diesel   Solar

Source:U.S. Office of Technology; Danish Wind Turbine Manufacturers Association

1. Which of the following would be <u>most likely</u> to use wind energy to produce electricity?

   (1) a huge metropolitan area
   (2) a factory
   (3) a wilderness research station
   (4) an industrial complex
   (5) a modern farm

2. Which is the greatest advantage to a farmer of having a wind generator even though electricity from a power plant is available?

   (1) Maintaining a wind generator is less work than getting electricity from a power plant.
   (2) Having a wind generator means having power if the main source of electricity fails.
   (3) Wind is a more reliable source of energy than a power plant.
   (4) Installing and running a wind generator is cheaper than getting energy from a power plant.
   (5) A wind generator uses a nonrenewable form of energy, unlike a power plant.

3. A rancher in the western United States for whom economy of operation is a major value wants to install an independent, self-contained energy system and selects wind power. What is the <u>best</u> explanation for this choice?

   (1) Wind is the cheapest source of power.
   (2) Diesel generators are expensive to run.
   (3) Solar energy costs more than wind energy.
   (4) A wind system is cheaper than diesel.
   (5) Water power is not available in that location.

TIP Bar graphs usually compare amounts. For example, a bar graph may show the prices of different cars. The tallest (or longest) bar represents the highest price.

WATER: THE LIMITS OF A RENEWABLE RESOURCE

Questions 4 through 6 refer to the passage and the graph below.

About 97.5 percent of the world's water is salt water in the oceans and seas. Most of the world's fresh water is frozen in ice caps and glaciers. Only 0.77 percent of the planet's fresh water is in lakes, rivers, swamps, aquifers, or the atmosphere. Much of it is not available for use.

Thus, a very small supply of renewable fresh water supports all life. Along with oxygen in the air, it is the most important resource on Earth.

In theory, the fact that water recycles through the biosphere means there is enough to meet basic human drinking, cooking, and sanitation needs for quite a long time. However, in reality water is distributed unevenly over the planet. There is an oversupply in some areas and scarcity in others. In addition, in many places pollution makes water unfit for drinking and cooking. Today more than a billion people do not have access to clean drinking water.

In recent times, water use has increased tremendously. The human population explosion has meant more water is used for basic needs. Producing food for the additional population has meant more water is needed for agriculture, the largest single use of water. Industrialization and urbanization have also increased the demand for water.

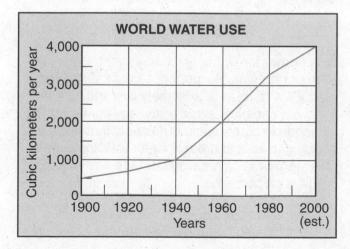

4. By how much did water use increase from 1900 to 2000?

    (1) remained the same
    (2) doubled
    (3) tripled
    (4) quadrupled
    (5) was eight times greater

5. If global warming caused partial melting of ice caps and glaciers, what effect would that have on the percentage of fresh water on Earth?

    (1) About 97.5 percent of water would still be fresh.
    (2) About 97.5 percent of water would still be salty.
    (3) The percentage of fresh water would decline as ice caps melted into the ocean.
    (4) The percentage of fresh water would increase as the ice caps melted.
    (5) There would be no effect on the percentage of fresh water on Earth.

6. Which of the following strategies is the best way to help us keep pace with the increasing demand for water all over the world?

    (1) increase the amount of water for agriculture to ensure an adequate food supply
    (2) improve water management, including water treatment, distribution, and conservation
    (3) divert water from agriculture to the growing cities to satisfy basic needs
    (4) increase the supply of fresh water in nations with desert climates
    (5) find ways to treat polluted water so it can be used again

TIP To find the value of a point on a line graph, draw lines from the point to each axis. Use both values to understand the graph.

Answers start on page 291.

GED Mini-Test • Lesson 12

Directions: This is a ten-minute practice test. After ten minutes, mark the last question you finished. Then complete the test and check your answers. If most of your answers were correct but you didn't finish, try to work faster next time. Choose the <u>one best answer</u> to each question.

<u>Questions 1 through 3</u> refer to the passage and the diagram below.

Soil is the portion of the land surface that supports plant growth. It consists of minerals, organic matter, water, and air in varying proportions. About half the volume of a good soil consists of minerals and organic matter. The remaining half consists of space. The space is important because it allows air and water to circulate through the soil.

If you were to dig a deep hole in the soil, you would see horizontal layers of differing characteristics. These layers, called horizons, make up a particular soil's profile.

• The *A* horizon is the surface layer. It is the part of the soil with the greatest organic activity and living organisms.
• The *B* horizon is the subsoil. In it accumulate the materials that leach out of the *A* horizon through the action of water. Living organisms are plentiful in the *B* horizon.
• The *C* horizon is a layer of weathered, broken bedrock with little organic matter.

Below the *C* horizon is the solid bedrock, the material from which the soil is formed.

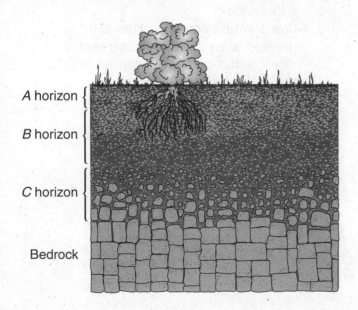

1. Why is a given volume of good soil less dense than the same volume of rock?

   (1) Soil is made of particles of mineral and organic matter.
   (2) About half the volume of soil consists of space, through which water and air circulate.
   (3) Both soil and rock contain mineral matter.
   (4) Soil contains organic matter, both living and dead.
   (5) The *C* horizon of soil consists of weathered bedrock.

2. Which of the following describes the exposed soil layer that would result if the *A* and *B* horizons were worn away by erosion?

   (1) The soil would be unable to support much plant and animal life.
   (2) The soil would have a finer consistency with greater mineral content.
   (3) The soil would be coarser with great amounts of organic activity.
   (4) The soil would be rich, consisting of about half water and air by volume.
   (5) There would be no soil, only a layer of solid bedrock with no organic activity.

3. A farmer for whom soil conservation is a very important value experiences a drought. The soil's *A* horizon is extremely dry and its top layers can blow away. In the spring the farmer needs to plant crops, but knows that tilling the soil can lead to greater water loss through evaporation. What would be the farmer's <u>most likely</u> response?

   (1) make no changes in farming technique
   (2) till the soil aggressively so that water will evaporate
   (3) plant fewer, more drought-resistant crops
   (4) water the crops less frequently
   (5) stop farming until the drought is over

Questions 4 through 6 refer to the information below.

The United States imports its entire supply of several minerals, including those in the chart.

Mineral	Major Uses
Bauxite	Aluminum production
Manganese	Steelmaking, batteries
Sheet mica	Electronic and electrical equipment
Strontium	Picture tubes, fireworks
Thallium	Superconductors, electronics

Source: U.S. Geological Survey

4. What is a good title for this information?

(1) Minerals
(2) Minerals and Their Uses
(3) The Five Most Important Minerals
(4) Some Imported Minerals and Their Uses
(5) Mineral Resources of the United States

5. Which of the minerals listed in the chart are of most interest to the electronics industry?

(1) bauxite and manganese
(2) bauxite and strontium
(3) manganese and strontium
(4) strontium and thallium
(5) sheet mica and thallium

6. Suppose a U.S. source of thallium were discovered, but recovering the mineral would be more expensive than importing it. What might be a reason for mining and processing thallium in the United States despite the extra cost?

(1) Thallium is one of the minerals used in the production of superconductors.
(2) Thallium is one of the minerals used in the production of electronic equipment.
(3) The United States has always imported thallium from foreign nations.
(4) The United States would reduce its dependence on foreign nations.
(5) The United States would be the only source of thallium in the world.

7. In recent years China has increased the amount of soft coal it burns in order to fuel its growing economy. As a result, China now leads the world in sulfur emissions, an air pollutant. A study of China's air pollution shows that the haze produced by burning soft coal acts as a filter, absorbing some of the sunlight that would normally be used by plants for photosynthesis.

Which of the following is a possible result of the air pollution in China?

(1) increased wind speeds during storms
(2) decreased agricultural production
(3) decreased level of sulfur emissions
(4) increased number of sunny days
(5) increased supply of soft coal

8. A watershed is a drainage area, a land area that catches rainwater and drains it by means of surface runoff, streams, rivers, lakes, and groundwater. In 1997 the Environmental Protection Agency issued an analysis of the water quality of the watersheds in the continental United States. The results are shown below.

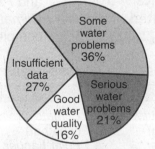

Source: U.S. Environmental Protection Agency

Which of the following statements is supported by the information given?

(1) Most watersheds had good quality water.
(2) Water pollution is not a major problem.
(3) About one-fifth of the watersheds had serious quality problems.
(4) More than half the watersheds had serious quality problems.
(5) Three-quarters of the watersheds were not tested.

Answers start on page 292.

Lesson 13

GED SKILL Identifying Implications

infer
to conclude something that is suggested by stated information

inference
a fact or idea that you conclude based on stated information

Remember that implications are suggested by the information. They follow logically from what is stated.

As you learned in Lesson 9, an implication is a fact that is not stated directly. Rather, it is suggested by the author's words or by information in a diagram, graph, or other illustration.

When you identify an implication, you figure out something that is likely to be true based on the information that is stated or shown. For example, suppose on the day a space mission is scheduled to end you read, "The National Weather Service is forecasting a 70% probability of severe thunderstorms over the Kennedy Space Center." You can **infer,** or figure out, that the shuttle landing will be postponed or rescheduled for a different location due to the weather.

You can improve your ability to identify implications by using common sense. By using your common sense, looking for generalizations, and thinking about consequences, you can make reasonable **inferences** based on the information given.

Read the passage. Then answer the question below.

The National Aeronautics and Space Administration (NASA) has planned a series of robotic missions to explore Mars. These missions gather data to help plan manned missions to the planet. *Global Surveyor* and *Pathfinder* were great successes. However, in 1999 both the *Mars Climate Orbiter* and *Polar Lander* missions failed. As a result, NASA is completely reviewing all of its systems and mission plans.

1996–1997	1998–1999	2001–2002	2003–2008	2007–2013
Global Surveyor (mapping) *Pathfinder* (surface exploration)	*Climate Orbiter* (weather) *Polar Lander* (search for water)	*2001 Mars Odyssey* (surface survey)	Series of missions to gather samples	Additional sampling missions

Put a check mark next to the sentence that is implied by the fate of *Climate Orbiter* and *Polar Lander*.

_____ a. The United States lacks the technology to send robotic missions to Mars and other planets.

_____ b. Future Mars missions are likely to be delayed while NASA rechecks its systems and plans.

You were correct if you checked *option b.* Common sense tells you that two mission failures in a row will disrupt plans for the future. NASA is likely to take extra time and care with its future mission.

Use the passage and the diagram to answer the questions below.

A **galaxy** is a group of billions of stars. Our sun is a star located in the **Milky Way** galaxy. From astronomical observations, scientists have inferred that the Milky Way is a spiral galaxy. It is shaped like a disk with arms spiraling out from the center. Our sun and the **solar system** are located in the Orion Arm.

It takes the sun about 225 million years to make one turn around the center of the galaxy. Measurements of the movements of different stars in the galaxy show that they move with respect to one another while turning around the dense center of the galaxy. Thus, people thousands of years ago saw the stars in slightly different patterns than the ones we see today.

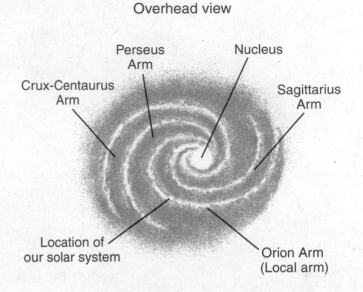

Overhead view

Perseus Arm

Nucleus

Crux-Centaurus Arm

Sagittarius Arm

Location of our solar system

Orion Arm (Local arm)

1. Put a check mark next to the reason scientists have inferred the shape of the Milky Way rather than observing its shape directly.

_____ a. Scientists are located in the Milky Way, so they do not have a distant view of the entire galaxy.

_____ b. Scientists would rather observe things directly than figure them out based on indirect evidence.

2. Put a check mark next to the statement that is implied by the information in the passage and diagram and the statement, "A star is located farther out on the Orion Arm than the sun."

_____ a. The star is likely to take longer than 225 million years to make one turn around the center of the galaxy.

_____ b. The star is likely to take less than 225 million years to make one turn around the center of the galaxy.

3. In 50,000 B.C., the group of stars known as the Big Dipper looked like an arrow. Today the group looks like a ladle with a long handle. Put a check mark next to the statement that describes what it will look like 50,000 years in the future.

_____ a. It will look like a ladle with a long handle.

_____ b. Its appearance will have changed.

4. According to the diagram, the Milky Way is shaped like a disk with spiral arms. Put a check mark next to the statement that describes what the Milky Way would look like from the side rather than from overhead.

_____ a. a circular group of stars with arms spiraling out from the center

_____ b. a relatively flat disk of stars seen from the edge

Answers start on page 293.

FORMATION OF THE SOLAR SYSTEM

Ring of gas and dust

Sun

The sun developed from a cloud of gas and dust about 4.6 billion years ago. Some of the gas and dust formed a flat disk around the sun. Eventually, the force of gravity caused clumps to form in this material. The clumps developed into large bodies called **planets** and smaller bodies called **asteroids.** The sun and all the bodies that revolve around it are known as our solar system.

At the center of the solar system is the sun. Orbiting the sun are the nine planets and their satellites, or moons. In addition, there are millions of smaller objects revolving around the sun, including asteroids, comets, and dust.

The four planets closest to the sun are Mercury, Venus, Earth, and Mars. Called the inner planets, these are all relatively small, rocky bodies. Earth is a watery planet with one satellite, called the moon. Earth is about 93 million miles from the sun. Mars is a much drier planet. However, like Earth, Mars has four seasons. Its day is about the same length as a day on Earth.

After Mars comes a gap in which countless asteroids, rocks, and particles of dust orbit the sun. Beyond the asteroid belt are the outer planets. With the exception of small, rocky Pluto, the four other outer planets—Jupiter, Saturn, Uranus, and Neptune—are gas giants. Composed mainly of gases, these planets have ring systems consisting of particles of rock and ice. Saturn's ring system is the most extensive.

Outside the orbit of Pluto is a band of rocky bodies that includes comets. A comet has an icy, rocky core. When its orbit approaches the sun, the heat vaporizes the ice, which streams out behind the comet in a long tail.

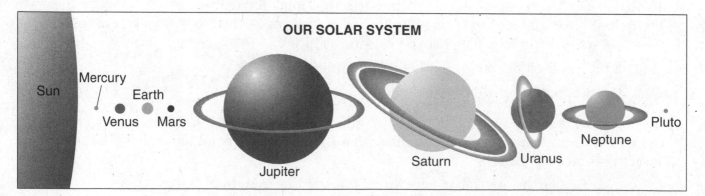

OUR SOLAR SYSTEM

Sun · Mercury · Venus · Earth · Mars · Jupiter · Saturn · Uranus · Neptune · Pluto

Directions: Choose the one best answer to each question.

Questions 1 through 5 refer to the passage and the diagrams on page 144.

1. What is the solar system?

   (1) the sun and the cloud of dust and gas around it
   (2) the sun and all the objects that revolve around it
   (3) the sun and the inner planets and outer planets
   (4) the inner planets, asteroid belt, and outer planets
   (5) the inner planets, asteroid belt, outer planets, and comets

2. Which of the following is not directly stated but is implied by the first paragraph of the passage or by the diagram of the formation of the solar system?

   (1) The solar system formed out of a cloud of gas and dust.
   (2) The cloud of gas and dust revolved around the sun.
   (3) The solar system will continue to develop and change.
   (4) The sun is at the center of the solar system.
   (5) Earth is the most important planet in the solar system.

3. According to the passage and the diagram of planets, which of the following planets has characteristics that differ from those of the other outer planets?

   (1) Jupiter
   (2) Saturn
   (3) Uranus
   (4) Neptune
   (5) Pluto

4. NASA has conducted an ambitious program to learn more about Mars. Which of the following statements can be inferred from this information and from information in the passage and diagram?

   (1) The outer planets do not interest scientists.
   (2) The ring systems on the gas giants prevent exploration of those planets.
   (3) The location and physical nature of Mars make its exploration feasible.
   (4) The asteroid belt beyond Mars makes exploration of the outer planets impossible.
   (5) NASA technology is not capable of exploring farther than Mars.

5. At present, the sun has a diameter of about 870,000 miles. Toward the end of its lifetime, the sun will swell into a much larger star with a diameter between 9.3 and 93 million miles. What is the likely effect of this development on the solar system?

   (1) The inner planets will become colder.
   (2) The outer planets will become colder.
   (3) The inner planets will be destroyed.
   (4) New planets will form in the solar system.
   (5) The solar system will continue in its present form.

6. In 1969 Americans first landed on the moon. More successful moon missions followed in the early 1970s. Beginning in the 1980s, U.S. crewed space missions have used the space shuttles, staying close to Earth. Which of the following is the most likely reason for this?

   (1) The moon has a harsh environment.
   (2) The moon is too far away to visit.
   (3) Previous crewed missions to the moon ended in failure.
   (4) The U.S. wanted to perform experiments concerning the effects of weightlessness.
   (5) The U.S. lacks the technology for crewed space travel.

Answers start on page 293.

Directions: Choose the <u>one best answer</u> to each question.

<u>Questions 1 through 3</u> refer to the passage and the diagram below.

Stars form from a cloud of gas and dust. As pressure increases in the core of the collapsing cloud, the temperature rises until nuclear fusion reactions begin. In fusion reactions, hydrogen is converted to helium, and huge amounts of radiation energy are given off. The radiation stops further collapse of the star. This stage, called the main sequence phase, is the longest period in a star's lifetime. Our sun is a yellow dwarf star in the main sequence stage.

Eventually, the hydrogen in a star is used up. The core then collapses under the force of gravity. Pressure and heat increase until fusion can take place in the shell surrounding the core. At this stage, the outer layers of the star expand, producing a giant or supergiant. When this second stage of fusion is complete, the star collapses and heats up again.

In low-mass stars like our sun, there is not enough heat for fusion to recur, and the star becomes a white dwarf, giving off little radiation. In high-mass stars, fusion recurs until the core is depleted and collapses, throwing off the outer layers in an explosion called a supernova. The resulting superdense core increases its gravitational pull, forming a neutron star or, if it is sufficiently massive, a black hole. Gravity is so strong in a black hole that even light cannot escape.

1. Which of the following is implied by the fact that the sun is a low-mass star?

   (1) The sun is in the main sequence phase.
   (2) The sun formed from gas and dust.
   (3) The sun gives off radiation from fusion.
   (4) The sun is at the end of its life cycle.
   (5) The sun is likely to end up a white dwarf.

2. Based on the passage and the diagram, which of the following would be the most spectacular sight?

   (1) a main sequence star
   (2) a neutron star
   (3) a white dwarf
   (4) a supernova
   (5) a black hole

3. Which of the following statements is supported by the information in the passage and the diagram?

   (1) Stars have planets during the main sequence stage.
   (2) Only low-mass yellow dwarf stars have planets.
   (3) Only a few low-mass stars become giants.
   (4) Eventually, stars run out of "fuel" and collapse.
   (5) White dwarfs give off huge amounts of radiation.

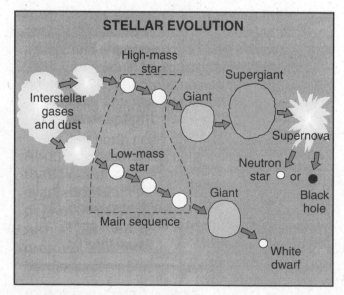

STELLAR EVOLUTION

TIP Always read the text that accompanies a diagram to better understand the details of the diagram.

Unifying Concepts and Processes

THE EVOLUTION OF THE UNIVERSE

Questions 4 through 6 refer to the passage and the graph below.

Most astronomers believe that the universe began about 10 to 20 billion years ago in an explosion called the **big bang.** Just after the big bang, the universe was a small cloud of extremely hot and compressed hydrogen and helium. As the universe expanded, it cooled unevenly, and the gases began to form clumps. Because of the force of gravity, the clumps contracted and became galaxies. Today, the universe consists of about 100 billion galaxies that continue to move away from one another.

There is much evidence to support the big bang theory. Galaxies are moving away from Earth in every direction, as if they all once came from the same place. The farther away a galaxy is, the faster it appears to move, which is consistent with an expanding universe. In addition, cosmic background radiation (CBR), left over from the big bang, has been observed by radio telescopes in every direction in space. Ripples in the CBR indicate areas of density needed for the formation of galaxies.

However, there is much disagreement about what will happen to the universe. Its fate depends on the amount of mass it contains and its gravitational effect. Will it continue to expand? Will it stop at a certain size? Will it start to contract? Three different possibilities are shown below.

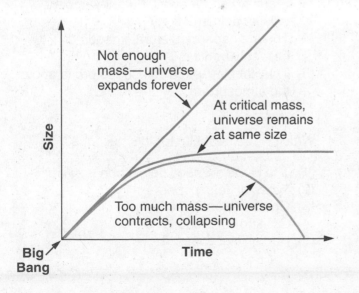

4. Which of the following situations most closely resembles the big bang?

  (1) A bonfire sends sparks and ashes up into the air.
  (2) Fireworks explode, sending sparks, ashes, and smoke in all directions.
  (3) Two cannonballs collide in midair, causing a fireball that quickly falls to the ground.
  (4) Several sparks fly as you light a match.
  (5) A candle burns until it is completely melted.

5. According to the graph, what is likely to happen if the universe contains enough matter to cause it to contract?

  (1) The universe would continue to expand.
  (2) The universe would collapse in on itself.
  (3) A parallel universe would begin elsewhere.
  (4) The universe would remain steady at a particular size.
  (5) Another big bang would take place in 10 billion years.

6. About 90 percent of the matter in the universe has mass and exerts gravity but cannot be seen. If this so-called dark matter is invisible, how can scientists know it is there?

  (1) They have observed it with orbiting space telescopes.
  (2) They have observed it from Earth.
  (3) They have observed its gravitational effects on visible objects.
  (4) They have observed distant galaxies moving away rapidly.
  (5) They have observed CBR in every direction.

TIP Always study and understand the scales of a graph. Some graphs do not show specific quantities, but rather, show relationships—such as size, time, and mass.

Answers start on page 293.

Directions: This is a ten-minute practice test. After ten minutes, mark the last question you finished. Then complete the test and check your answers. If most of your answers were correct but you didn't finish, try to work faster next time. Choose the one best answer to each question.

Questions 1 and 2 refer to the chart below.

Planet	Distance from Sun In Astronomical Units*
Mercury	0.39
Venus	0.72
Earth	1.0
Mars	1.5
Jupiter	5.2
Saturn	9.2
Uranus	19.2
Neptune	30.0
Pluto	39.4

*One astronomical unit is the distance from Earth to the sun.

1. If a planet is more than one astronomical unit from the sun, what does that imply?

    (1) It is closer to the sun than Earth is.
    (2) It is the same distance from the sun as Earth is.
    (3) It is farther from the sun than Earth is.
    (4) It is likely to receive more solar energy than Earth does.
    (5) It is likely to be a planet with no satellites.

2. It takes the sun's light 8 minutes to reach Earth. How long does it take the sun's light to reach Neptune?

    (1)   0.3 minutes
    (2)   8 minutes
    (3)   24 minutes
    (4)   30 minutes
    (5) 240 minutes

Questions 3 and 4 refer to the following passage.

Optical telescopes use light to produce images of objects that are far away. In 1610, Galileo discovered four of Jupiter's moons by using an optical telescope. However, optical telescopes cannot produce large images of objects outside the solar system. No matter how powerful the telescope, stars are so distant that they look like points of light. In addition, the atmosphere distorts the light passing through it, making images fuzzy.

Today there are optical telescopes that orbit above Earth's atmosphere. The largest of these, the Hubble Space Telescope, was launched in 1990. It has provided stunning, clear images of planets and moons in the solar system as well as of distant stars and galaxies.

3. Which of the following is an unstated assumption important for understanding the passage?

    (1) Galileo discovered four of Jupiter's moons in 1610 using a telescope.
    (2) Optical telescopes magnify images of distant objects.
    (3) Stars are so far away that they appear only as points of light.
    (4) The atmosphere distorts images of heavenly bodies.
    (5) The Hubble Space Telescope orbits above the atmosphere.

4. Which is the best title for this passage?

    (1) The Hubble Space Telescope
    (2) Types of Telescopes
    (3) Optical Telescopes
    (4) Orbiting Telescopes
    (5) Radio Telescopes

FORMATION OF CRATERS

Path of rocky ejected material

Path of meteorite

Earth's surface

Primary crater

Secondary craters

5. According to the diagram, what causes the formation of secondary craters?

    (1) small meteorites hitting the surface near the larger meteorite
    (2) large meteorites breaking into many small meteorites before hitting the surface
    (3) a comet rather than a meteorite hitting the surface
    (4) debris thrown out of the large crater by the meteorite's impact
    (5) the sinking of small areas as the ground settles after the meteorite's impact

6. Most small objects burn up in the atmosphere and never hit the surface of Earth. Which of the following facts supports this conclusion?

    (1) Jupiter, which is a gas giant, has many storms in its atmosphere, including the Great Red Spot.
    (2) Saturn has a complex ring system consisting of particles of ice and rock.
    (3) Earth has fewer craters than the moon, which has no atmosphere.
    (4) Some craters on Earth are produced as a result of volcanic activity.
    (5) Craters on Earth are sometimes filled with water, forming round lakes.

A pair of stars viewed through a telescope may seem to be very close together because of the angles at which they are seen from Earth, even though in reality they are millions of light years apart.

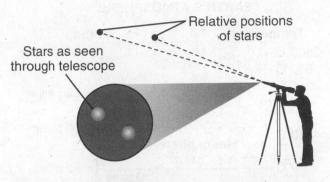

Relative positions of stars

Stars as seen through telescope

7. Which of the following people would probably be most interested in this information?

    (1) a planetary scientist
    (2) an amateur astronomer
    (3) an optician
    (4) a telescope manufacturer
    (5) a scientist who studies the sun

8. Some astronomers think the planet Pluto and its moon, Charon, may not be a planet and moon at all. Instead they hypothesize that Pluto and Charon are a double planet system—two planets orbiting around a common point. This is because Pluto and Charon appear to be very similar in mass, whereas usually the planet is much larger than its moon(s). However, telescope images of Pluto are not good enough to determine the relative masses of the two bodies with any certainty.

Which type of evidence might provide enough information to determine whether Pluto and Charon are a double planet system or a planet and a moon?

    (1) data from a space probe to Pluto
    (2) images from the Hubble Space Telescope
    (3) images from land-based telescopes
    (4) data from another double-planet system
    (5) data from the Earth-moon system

Answers start on page 294.

Unit 2 Cumulative Review Earth and Space Science

Directions: Choose the <u>one best answer</u> to each question.

Questions 1 through 3 refer to the diagram below.

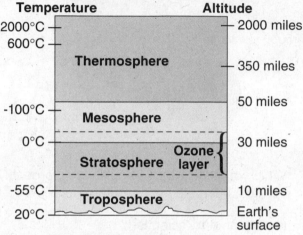

EARTH'S ATMOSPHERE

1. According to the diagram, what occurs 50 miles above Earth?

   (1) The ozone layer ends.
   (2) The temperature is 600°C.
   (3) The mesosphere ends.
   (4) The thermosphere ends.
   (5) Air molecules disappear.

2. Which of the following summarizes the relationship between altitude and temperature in Earth's atmosphere?

   As altitude increases, temperature

   (1) remains the same
   (2) increases
   (3) decreases
   (4) first decreases and then increases
   (5) decreases, then increases, then decreases and increases again

3. As you go higher in the troposphere, the air becomes "thinner," or less dense. There is much less oxygen in a given volume of air than there is at sea level. Which of the following experiences gives adequate evidence to confirm this statement?

   (1) A runner from Boston, which is at sea level, has trouble breathing while jogging in the Rocky Mountains.
   (2) A person exposed to the ultraviolet rays of the sun is much likelier to get burned at higher altitudes than at sea level.
   (3) A hiker in the mountains is much more likely to experience cold temperatures than a hiker at sea level.
   (4) A person who climbs high mountains trains for an expedition by re-creating atmospheric conditions at sea level.
   (5) Before opening a parachute, a skydiver experiences free-fall from 12,000 feet to about 2500 feet above the ground.

4. The Search for Extraterrestrial Intelligence (SETI) uses radio telescopes to scan the sky for evidence of intelligent life in the form of patterned radio waves. It is difficult for SETI scientists to obtain time on the world's largest radio telescopes, because many people in the scientific community consider their project to be science fiction rather than valid scientific research.

   Which of the following is an opinion about SETI rather than a fact?

   (1) Some scientists are searching for signs of extraterrestrial intelligence.
   (2) Radio telescopes pick up radio waves from space.
   (3) Radio waves sent by intelligent beings would show regular patterns.
   (4) It is difficult for SETI scientists to get observation time on the large telescopes.
   (5) SETI projects are based on dreams rather than realistic possibilities about space.

Questions 5 through 8 refer to the following paragraph and diagram.

There are three types of rock: igneous, sedimentary, and metamorphic. Over long periods of time, external conditions such as weathering, pressure, and extreme heat can transform rocks from one type to another. These changes occur again and again, in a process called the rock cycle.

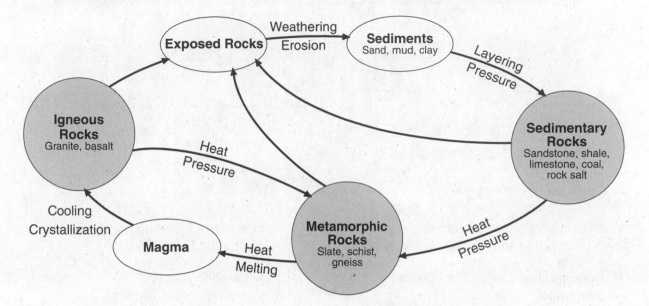

5. What is a good title for this information?

   (1) Overview of the Rock Cycle
   (2) The Formation of Metamorphic Rocks
   (3) Uses of Rock
   (4) The Effect of Pressure on Rock
   (5) Types of Rocks

6. Which of the following conclusions is supported by the information in the diagram?

   (1) Metamorphic rocks are formed only from igneous rocks.
   (2) Sedimentary rocks are formed by heat.
   (3) Some igneous rocks are formed directly from sediments.
   (4) Weathering and erosion can affect all kinds of rocks on Earth's surface.
   (5) Heat and pressure cause sedimentary rocks to form igneous rocks.

7. A hiker finds a rock that includes light and dark stripes. What type of rock is this likely to be?

   (1) clay
   (2) sedimentary
   (3) magma
   (4) igneous
   (5) granite

8. What kind of rock would you be most likely to find at a place where there had once been a volcano?

   (1) igneous
   (2) metamorphic
   (3) sedimentary
   (4) limestone
   (5) slate

TIP

A flowchart shows one event leading to another—the arrows show causes and point to the circles and ovals showing effects.

Questions 9 through 14 refer to the information below.

Scientists have developed a geologic time line to record the history of Earth. Geologic time is often described in terms of four eras.

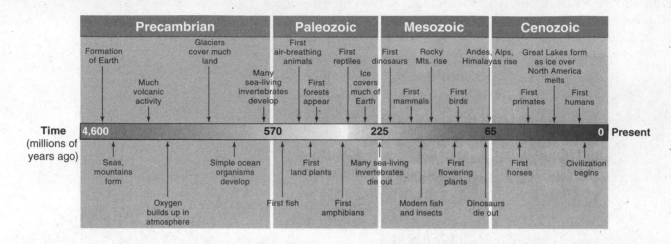

9. Which of the following statements is a conclusion rather than a supporting detail?

   (1) Primates appeared about 50 million years ago.
   (2) Humans appeared in the late Cenozoic.
   (3) Horses appeared in the Cenozoic.
   (4) Humans did not exist for most of geologic time.
   (5) The Great Lakes formed during the Cenozoic.

10. Which of the following kinds of fossils would most likely be found in Mesozoic rocks?

   (1) only simple ocean organisms
   (2) land plants, dinosaurs, and horses
   (3) fish, land plants, and dinosaurs
   (4) primates and humans
   (5) flowering plants and primates

11. About how long did dinosaurs exist?

   (1)   65 million years
   (2) 160 million years
   (3) 225 million years
   (4) 4,535 million years
   (5)   1 billion years

12. Which of the following might have been eaten by the first fish?

   (1) flowering plants
   (2) sea-living invertebrates
   (3) insects
   (4) amphibians
   (5) land plants

13. Which of the following most likely contributed to the dying out of sea invertebrates at the end of the Paleozoic era?

   (1) the rise of the Andes, Alps, and Himalayas
   (2) the dying out of the dinosaurs
   (3) global climate change
   (4) buildup of oxygen in atmosphere
   (5) increasing volcanic activity

14. Which of the following statements is supported by the information in the timeline?

   (1) The first air-breathing animals were amphibians.
   (2) Dinosaurs were the chief form of life during the Paleozoic Era.
   (3) The Great Lakes are younger than the Rocky Mountains.
   (4) Dinosaurs died out five million years ago.
   (5) The first forms of life originated on land and then developed in the sea.

Questions 15 and 16 refer to the paragraph and the map below.

Most earthquakes and volcanic activity occur along the boundaries of Earth's tectonic plates. In these areas, the plates are crunching together, pulling apart, or sliding past one another.

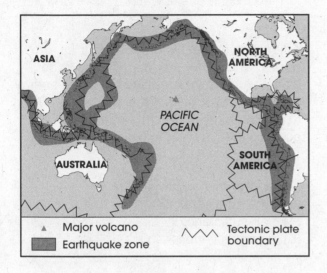

15. Which continent is generally free of major earthquakes?

    (1) North America
    (2) South America
    (3) Asia
    (4) Australia
    (5) Europe

16. In 1994, a robot named Dante II was sent into the crater of an active volcano to collect data for scientists. In which location was this expedition most likely to have taken place?

    (1) the east coast of North America
    (2) an island in the southern Pacific
    (3) northern Asia
    (4) an island in the northern Pacific
    (5) northern Australia

TIP Always look at the map key to learn what the symbols and colors or shadings on the map represent.

Questions 17 and 18 refer to the information below.

A mineral is a substance that has five basic characteristics, or properties:

1. It is found naturally on Earth.
2. It is a solid.
3. It was never alive.
4. It is made of particular elements.
5. Its particles are arranged in a definite pattern called a crystal.

Minerals are often found mixed together in rocks. Rock deposits that contain certain minerals are called ores. Removing a mineral from ore involves mining the ore and then smelting it. During smelting, the ore is heated in such a way that the particular mineral separates from the other substances in the rock.

17. One piece of granite was formed from tiny particles of three different colors. Another piece of granite was formed from particles of four different colors. Which of the following statements best supports the conclusion that granite is merely a rock, not a mineral?

    (1) Granite occurs naturally on Earth.
    (2) Granite is one of the most common rocks on Earth's surface.
    (3) There are different types of granite, each made of different minerals.
    (4) Granite forms from cooling magma.
    (5) Granite is a solid.

18. Which of the following is based on an unstated assumption?

    (1) A substance must have five basic properties to be a mineral.
    (2) The particles of a mineral are arranged in crystals.
    (3) The minerals removed from ores are valuable resources.
    (4) Ores are first mined and then smelted.
    (5) In smelting, a mineral is removed from its ore.

Questions 19 through 21 refer to the following passage and diagram.

The tide is the periodic rise and fall of the sea. High and low tides occur about twice a day. In areas in which the water rises and falls more than 4.6 meters, the water flow can be used to generate electricity.

A tidal power station is part of a dam built across the mouth of a river. Channels in the dam allow water to flow through when the tide rises and flow back out when the tide falls. The water flow turns turbines that operate generators that produce electricity.

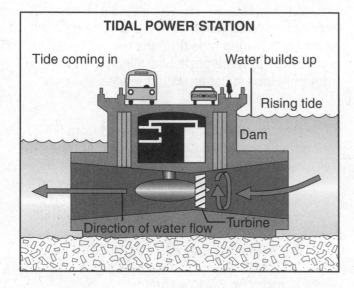

TIDAL POWER STATION

The energy harnessed by tidal power is very clean in that no pollutants are given off. However, tidal power plants disrupt the ecology of the river system they block.

19. Which of the following locations would be most suitable for a tidal power station?

　(1) the source of the Mississippi River, in the Upper Midwest
　(2) the mouth of the Hudson River, in New York Harbor, with small variation in high and low tides
　(3) the mouth of the Annapolis River, Nova Scotia, with large variation in high and low tides
　(4) the falls of the Missouri River, in the Great Plains
　(5) Hoover Dam, in the southwestern United States

20. What is the source of energy in a tidal power station?

　(1) wave action
　(2) rising and falling tides
　(3) turbines
　(4) river currents
　(5) the mixing of salt water and fresh water

21. A tidal power plant is proposed for a particular location. People who favor the plant value the inexpensive electrical energy it will provide. Which of the following is likely to be valued by opponents of the tidal power plant?

　(1) profitability
　(2) environmental protection
　(3) local political power
　(4) self-sufficiency
　(5) competitiveness

Question 22 refers to the following diagram.

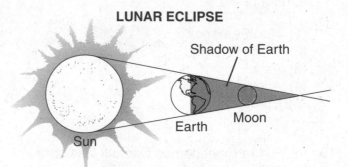

LUNAR ECLIPSE

22. A lunar eclipse occurs when Earth moves into a certain position relative to the sun. Why is this statement an oversimplification?

　(1) The position of the moon is also a factor in the occurrence of a lunar eclipse.
　(2) A lunar eclipse occurs only during the spring and the autumn months.
　(3) A lunar eclipse is not visible while Earth is revolving around the sun.
　(4) A lunar eclipse is visible only at night.
　(5) The position of Earth is not a factor in the occurrence of a lunar eclipse.

Answers start on page 294.

Cumulative Review Performance Analysis
Unit 2 • Earth Science

Use the Answers and Explanations starting on page 294 to check your answers to the Unit 2 Cumulative Review. Then use the chart to figure out the skill areas in which you need more practice.

On the chart, circle the questions that you answered correctly. Write the number correct for each skill area. Add the number of questions that you got correct on the Cumulative Review. If you feel that you need more practice, go back and review the lessons for the skill areas that were difficult for you.

Questions	Number Correct	Skill Area	Lessons for Review
1, 2, 5, 10, 11, 15, 20	____/7	Comprehension	1, 2, 6, 9, 13
4, **8, 9, 12, 13**, 18	____/6	Analysis	3, 4, 7, 10
7, 16, 19	____/3	Application	8
3, 6, 14, 17, **21, 22**	____/6	Evaluation	5, 11, 12
TOTAL CORRECT	____/22		

Question numbers in **boldface** are based on graphics.

UNIT 3

Physical Science

Physical scientists study the most basic questions about the universe. What is matter? What is energy? How are they related? The answers affect every area of science and technology, the workforce, and everyday life—from cooking and baking to understanding how atoms and molecules work, from designing cars, cosmetics, and nuclear power plants to daily laboratory tasks. Physical science is often divided into chemistry, the study of matter, and physics, the study of the relationship between matter and energy. Increasingly, however, knowledge from both chemistry and physics is required to make and use new scientific discoveries and innovations.

Understanding physical science is very important for success on the GED Science Test. Physical science topics are the basis for about 35 percent of the questions on the test.

Many jobs, such as this blood bank technician, use the principles of both chemistry and physics every day.

The lessons in this unit include:

Lesson 14:   **Matter**
Matter is any substance that occupies space. Almost all matter exists in one of three states—solid, liquid, or gas. Most matter can be changed from one state to another.

Lesson 15:   **Structure of Atoms and Molecules**
All matter consists either of atoms (elements) or of molecules (compounds made from elements). The periodic table shows elements arranged according to their atomic numbers and by similar physical and chemical properties.

Lesson 16:   **Chemical Reactions**
Much of what we depend upon in daily life is based on producing and transforming substances through chemical reactions. These reactions take place when atoms or molecules rearrange to form new products with different properties.

Lesson 17:   **Motion and Forces**
A force is a push or pull that acts on matter, changing an object's speed or direction of movement. Many actions in the physical world depend upon the relationship between force and the motion of objects.

Lesson 18:   **Work and Energy**
Energy is the ability to do work—to move matter from one place to another. When work is done, energy is transferred from one object to another and is changed from one form to another.

Lesson 19:   **Electricity and Magnetism**
Electricity is the result of the interaction of positive and negative charges in atoms. Magnetism is the attraction and repulsion between two different objects. The relationship between electricity and magnetism is known as electromagnetism.

Lesson 20:   **Waves**
A wave is a disturbance that travels through space or matter. Energy is transmitted by waves, such as sound waves and light waves.

THINKING SKILLS

- Comparing and contrasting
- Applying ideas
- Assessing the adequacy of written information
- Recognizing unstated assumptions
- Assessing the adequacy of visual information
- Analyzing cause and effect
- Identifying faulty logic

GED SKILL Comparing and Contrasting

compare
to identify how things are alike

contrast
to identify how things are different

In science as well as in everyday life, you are often faced with looking at two items that appear alike. First you might **compare** them, or identify their similarities. In the Venn diagram below, ethane and ethene are both hydrocarbons made from carbon and hydrogen. Next, you might **contrast** the two items to identify their differences. In this case, ethane is saturated and ethene is unsaturated. You can show these similarities and differences in a Venn diagram.

Comparing and contrasting are skills that can help you understand science materials. To compare things, ask, "How are these alike?" To contrast things, ask, "How are these different?"

Read the passage. Then answer the questions that follow.

Glass is a **solid** because it has a definite shape and a definite **volume.** However, at the molecular level glass is similar to a **liquid.** Glass is formed from melted materials that have been cooled very quickly. This cooling process does not give the molecules that form glass time to organize into a regular pattern characteristic of most solids. Instead, the molecules are disorganized, more like those of a liquid. However, at ordinary temperatures, glass is not a liquid. It cannot flow as liquids can. Only when heated to high temperatures does glass melt and become a true liquid.

Ethane
saturated
single bonds only
6 H atoms

organic compound
hydrocarbon
covalent bonding
C and H atoms only
2 C atoms
gas at room temperature

unsaturated
one C=C double bond
4 H atoms
Ethene

1. Compare glass to liquids. Put a check mark next to each statement that tells how they are similar.

   _____ a. Glass and liquids both have a definite shape and volume.

   _____ b. Glass and liquids both have a disorganized molecular structure.

You were correct if you checked *option b*. The paragraph explains that molecules of glass are arranged randomly, not in a pattern, which is similar to the molecular arrangement of liquids. *Option a* is incorrect. Glass—a solid—has a definite shape and volume; liquids have only a definite volume.

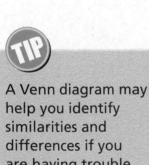

TIP

A Venn diagram may help you identify similarities and differences if you are having trouble comparing and contrasting two or more things.

2. Contrast glass and liquids. Put a check mark next to the statement that tells how they are different.

   _____ a. Glass does not flow at ordinary temperatures; liquids do.

   _____ b. Glass can be cooled quickly and liquids cannot.

You were correct if you chose *option a*. Glass, unlike liquids, does not flow at ordinary temperatures. *Option b* is incorrect because both liquids and glass can be cooled quickly.

Use the passage and the diagram to answer the questions below.

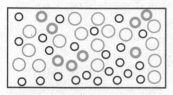

Mixture: uneven distribution of substances

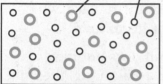

Solution: even distribution of solute and solvent

When two or more substances are combined mechanically, the result is a **mixture.** In a mixture, each substance keeps its own properties. The substances may be mixed in any proportion and they may be mixed unevenly or evenly. Substances in a mixture may be separated from the mixture by mechanical means such as filtration or evaporation. Examples of mixtures are seawater, air, gravel, and mayonnaise.

A special type of mixture is a **solution.** In a solution, one substance is dissolved in another and both substances are distributed evenly throughout. Solutions can involve solids, liquids, or gases. The dissolved substance is called the **solute.** The substance doing the dissolving is called the **solvent.** In a sugar-water solution, sugar, a solid, is the solute and water, a liquid, is the solvent. In carbonated water, carbon dioxide gas is the solute dissolved in a liquid solvent.

1. Put a check mark next to the statement that tells what all mixtures and solutions have in common.

   _____ a. Both are made up of different substances that keep their properties.

   _____ b. Both involve the dissolving of a solute in a solvent.

2. Put a check mark next to the statement that tells how a solution differs from other mixtures.

   _____ a. In a solution, the substances are distributed evenly throughout, and in other mixtures they may be distributed unevenly.

   _____ b. In a solution, the substances are distributed unevenly throughout, and in other mixtures they may be distributed evenly.

3. Complete the Venn diagram below. Note similarities between the mixtures gravel and salt water in the overlapping portion of the two circles. Note differences in the portions of the circles that are not shared.

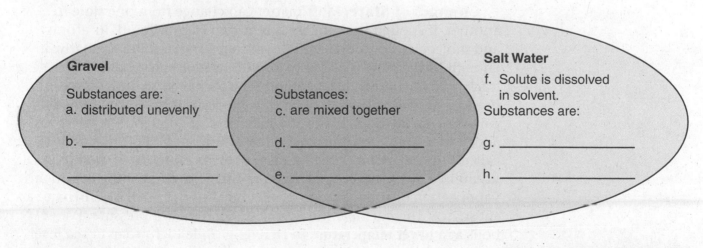

Gravel

Substances are:
a. distributed unevenly

b. _____

_____

Substances:
c. are mixed together

d. _____

e. _____

Salt Water
f. Solute is dissolved in solvent.
Substances are:

g. _____

h. _____

Answers start on page 296.

Matter can exist in any of three physical states: solid, liquid, or gas. The **atoms** and molecules that make up matter are constantly in motion. Whether matter is solid, liquid, or gas depends on the motion of its atoms and molecules.

Solid. A solid is matter that has a definite shape and volume. A bar of gold is an example of a solid. If you try to put a square bar of gold into a round hole, it will not fit. The gold has a definite shape. If you try to put the bar of gold into a space that is too small, it also will not fit. The bar of gold has a definite volume.

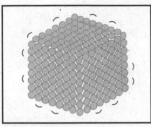
Solid

Molecules in a solid barely move. They only vibrate. Forces of attraction hold the molecules of a solid very tightly in place, which is why solids have both definite shape and definite volume.

Liquid. A liquid has a definite volume, but it does not have a definite shape. If you pour a quart of milk into a gallon jug, the milk will fill only one-fourth of the jug. If you pour the same quart of milk into an eight-ounce glass, the milk will overflow. The volume of the milk does not change. However, its shape changes each time you pour it into a different container.

Liquid

The molecules in a liquid move more freely and have more energy than those of a solid. Although weaker than in solids, the forces of attraction among molecules of the liquid are strong enough to hold them together loosely. That is why a liquid has a definite volume. But, the forces are too weak to hold the molecules in a definite shape.

Gas. A **gas** has neither definite shape nor definite volume. A gas will spread out to fill the volume of a container that it is placed in. You can understand this property of a gas if you think of how quickly the smell of an apple pie baking in the oven fills the whole kitchen.

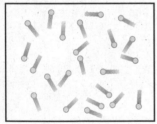
Gas

Molecules of a gas move freely and randomly. There are almost no forces of attraction among gas molecules. A gas will escape from an open container and spread out into the air.

Changes of State. Most matter can change from one state to another. If enough heat energy is removed from a liquid, its atoms and molecules slow down and it will freeze into a solid. Similarly, if enough heat energy is added to a solid, its molecules move more freely and it will melt into a liquid. The temperature under a specific pressure at which these changes of state occur is called the **freezing point** or **melting point** of the substance. If enough heat energy is added to a liquid, the liquid will change into a gas. This process is called **vaporization.** When a gas is cooled enough, it changes into a liquid in a process called **condensation.** The temperature at which vaporization or condensation occurs is called the **boiling point** of a substance. These temperatures vary under different pressure. Water boils at a lower temperature in Denver (1 mile high) than at sea level.

Directions: Choose the one best answer to each question.

Questions 1 through 7 refer to the passage and the diagrams on page 160.

1. Which properties characterize a solid?

   (1) definite shape; definite volume
   (2) definite shape; no definite volume
   (3) no definite shape; no definite volume
   (4) no definite shape; definite volume
   (5) definite shape; no molecular motion

2. How are gases and liquids similar?

   (1) Both have molecules that move randomly.
   (2) Both have molecules held together in a rigid pattern.
   (3) Both have molecules with very high forces of attraction.
   (4) Both can evaporate when sufficient heat is added to them.
   (5) Both can melt when sufficient heat is added to them.

3. A heart-shaped cake is made by pouring cake batter into a heart-shaped mold. Which property of matter is illustrated by the pouring?

   (1) A solid takes the shape of the container into which it is placed.
   (2) A solid has a definite shape but not a definite volume.
   (3) A liquid has a definite shape and volume.
   (4) A liquid has no definite shape; it takes the shape of its container.
   (5) A gas has a definite shape and volume.

4. Which of the following actions would produce a change in the state of matter?

   (1) adding food coloring to water
   (2) leaving ice cream on a hot stove
   (3) poking a hole in a large helium balloon
   (4) placing a candy bar on a scale
   (5) cutting a square block of wood in half

5. Condensation and vaporization are opposites. Which of the following occurs in condensation?

   (1) a solid changes to a liquid
   (2) a liquid changes to a gas
   (3) a gas changes to a liquid
   (4) a liquid changes to a solid
   (5) a solid changes to a gas

6. At what temperature does a particular liquid become a gas?

   (1) at its melting point
   (2) at its freezing point
   (3) at its boiling point
   (4) at its condensation point
   (5) at its change in state

7. Which of the following conclusions is supported by the diagram on page 160?

   (1) Large molecules move faster than small molecules.
   (2) Molecules in gases have less energy if the gas is in a small container.
   (3) You can feel molecules vibrating in a solid.
   (4) Molecules in gases move faster than molecules in liquids.
   (5) Molecules of a solid will spread out and fill a container.

TIP Create a picture in your mind of what you are reading about. Visualizing a process that is occurring or being described can help you answer questions about it.

Answers start on page 296.

Directions: Choose the one best answer to each question.

Questions 1 through 3 refer to the following paragraph and graph.

If you hold a book in one hand and a comparably sized piece of foam packing material in the other, the book feels heavier. The book feels heavier because it has more mass in the same amount of space. This property of matter is referred to as density. **Density** is defined as the mass per unit volume of a material. It is an important property, one that when combined with other properties helps distinguish one substance from another. In general, gases are less dense than liquids, which are less dense than solids. The bar graph shows the density of some common substances.

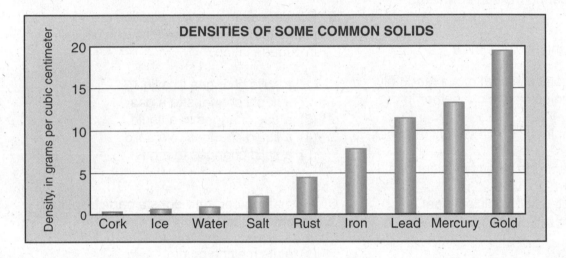

1. Which of the following substances is denser than lead?

   (1) water
   (2) salt
   (3) rust
   (4) iron
   (5) gold

2. According to the graph, if you melt ice, what is the effect on its density?

   (1) Its density increases.
   (2) Its density decreases.
   (3) Its density increases, then decreases.
   (4) Its density decreases, then increases.
   (5) Its density remains the same.

3. A materials scientist must identify a sample of matter. She measures its density at 7.9 grams per cubic centimeter. The sample is made of which of the following substances?

   (1) rust
   (2) iron
   (3) lead
   (4) mercury
   (5) Density alone cannot be used to identify a particular substance.

Bar graphs are used to compare amounts. Usually, bars represent items in a category, and the length of each bar represents a measurable characteristic. Taller or longer bars have more of the characteristic than shorter bars.

Unifying Concepts:

CONSTANCY AND CHANGE
THE BEHAVIOR OF GASES

Questions 4 through 6 refer to the following passage and diagrams.

Gases behave differently under different conditions of temperature, volume, and pressure (the force per unit area of the molecules' collisions with the container) because of the way their molecules move.

As shown in diagram A, the pressure of a gas doubles if the temperature doubles and the volume remains the same. The rise in temperature causes the molecules to move twice as fast in the same amount of space. This increases the pressure. The pressure of a gas also doubles if its volume is cut in half and its temperature remains constant, as shown in diagram B. This is because, in the smaller space, the molecules have twice the number of collisions. The pressure of a gas remains the same if the temperature and volume both double, as shown in diagram C. This is because the molecules move faster at higher temperatures, but, with the volume doubled, they have twice the space to move in.

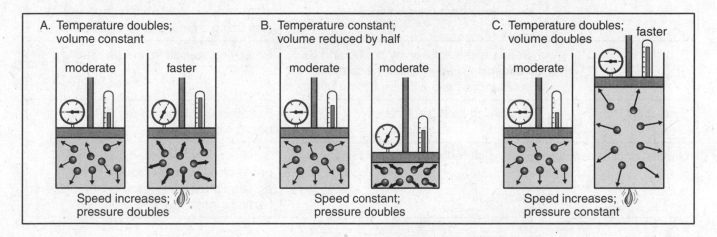

4. What is the pressure of a gas?

   (1) the heat energy of its molecules
   (2) the effect of molecules as they hit the sides of their container
   (3) the volume of the container multiplied by the temperature
   (4) the temperature of a given volume of gas
   (5) the volume of the gas compared to the size of the container

5. Under which conditions would a gas have the least pressure?

   (1) high temperature, large volume
   (2) high temperature, small volume
   (3) medium temperature, medium volume
   (4) low temperature, large volume
   (5) low temperature, small volume

6. Which of the following statements about gases is supported by the information given in the diagrams?

   (1) Pressure decreases when temperature and volume remain the same.
   (2) Pressure decreases when temperature increases and volume remains the same.
   (3) Pressure increases when volume decreases and temperature remains the same.
   (4) Pressure decreases when temperature and volume both double.
   (5) Pressure remains the same when temperature increases and volume decreases.

Answers start on page 297.

GED Mini-Test • Lesson 14

Directions: This is a ten-minute practice test. After ten minutes, mark the last question you finished. Then complete the test and check your answers. If most of your answers were correct but you didn't finish, try to work faster next time. Choose the <u>one best answer</u> to each question.

<u>Questions 1 through 4</u> refer to the following paragraph and table.

The ingredients of a mixture keep their own properties, and they can be separated from a mixture by physical means as described below.

Method	Description	Example
Sorting	Selecting the desired substance from the mixture	In coal mining, sorting coal from rock by hand
Magnetic separation	Using a magnet to separate a magnetic substance from the mixture	In iron ore processing, separating the magnetic iron from nonmagnetic waste rock using a magnetized conveyor belt
Distillation	Separating a solution by boiling and condensing; works because different substances have different boiling points	Removing the salt from seawater
Extraction	Dissolving an ingredient out of a mixture by using a specific solvent	Extracting vanilla flavoring from vanilla beans with alcohol
Gravitational separation	Sorting ingredients by the density of each	In panning for gold, the dense gold particles settle to the bottom of the pan and the lighter (less dense) rock particles wash away

1. Which of the following is the best title for the table?

   (1) Types of Mixtures
   (2) Sorting and Extraction
   (3) Industrial Uses of Mixture Separation
   (4) The Ingredients of Mixtures
   (5) Methods of Separating Mixtures

2. What do distillation and extraction have in common?

   (1) They both involve solutions.
   (2) They both involve magnetism.
   (3) They both involve density.
   (4) They both involve appearance.
   (5) They both remove salt from seawater.

3. Brittany used the chemical trichloroethylene to remove a salad dressing stain from a tablecloth. Which method of separating mixtures did Brittany use?

   (1) sorting
   (2) magnetic separation
   (3) distillation
   (4) extraction
   (5) gravitational separation

4. Petroleum is separated into products such as gasoline and kerosene by heating them to the boiling point and allowing them to cool again. Which method of separating mixtures is used to process petroleum?

   (1) sorting
   (2) magnetic separation
   (3) distillation
   (4) extraction
   (5) gravitational separation

A colloid is a type of mixture in which particles of matter measuring from one ten millionth of an inch to one thousandth of an inch are scattered throughout a liquid or a gas. Examples of colloids include smoke (solid particles in a gas); cytoplasm (solid particles in a liquid); and foam (gas particles in a liquid or solid).

Colloids differ from solutions in that the colloidal particles are larger than the solute molecules of solutions. This can be shown with a semipermeable membrane, which allows small molecules like those of water and the dissolved solute to pass through, but blocks larger colloidal particles, such as those of proteins. If you pour cream, a colloid, through a semipermeable membrane, the solid particles in the cream do not pass through the membrane, but the water does. In contrast, when you pour a food coloring solution through a semipermeable membrane, both the solute—the food coloring—and the solvent—water—pass through.

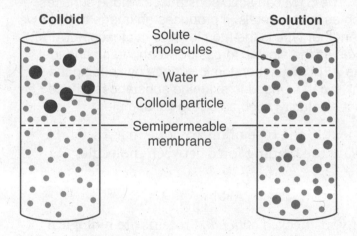

Colloid   **Solution**

Solute molecules

Water

Colloid particle

Semipermeable membrane

5. Based on the passage and the diagrams, how do colloids and solutions differ?

(1) A colloid is a gas and a solution is a liquid.
(2) The freezing point of a colloid is lower than the freezing point of a solution.
(3) The molecules in solutions are smaller than the particles in colloids.
(4) Colloid particles can pass through a semipermeable membrane and the solute molecules in a solution cannot.
(5) Colloids are usually solids, and solutions are always liquids.

6. If you were to substitute wire mesh for the semipermeable membranes in the diagram, which of the following would be likely to occur?

(1) Solid particles of the colloid would flow through, but molecules of the solute would not.
(2) Solid particles of the colloid would not flow through, but molecules of the solute would.
(3) Both the colloid particles and the solute molecules would flow through.
(4) Neither particles of the colloid nor molecules of the solute would flow through.
(5) Only water molecules would be able to flow through the mesh.

7. A suspension is a type of mixture, like muddy water, whose particles are even larger than those of colloids. What is implied by this?

(1) The particles of a suspension are larger than the molecules of a solution.
(2) The particles of a suspension would flow through the semipermeable membrane.
(3) Suspensions are always solids suspended in liquids.
(4) A suspension can be identified by its color.
(5) A suspension is the only type of mixture that can be separated into its ingredients.

8. The freezing point of water can be lowered a few degrees by adding a solute to form a solution. The molecules of solute spread through the solvent, in this case water. That makes it more difficult for the water to freeze and form crystals. Which of the following observations supports this information?

(1) When it snows, calcium chloride is applied to roads to prevent the formation of ice.
(2) Ice crystals form on windows when the temperature is below freezing.
(3) A glass jar of soup cracks when the soup freezes.
(4) When you place ice cubes in a glass of water, they melt.
(5) When water freezes, it expands and takes up more space.

Answers start on page 298.

Lesson 15

GED SKILL Applying Ideas

One way we make sense of the world is to place things in general categories, or groups. For example, we all know what a dog is. Even though we may not have seen every breed of dog that exists, when we see a new type of dog we still recognize that it is a dog. We apply what we know about dogs in general to the new dog.

In science, many things are defined in general terms. For example, you learned that a liquid is matter with a definite volume but no definite shape. When you see milk or motor oil, you recognize these specific types of matter as liquids because they too have a definite volume but no definite shape. They share the properties of liquids. In science, general ideas or categories, such as liquids, can be easier to understand if you apply them to specific examples such as milk or oil.

Read the passage and answer the questions below.

In the mid-1980s, it became possible to see atoms and molecules with new kinds of microscopes. One type is the scanning tunneling microscope (STM). It uses a constant flow of electric current to scan a substance from a constant height. The STM can scan substances whose surfaces conduct electricity, such as many metals. It produces an image that shows the shapes of atoms. Another type is the atomic force microscope (AFM). The tip of the AFM flexes as the electric forces between the tip and the atoms push or pull. The AFM maps the atomic surface by keeping the force on its tip constant. It can be used to examine substances whose surfaces do not conduct electricity, such as biological samples.

1. Put a check mark next to the type of microscope that a scientist would use to measure the binding force between molecules of proteins.

    _____ a. STM   _____ b. AFM

You were correct if you checked *option b*. Proteins are biological samples, so the scientist would use the type of microscope that is suited to examine biological molecules—the AFM.

2. Put a check mark next to the type of microscope scientists probably used to distinguish between clusters of gold and silver atoms by measuring emitted light and voltage.

    _____ a. STM   _____ b. AFM

You were correct if you checked *option a*. The passage indicates that STMs can scan materials that conduct electricity, such as metals like gold and silver.

TIP

To understand general ideas or categories in science, ask yourself:

- What central idea or concept is being presented?
- What are its elements or characteristics?
- What are some specific examples?

Use the passage and the diagram to answer the questions below.

All matter is made up of elements. An **element** is a substance that cannot be broken down into simpler substances by chemical means. Helium, carbon, oxygen, neon, and iron are examples of elements.

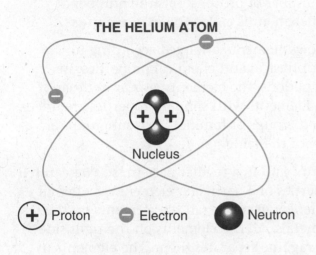

THE HELIUM ATOM

Nucleus

(+) Proton   (−) Electron   ● Neutron

Can an element like copper be broken into smaller and smaller pieces forever and still be the element copper? The answer is no. Eventually a submicroscopic piece would remain— a piece that could not be divided and still be copper. This smallest piece of an element is called an **atom.**

An atom is the smallest piece of an element that still has the properties of that element. All elements are made of atoms. The element copper is made of copper atoms. The element helium is made of helium atoms, and so on.

What is an atom made of? Each atom has a small, dense core called a **nucleus.** The nucleus contains particles called **protons,** which have a positive electric charge, and **neutrons,** which have no charge. Moving in "orbitals" (differently shaped areas in space) around the nucleus and forming a "cloud" are submicroscopic negatively charged particles called **electrons.** A neutron and a proton have about the same mass. Their mass is about 1,800 times greater than the mass of an electron.

1. Put a check mark next to the phrase that defines an element.

    ____ a. a substance that cannot be broken down into simpler substances by chemical means

    ____ b. a substance that is made up of many types of atoms

2. Write *E* next to each of the following that is an example of an element.

    ____ a. helium, which can be broken down only into helium atoms by chemical means

    ____ b. water, which is made up of hydrogen and oxygen atoms

    ____ c. copper, which is made up of copper atoms

    ____ d. brass, which is made up of copper and zinc

    ____ e. salt, which is made up of sodium and chlorine atoms

    ____ f. mercury, which can be broken down only into mercury atoms by chemical means

3. Neon is a gaseous element similar to helium, except that neon has 10 protons, 10 neutrons, and 10 electrons. Put a check mark next to the location of the protons and neutrons in a neon atom.

    ____ a. in the nucleus

    ____ b. in the orbits around the nucleus

Answers start on page 299.

GED CONTENT The Structure of Atoms and Molecules

The atoms of each element have a certain number of protons in the nucleus. The number of protons in the nucleus of an atom of an element is called the **atomic number.** Thus, each element has its own atomic number. The number of protons plus the number of neutrons in the atom of an element is called the **atomic mass.**

The **periodic table** shows elements arranged according to atomic number and similar physical and chemical properties. In the horizontal rows, called periods, the elements appear in order of increasing atomic number. Elements with similar properties are lined up in vertical columns called groups or families. Two subgroups are shown below the main part of the table.

The properties of elements vary in a regular pattern, so you can tell a great deal about the properties of a particular element by where it appears in the periodic table. For example, all the elements on the left side and in the center are metals. All the elements on the right side are nonmetals. A heavy zigzag line separates them. The elements in each column have similar chemical and physical properties, such as the state of matter it exists in under natural conditions and degree of reactivity with other elements.

A PERIODIC TABLE OF THE ELEMENTS

periods →   ← periods

groups   groups

atomic number → 12
symbol of element → Mg
element name → Magnesium

Elements above and to the right of this line are nonmetals.

Elements below and to the left of this line are metals.

Elements in this column are noble gases. →

IA	IIA	IIIB	IVB	VB	VIB	VIIB	8			IB	IIB	IIIA	IVA	VA	VIA	VIIA	VIIIB
1 H Hydrogen																	2 He Helium
3 Li Lithium	4 Be Beryllium											5 B Boron	6 C Carbon	7 N Nitrogen	8 O Oxygen	9 F Fluorine	10 Ne Neon
11 Na Sodium	12 Mg Magnesium											13 Al Aluminum	14 Si Silicon	15 P Phosphorus	16 S Sulfur	17 Cl Chlorine	18 Ar Argon
19 K Potassium	20 Ca Calcium	21 Sc Scandium	22 Ti Titanium	23 V Vanadium	24 Cr Chromium	25 Mn Manganese	26 Fe Iron	27 Co Cobalt	28 Ni Nickel	29 Cu Copper	30 Zn Zinc	31 Ga Gallium	32 Ge Germanium	33 As Arsenic	34 Se Selenium	35 Br Bromine	36 Kr Krypton
37 Rb Rubidium	38 Sr Strontium	39 Y Yttrium	40 Zr Zirconium	41 Nb Niobium	42 Mo Molybdenum	43 Tc Technetium	44 Ru Ruthenium	45 Rh Rhodium	46 Pd Palladium	47 Ag Silver	48 Cd Cadmium	49 In Indium	50 Sn Tin	51 Sb Antimony	52 Te Tellurium	53 I Iodine	54 Xe Xenon
55 Cs Cesium	56 Ba Barium	57–71* See Below	72 Hf Hafnium	73 Ta Tantalum	74 W Tungsten	75 Re Rhenium	76 Os Osmium	77 Ir Iridium	78 Pt Platinum	79 Au Gold	80 Hg Mercury	81 Tl Thallium	82 Pb Lead	83 Bi Bismuth	84 Po Polonium	85 At Astatine	86 Rn Radon
87 Fr Francium	88 Ra Radium	89–103** See Below	104 Rf Rutherfordium	105 Db Dubnium	106 Sg Seaborgium	107 Bh Bohrium	108 Hs Hassium	109 Mt Meitnerium	110 (unnamed)	111 (unnamed)	112 (unnamed)						

*Lanthanide series

57 La Lanthanum	58 Ce Cerium	59 Pr Praseadymium	60 Nd Neodymium	61 Pm Promethium	62 Sm Samarium	63 Eu Europium	64 Gd Gadolinium	65 Tb Terbium	66 Dy Dysprosium	67 Ho Holmium	68 Er Erbium	69 Tm Thulium	70 Yb Ytterbium	71 Lu Lutetium

**Actinide series

89 Ac Actinium	90 Th Thorium	91 Pa Protactinium	92 U Uranium	93 Np Neptunium	94 Pu Plutonium	95 Am Americium	96 Cm Curium	97 Bk Berkelium	98 Cf Californium	99 Es Einsteinium	100 Fm Fermium	101 Md Mendelevium	102 No Nobelium	103 Lr Lawrencium

Directions: Choose the <u>one best answer</u> to each question.

Questions 1 through 3 refer to the passage and the table on page 168.

1. Look at the periodic table. Which of the following elements has the fewest protons in its nucleus?

   (1) zinc (Zn)
   (2) cobalt (Co)
   (3) potassium (K)
   (4) arsenic (As)
   (5) iron (Fe)

2. According to the periodic table, which of the following combination of elements has similar properties?

   (1) sodium (Na), chlorine (Cl), hydrogen (H)
   (2) neon (Ne), argon (Ar), krypton (Kr)
   (3) lithium (Li), magnesium (Mg), sulfur (S)
   (4) beryllium (Be), carbon (C), fluorine (F)
   (5) aluminum (Al), sulfur (S), chlorine (Cl)

3. According to the passage, the periodic table is based on a relationship between which two factors?

   (1) atomic number and atomic mass
   (2) atomic number and total number of electrons
   (3) atomic number and properties
   (4) atomic mass and number of electrons
   (5) whether an element is metallic or nonmetallic

TIP Items found in a classification share certain characteristics. Knowing these common characteristics will help you classify "new" items.

Questions 4 and 5 refer to the following passage.

Elements in the same group in the periodic table have many similar properties. Five groups of elements are described below.

- group I = very reactive metals; react violently with water
- group II = fairly reactive metals; often found in salts
- transition elements = metals, many of which can react with oxygen to form more than one compound
- group VII = very reactive nonmetals; combine with hydrogen to form acids
- group VIII = inert ("Noble") gases that rarely take part in chemical reactions

Each of the following questions describes an element that belongs to one of these groups. Classify each element into one of the groups.

4. Element X combines with hydrogen to form hydrochloric acid.

   (1) group I
   (2) group II
   (3) transition elements
   (4) group VII
   (5) group VIII

5. Element Y is a silvery-gray solid that can cause an explosion when dropped into water.

   (1) group I
   (2) group II
   (3) transition elements
   (4) group VII
   (5) group VIII

Answers start on page 299.

GED Practice • Lesson 15

Directions: Choose the one best answer to each question.

Questions 1 and 2 refer to the passage below.

Atoms of most elements can bond with other atoms. When atoms bond they either transfer or share electrons. If electrons are transferred from one atom to another, each atom takes on a charge; charged atoms are called **ions.** A bond between ions is an **ionic bond.** Ionic bonds form only between two different elements; the substances that result are ionic compounds. Elements on opposite sides of the periodic table are most likely to join by ionic bonding.

Elements closer to each other in the periodic table tend to bond by sharing electrons. Bonds that result when electrons are shared are called **covalent bonds.** A single covalent bond requires a pair of electrons be shared; one electron comes from each atom. Two or more atoms joined by a covalent bond form a molecule.

Covalent bonds can form between atoms of the same element or between atoms of two or more different elements. When atoms of different elements are joined by covalent bonds, the result is a covalent compound.

Question 3 refers to the following passage and diagram.

Compounds can be represented by **chemical formulas, structural formulas,** and diagrams. For example, the compound methane is shown by the chemical formula CH_4. C stands for carbon, and H stands for hydrogen. The numbers tell you how many atoms are in one molecule of methane. When there is no number, that means there is one atom. Thus, a molecule of methane has one atom of carbon and four atoms of hydrogen.

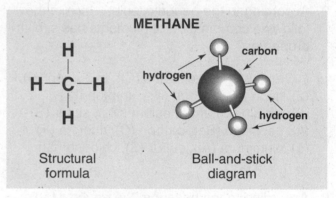

METHANE

Structural formula

Ball-and-stick diagram

1. Which situation involves ionic bonding?

   (1) two hydrogen atoms and an oxygen atom sharing two pairs of electrons
   (2) sugar and water mixed together
   (3) calcium giving up two electrons to two fluorine atoms
   (4) oxygen and nitrogen together in air
   (5) water and carbon dioxide in a soft drink

2. Which of the following is an unstated assumption suggested by the passage?

   (1) Compounds form from atoms of different elements.
   (2) Covalent bonds require electron sharing.
   (3) A molecule is made up of atoms bonded covalently.
   (4) Ions are atoms that carry a charge.
   (5) A molecule can have ionic bonds.

3. The structural formula for propane is shown here.

PROPANE

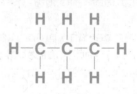

Which of the following statements is supported by the structural formula for propane?

   (1) Propane contains nitrogen atoms.
   (2) Propane has three atoms of carbon and three atoms of hydrogen.
   (3) Propane has three atoms of carbon and four atoms of oxygen.
   (4) The chemical formula for propane is C_3H_8.
   (5) The chemical formula for propane is C_3H_6.

Science as Inquiry

THE SEARCH FOR SUBATOMIC PARTICLES

Questions 4 through 6 refer to the following passage.

At the beginning of the twentieth century, scientists thought that the smallest particles were the protons, neutrons, and electrons that make up atoms. However, in the 1920s showers of **subatomic particles** produced by cosmic rays were detected in the atmosphere. Scientists soon realized that protons and neutrons were themselves made up of smaller particles which were named **quarks.** In addition, scientists found evidence of a category of force-carrying subatomic particles known as **bosons.**

To study subatomic particles such as quarks and bosons, scientists use **particle accelerators.** These huge machines consist of ring- or donut-shaped tunnels that are miles in circumference. An accelerator launches particles such as protons into the ring. As they travel the miles around the ring, the particles are accelerated almost to the speed of light. Then they arrive at the detector, where they collide with other particles. When particles collide, they release energy that immediately turns into new particles of matter. By analyzing the collisions that take place in particle accelerators, scientists help prove or disprove the latest theories about the structure of matter and the forces that bind matter.

Today, two of the largest particle accelerators are engaged in a race. Scientists at Fermi National Accelerator Laboratory (Fermilab) in Illinois and the European Laboratory for Particle Physics (CERN) in Switzerland hope to be the first to prove the existence of the Higgs boson. Scientists have predicted that the interactions of Higgs bosons are what give matter its mass. A great deal of energy is required to produce a Higgs boson in a particle collision. So far neither accelerator has been able to generate sufficient energy to produce direct evidence that the Higgs boson exists.

4. Based on the passage, which subatomic particles are protons and neutrons made of?

   (1) cosmic rays
   (2) quarks
   (3) bosons
   (4) Higgs bosons
   (5) electrons

5. Suppose that a collision in an accelerator briefly produces a subatomic particle that carries a force called a gluon. What type of particle is a gluon?

   (1) cosmic ray
   (2) quark
   (3) boson
   (4) neutron
   (5) electron

6. Particle accelerators are huge, complex machines that are controversial because they are usually built with public funds. Which of the following arguments would be used by a person favoring the building of a new accelerator?

   (1) An accelerator would occupy land better put to other uses.
   (2) The collisions in an accelerator could pose a hazard to people in the area.
   (3) The cost of an accelerator greatly outweighs its benefits.
   (4) Scientists should be investigating matters with immediate practical applications.
   (5) Understanding subatomic particles may lead to advances in technology.

TIP Values are often reflected in fact-opinion and support-for-conclusion type questions. Values are often a clue to opinion.

Answers start on page 299.

Directions: This is a ten-minute practice test. After ten minutes, mark the last question you finished. Then complete the test and check your answers. If most of your answers were correct but you didn't finish, try to work faster next time. Choose the one best answer to each question.

Questions 1 through 3 refer to the following passage and chart.

All living things contain carbon. Compounds containing carbon and hydrogen are called organic compounds. An organic compound that contains only the two elements hydrogen and carbon is called a hydrocarbon. There are thousands of different hydrocarbons, including fossil fuels. Even though they contain just two elements, hydrocarbons vary greatly in their properties. Scientists classify hydrocarbons into subgroups called series.

Members of one group, called the alkane series, are the most abundant hydrocarbons. You're probably familiar with many of them. If you've been camping, you may have used propane or butane. These two gases are often sold in canisters for use in barbecue grills, camp stoves, and lanterns. The gasoline that fuels a car usually contains pentane, hexane, heptane, and octane. Some alkanes are listed below.

THE ALKANE SERIES			
Name	Formula	Physical State at Room Temperature	Boiling Point (°C)
Methane	CH_4	gas	−162
Ethane	C_2H_6	gas	−89
Propane	C_3H_8	gas	−42
Butane	C_4H_{10}	gas	−1
Pentane	C_5H_{12}	liquid	36
Hexane	C_6H_{14}	liquid	69
Heptane	C_7H_{16}	liquid	98
Octane	C_8H_{18}	liquid	126
Nonane	C_9H_{20}	liquid	151
Decane	$C_{10}H_{22}$	liquid	174
Eicosane	$C_{20}H_{42}$	solid	344

1. According to the passage and the chart, which of the following is a characteristic of all members of the alkane series?

   (1) They are living things because they contain hydrogen and carbon.
   (2) They are both organic compounds and hydrocarbons.
   (3) They are all liquid when they are at room temperature.
   (4) They all contain the same number of carbon atoms.
   (5) They are made up of helium atoms.

2. If you open the valve on the fuel tank of a gas barbecue grill, the fuel that escapes is in the gaseous state. Which of the following is likely to be the fuel in the grill?

   (1) C_3H_8
   (2) C_8H_{18}
   (3) C_9H_{20}
   (4) $C_{10}H_{22}$
   (5) $C_{20}H_{42}$

3. Which of the following conclusions can you draw based on the data in the chart?

   (1) Heptane boils at a lower temperature than hexane.
   (2) Butane boils at a higher temperature than ethane.
   (3) Butane melts at a lower temperature than ethane.
   (4) Eicosane contains the fewest carbon atoms.
   (5) Pentane contains fewer carbon and hydrogen atoms than butane does.

Questions 4 through 6 refer to the following passage and diagram.

A polymer consists of large molecules made of many small, repeating units called monomers which are joined together by covalent bonds. Most of the organic compounds found in living things are polymers. These include cellulose, carbohydrates, fats, and proteins. Many synthetic materials are also polymers. Plastics, nylon and other synthetic fibers, and adhesives are all polymers.

Polymers form structures that take several shapes. A linear polymer consists of long chains of monomers. A branched polymer consists of a long chain molecule with side chains. A cross-linked polymer consists of two or more chains joined together by side chains.

STRUCTURES OF POLYMERS

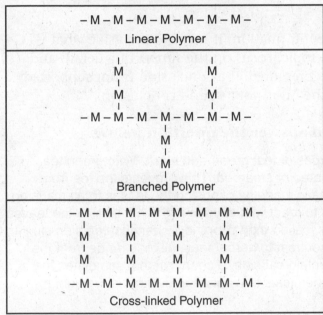

M = monomer unit

4. Based on the passage, which of the following is characteristic of the monomers that make up polymers?

Monomers in polymers are

(1) repetitive.
(2) large.
(3) ionic.
(4) metallic.
(5) gaseous.

5. Deoxyribonucleic acid (DNA) consists of a double helix of sugar-phosphate units connected by linked pairs of nitrogen bases. This structure suggests that DNA can be classified as which of the following?

(1) a monomer
(2) a linear polymer
(3) a branched polymer
(4) a cross-linked polymer
(5) a sugar molecule

6. Plastics like polyethylene are linear polymers. When heated, they melt. Other plastics like Bakelite™ are cross-linked polymers. When heated, they burn or decompose rather than melt. Which of the following is the most likely cause of this difference in properties?

(1) the fact that Bakelite is a monomer and polyethylene is a polymer
(2) the absence or presence of links between the chains
(3) the low melting point of linear polymer plastics
(4) the amount of cellulose in Bakelite
(5) the branches on the polyethylene polymer

Question 7 refers to the following diagram.

WATER MOLECULE (H_2O)

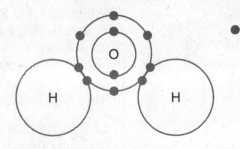

● = electron

7. Covalent bonding involves each atom contributing one electron to form the bond. Therefore, how many total electrons did the oxygen atom have before it bonded covalently with the hydrogen atoms to form a water molecule?

(1) one
(2) two
(3) six
(4) eight
(5) ten

Answers start on page 300.

If you pay attention to science and health news, you know that scientists publish their data and conclusions in professional journals read by other scientists. For example, a new study may provide evidence that children who drink bottled water have more cavities than children who drink fluoridated tap water. Other scientists then examine or repeat the study to see whether new data actually support the conclusion that the authors reached.

Whenever you read anything factual, as on a scientific topic or otherwise, you should examine whether the written information presented is adequate to support the conclusions. Ask yourself, "What conclusions are being reached? Which facts and observations are given to support these conclusions? Does this information give adequate support?"

evaluate

to examine something in order to judge its worth or significance

When you **evaluate** information, it helps to put aside what you already know about the topic. Focus on the supporting details and the conclusions that are presented. If a conclusion is not supported by adequate evidence, then it is not a sound conclusion.

Read the passage and answer the question below.

There are two main types of tea: green and black. With green tea, the leaves are quickly heated or steamed. This prevents the tea from reacting with air. Black tea is made by exposing the leaves to air, causing substances in the leaves to react with oxygen in the air, turning the leaves dark brown. This process, called **oxidation,** is a chemical reaction similar to the rusting of iron. In contrast to herbal teas, all teas made from the leaves of the tea plant contain caffeine, a chemical that stimulates the body, and polyphenols, chemicals that act as antioxidants, thought to prevent cell damage.

TIP

Think of a conclusion as a main idea. Then look for the details that support that main idea.

Put a check mark next to each fact from the passage that supports the conclusion that drinking tea has health benefits.

_____ a. Tea has been shown to reduce the likelihood of developing digestive tract cancer.

_____ b. Black tea is processed by exposure to the air, which causes oxidation.

_____ c. The polyphenols in tea act as antioxidants and help prevent cell damage.

You were correct if you checked *option c.* The last sentence of the passage describes the beneficial effects of polyphenols on cells. *Option a* might be true, but you can't tell because it is not discussed in the passage. *Option b* is true and is stated in the passage, but it does not support the conclusion that drinking tea benefits health.

Use the passage and the diagram to answer the questions below.

In a **chemical reaction,** the atoms of substances are rearranged to produce new substances with different chemical and physical properties. The substances you start out with are called the **reactants.** The new substances that are formed are called the **products.**

A **chemical equation** uses formulas and symbols to show what happens during a chemical reaction. The general form of a chemical equation is:

reactants → products

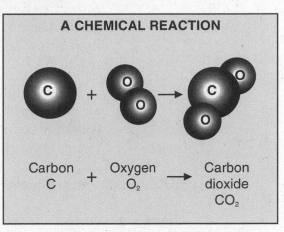

A CHEMICAL REACTION

Carbon + Oxygen → Carbon
   C O_2 dioxide
                              CO_2

1. Put a check mark next to the statement that is a conclusion supported by the information in the first paragraph.

    _____ a. Chemical reactions involve substances changing into other substances.

    _____ b. Chemical reactions involve products changing into reactants.

2. Write a sentence telling what information in the first paragraph supports the conclusion you chose in question 1.

    _____

    _____

3. The second paragraph states that chemical equations are used to represent chemical reactions. Write *S* next to the description of information in the passage and the diagram that supports this statement.

    _____ a. definitions of products and reactants

    _____ b. the format of a typical chemical equation: reactants → products

    _____ c. a specific chemical equation: $C + O_2 \rightarrow CO_2$

4. Put a check mark next to the conclusion that can be supported by the details provided in the diagram.

    _____ a. CO_2 is present in the atmosphere.

    _____ b. CO_2 is a product of the chemical reaction.

5. Write a sentence telling what information in the diagram supports your conclusion from question 4.

    _____

    _____

Answers start on page 301.

In some chemical reactions, molecules split apart into atoms. In other reactions, atoms join together to form molecules. In yet other reactions, atoms change places with other atoms to form new molecules. Atoms are neither created nor destroyed in chemical reactions.

For example, consider what happens when methane burns in air. In this reaction, the reactants methane (CH_4) and oxygen (O_2) combine to form the products carbon dioxide (CO_2) and water (H_2O). Here are two possible chemical equations for this reaction.

Unbalanced Chemical Equation

$$CH_4 + O_2 \rightarrow CO_2 + H_2O$$

Balanced Chemical Equation

$$CH_4 + 2O_2 \rightarrow CO_2 + 2H_2O$$

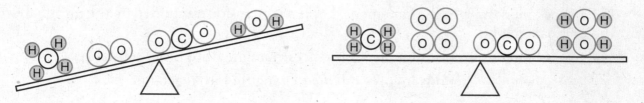

Why is the first equation above unbalanced? In math you learn that the expressions on both sides of an equation must be equal. The same is true of chemical equations. In the first equation, there are four hydrogen atoms on the left side of the equation and only two on the right. There are two atoms of oxygen on the left side and three on the right. However, a chemical equation must show that no atoms are created or destroyed in a chemical reaction. Thus the number of atoms of each element on each side of the equation must match. We do this by changing the number of units of a compound. We add an oxygen molecule (O_2) to the left side. Then for the quantities to come out even, there must be two water molecules (H_2O) on the right side.

Chemical reactions either release or absorb heat energy. A chemical reaction that releases heat energy is called an **exothermic reaction.** For example, when wood or oil is burned, large amounts of heat energy are released. A chemical reaction that absorbs heat energy is called an **endothermic reaction.** Cooking an egg is an endothermic reaction, because the egg absorbs heat energy as it changes. Note that other processes, such as changes of state, can be endothermic or exothermic. For example, the condensation of water vapor is an exothermic process because heat energy is released.

Energy must be added to start many reactions. The energy is necessary to begin to break the bonds in the reactant molecules. The energy that must be added to start a chemical reaction is called the **activation energy.** When you use a match to start a charcoal grill, you are supplying activation energy.

Directions: Choose the one best answer to each question.

Questions 1 through 6 refer to the passage, the equations, and the diagram on page 176.

1. Which of the following happens in a chemical reaction?

   (1) Matter is created.
   (2) Matter is destroyed.
   (3) Matter changes state.
   (4) Atoms change into other atoms.
   (5) Atoms combine or rearrange to form molecules.

2. Which of the following best restates the chemical equation below?

   $$CH_4 + 2O_2 \rightarrow CO_2 + 2H_2O$$

   (1) Methane combines with oxygen to yield carbon dioxide and water.
   (2) Carbon, hydrogen, and oxygen atoms combine to form carbon and oxygen atoms and water molecules.
   (3) One molecule of methane combines with two molecules of oxygen to yield one molecule of carbon dioxide and two molecules of water.
   (4) Four molecules of methane and two molecules of oxygen yield two molecules of carbon dioxide and one molecule of water.
   (5) Carbon and hydrogen form methane; carbon and oxygen form carbon dioxide; and hydrogen and oxygen form water.

3. To balance the equation $2Fe + 3O_2 \rightarrow 2Fe_2O_3$ what should the 2Fe be changed to?

   (1) Fe
   (2) 3Fe
   (3) 4Fe
   (4) 5Fe
   (5) 6Fe

TIP Sketching the atoms and molecules of a chemical equation can help you understand it.

4. Which of the following statements supports the idea that rusting is an exothermic reaction?

   (1) During the process of rusting, small amounts of heat energy are released.
   (2) Activation energy produces rust on metals such as iron.
   (3) Rusting affects only certain substances exposed to oxygen.
   (4) During the process of rusting, metal absorbs heat energy.
   (5) Rusting occurs more quickly in humid conditions than in dry conditions.

5. Which of the following conclusions can be supported by the information in the passage?

   (1) Electricity and magnetism result from both endothermic and exothermic reactions.
   (2) Covalent bonds are formed during exothermic reactions, and ionic bonds are formed during endothermic reactions.
   (3) Boiling water is an exothermic process that releases heat energy as water molecules heat up.
   (4) Some exothermic reactions are more useful for the energy they release than for their products.
   (5) Any chemical reaction can start with or without activation energy.

6. In a gas burner, natural gas combines with oxygen to yield carbon dioxide and water, giving off large amounts of heat. Many gas burners have electrical ignition, which generates a spark as the burner is turned on. What role does the spark play in the chemical reaction?

   (1) It is a reactant.
   (2) It is a product.
   (3) It provides activation energy.
   (4) It slows the reaction.
   (5) It stops the reaction.

Answers start on page 301.

GED Practice • Lesson 16

Directions: Choose the one best answer to each question.

Questions 1 through 4 refer to the following passage.

You may not think of the kitchen as being a chemistry lab, but many chemicals can be found right on your kitchen shelf. One substance that contains several interesting chemicals is baking powder, which is used to make cake batter rise.

The principal ingredient in baking powder is sodium bicarbonate, $NaHCO_3$. When sodium bicarbonate reacts with an acid, it produces water and the gas carbon dioxide (CO_2). When sodium bicarbonate is heated to baking temperatures, it breaks down to form carbon dioxide and sodium carbonate (Na_2CO_3), a bland tasting salt. Baking powder also contains a compound, such as a tartrate, that will react with water to form acids.

1. What is the purpose of the tartrate in baking powder?

    (1) to provide an acid for sodium bicarbonate to react with
    (2) to break down to form carbon dioxide
    (3) to react with carbon dioxide
    (4) to provide a salt that makes dough rise
    (5) to react with water to form sodium bicarbonate

2. To make some kinds of baked goods rise, bakers mix sour milk with sodium bicarbonate. Based on the passage, which statement supports the idea that sour milk contains an acid?

    (1) It is found in baking powder.
    (2) It can be heated to baking temperatures.
    (3) It reacts with water.
    (4) It reacts with sodium bicarbonate to produce CO_2 and H_2O.
    (5) It breaks down to form CO_2 and Na_2CO_3 when heated to baking temperatures.

3. When baking powder is added to batter, which substance causes the cake to rise?

    (1) salt
    (2) oxygen gas
    (3) water
    (4) tartrate
    (5) carbon dioxide gas

4. When baking powder is left uncovered in damp weather, it quickly loses its effectiveness. Which of the following statements helps explain why this happens?

    (1) Moisture in the air causes sodium bicarbonate to break down.
    (2) Oxygen in the air causes the tartrate to break down.
    (3) Moisture in the air reacts with the tartrate.
    (4) Oxygen in the air reacts with carbon dioxide.
    (5) Oxygen in the air reacts with sodium bicarbonate.

Question 5 refers to the following table.

Heat Energy Released by Combustion with Oxygen	
Fuel	Heat Energy Released per gram of fuel (in kilocalories)
Methane	13.3
Natural Gas	11.6
Heating Oil	11.3
Coal (anthracite)	7.3
Wood	4.5

5. Which of the following comparisons is supported by the information in the table?

    (1) Natural gas releases less heat than oil.
    (2) Methane provides the most heat.
    (3) Wood gives off half as much heat as oil.
    (4) Wood gives off more heat than coal.
    (5) Coal gives off more heat than oil.

CONTROLLING CHEMICAL REACTIONS

Questions 6 through 8 refer to the following passage.

Over the years, chemists have developed many ways to control chemical reactions. For example, they can vary temperature, pressure, concentration, acidity, and other factors to control the rate and outcome of a reaction. However, these techniques are often imprecise. They usually work by exciting the molecules, increasing their vibrations, causing the weakest bonds to break first.

There are situations in which more precise control is needed. For example, a chemist may want to break the strongest bonds first in order to ensure that a chemical reaction takes the desired course. In this type of situation, a new method holds promise.

In the new technique, interacting beams of light from two lasers are used to control a chemical reaction. By varying the intensity of the lasers' interactions, scientists can control which bonds in the molecules break apart first. This procedure gives scientists more control over the products of the reaction.

Although this method is experimental, it has the potential for practical application. Many chemical reactions proceed simultaneously along different pathways to yield a mixture of compounds. This can be a problem for drug manufacturers and others who are trying to produce one pure compound without other compounds in the product.

For example, some reactions produce chiral molecules. These are pairs of molecules that have the same chemical formula but are mirror-images in structure. One chiral molecule is designated the "right-handed" molecule and the other is designated the "left-handed" molecule. The left-handed and right-handed molecules often have very different properties. For example, the right-handed form of the drug thalidomide is a fairly safe sedative. The left-handed form, however, caused many birth defects in the 1960s. For the manufacture of such chemicals, the new laser technique may improve quality control.

6. Which is the most important way in which the laser technique for controlling chemical reactions differs from earlier methods?

   (1) It uses light beams.
   (2) It uses modern technology.
   (3) It is more precise.
   (4) It has practical applications.
   (5) It controls pressure and temperature.

7. What is the role of the interacting laser beams in the new technique?

   (1) To supply more reactants.
   (2) To function as products.
   (3) To provide activation energy.
   (4) To create mixtures.
   (5) To create compounds.

8. Some chemical reactions can be controlled at the molecular level. According to the passage, which statement is evidence of this?

   (1) Scientists vary temperature, pressure, concentration, and other factors to control reactions.
   (2) Laser control of reactions allows scientists to break specific bonds between atoms.
   (3) Thalidomide manufacturers produced both left-handed and right-handed versions of the drug.
   (4) Control of chemical processes is possible using different forms of technology.
   (5) The laser technique may be used by drug and other manufacturers to ensure that they produce quality products.

TIP When you are asked to identify evidence that supports a conclusion, look for logical relationships linking the evidence and the conclusion.

Answers start on page 301.

Directions: This is a ten-minute practice test. After ten minutes, mark the last question you finished. Then complete the test and check your answers. If most of your answers were correct but you didn't finish, try to work faster next time. Choose the <u>one best answer</u> to each question.

<u>Questions 1 through 4</u> refer to the following passage and diagram.

Three important groups of chemical compounds are acids, bases, and salts. When dissolved in water, these compounds produce ions. Ions are atoms or molecules with an electric charge. In water, acids produce hydrogen, or H^+ ions. In water, bases produce hydroxide, or OH^- ions. Citric acid is found in citrus fruits. Vitamin C is ascorbic acid. Magnesium hydroxide is a base that is the active ingredient in many stomach remedies. Sodium bicarbonate is a base in baking soda and baking powder.

A strong acid, such as sulfuric acid, or a strong base, such as sodium hydroxide, is poisonous and can burn the skin. Yet a weak acid, such as citric acid, or a weak base, such as magnesium hydroxide, can be safely handled and even ingested (eaten).

The strength of an acid or base is measured on a scale called the pH scale. The pH scale generally ranges from 0 to 14. The number 7 is the neutral point. Substances with a pH below 7 are acidic, and substances with a pH above 7 are basic. Extremely strong acids have a pH of 0; extremely strong bases have a pH of 14.

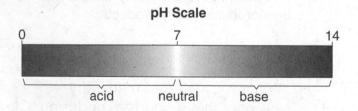

pH Scale

When an acid and a base combine chemically, the results are two neutral compounds: water and a salt. One familiar salt is sodium chloride, table salt.

1. Which of the following is correctly ordered from lowest to highest pH?

   (1) magnesium hydroxide, citric acid, pure water, sulfuric acid, sodium hydroxide
   (2) pure water, sulfuric acid, citric acid, sodium hydroxide, magnesium hydroxide
   (3) sulfuric acid, sodium hydroxide, citric acid, magnesium hydroxide, pure water
   (4) sulfuric acid, citric acid, pure water, magnesium hydroxide, sodium hydroxide
   (5) sodium hydroxide, magnesium hydroxide, pure water, citric acid, sulfuric acid

2. An antacid is a medication that relieves indigestion caused by stomach acid. Which ingredient in an antacid has this soothing effect?

   (1) a salt
   (2) an acid
   (3) a base
   (4) H^+ ions
   (5) water

3. When calcium hydroxide, a base, reacts with citric acid, the reaction produces calcium citrate and water. What is calcium citrate?

   (1) a strong acid
   (2) a weak acid
   (3) a salt
   (4) a weak base
   (5) a strong base

4. What would be the pH of a solution of table salt and water?

   (1) 0
   (2) 4
   (3) 7
   (4) 10
   (5) 14

Questions 5 through 9 refer to the following passage and chart.

Labels on food often list amounts of saturated and unsaturated fats. A saturated molecule is one that contains only single bonds, in which one pair of electrons is shared in each bond. Unsaturated molecules contain other types of bonds, in which more than one pair of electrons are shared.

A saturated hydrocarbon is saturated with hydrogen. That is, it contains more hydrogen than an unsaturated hydrocarbon with the same number of carbon atoms. One example of a saturated hydrocarbon is ethane, C_2H_6. An example of an unsaturated molecule is ethene, C_2H_4. In the unsaturated hydrocarbon ethene, two electrons of one carbon atom are paired with two electrons of another carbon atom, forming a double bond.

In certain reactions, the double and triple bonds of an unsaturated hydrocarbon can be broken. Hydrogen can then be added to the molecule. A reaction in which hydrogen is added to an unsaturated hydrocarbon is called an addition reaction.

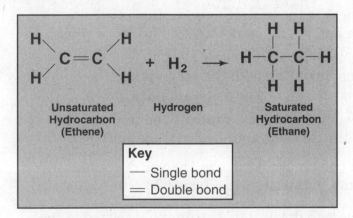

Unsaturated Hydrocarbon (Ethene)   Hydrogen   Saturated Hydrocarbon (Ethane)

Key
— Single bond
= Double bond

5. Which of the following elements is involved in an addition reaction involving hydrocarbons?

(1) oxygen
(2) nitrogen
(3) lithium
(4) neon
(5) hydrogen

6. In contrast to a saturated molecule, what does an unsaturated molecule contain?

(1) hydrogen atoms
(2) only single bonds
(3) shared electrons
(4) double (or triple) bonds
(5) carbon atoms

7. Which of the following is a fact stated about ethane?

(1) It is an unsaturated hydrocarbon molecule.
(2) Single bonding occurs between its carbon atoms.
(3) Double bonding occurs between its carbon atoms.
(4) Its atoms contain only two electrons.
(5) It has four hydrogen atoms.

8. Which statement does the diagram support about the addition reaction shown?

(1) One reactant is a saturated hydrocarbon.
(2) Both reactants are hydrocarbons.
(3) The reactants are H_2 and C_2H_6.
(4) The product contains a double bond.
(5) The product is C_2H_6.

9. Which of the following conclusions is supported by the information presented?

(1) Saturated hydrocarbons can be produced from unsaturated hydrocarbons through addition reactions.
(2) Unsaturated hydrocarbons can be produced from saturated hydrocarbons by means of addition reactions.
(3) In addition reactions, the number of carbon atoms in the original molecule increases.
(4) Ethene can be made from ethane by means of an addition reaction.
(5) Under certain conditions, hydrocarbons react with chlorine to form compounds containing hydrogen, carbon, and chlorine.

Answers start on page 302.

We bring our knowledge and experience of the world to bear on everything we do. For example, when a person writes a science article, he or she brings a lot of relevant knowledge to the task of writing. You bring a lot of relevant knowledge to the task of reading. Therefore, the writer does not explain everything in great detail. He or she assumes that you know a lot already. Thus when you read, it's important to recognize the unstated assumptions of a passage. Recognizing unstated assumptions will help you understand what you read.

TIP

When looking for unstated assumptions, draw on the things you already know and your experiences of the world.

Read the passage. Then answer the questions that follow.

When you are a passenger in a car, you are free to watch things whiz by on the side of the highway. Telephone poles, trees, houses, buildings all speed by you. In contrast, the car door and the driver don't seem to move at all. They stay right next to you.

Now, suppose you are standing on the side of the same road. The cars, with their drivers, move quickly past you, but the telephone poles, trees, houses, and buildings don't move an inch.

1. Put a check mark next to the unstated assumption related to the reason the car door and the driver do not seem to move when you are in the car.

_____ a. You are moving along with the car door and the driver and dashboard, so they appear stationary to you.

_____ b. Your view out the window distracts you from the fact that you, the car door, and the driver are all moving.

You were correct if you checked *option a*. The writer assumes you understand that all motion is relative to a person's point of view.

2. Put a check mark next to the unstated assumption related to the reason the cars appear to move when you are standing on the side of the road, but the trees and poles do not appear to move.

_____ a. The cars only appear to be moving, and the trees and poles are not actually moving.

_____ b. The cars are moving relative to your position, and the trees and poles are not.

You were correct if you checked *option b*. Again, the writer assumes you know that all motion is relative to your frame of reference. Thus, objects that are moving at the same rate you are appear to be motionless; you perceive motion only in objects whose motion differs from your own.

Use the passage and the graphs to answer the questions below.

When you describe the motion of an object, you can discuss how far the object moved. Or you can discuss how fast the object moved. Or you can tell how much time the object was in motion. One way to describe an object's motion is with a graph.

The graph on the left shows the distance a train traveled during a particular period of time. The graph on the right shows the train's average speed during that time period.

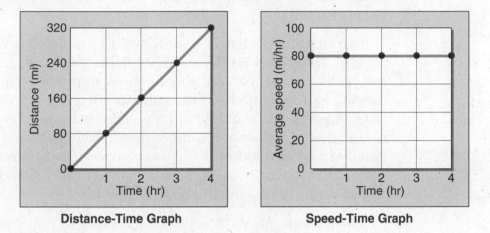

Distance-Time Graph   **Speed-Time Graph**

1. Put a check mark next to the distance the train had traveled after three hours.

   _____ a. 80 miles

   _____ b. 240 miles

2. Put a check mark next to the average speed at which the train was traveling during the four hours.

   _____ a. 80 miles per hour

   _____ b. 320 miles per hour

3. In the speed-time graph, the speed shown is constant. Put a check mark next to an unstated assumption suggested about the speed of the train.

   _____ a. The actual speed of the train did not vary during the course of the four-hour trip.

   _____ b. The average speed of the train is not the same thing as the actual speed of the train.

4. Put a check mark next to an unstated assumption about the relationship between the two graphs.

   _____ a. Time is shown on one axis of each graph.

   _____ b. Speed is shown on one axis of each graph.

   _____ c. The graphs show two aspects of the same trip.

Answers start on page 303.

GED CONTENT Motion and Forces

A **force** is a push or pull that acts on matter, changing an object's speed or direction of movement. For example, if you are pushing a child in a stroller, you can make the stroller go faster by increasing the amount of force you are applying. You can also change the direction in which the stroller is going by changing the angle at which you apply the force. Any change (either increase or decrease) in the speed of an object or in its direction of motion is called **acceleration.**

The English scientist Sir Isaac Newton formulated laws about motion. **Newton's First Law of Motion** states that an object at rest tends to remain at rest, and an object in motion tends to keep moving in a straight line at the same speed, unless acted upon by outside forces. For example, when you throw a ball, it eventually falls to the ground and stops rolling. It stops moving because the force of gravity has pulled it down, and the friction from the air and the ground has slowed it down. Without gravity or friction, the ball would continue moving in a straight line forever.

The tendency of an object to keep moving or remain at rest is called **inertia.** You notice inertia when a bus in which you are riding suddenly stops and the standing passengers lurch forward and must struggle to stay on their feet. Because of inertia, the people on the bus keep moving forward.

Newton's Second Law of Motion states that an object accelerates, changing speed and/or direction, when a force acts upon it. The mass of the object and the size and direction of the force that acts upon it will affect how fast and in what direction the object accelerates. For example, a large truck requires more force than a small car to accelerate away from a stoplight at the same rate. Newton's second law can be expressed by the formula:

$$\text{force} = \text{mass} \times \text{acceleration}$$

NEWTON'S FIRST LAW OF MOTION

No force acts on skateboard; skateboard is stationary.

No force acts on skateboard; skateboard moves at constant speed. (Not really possible because friction acts to slow the speed.)

NEWTON'S SECOND LAW OF MOTION

A force acts on skateboard; the skateboard increases in speed (accelerates).

Directions: Choose the one best answer to each question.

Questions 1 through 6 refer to the passage and the diagrams on page 184.

1. Which of the following situations is an example of Newton's First Law of Motion?

   (1) A man finds that pushing a full wheelbarrow takes more force than pushing an empty one.
   (2) A package on the seat of a car going 60 miles per hour slides forward when the car stops suddenly.
   (3) Passengers notice that a bus travels more smoothly at 50 miles per hour than at 25 miles per hour.
   (4) A car stuck on an ice patch is able to move when a rough mat is placed under the back wheels.
   (5) A football player intercepts a pass and runs in the opposite direction from which the ball was thrown.

2. Once a spacecraft reaches outer space, inertia keeps it moving in a straight line at a constant speed, even without its engine. Which of the following is most likely to cause the spacecraft to change direction?

   (1) running out of fuel
   (2) energy from the sun
   (3) the force of friction
   (4) the force of gravity
   (5) acceleration

3. An engineer designs a racing car with a powerful engine and a lightweight body. What assumption is she making?

   (1) An object at rest tends to remain at rest.
   (2) An object in motion tends to remain in motion.
   (3) Large force and small mass yield rapid acceleration.
   (4) Large force and small mass yield constant motion.
   (5) Large force and small mass yield great inertia.

4. According to Newton's laws, an outside force would be required to make which of the following situations occur?

   (1) A cyclist coasting at 5 miles per hour continues to coast at the same speed in the same direction.
   (2) A person who stood through the first hour of a sold-out concert stands through the second hour.
   (3) A passenger sits on the subway as the train travels at a constant speed for four minutes.
   (4) A rocket traveling through space continues to maintain its speed and move in a forward direction.
   (5) A car traveling at 40 miles per hour goes around a curve at the same speed.

5. Newton's Second Law of Motion describes the relationship among which factors?

   (1) mass and acceleration
   (2) direction and force
   (3) direction, force, and acceleration
   (4) mass, force, and acceleration
   (5) mass, direction, and acceleration

6. Football teams use large, heavy players in the defense lines and smaller, lighter players in the backfield to run and catch passes. What is the assumption behind this assignment strategy?

   (1) Small players accelerate quickly, while large players apply force to stop opponents.
   (2) Large players tend to remain at rest, while light players tend to remain in motion.
   (3) Light players can catch passes, while large players can tackle.
   (4) Large players tend to move in a straight line, while light players change direction easily.
   (5) The force needed to stop a large player is greater than that needed to stop a small one.

Answers start on page 303.

Directions: Choose the one best answer to each question.

Questions 1 and 2 refer to the following passage and diagram.

According to **Newton's Third Law of Motion,** if one object exerts a force on a second object, then the second object exerts an equal and opposite force, called the reaction force, on the first object.

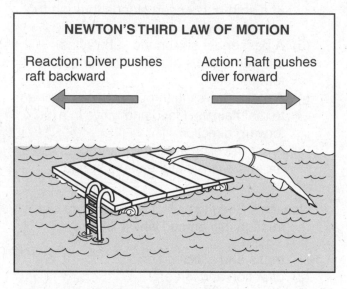

NEWTON'S THIRD LAW OF MOTION

Reaction: Diver pushes raft backward

Action: Raft pushes diver forward

You can feel the effects of Newton's Third Law if you dive off the side of an unanchored or lightly tethered raft. Your feet push off the raft; the raft pushes you forward at the same time that you are pushing the raft backward.

1. Which of the following is an example of a reaction force?

   (1) hot air rushes out of a balloon
   (2) wind blowing against a kite
   (3) a ball hitting a wall
   (4) the backward "kick" of a fired rifle
   (5) a swimmer's stroke against the water

TIP

When you are looking for a specific example of a general law in science, substitute the specific elements of the example for the general elements of the law to see whether they fit.

2. A rocket engine is designed to take advantage of Newton's Third Law of Motion. Which of the following causes a rocket engine to move forward?

   (1) air flowing through the engine from the front to the back
   (2) the lift caused by differences in air speed over the top and bottom of the engine
   (3) the force exerted by gases escaping the rear of the engine
   (4) the force of gravity pulling the rocket back to Earth
   (5) the force of friction exerted by the air past which the rocket travels

3. According to Isaac Newton, the **momentum** of an object can be found by multiplying its mass by its **velocity** (speed). For example, if someone taps your hand with a ruler, you barely feel it. However, if someone brings the ruler down fast on your hand, the blow hurts. The ruler has not gotten heavier, but its velocity has increased, increasing its momentum. Newton showed that to change an object's momentum you must apply a force. When the ruler hits your hand, you supply the force to stop the ruler, which is why the blow hurts.

Which of the following statements supports the idea that a speeding truck has more momentum than a small car moving at the same speed?

   (1) The truck has a larger mass than the car does.
   (2) The car has a larger mass than the truck does.
   (3) The truck has a larger velocity than the car does.
   (4) The car has a larger velocity than the truck does.
   (5) The truck and the car experience relative motion.

THE PHYSICS OF SEATBELTS AND AIR BAGS

Questions 4 through 6 refer to the following passage and diagram.

According to Newton's First Law of Motion, a body in motion tends to stay in motion unless acted upon by an outside force. Thus when a car collides with a tree, it stops abruptly. Inside the car, however, the driver's inertia keeps him moving forward until his motion is stopped by the steering column, dashboard, or windshield— or his seatbelt.

Let's use a specific example to see how a seatbelt works. Suppose a car going 30 miles per hour collides with a tree and crumples 1 foot (that is, from point of impact to where the car stops is 1 foot). If the driver, who weighs 160 pounds, is not wearing a seatbelt, he keeps moving forward rapidly and meets the windshield. His motion from point of impact until his body's motion stops is only a few inches because the windshield does not continue moving after the car stops. In this case the force of the impact on the driver is about 12 tons.

Now suppose this accident occurred while the driver was wearing a seatbelt. The seatbelt would restrain his forward motion after the collision. But from initial impact with the seatbelt he continues to move with the car and a little farther before stopping, about 1.5 feet. In this case the force of the impact would be about 1.6 tons. Wearing a seatbelt reduces the impact force dramatically.

What does an air bag do? The air bag does not affect the force of the impact. Instead, it distributes the impact force over a large area, decreasing the pressure on any given point of the driver's body.

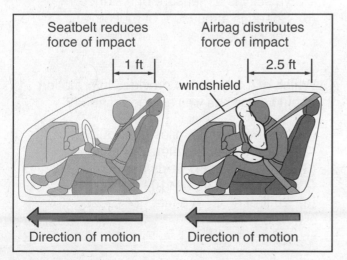

Seatbelt reduces force of impact | Airbag distributes force of impact
1 ft | 2.5 ft
windshield

Direction of motion | Direction of motion

4. Which of the following is an unstated assumption suggested by this passage?

(1) Inertia keeps the driver moving forward when the car is stopped in a collision.
(2) In a collision, a driver not wearing a seatbelt is stopped by a part of the car.
(3) Air bags have caused as much harm as good in car crashes.
(4) The less the impact force on the driver, the less serious his injuries are likely to be.
(5) Air bags spread the impact force over a large area of the driver's body.

5. How does a seatbelt work?

(1) by restraining forward motion and increasing the impact force
(2) by restraining forward motion and decreasing the impact force
(3) by allowing forward motion and decreasing the impact force
(4) by allowing forward motion and increasing the impact force
(5) by concentrating the impact force on a small area of the body

6. The principle by which an air bag works is most similar to which of the following?

(1) a hot air balloon, which rises because the gases inside the balloon are less dense than the gases outside it
(2) a jet engine, which moves an airplane forward with a force equal and opposite to that of the hot gases escaping out the back
(3) a system of pulleys, which reduces the force needed to move a load a certain distance
(4) ball bearings, which reduce the friction between the moving parts of a machine, increasing its efficiency
(5) snowshoes, which spread the weight of a person over a large area, allowing her to walk on the surface of the snow

Answers start on page 304.

Directions: This is a ten-minute practice test. After ten minutes, mark the last question you finished. Then complete the test and check your answers. If most of your answers were correct but you didn't finish, try to work faster next time. Choose the <u>one best answer</u> to each question.

<u>Questions 1 and 2</u> refer to the following passage and diagram.

Gravity is a force of attraction that affects all matter. The force of gravity between any two objects depends on their mass and the distance between them.

For example, Earth exerts gravity on objects near its surface, pulling them toward its center. When you release an object like a ball, it falls straight down. Earth also exerts gravity on distant objects like the moon. Because the moon is far away, the force of Earth's gravity is weaker. Earth's gravity is too weak to cause the moon to fall to Earth. However, it is strong enough to exert a pull on it. If Earth were not exerting gravity, the moon would travel in a straight line according to Newton's First Law of Motion. Instead, it travels in an orbit around Earth.

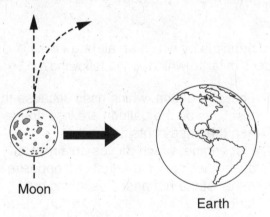

Moon

Earth

1. How does the diagram show the force of gravity acting between Earth and the moon?

(1) The straight, dashed arrow shows the force of Earth's gravity propelling the moon.
(2) The curved, dashed arrow shows the force of Earth's gravity propelling the moon.
(3) The solid arrow shows the pull of Earth on the moon.
(4) The solid arrow shows that the moon is moving straight toward Earth.
(5) The distance between the moon and Earth indicates that a force is acting to push them apart.

2. Which of the following is an unstated assumption about mass that is important for understanding the passage?

(1) Mass is the volume of an object.
(2) Mass is the amount of matter in an object.
(3) The force of gravity is related to an object's mass.
(4) Some objects do not have any mass.
(5) The mass of objects cannot be measured.

<u>Questions 3 and 4</u> refer to the following paragraph.

Speed is the distance an object travels in a given amount of time. Velocity is different from speed because it includes both speed and direction of motion.

3. What is the difference between speed and velocity?

(1) Speed involves distance, and velocity involves time and distance.
(2) Speed involves distance divided by time, and velocity involves distance.
(3) Speed involves distance divided by time, and velocity involves speed as well as direction.
(4) Speed is a measure of motion, and velocity is a measure of distance.
(5) Speed is a measure of motion, and velocity is a measure of time.

4. Which of the following provides information about velocity as well as about speed?

(1) 100 miles at 60 miles per hour
(2) 17 meters at 3 meters per second
(3) 100 yards at 10 yards per minute
(4) 900 kilometers at 110 kilometers per hour
(5) 20 feet north at 5 feet per second

Questions 5 and 6 refer to the following passage.

A force that slows down or prevents objects from moving is friction. One example of friction is air resistance, which you can feel if you stick your hand out the window of a moving car.

A more exciting way to experience air resistance is the sport of sky diving. When a sky diver first jumps from a plane, the only force affecting her is gravity, which pulls her downward. As she falls faster, friction from the passing air increases, slowing her acceleration. Eventually, at about 100 to 150 miles per hour, the force of friction balances the force of gravity, and she stops accelerating. This is called her terminal velocity. Terminal velocity depends mainly on the sky diver's mass and the body position she holds.

When the sky diver opens her parachute, she increases the area affected by air resistance. She slows to about 25 miles per hour, a much safer terminal velocity for a landing.

5. A sky diver landed with a terminal velocity of 27 miles per hour. On his next jump the next day, his terminal velocity was only 24 miles per hour. Which of the following was most likely to have decreased his terminal velocity?

   (1) He jumped from a higher altitude.
   (2) His body mass was lower.
   (3) He chose a different landing site.
   (4) He used a parachute with a larger surface area.
   (5) The plane was traveling at a slower speed.

6. In order to calculate the time it would take for a sky diver to reach Earth, you need to know the distance she must fall and the surface area and mass of her parachute. What other information are you likely to need?

   (1) her mass
   (2) her volume
   (3) her height
   (4) speed of airplane
   (5) type of airplane

7. Friction between two solid objects can be reduced by lubricating them—inserting a layer of fluid between them. Because the molecules in fluids like oil flow freely, they allow easier movement between the two surfaces.

What would be the result of running an engine that is low on oil?

   (1) decreased friction on the moving parts
   (2) increased friction on the moving parts
   (3) decreased friction on the stationary parts
   (4) increased friction on the stationary parts
   (5) easier movement of the engine's parts

8. An object moving in a circle is always changing direction. The force that keeps an object moving in a circle is called centripetal force. For example, when you whirl a ball at the end of a string, the force of the string pulls the ball to the center. The ball's inertia keeps it from falling into the center.

Which of the following is most similar to centripetal force described above?

   (1) a bullet eventually falling to Earth
   (2) the force of friction on a slide
   (3) the pull of Earth's gravity on a space station
   (4) the attraction between opposite electric charges
   (5) a sky diver reaching terminal velocity

9. The average speed of an object is found by dividing the total distance traveled by the time. Instantaneous speed is the object's speed at any given moment. Which of the following is an example of instantaneous speed?

   (1) a bird flitting from branch to branch
   (2) a baseball traveling 90 feet in 3 seconds
   (3) a 1,000-mile drive that takes two days
   (4) a car accelerating from 0 to 30 miles per hour
   (5) a car whose speedometer reads 65 miles per hour

Answers start on page 305.

Lesson 18

GED SKILL Assessing the Adequacy of Visual Information

In science, diagrams, charts, and drawings can help you understand objects, processes, and ideas. However, be careful about the conclusions you draw from this type of information. For example, a diagram may show the parts of a machine. You can figure out how the machine works by studying the diagram. But the diagram won't enable you to figure out how *well* the machine works. To do that, you would need more data. To assess the adequacy of data in visuals to support a generalization or conclusion, concentrate on what is actually shown rather than adding your own interpretation or drawing conclusions that are not supported by the information.

Study the passage and the diagrams. Then answer the questions that follow.

A group of scientists, design students, and people working in Antarctica are designing a bicycle suitable for polar conditions. The extreme cold and drifting snow make conventional mountain bikes useless there. The designs being tested include three types of wide-tread wheels and tires.

TIP

When determining whether a conclusion is supported by a diagram, think of the diagram as a source of data. Ask yourself whether these data are sufficient to enable you to draw that conclusion.

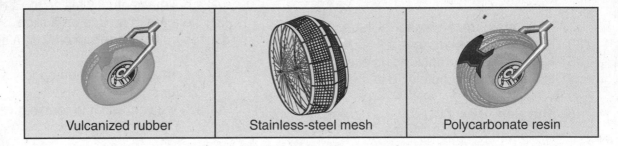

| Vulcanized rubber | Stainless-steel mesh | Polycarbonate resin |

1. Put a check mark next to the wheel type that is <u>most similar</u> to that of a regular bicycle.

_____ a. wheel with vulcanized rubber tires

_____ b. stainless steel mesh wheel

_____ c. hollow, polycarbonate resin wheel

You were correct if you checked *option a*. The diagrams show that the wheel with rubber tires is <u>most similar</u> to those of a regular bicycle.

2. Put a check mark next to the information you would need to decide which wheel design works best.

_____ a. detailed drawings of how the wheels look and work

_____ b. results of the tests conducted on each wheel type

You were correct if you checked *option b*. Only data from an actual test can prove one wheel works better than the others.

Use the passage and the diagrams to answer the questions below.

Lifting an object straight up requires a great deal of **effort,** or force. However, the distance you must lift the object, or **load,** is short. On the other hand, moving the same object up a sloping ramp takes much less effort, but the distance to the top is greater.

COMPARING FORCE AND DISTANCE

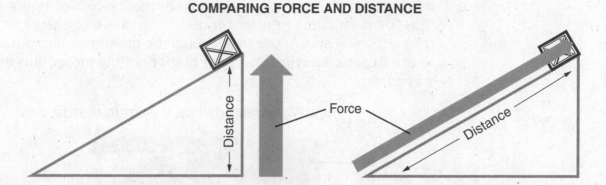

In both cases the amount of work you do is the same. In physics, **work** is done when a force moves an object over a distance in the direction of that force. This relationship can be expressed as

work = force × distance

1. Write *M* next to the main idea of this passage.

   _____ a. It takes more effort to lift an object straight up than to move it over a greater distance to the same point.

   _____ b. Work is done when a force moves an object over a distance, and it can be expressed by the formula *work = force × distance*.

2. Write *D* next to a detail in the passage that supports the main idea.

   _____ a. Moving a heavy object along a ramp to the top takes less effort than lifting it straight up.

   _____ b. *work = force × distance*

3. Write *D* next to a detail in the diagrams that supports the main idea.

   _____ a. The distance along the slope is greater than the distance straight up the side.

   _____ b. The vertical face of the ramp is on the right side of the diagram.

4. Put a check mark next to each bit of data you would need in order to calculate the amount of work done in the diagrams.

   _____ a. the force applied to the crate

   _____ b. the distance the crate travels

   _____ c. the volume of the crate

Answers start on page 305.

Energy is the ability to do work—to move matter from one place to another. It is measured in joules (J) in the metric system and in foot-pounds in the English system. When work is done, energy is transferred from one object to another and is often changed from one form to another in the process. However, the total amount of energy in a system remains the same. Energy cannot be created or destroyed. This is known as the principle of the conservation of energy. As the diagram below shows, the total energy the motor supplies is the sum of the **kinetic energy** (energy of motion) of the motor plus its waste heat.

ENERGY TRANSFER IN AN ELECTRIC MOTOR

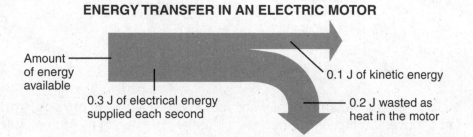

Amount of energy available

0.3 J of electrical energy supplied each second

0.1 J of kinetic energy

0.2 J wasted as heat in the motor

Let us look at an example of energy transfer. To lift an object such as a hammer, you use the energy stored in your arm muscles. Some of your energy is changed into kinetic energy, as you move the hammer. Some of the energy in your arm is changed into **potential energy**, or the energy of position. Potential energy is stored energy. The higher you lift the hammer, the more potential energy you give it. Potential energy is released when matter moves. Drop the hammer and its potential energy changes into kinetic energy as it falls.

Kinetic energy   Potential energy   Kinetic energy

You learned about other examples of energy transfer when you studied how substances change state (see Lesson 14). For instance, when you apply heat energy to a pot of water, the kinetic energy of the water molecules increases and they move more rapidly. The water boils. At that point, some of the molecules have enough kinetic energy to break away from the liquid, escaping as a gas.

Directions: Choose the one best answer to each question.

Questions 1 through 6 refer to the passage and the diagrams on page 192.

1. Which of the following is an example of kinetic energy?

   (1) a boy sitting still
   (2) a turning Ferris wheel
   (3) a cat sleeping on a window ledge
   (4) a plate on the edge of a table
   (5) a coat hanging in a closet

2. Which of the following is an example of potential energy?

   (1) a woman jogging
   (2) a moving bicycle
   (3) a car parked on a hill
   (4) wind
   (5) a swiftly flowing stream

3. A person lifts up a book and places it on a table. Which of the following conclusions about the book's energy is supported by the information in the diagrams of the hammer?

   (1) The book has no energy while it is moving.
   (2) Once it stops moving, the book has no energy.
   (3) The book loses energy when it is lifted onto the table.
   (4) The book has potential energy during lifting; it has kinetic energy at rest on the table.
   (5) The book has kinetic energy during lifting; it has potential energy at rest on the table.

TIP
When examining a diagram to see whether its data support a conclusion, read the labels. They usually point out important details.

4. A roller coaster ride begins as a chain slowly pulls the cars to the top of the first hill. How does the energy of the cars change during this time?

   (1) The cars gain potential energy gradually as they move higher.
   (2) The cars have the same amount of potential energy until they reach the top of the hill, and then potential energy increases.
   (3) The cars gain kinetic energy gradually as they move higher.
   (4) The cars lose potential energy gradually as they move higher.
   (5) The cars transfer some of their potential energy to the chain.

5. In which of the following changes of state are molecules of matter losing kinetic energy?

   (1) melting from solid to liquid
   (2) boiling from liquid to gas
   (3) evaporation from liquid to gas
   (4) condensation from gas to liquid
   (5) in superheating steam

6. In the diagram of energy transfer in an electric motor, near the top of page 192, the width of the shaft of the electrical energy arrow is the same as the total width of the shafts of the kinetic energy and heat energy arrows. What principle does this represent?

   (1) Electrical energy is more powerful than kinetic and heat energy.
   (2) Energy is needed to move matter, or do work.
   (3) Potential energy is the energy of a stationary object.
   (4) Kinetic energy is the energy of an object in motion.
   (5) Energy is conserved in a system; it is neither created nor destroyed.

Answers start on page 306.

GED Practice • Lesson 18

Directions: Choose the <u>one best answer</u> to each question.

<u>Questions 1 through 3</u> refer to the following paragraph and diagram.

Humans have learned to change one form of energy into another in order to power machines. For example, the chemical energy in gasoline is converted to heat energy in a car's engine and then to mechanical energy to move the car. Electrical energy is converted to light energy in the headlights and to sound energy in the car stereo. Still, we are not very efficient converters of energy. Most of the energy escapes into the environment as heat.

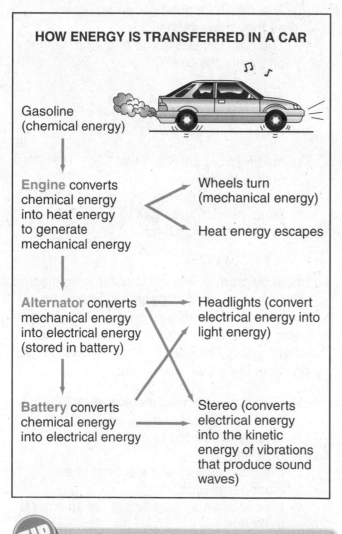

HOW ENERGY IS TRANSFERRED IN A CAR

Gasoline (chemical energy)

Engine converts chemical energy into heat energy to generate mechanical energy

Wheels turn (mechanical energy)

Heat energy escapes

Alternator converts mechanical energy into electrical energy (stored in battery)

Headlights (convert electrical energy into light energy)

Battery converts chemical energy into electrical energy

Stereo (converts electrical energy into the kinetic energy of vibrations that produce sound waves)

TIP
The main idea of a diagram is often stated in its title. Arrows may be used to indicate relationships between various parts of the diagram.

1. What are the sources of chemical energy that help a car run?

   (1) the battery and lubricating oil
   (2) lubricating oil and gasoline
   (3) gasoline and the battery
   (4) the battery and the engine
   (5) the engine and the drive train

2. Which of the following data would give you the best indication of a car's efficiency?

   (1) the amount of heat that escapes
   (2) the capacity of its gasoline tank
   (3) the miles it travels per gallon of gasoline
   (4) the miles between rotating tires
   (5) the mix of air and gas in the car's engine

3. Which machine is powered directly by mechanical energy from a human being?

   (1) a motorcycle
   (2) a bicycle
   (3) an automatic garage door opener
   (4) an electric lawn mower
   (5) a clothes dryer

4. Energy on Earth comes from nuclear reactions in the sun. The sun's energy reaches Earth in the form of heat and light. On Earth, green plants convert light energy to chemical energy through photosynthesis. Animals get their energy by eating plants or other animals.

   If this energy conversion through photosynthesis decreased, what would be the effect on Earth?

   Earth would have

   (1) greater light energy from the sun
   (2) less light energy from the sun
   (3) greater heat energy from the sun
   (4) less energy available for living things
   (5) more energy available for living things

GASOLINE-ELECTRIC HYBRID CARS

Questions 5 through 7 refer to the following passage.

The automobile may be one of the best-loved machines on Earth, but it uses a great deal of an important nonrenewable resource: gasoline, refined from oil, a valuable fossil fuel. Autos also contribute to environmental problems, releasing many pollutants and waste heat into the air.

In a conventional automobile, gasoline burned in the engine provides heat energy, which is converted to mechanical energy to power the drive train. The battery is used simply to provide electrical energy to start the vehicle and to help power parts such as headlights. Almost all of the energy in a traditional automobile comes from burning gasoline.

An all-electric car is much cleaner than a conventional car. It powers the engine with electrical energy produced by batteries. The main drawback of all-electric cars is their limited driving range. Most can drive only about 80 miles before their batteries need recharging. And recharging the batteries is time-consuming— taking from three to eight hours.

A more practical design is a vehicle that combines a small gasoline engine with an electric motor powered by batteries that are recharged automatically by the running of the gasoline engine; so with the gasoline-electric hybrid car, the batteries do not need to be plugged in to be recharged. These hybrid vehicles are of two basic types. In a series hybrid, the gasoline engine provides heat energy to generate electrical energy that is stored as chemical energy in the batteries. The batteries, in turn, provide electrical energy to run the motor that produces mechanical energy to power the drive train. In a parallel hybrid, both the gasoline engine and electric motor can power the drive train directly.

Gasoline-electric hybrid cars use less gasoline than comparable conventional cars. Because they burn less gasoline, they produce less heat and air pollution as well. Auto manufacturers sold the first gasoline-electric hybrid cars in the United States in 1999.

5. Which type of energy powers the drive train in a parallel gasoline-electric hybrid car?

   (1) heat energy only
   (2) electrical energy only
   (3) either heat or electrical energy
   (4) light energy
   (5) nuclear energy

6. Why are gasoline-electric hybrid cars more practical than all-electric cars?

   (1) They have a greater driving range and their batteries recharge automatically.
   (2) They get more miles per gallon than all-electric cars.
   (3) They give off less heat pollution than all-electric cars.
   (4) They give off less air pollution than electric cars.
   (5) In both types of cars, an electric motor can power the drive train.

7. The sales history of all-electric cars has been poor, even in places like Europe and Japan, where gas costs several times what it costs in the United States. What does this indicate that car buyers value the most?

   (1) contributing to a cleaner environment
   (2) conserving nonrenewable resources
   (3) the convenience of a conventional car
   (4) the lower operating costs of electric cars
   (5) setting trends with new technology

TIP

When things are being compared and contrasted, make a chart listing the characteristics of each thing. That will help you sort out the similarities and differences between or among them.

Answers start on page 306.

GED Mini-Test • Lesson 18

Directions: This is a ten-minute practice test. After ten minutes, mark the last question you finished. Then complete the test and check your answers. If most of your answers were correct but you didn't finish, try to work faster next time. Choose the <u>one best answer</u> to each question.

<u>Questions 1 through 4</u> refer to the following paragraph and diagrams.

The transfer of heat from one object to another can be explained in terms of moving molecules. The molecules in hot objects have more kinetic energy and move faster than the molecules in cold objects. When two objects come in contact with each other, the higher-energy molecules in the warmer object begin to collide with the molecules in the cooler object. Energy is transferred in the process. This process shows that coldness is actually the absence of heat. As heat energy leaves an object, the object becomes less warm, or cold.

HEAT TRANSFER BETWEEN TWO OBJECTS

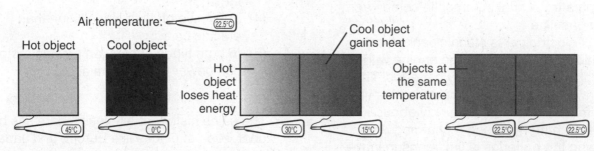

1. According to the diagrams, when does the heat transfer stop?

   (1) when all the molecules stop moving
   (2) when the two objects are at the same temperature
   (3) when the two objects are pulled apart
   (4) when the cold object loses heat to the hot object
   (5) when the cold object begins to warm up

2. Which of the following is <u>most similar</u> to the action of molecules in a <u>heated substance</u>?

   (1) a car traveling in a straight line
   (2) a ball rolling
   (3) popcorn popping
   (4) Earth rotating on its axis
   (5) a truck coming to a sudden stop

3. As an ice cube in your hand melts, your hand begins to feel cold. Which of the following conclusions about heat transfer is supported by the information in the passage and the diagram?

   (1) Cold from the ice flows into your hand.
   (2) Your hand's heat is absorbed by the ice.
   (3) The ice loses heat energy and melts.
   (4) Molecules in your hand gain energy.
   (5) Molecules in the ice lose energy.

4. What other heat transfer involving the objects in the diagrams is likely to take place?

   (1) The cold object transfers heat to the hot object.
   (2) The cold object transfers heat to the air.
   (3) The air transfers heat to the hot object.
   (4) The hot object transfers heat to the air.
   (5) No other heat transfer is likely to occur.

Questions 5 and 6 refer to the following paragraph and diagram.

In a single-pulley system, the load moves the same distance as the rope that is pulled. A pulley does not increase the effort force, but it changes its direction. Instead of lifting something up, you are pulling something down.

HOW A SINGLE PULLEY WORKS

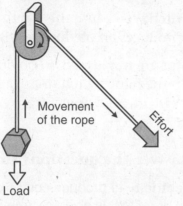

5. Which information would you need in order to calculate the distance the load moves in this pulley system?

   (1) size of the pulley wheel
   (2) distance the rope is pulled
   (3) weight of the load
   (4) effort force
   (5) total length of the rope

6. In an ideal single-pulley system, the effort equals the load. In real life, the effort is always slightly greater than the load. Why?

   (1) The distance pulled on the rope is equal to the distance the load moves.
   (2) The distance pulled on the rope is greater than the distance the load moves.
   (3) The distance pulled on the rope is less than the distance the load moves.
   (4) As the load moves up, it becomes heavier, so the rope puller exerts more effort.
   (5) The friction from the pulley wheel must be overcome by the effort used in pulling the rope.

7. Most of the heat energy from gasoline powered engines is not converted to mechanical energy. Instead, it is wasted.

   Based on this information, why is the temperature on heavily traveled streets higher than the temperature on streets with less traffic?

   (1) The heavily traveled streets absorb more sunlight than the less traveled streets.
   (2) Heat released from many cars raises the temperature of heavily traveled streets.
   (3) The wearing away of road surfaces increases the heat on heavily traveled streets.
   (4) Heavily traveled streets have fewer trees to provide shade.
   (5) More heat-generating industries are near heavily traveled streets.

8. Power is the rate at which work is done. If a 165-pound man runs up a 10-foot high flight of stairs, he does 1650 foot-pounds of work. If he does this in 3 seconds, his power is 550 foot-pounds per second (1650 foot-pounds divided by 3 seconds). This is equal to one horsepower.

   Horsepower is used to describe the power of an engine. In cars, engines that produce more horsepower can carry a greater load and can accelerate into traffic more easily. However, these engines use more fuel than lower-horsepower engines.

   Which of the following situations would be most likely to require you to replace a low-horsepower car with one that has a more powerful engine?

   (1) You changed jobs and now drive a longer distance to work.
   (2) You want to save money on fuel.
   (3) You are moving to a place that gets a lot of snow and are concerned about driving on slippery roads.
   (4) Your new job requires you to transport heavy supplies in your car.
   (5) You are concerned about air pollution.

Answers start on page 307.

Lesson 19

GED SKILL Analyzing Cause and Effect

When you think about cause and effect, you are thinking about how one thing influences another. A cause is what makes something happen. An effect is what happens as a result of the cause.

When you flip on a light switch, you cause the lights to come on. This obvious action, or cause, produces an obvious result, or effect.

Cause-and-effect relationships are not always so obvious. What is really happening when you flip the light switch, for example, is that you are completing an electric circuit, allowing current to flow into the bulb and produce light.

Study the passage. Then answer the questions that follow.

A photocopier uses **static electricity** to produce copies of documents. Inside the photocopier is a metal drum that is given a negative electric charge. Lenses project an image of the document onto the drum. Where light strikes the metal drum, the electric charge disappears. Only the dark parts of the image on the drum remain negatively charged. The copier contains a dark powder called toner. The positively charged toner is attracted to the negatively charged dark parts of the image on the drum. Then a piece of paper rolls over the drum. The toner is transferred to the paper and sealed by heat. A warm photocopy comes out of the machine.

1. Put a check mark next to the statement that explains why toner forms an image of the document on the drum.

    _____ a. The positively charged toner is attracted to the negatively charged areas of the drum.

    _____ b. Heat from the machine causes the toner to form the image of the document.

You were correct if you checked *option a*. The dark parts of the image are negatively charged on the drum. They attract the positively charged particles of toner.

2. Put a check mark next to the statement that tells what would happen if just light were projected onto the drum when you were making a photocopy.

    _____ a. A blank sheet of copy paper would emerge.

    _____ b. A grayish-black sheet of copy paper would emerge.

You were correct if you checked *option a*. Since light would reach all areas of the drum, the negative charge would disappear, leaving nothing to attract the toner. Thus the copy would be blank.

TIP

When evaluating cause-and-effect situations, read the passage carefully to discover possible causes and effects. Use definitions and equations in the passage to figure out these relationships.

Use the passage and the diagrams to answer the questions below.

As you know, atoms are made up of particles called protons, electrons, and neutrons. Protons and electrons have a property called electric charge. Protons are positively charged (+) and electrons are negatively charged (−). Neutrons have no charge; they are neutral (0).

The forces of attraction between the positively charged protons and the negatively charged electrons help hold an atom together. There is a basic rule of electric charge: Unlike charges attract each other, while like charges repel each other.

When electrons move from the atoms of one object to another, the objects take on a temporary charge called static electricity. For example, if you rub a comb with a cloth, the friction causes the comb to gain electrons and become negatively charged. When the negatively charged comb is placed near small pieces of paper, the paper's electrons are repelled, and its surface gains a positive charge. The diagram shows how the comb and paper bits then interact.

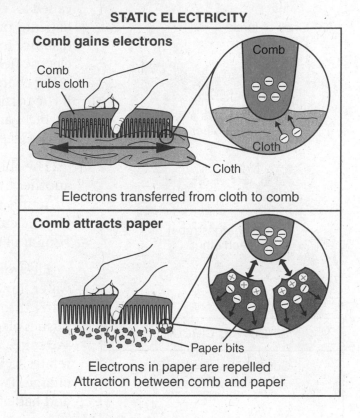

STATIC ELECTRICITY

Comb gains electrons
Comb rubs cloth
Comb
Cloth
Cloth
Electrons transferred from cloth to comb

Comb attracts paper
Paper bits
Electrons in paper are repelled
Attraction between comb and paper

1. An atom that has an equal number of protons and electrons has an overall neutral charge. Put a check mark next to the charge the atom would have if it gained an electron.

_____ a. It would have a negative charge.

_____ b. It would have a positive charge.

2. According to the passage and the diagram, when the negatively charged comb is placed near the paper, the electrons in the paper move away from the surface, which becomes positively charged. Put a check mark next to the results.

_____ a. The paper moves away from the comb.

_____ b. The paper moves closer to the comb.

3. Atoms and molecules with an overall electric charge are called ions. Place a check mark next to the likely result of mixing positively and negatively charged ions.

_____ a. The negative and positive ions will attract each other.

_____ b. The positive ions will remain grouped together.

Answers start on page 308.

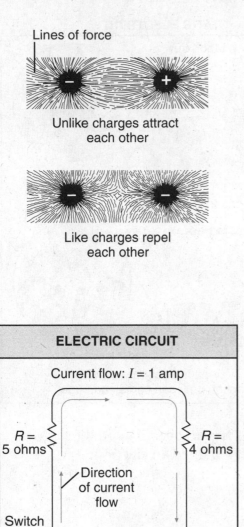

Lines of force

Unlike charges attract
each other

Like charges repel
each other

ELECTRIC CIRCUIT

Current flow: I = 1 amp

$R =$
5 ohms

$R =$
4 ohms

Direction
of current
flow

Switch

9 Volt
Battery

The area of force that surrounds a charged particle is called an **electric field.** The strength of an electric field depends on the distance from the charged particle—as the distance increases, the strength of the field decreases. The electric field of a charged particle exerts a force on any other charged particle. The force will be one of attraction if the particles are of unlike charge, and repulsion if the particles are of like charge. The force of an electric field causes electrons to move.

The ability of electrons to move from one place to another makes **electric current** possible. Electric current is the flow of electrons or other charged particles. Electric current flowing through wires is what powers your appliances.

Electrons flow through a wire in much the same way as water flows through a hose. Just as water pressure pushes water through a hose, a type of electrical "pressure" pushes electrons through a wire. This "pressure" is called **voltage.** Voltage is measured in units called volts, which relates to the energy the voltage source provides per charge. Two common sources of voltage are generators and batteries.

For electric current to flow, electrons must have a closed, continuous pathway over which to travel. Such a pathway is provided by an **electric circuit.** An electric circuit usually consists of a source of electrons, a load or resistor, and a switch to open and close the circuit. In the diagram the source of electrons is a 9-volt battery. The wavy lines are resistors. A resistor can be a light bulb, an appliance, or a motor—anything that uses or slows the flow of electrical energy.

Electric current (I) is measured in amperes (amps for short). Resistance (R) is measured in ohms. Current, resistance, and voltage (V) are related by the following equation:

$$V = I \times R$$
$$9V = I \times (4\ ohms + 5\ ohms)$$
$$9 = I \times 9$$
$$1 = I$$

Directions: Choose the <u>one best answer</u> to each question.

<u>Questions 1 through 7</u> refer to the passage and the diagrams on page 200.

1. What is an electric field?

   (1) a charged particle
   (2) a flow of electrons
   (3) a group of electrons
   (4) a group of protons
   (5) an area of force

2. What would be the effect of decreasing the distance between the unlike charged particles in the top diagram on page 200?

   (1) increasing their electric charges
   (2) decreasing their electric charges
   (3) increasing the flow of electricity
   (4) increasing their force of attraction
   (5) decreasing their force of attraction

3. In the passage, why is voltage compared to water pressure?

   (1) Both provide energy to move electrons from one place to another.
   (2) Both make possible the flow of something from one place to another.
   (3) Both are measured in units of energy called volts.
   (4) Both involve the transfer of charged particles.
   (5) Both can be used to power a chemical battery.

TIP To answer a question asking "why" something occurs, you should look for a cause in the passage or diagram.

4. What is electric current?

   (1) the attraction of opposite charges
   (2) the attraction between protons and electrons
   (3) the flow of electrons or other charged particles
   (4) something that slows the flow of electrons
   (5) the voltage of an energy source

5. What is the purpose of a switch in an electric circuit?

   (1) to open and close the circuit, controlling the flow of current
   (2) to provide energy to start the flow of electrons
   (3) to speed up the flow of electric current
   (4) to slow the flow of electric current
   (5) to provide energy to power the resistance

6. If the voltage in the circuit on page 200 were increased to 18 volts and the resistor remained the same, what would be the effect on the current?

   (1) It would stay the same.
   (2) It would be cut in half.
   (3) It would double.
   (4) It would decrease to zero.
   (5) It would be equal to the voltage.

7. If more resistance were added to the circuit on page 200 and the voltage remained the same, what would be the result?

   (1) an increase in current
   (2) a decrease in current
   (3) the current would stop flowing
   (4) the switch would open
   (5) a greater number of electrons would pass through each resistor

Answers start on page 308.

GED Practice • Lesson 19

Directions: Choose the one best answer to each question.

Questions 1 through 4 refer to the following passage and diagram.

As the diagram shows, a magnetic field forms around a wire when electric current flows through the wire. This relationship between electricity and magnetism is known as **electromagnetism.**

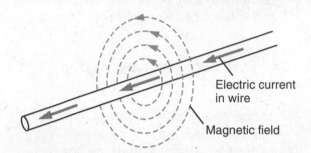

Electric current in wire

Magnetic field

Powerful temporary magnets called electromagnets can be made by wrapping coils of wire around soft iron and passing an electric current through the wire. When the current passing through the wire is turned off, the electromagnet loses its magnetic properties. When the current is turned back on, the electromagnet regains its magnetic properties. The strength of an electromagnet depends on the number of loops of wire and the size of the current.

1. The relationship between electricity and magnetism described in the passage is best expressed by which of the following statements?

   (1) Electromagnets form magnetic fields.
   (2) Magnets cause electricity.
   (3) Wrapping wire around iron causes magnetism.
   (4) An electric current produces a magnetic field.
   (5) A magnetic field can be produced by an iron magnet.

2. A crane at a construction site has a large electromagnet. The electromagnet will make the crane most useful for which of the following tasks?

   (1) carrying pieces of iron to distant sites
   (2) picking up pieces of metal on the site and depositing them elsewhere on the site
   (3) generating electricity for the area surrounding the site
   (4) melting pieces of scrap metal at the site
   (5) lifting all objects too heavy for other types of machines on the site to move

3. Every magnet has a north pole and a south pole. Opposite poles attract, and like poles repel. Thus the south pole of a compass needle points to Earth's magnetic north pole. When a compass is placed near a current-carrying wire, the compass needle turns away from north. Why does this happen?

   (1) The needle can no longer point north.
   (2) The wire in the circuit is pointing north.
   (3) The needle responds to the magnetic field produced by the current in the wire.
   (4) Electrons in the needle are moving back and forth.
   (5) The compass needle has become an electromagnet.

4. Which hypothesis can be supported by the information in the passage and the diagram?

   (1) Electromagnets are stronger than natural magnets.
   (2) Once electromagnets were invented, natural magnets no longer had any use.
   (3) A magnet can reverse the direction of an electric current.
   (4) The strength of an electromagnet depends upon the material used to make the magnet.
   (5) Magnetism is related to the movement of electrons.

THE DISCOVERY OF ELECTROMAGNETISM

Questions 5 through 7 refer to the following passage.

During a lecture in 1820, the Danish physicist Hans Oersted noticed that an electric current he produced changed the direction of a nearby compass needle. He concluded that an electric current could produce a magnetic field. Thus, Oersted was the first to demonstrate that electricity and magnetism are related—a discovery that changed human history because it made possible machines that employ electromagnetism.

Shortly afterward, a French scientist, André-Marie Ampère, proved that wires could behave like magnets when electrical current passed through them. He also showed that reversing the direction of the current reversed the polarity of the magnetic field.

In 1821, English scientist Michael Faraday showed the reverse of what Oersted had observed: that a magnet could cause a current-carrying wire to move. This phenomenon is the underlying principle of the electric motor, which converts electrical energy into mechanical energy. By 1840, several inventors had produced electric motors of varying designs and efficiency. Faraday also discovered that a moving magnetic field causes electric current to flow in a wire. This phenomenon underlies the production of electricity in generators.

5. Which important discovery did Oersted make?

    (1) An electric current flowing through a wire produces a magnetic field.
    (2) Earth has a magnetic field that causes compass needles to point north.
    (3) A magnetic field causes an electric current to flow.
    (4) A magnet causes a current-carrying wire to move.
    (5) An electric motor converts electrical energy to mechanical energy.

6. Which of the following is an unstated assumption based on the passage?

    (1) An electric current produces a magnetic field.
    (2) An electric motor is based on electromagnetism.
    (3) A compass needle is magnetic.
    (4) Electricity and magnetism are related.
    (5) Oersted discovered electromagnetism.

7. Which of the following was a result of the discovery of electromagnetism?

    (1) the use of fossil fuels to power internal combustion engines
    (2) the use of steam to power locomotives
    (3) the use of windmills to pump water
    (4) the large-scale generation of electricity by means of moving magnetic fields
    (5) the use of batteries to produce electrical energy

8. The ancient Chinese, Greeks, and Romans were familiar with magnetism as a natural property of certain rocks such as lodestones. However, until the 1200s, magnetism had few practical uses aside from compasses, which were first used in navigation around that time. However, with the discoveries of Oersted, Ampère, and Faraday in the 1800s, interest in magnetism increased sharply.

Which of the following most likely accounts for the increased interest in magnetism in the 1800s?

    (1) New uses for lodestones were found.
    (2) Navigation was much more accurate with magnetic compasses.
    (3) There were more scientists in the 1800s than in previous centuries.
    (4) A renewed interest in ancient civilizations sparked scientific discoveries.
    (5) Electromagnetism had many potentially valuable applications.

Answers start on page 308.

GED Mini-Test • Lesson 19

Directions: This is a ten-minute practice test. After ten minutes, mark the last question you finished. Then complete the test and check your answers. If most of your answers were correct but you didn't finish, try to work faster next time. Choose the <u>one best answer</u> to each question.

Questions 1 through 3 refer to the following paragraph.

A conductor is a substance that allows electric current to flow through it easily. Metals such as copper, gold, and aluminum are the best conductors. An insulator is a substance that resists the flow of electrons. Insulators tend to be nonmetals such as glass, plastic, and porcelain.

1. Which of the following is a good insulator?

    (1) aluminum
    (2) copper
    (3) gold
    (4) rubber
    (5) silver

2. Which of the following would be the best use for a conductor?

    (1) electrical wire for a lamp
    (2) an electrical outlet cover
    (3) shoe soles for electrical line repairers
    (4) decorative base for a lamp
    (5) the outside of a light bulb

3. Which of the following conclusions is supported by the information in the paragraph?

    (1) A silver pipe is likely to have a lower resistance than a plastic pipe.
    (2) How well a substance conducts electricity depends on its temperature.
    (3) Silver is a better insulator than porcelain.
    (4) A glass tube is likely to have a lower resistance than a copper tube.
    (5) Electrons move more readily through nonmetals than through metals.

Questions 4 and 5 refer to the following paragraph and diagrams.

In a series circuit, there is only one path for the electric current. When the circuit is broken, the current stops flowing. In a parallel circuit, the current flows in two or more separate paths. If the current in one path is interrupted, it still flows in the other branches.

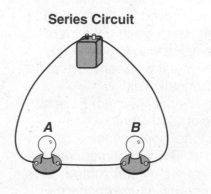 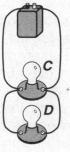

Series Circuit   **Parallel Circuit**

4. Look at the diagrams. Assume that the light bulbs labeled *A* and *C* have burned out. Which of the following will occur as a result?

    (1) The wire between *A* and *B* needs to be replaced.
    (2) Bulb *B* also will not light.
    (3) Bulb *D* also will not light.
    (4) The parallel circuit needs to be rewired.
    (5) Both circuits need a new battery.

5. One light bulb in a kitchen circuit burns out, but the other lights on the same circuit still work. Which statement supports the conclusion that the kitchen uses a single parallel circuit?

    (1) A power failure caused the light to go out.
    (2) The current stopped in the entire circuit.
    (3) The current continues in all but one path of the circuit.
    (4) A circuit breaker shut off the current.
    (5) The burned-out bulb was on its own series circuit.

Questions 6 and 7 refer to the following paragraph and diagram.

In a simple electric motor, direct current from a battery flows through a coil inside a fixed magnet. When current flows through the coil, it becomes magnetic, with a north and south pole. Since like poles repel and unlike poles attract, the coil makes a half turn so its north pole faces the magnet's south pole. The flow of current through the coil is then reversed, reversing the magnetic field. The coil makes another half turn. As the current continues to reverse, the coil, which is attached to the shaft of the motor, keeps turning.

ELECTRIC MOTOR

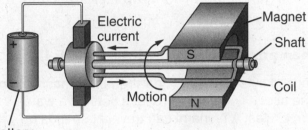

6. Based on the passage and the diagram, what turns the shaft of the motor?

   (1) the battery
   (2) the rotation of the coil
   (3) the rotation of the magnet
   (4) the poles of the magnet
   (5) the center of the magnet

7. What would happen if current in the coil flowed continuously in the same direction?

   (1) The coil would stop turning.
   (2) The coil would turn more rapidly.
   (3) The magnetic field of the fixed magnet would reverse.
   (4) The magnetic field of the coil would reverse.
   (5) The battery would never run down.

8. Electromagnetic induction is the use of magnetism to produce electricity. A bar magnet is pushed through a wire coil, producing an electric current as long as the magnet keeps moving.

Which of the following makes use of the principle of electromagnetic induction?

   (1) an electromagnet, which uses electricity to produce a magnetic field
   (2) a turbine, which is powered by moving fluid
   (3) an internal combustion engine, which burns fuel to produce heat energy
   (4) a battery, which uses chemical energy to produce electricity
   (5) a generator, which uses a magnetic field to produce electricity

Question 9 refers to the following chart.

FORCE	DESCRIPTION
Gravity	Force of attraction between a star, planet, or moon and the objects on and near it
Electro-magnetic	Force of attraction between negatively charged electrons and positively charged protons, which holds atoms together
Weak nuclear	Force that causes radioactive decay of atomic nuclei
Strong nuclear	Force that holds protons and neutrons together in atomic nuclei

9. Which of the following fundamental forces involves attraction between objects that can be easily seen every day in the world around you?

   (1) gravity
   (2) electromagnetism
   (3) the weak nuclear force
   (4) the strong nuclear force
   (5) All of the forces operate only on the subatomic level.

Answers start on page 309.

GED SKILL Identifying Faulty Logic

When you read science materials, you need to watch for instances of faulty logic. One type of faulty logic is called the **circular argument.** In a circular argument, the reasons supporting a conclusion simply restate the conclusion itself. Suppose Janna said that Lowell is handsome because he is good looking. This is a circular argument. The meaning of handsome is good looking, so Janna is not providing any evidence or reasons to conclude that Lowell is indeed good looking.

Another form of faulty logic is the **hasty generalization.** In a hasty generalization, a conclusion is based on insufficient evidence. If Janna sees Lowell once from afar and concludes he is handsome, that is a hasty generalization. Janna didn't see Lowell clearly enough to conclude that he was handsome.

circular argument
a form of faulty logic in which a conclusion is supported by reasons that simply restate the conclusion

hasty generalization
a form of faulty logic in which a conclusion is based on insufficient evidence

Study the passage. Then answer the questions that follow.

A tsunami is a **wave** caused by an undersea earthquake, landslide, or volcanic eruption. When the ocean floor is disturbed, it sets off a water wave that travels outward in circles. A tsunami can travel at speeds up to 500 miles per hour. Out at sea, the wave may be only one or two feet high. When it reaches shallow coastal water, the wave rapidly grows much higher. By the time it reaches shore, a tsunami may be 50 feet or higher. Such waves can wipe out coastal areas. From 1992 to 1997, tsunamis killed more than 1800 people around the Pacific Ocean.

When reading, check the logic of the facts, ideas, and conclusions presented. Ask yourself, does this make sense? Is this conclusion what the facts show?

1. Put a check mark next to the reason tsunamis are dangerous.

_____ a. They pose many hazards.

_____ b. They cause floods, kill people, and damage property.

You were correct if you checked *option b.* It cites specific reasons tsunamis are dangerous. *Option a* is incorrect because it's a circular argument. It is simply another way of saying tsunamis are dangerous.

2. Write C next to the conclusion that is supported by sufficient evidence from the passage.

_____ a. Most tsunamis occur in the Pacific Ocean.

_____ b. A tsunami is not very dangerous while it is out at sea.

You were correct if you chose *option b.* A one- or two-foot wave is not dangerous. *Option a* is a hasty generalization. The Pacific death toll is not sufficient evidence to conclude that tsunamis usually occur there.

Use the passage and diagram to answer the questions below.

A wave is a disturbance that travels through space or matter. Waves transfer energy from one place to another. All waves, including water waves, have certain basic characteristics.

When the sea is absolutely calm, the water is at its rest position. As a wave rises, the water reaches a high point. The high point is called the **crest.** The distance from the rest position to the crest is the **amplitude.** The greater the amplitude, the greater the energy of the wave.

As the wave falls, it reaches a low point called the **trough.** The trough is the same distance from the rest position as the crest is. The **wavelength** is the distance between two similar points in a wave cycle. For instance, the wavelength can be measured from one trough of the wave to the next.

A WAVE

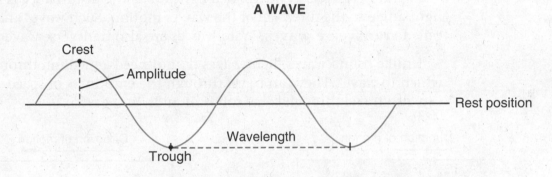

1. Put a check mark next to the best explanation of what a wave is.

   _____ a. a disturbance that travels through space or matter

   _____ b. a shape or outline having curves one after another

2. Put a check mark beside the conclusions that are hasty generalizations based on the information in the passage and diagram.

   _____ a. All waves have certain basic characteristics such as amplitude and wavelength.

   _____ b. Every wave has a wavelength that is at least twice its amplitude.

   _____ c. A 10-foot-high wave has more energy than a 5-foot-high wave.

   _____ d. Wavelength can be determined by measuring the distance between two consecutive crests or troughs.

   _____ e. To accurately measure wavelength, you need at least two troughs.

3. "Most surfers prefer waves with a great amplitude because they are high." The previous sentence is an example of circular reasoning. Put a check mark beside the statement below that <u>best</u> explains how the reasoning is circular.

   _____ a. The waves have great energy and are fun to ride.

   _____ b. Saying a wave has great amplitude is the same as saying it is high.

   _____ c. There is not enough evidence that surfers prefer high waves.

Answers start on page 310.

Sounds travel as waves. For a sound wave to travel, it must have a medium, a substance capable of transmitting the wave. The medium can be a solid, a liquid, or a gas. Most of the sounds we hear travel through air, a gas. However, we can also hear sounds underwater and through solids like walls.

A sound wave pushes the molecules of the medium back and forth parallel to the sound wave's line of motion. During one complete cycle of a sound wave, the molecules are pushed together in a compression, then spread out in a rarefaction. You can think of the wave's motion as push forward–pull back. Such waves are called **longitudinal waves.**

Light also travels as waves. In a light wave, the disturbance is at a right angle to the direction of the wave's motion. Such waves are called **transverse waves.** Water waves are also transverse waves.

Unlike sound waves, light waves do not need a medium through which to travel. They can travel through the emptiness of space. They can also travel through some solids, liquids, and gases.

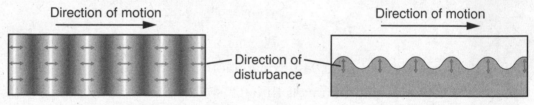

Ordinary light, called white light, has waves of many different wavelengths. Each color has its own wavelength. When white light passes through a triangular piece of glass called a prism, each color of light bends at a specific angle. As a result, the light emerging from the prism shows the colors of the visible spectrum: red, orange, yellow, green, blue, indigo (blue-violet), and violet.

LIGHT THROUGH A PRISM

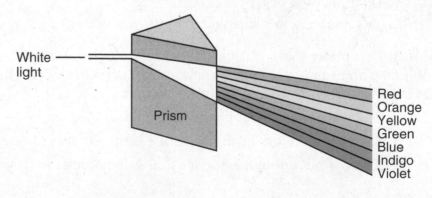

Directions: Choose the <u>one best answer</u> to each question.

<u>Questions 1 through 6</u> refer to the passage and the diagrams on page 208.

1. What does the motion of a longitudinal wave most resemble?

   (1) an ocean wave as it approaches the shore
   (2) a pulsating rope held between two people
   (3) an accordion being played
   (4) a ball bouncing along a paved street
   (5) a bicycle traveling on a bumpy road

2. The moon has no atmosphere. Which item would be useless to take along on a trip to the moon?

   (1) a flashlight
   (2) thermal underwear
   (3) an oxygen supply attached to a space suit
   (4) a space helmet with built-in CD player and earphones
   (5) a stereo and speaker system

3. What forms white light?

   (1) one color of visible light
   (2) the colors of a prism
   (3) colorless light that varies in brightness
   (4) a mix of all the colors of visible light
   (5) longitudinal waves in space

TIP Preview the diagram that accompanies text. Then refer to the diagrams whenever necessary, to help you better understand the passage.

4. As white light passes through a prism, of all the emerging colors of light, violet light is bent the most. Which of the following statements is supported by information from the passage and from the bottom diagram on page 208?

   (1) Green light is bent the least.
   (2) Orange light forms three separate beams of light split by other colors.
   (3) Red light is bent the least.
   (4) Yellow light is bent to the same angle as blue light.
   (5) Indigo light is bent the least.

5. "All transverse waves can travel through empty space." Which of the following statements provides evidence that this is a hasty generalization?

   (1) Light waves can travel through empty space.
   (2) Water waves require water through which to travel.
   (3) Sound waves can travel through liquid, solid, or gas.
   (4) White light from the sun travels through a vacuum to Earth.
   (5) White light bends as it passes through a prism.

6. As sound waves move away from their source, their energy decreases. What is the result of this decrease in energy?

   (1) The sound waves travel faster.
   (2) The sound waves travel slower.
   (3) The sound waves travel in a straight line.
   (4) The sound becomes louder.
   (5) The sound becomes softer.

Answers start on page 311.

GED Practice • Lesson 20

Directions: Choose the one best answer to each question.

Questions 1 through 4 refer to the following passage and diagram.

Electromagnetic radiation is a wave motion of oscillating electric and magnetic fields. The electric and magnetic fields are perpendicular to one another and to the direction in which the wave is traveling.

Electromagnetic waves range from the very long wavelengths of radio waves to the extremely short wavelengths of gamma waves. The range of electromagnetic waves is called the **electromagnetic spectrum**. The only waves in the spectrum that we can see are visible light.

All electromagnetic waves travel at the same speed through a vacuum. The speed of light in a vacuum is 186,282 miles per second.

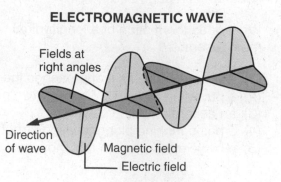

ELECTROMAGNETIC WAVE

Fields at right angles

Direction of wave

Magnetic field

Electric field

ELECTROMAGNETIC SPECTRUM

Wavelength in meters

10^{-11} 10^{-10} 10^{-9} 10^{-8} 10^{-7} 10^{-6} 10^{-5} 10^{-4} 10^{-3} 10^{-2} 10^{-1} 1 10 10^2 10^3 10^4

Gamma rays

X rays

Ultraviolet — Visible spectrum — Infrared

Microwaves

Radiowaves

1. What is electromagnetic radiation?

   (1) electromagnetic waves of varying wavelengths
   (2) a wave with disturbance in one direction
   (3) a longitudinal wave with alternating compressions and rarefactions
   (4) electric and magnetic fields that oscillate in a wave
   (5) one type of visible light

2. In what direction is the disturbance in an electromagnetic wave?

   (1) parallel to the direction of motion
   (2) at right angles to the direction of motion
   (3) at 45-degree angles to the direction of motion
   (4) back and forth in the same direction as motion
   (5) in circles around the direction of motion

3. How do visible light waves differ from radiowaves?

   (1) Light waves consist only of moving magnetic fields.
   (2) Light waves consist only of moving electric fields.
   (3) Light waves have shorter wavelengths.
   (4) Radio waves must travel through air.
   (5) Radio waves are sound waves.

4. Based on the diagram and the passage, which of the following statements is true of infrared waves?

   (1) They are produced by X-ray machines.
   (2) They travel through a vacuum at 186,282 miles per second.
   (3) They travel faster through space than radio waves do.
   (4) Some have a wavelength of 100 meters.
   (5) They are not electromagnetic waves.

CELL PHONES AND BRAIN CANCER?

Questions 5 through 7 refer to the following passage.

Cell phones give off low levels of electromagnetic radiation in the microwave range. High levels of this type of radiation can produce biological damage through heating—that's how a microwave oven works. But can the low levels emitted by cell phones cause health problems in humans? Of particular concern is a possible link between cell phones with built-in antennas, which are held close to the head, and brain cancer.

To date, there is no definitive judgment on the safety of cell phones. The scientific evidence from animal studies is conflicting. In one study, mice that had been genetically altered to be predisposed to develop a certain type of cancer did develop more cases of that cancer when exposed to low-level microwave radiation than did the control group. In other animal studies, the results have been inconclusive.

Studies of humans have not found any association between brain cancer and cell phone use. It is true that some people who use cell phones develop brain cancer. But people who do not use cell phones also develop brain cancer. About 80,000,000 people use cell phones in the United States today. About 4,800 cases of brain cancer would be expected to develop each year among those 80,000,000 people, whether or not they use cell phones. As long-term use of cell phones increases, further studies, of both animals and humans, will be needed to clarify the relationship—if any—between cell phone use and the development of brain cancer.

TIP When deciding whether you have enough information to support a conclusion, ask yourself, is the information adequate to support the conclusion or if it only suggests that it *might* be true.

5. Why do some people think cell phone use may lead to brain cancer?

(1) Cell phones emit microwaves near the head.
(2) Distance causes transmission to break up.
(3) Mice exposed to operating cell phones have developed cancer.
(4) Cell phone use has grown dramatically in the last five years.
(5) Cell phones are wireless.

6. Which of the following steps could a cell phone user take to minimize exposure to microwave radiation?

(1) Use the cell phone outdoors in wide open spaces.
(2) Use a cell phone with a remote antenna to lessen microwave intensity near the head.
(3) Alternate the side of the head to which the cell phone is held.
(4) Use the cell phone to receive incoming calls only.
(5) Use the cell phone to make outgoing calls only.

7. Which of the following conclusions is supported by the information in the passage?

(1) In all studies, low levels of microwave emissions caused cancer in laboratory animals.
(2) Cell phone use is associated with certain types of brain cancer in humans.
(3) Low levels of microwaves are sufficient to heat foods in microwave ovens.
(4) No definitive link has been found between cell phone use and brain cancer.
(5) People who use cell phones have a higher risk of developing brain cancer.

Answers start on page 311.

Directions: This is a ten-minute practice test. After ten minutes, mark the last question you finished. Then complete the test and check your answers. If most of your answers were correct but you didn't finish, try to work faster next time. Choose the one best answer to each question.

Questions 1 and 2 refer to the following passage.

Frequency is the number of waves that pass a given point in a specific unit of time. For example, if you watched an object in the ocean bob up and down ten times in one minute, the frequency of the wave would be ten cycles per minute. In order to count one complete cycle, both a crest and a trough of the wave must pass.

If you know the wavelength (distance between two consecutive crests) and frequency of a wave, you can find its speed. If the frequency of the wave is measured in Hertz (waves per second), and the wavelength is measured in meters, then the speed in meters per second is given by this equation:

$$\text{speed} = \text{wavelength} \times \text{frequency}$$

1. What relationship does a wave's frequency involve?

   (1) height and distance between crests
   (2) height and distance between troughs
   (3) distance between crests and amplitude
   (4) number of cycles that pass a given point and unit of time
   (5) number of cycles that pass a given point and distance

2. What is the result of decreased wavelength or decreased frequency?

   (1) decreased speed
   (2) the same speed
   (3) increased speed
   (4) increased distance
   (5) decreased distance

Questions 3 and 4 refer to the following paragraph and diagram.

In a microwave oven, a magnetron produces a beam of microwaves, a type of electromagnetic radiation. The microwaves strike molecules of water in food, causing the water molecules to align and reverse alignment. The rapid and repeated twisting of the water molecules produces heat.

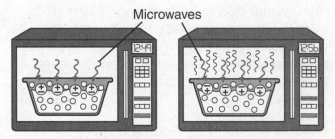

Microwaves

1. Water molecules align   2. Water molecules reverse alignment

3. What is the best title for this diagram?

   (1) Cooking with Electromagnetic Radiation
   (2) The Effect of Microwaves on Water Molecules
   (3) The Purpose of a Magnetron
   (4) Microwaves Change Over Time
   (5) The Design of the Microwave Oven

4. Which of the following conclusions is supported by information in the passage and diagram?

   (1) All types of electromagnetic radiation can cause water molecules to twist.
   (2) A microwave oven converts heat energy to electromagnetic energy.
   (3) A microwave oven heats food using the same principle as a conventional oven.
   (4) Food with a high water content heats more rapidly in a microwave oven than dry food does.
   (5) Microwave ovens pose a radiation hazard to people near them.

Questions 5 and 6 refer to the following paragraph.

Sound waves travel best through solids, because the molecules are packed tightly together. Elastic solids, such as nickel, steel, and iron, carry sound especially well; inelastic solids, such as sound-proofing materials, carry sound less well. Liquids are second-best in carrying sound, and gases are least effective.

5. Why is gas the least effective medium for the transmission of sound waves?

   (1) Its molecules are too close together.
   (2) Its molecules are too far apart.
   (3) It is too dense.
   (4) It is elastic.
   (5) Sound waves travel more slowly through it.

6. Which of the following expressions relates to the fact that sound waves travel fastest through solids?

   (1) The hills are alive with the sound of music.
   (2) It's music to my ears.
   (3) If a tree falls where no one hears it, does it make a sound?
   (4) Put your ear to the ground.
   (5) Children should be seen and not heard.

7. During a baseball game, a spectator sitting in the farthest bleachers sees the ball in the air well before hearing the crack of the bat. Which statement offers the best explanation for this?

   (1) The person's ears are stopped up.
   (2) The player hit the ball more slowly than usual.
   (3) The player hit the ball more quickly than usual.
   (4) The baseball is made of elastic materials.
   (5) Sound waves travel more slowly than light waves do.

Questions 8 and 9 refer to the following passage and diagram.

An ear thermometer contains a sensor whose electrical conductivity is affected by infrared radiation. The infrared radiation given off by the eardrum is converted to an electrical signal that is interpreted by a microprocessor in the handle. The body's temperature is then displayed.

EAR THERMOMETER

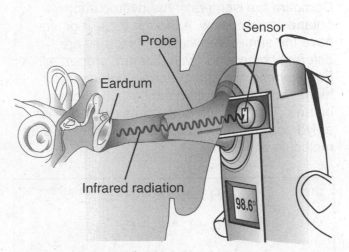

8. What property of infrared radiation allows it to change the electrical conductivity of the sensor?

   (1) its mass
   (2) its density
   (3) its electromagnetic fields
   (4) its wavelength
   (5) its frequency

9. Which is the most likely cause for an ear thermometer to give an incorrect temperature reading?

   (1) The temperature display shows the wrong temperature.
   (2) The wavelength of the infrared radiation changes dramatically.
   (3) The eardrum does not give off infrared radiation.
   (4) The probe is not pointed directly at the eardrum.
   (5) The mercury in the thermometer does not expand properly.

Answers start on page 312.

Unit 3 Cumulative Review Physical Science

Directions: Choose the one best answer to each question.

Questions 1 through 3 refer to the following paragraph and structural formulas.

Two compounds whose molecules have the same number and kind of atoms but different arrangements of atoms are called isomers. Compare the isomers of the hydrocarbon butane shown below. Although these isomers have the same chemical formula, they are different compounds with different properties. For example, the straight-chain butane has a higher boiling point than the branched-chain butane. The more carbon atoms contained in a hydrocarbon molecule, the more isomers that molecule can form.

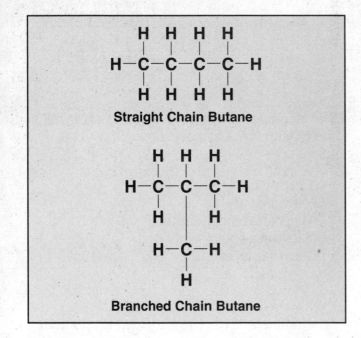

Straight Chain Butane

Branched Chain Butane

1. Which of the following chemical formulas restates the structural formula for both isomers of butane?

    (1) $C_3H_7CO_3$
    (2) C_4H_8
    (3) C_4H_{10}
    (4) $C_4H_{10}O_2$
    (5) C_5H_{12}

2. Pentane (C_5H_{12}), a member of the alkane series of hydrocarbons, has three isomers. Based on information from the paragraph, how does another member of this series, decane ($C_{10}H_{22}$), contrast with pentane?

    (1) Decane has fewer hydrogen atoms.
    (2) Decane has no isomers.
    (3) Decane has fewer isomers.
    (4) Decane has the same number of isomers.
    (5) Decane has more isomers.

3. Gasoline containing straight-chain hydrocarbons burns more quickly than gasoline containing branched-chain hydrocarbons. Which of the following statements is most likely to account for this?

    (1) Oxygen more easily reaches the parts of a straight-chain molecule.
    (2) The branched-chain molecule has a higher oxygen content.
    (3) The branched-chain molecule has a different chemical formula.
    (4) The branched-chain molecule has a higher carbon content.
    (5) The straight-chain molecule has a higher carbon and hydrogen content.

4. A longitudinal wave traveling through a medium disturbs the molecules as it passes, causing them to move back and forth in the same direction as the wave moves. Which of the following would make the best model of a longitudinal wave?

    (1) Grasp a jump rope and shake the end vigorously up and down.
    (2) Turn a jump rope in time to a peppy song.
    (3) Pull a few coils of a loose spring toward you and then quickly release them.
    (4) Skip a stone across a pond.
    (5) Throw a bounce pass during a basketball game.

Questions 5 through 7 refer to the following paragraph and diagrams

Depending on the size of the atom, atomic nuclei need certain proportions of protons and neutrons to be stable. If an atomic nucleus does not have the correct proportion of these subatomic particles, the atom will be radioactive. A radioactive atom decays and gives off particles until the nucleus is stable. The time needed for half the nuclei in a sample of radioactive material to decay is called its half-life. The half-life of carbon-14, for example, is about 5,730 years. This means that after 5,730 years, half the carbon-14 in a given sample will have decayed into another substance, the element nitrogen.

HALF-LIFE OF CARBON-14

1 gram
carbon-14

0 years

1/2 gram
carbon-14

5,730 years

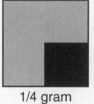

1/4 gram
carbon-14

11,460 years

1/8 gram
carbon-14

17,190 years

5. Which characteristic causes an atom to be radioactive?

   (1) too many electrons
   (2) too many nuclei
   (3) the length of its half-life
   (4) an unstable nucleus
   (5) particles given off by the nucleus

6. Using information about the half-life of radioactive substances would be of most interest to which scientist?

   (1) a metallurgist looking for ways to remove metals from ores
   (2) a chemist developing new products from organic compounds
   (3) a biochemist studying photosynthesis in algae
   (4) an oceanographer studying wave motion near shore
   (5) a geologist interested in estimating the age of rock samples

7. Which of the following conclusions is supported by the passage and the diagram?

   (1) After 22,920 years, none of the carbon-14 will remain.
   (2) After 22,920 years, $\frac{1}{8}$ gram of carbon-14 will remain of the original 1 gram.
   (3) After 22,920 years, $\frac{1}{16}$ gram of carbon-14 will remain of the original 1 gram.
   (4) The length of carbon-14's half-life is typical for radioactive elements.
   (5) Carbon-14 is radioactive for a million years.

8. Brownian motion occurs when the smaller molecules of a fluid hit the larger particles suspended in it, causing the larger particles to move randomly.

Which of the following is an unstated assumption important for understanding the information above?

   (1) Brownian motion occurs in a fluid.
   (2) A fluid is a liquid or a gas.
   (3) The fluid's molecules are small.
   (4) Small particles bombard large ones.
   (5) Brownian motion is random.

Questions 9 and 10 refer to the following paragraph and diagrams.

The friction created when objects move in air is called drag. Drag acts to slow down a moving object. The amount of drag depends on the shape of the object. Air flows more smoothly around objects with a tapered shape.

AIRFLOW AROUND OBJECTS

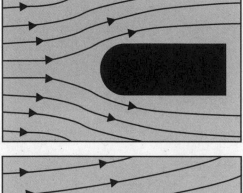

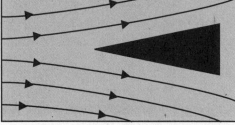

9. Which of the following would result if the drag acting on a moving object were increased?

   (1) decreased speed
   (2) increased speed
   (3) smoother airflow
   (4) increased airflow
   (5) decreased friction

10. Which of the following design changes would increase the fuel efficiency of a car?

   (1) provide a larger gas tank
   (2) taper the hood and fenders to streamline the design
   (3) increase the height and give the car a more rounded shape
   (4) lengthen the passenger compartment
   (5) restyle it from a 4-door to a 2-door model

Questions 11 and 12 refer to the following paragraph.

Resistance is a material's opposition to the flow of electric current. Some materials provide more resistance to current flow than others do and can be used as insulators. Resistance depends on many factors, including the material, its size, shape, and temperature. Resistance is measured in ohms. Resistance, voltage, and current are related in a formula called Ohm's Law:

$$\text{Resistance} = \frac{\text{Voltage}}{\text{Current}}$$

11. What is the main idea of the paragraph?

   (1) Ohm's Law states that resistance equals voltage divided by current.
   (2) A good conductor has low resistance to the flow of current.
   (3) A material's opposition to the flow of electric current is known as its resistance.
   (4) Resistance is measured in units called ohms.
   (5) When voltage increases and current decreases, resistance increases.

12. Gold has a lower resistance than copper, and copper has a lower resistance than steel. The thicker the wire, the lower the resistance.

Which of the following changes would increase the current, assuming that the voltage remains the same? (Hint: Rearrange the formula to determine how resistance must change to increase current.)

   (1) Replace a thick gold wire with a thin gold wire.
   (2) Replace a thin copper wire with a thin steel wire.
   (3) Replace a thick steel wire with a thin steel wire.
   (4) Replace a thick gold wire with a thick copper wire.
   (5) Replace a thin steel wire with a thick copper wire.

Questions 13 through 15 refer to the following passage and diagram.

Great amounts of energy are released by atoms when their nuclei rearrange themselves. In a nuclear fission reaction, an atomic nucleus splits into two smaller, approximately equal-sized nuclei, releasing a great deal of energy. The rapid splitting of many nuclei is a nuclear fission chain reaction.

A NUCLEAR FISSION REACTION

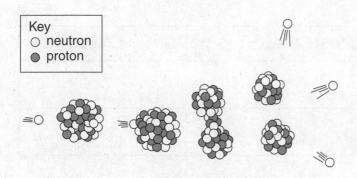

Key
○ neutron
● proton

Nuclear fission can occur naturally or be forced. The first sustained and controlled fission reaction was engineered in 1942. In July 1945, a team of physicists at Los Alamos, New Mexico, created the first nuclear explosion. The following month, two atomic bombs were dropped on Japan, devastating two cities and ending World War II. In the years after the war, many of the physicists came to feel they had been wrong to develop a weapon of such mass destruction. They opposed the continued spread of nuclear weapons.

13. Which of the following best summarizes what is shown in the diagram?

   (1) Electrons are released when a nucleus is hit by a neutron.
   (2) Two nuclei and several neutrons are released when a nucleus is hit by a neutron.
   (3) When a neutron hits a nucleus, several protons are released and a larger nucleus results.
   (4) In a chain reaction, one nucleus after another is hit.
   (5) A nuclear fission chain reaction can easily go out of control.

14. Which of the following expresses an opinion rather than a fact?

   (1) A fission chain reaction is the rapid splitting of many atomic nuclei.
   (2) Nuclear fission can occur naturally or be forced.
   (3) Scientists' goal was to achieve a sustained and controlled fission reaction.
   (4) Scientists tested the first nuclear explosion during the summer of 1945.
   (5) It was morally wrong for scientists to develop nuclear weapons.

15. Which was probably a primary value of the physicists working on the atomic bomb?

   (1) the opportunity to work independently
   (2) nonviolent means of conflict resolution
   (3) scientific and technical challenge
   (4) large monetary reward
   (5) the power to destroy

16. The law of reflection states that the angle at which a light ray strikes a surface (the angle of incidence) is equal to the angle at which the ray is reflected (the angle of reflection). Both angles are measured in relation to the normal, the line perpendicular to the surface.

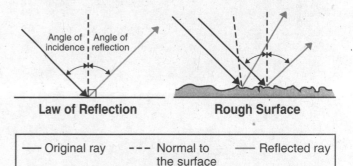

Angle of incidence | Angle of reflection

Law of Reflection   **Rough Surface**

— Original ray   - - - Normal to the surface   — Reflected ray

Which statement do the diagrams support?

   (1) A rough surface cannot reflect light, if the original rays come in parallel.
   (2) A rough surface reflects parallel light rays at different angles.
   (3) The law of reflection does not hold for rough surfaces.
   (4) Reflection of one light ray is not normal.
   (5) Reflection of many light rays is not normal.

Answers start on page 313.

Cumulative Review Performance Analysis
Unit 3 ● Physical Science

Use the Answers and Explanations starting on page 313 to check your answers to the Unit 3 Cumulative Review. Then use the chart to figure out the skill areas in which you need more practice.

On the chart, circle the questions that you answered correctly. Write the number correct for each skill area. Add the number of questions that you got correct on the Cumulative Review. If you feel that you need more practice, go back and review the lessons for the skill areas that were difficult for you.

Questions	Number Correct	Skill Area	Lessons for Review
1, 5, 11, **13**	_____/4	Comprehension	1, 2, 6, 9, 13
2, 8, **9, 10, 14**	_____/5	Analysis	3, 4, 7, 10, 14, 17, 19
4, **6**, 12	_____/3	Application	8, 15
3, 7, **15, 16**	_____/4	Evaluation	5, 11, 12, 16, 18, 20
TOTAL CORRECT	_____/16		

Question numbers in **boldface** are based on graphics.

SCIENCE

Directions

The Science Posttest consists of multiple-choice questions intended to measure your understanding of general concepts in science. The questions are based on short readings or on graphs, charts, or diagrams. Study the information given, and then answer the questions that follow. Refer to the information as often as necessary in answering the questions.

You should spend no more than 80 minutes answering the 50 questions on the Science Posttest. Work carefully, but do not spend too much time on any one question. Do not skip any items. Make a reasonable guess when you are not sure of an answer. You will not be penalized for incorrect answers.

When time is up, mark the last item you finished. This will tell you whether you can finish the real GED Test in the time allowed. Then complete the test.

Record your answers to the questions on a copy of the answer sheet on page 340. Be sure that all required information is properly recorded on the answer sheet.

To record your answers, mark the numbered space on the answer sheet that corresponds to the answer you choose for each question on the test.

Example:

Which of the following is the smallest unit in a living thing?

(1) tissue
(2) organ
(3) cell
(4) muscle
(5) capillary ① ② ● ④ ⑤

The correct answer is "cell"; therefore, answer space 3 should be marked on the answer sheet.

Do not rest the point of your pencil on the answer sheet while you are considering your answer. Make no stray or unnecessary marks. If you change an answer, erase your first mark completely. Mark only one answer space for each question; multiple answers will be scored as incorrect. Do not fold or crease your answer sheet.

When you finish the test, use the Performance Analysis Chart on page 238 to determine whether you are ready to take the real GED Test, and, if not, which skill areas need additional review.

Directions: Choose the one best answer to each question.

Questions 1 and 2 refer to the following information.

One way matter can change is through a chemical reaction. When matter undergoes a chemical change, the old substances are replaced by new substances with new properties, or characteristics. The energy needed to start a chemical reaction is called activation energy. Once they have started, some chemical reactions release heat energy. These are called exothermic reactions. Other chemical reactions absorb energy. These are called endothermic reactions.

1. What is an endothermic reaction?

   (1) a chemical reaction in which the properties of matter remain the same
   (2) a chemical reaction in which heat energy is released
   (3) a chemical reaction in which heat energy is absorbed
   (4) the application of energy to start a chemical reaction
   (5) a reaction that does not need activation energy to start

2. Lighter fluid is poured on charcoal in a barbecue grill, and a lighter is used to light the coals. In this chemical reaction, what is the flame of the lighter?

   (1) a property of the reaction
   (2) an endothermic reaction
   (3) a physical change
   (4) the resulting form of matter
   (5) the source of activation energy

Question 3 refers to the following diagram.

LAYERS OF EARTH

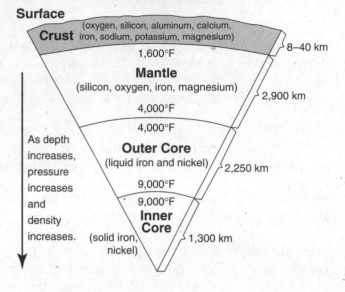

3. Scientists have calculated Earth's average density, or amount of matter per unit of volume. They estimate the average density at more than 5 grams per cubic centimeter. However, the density of rocks in Earth's crust is less than 3 grams per cubic centimeter.

   Which statement best explains the difference between the average density of Earth as a whole and the average density of the crust?

   (1) Earth's interior is composed of material much denser than the material in the crust.
   (2) Earth's interior is composed in part of molten metals.
   (3) The crust is made primarily of iron and nickel, and the interior of silicon and oxygen.
   (4) In order to calculate density, the volume of matter must be known.
   (5) The lower density of the oceans was left out of the calculation for Earth's crust.

Questions 4 and 5 refer to the following diagram.

THE HUMAN EYE

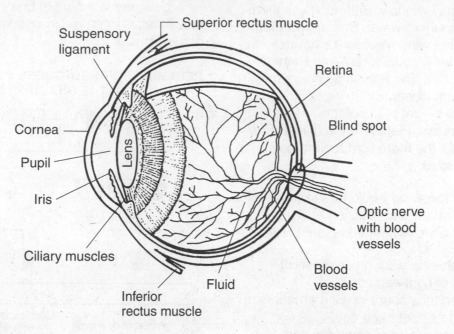

4. The lens in the human eye must change shape in order to focus images properly. Which part of the eye functions to control the shape of the lens?

   (1) the superior rectus muscle
   (2) the inferior rectus muscle
   (3) the ciliary muscles
   (4) the cornea
   (5) the optic nerve

5. Light enters the eye through the pupil. The iris is the colored area around the pupil that makes the pupil larger or smaller. What is the effect of the adjustments made by the iris?

   (1) The pupil changes color.
   (2) The blind spot of the eye changes position.
   (3) The amount of light entering the eye varies.
   (4) The cornea bulges.
   (5) The ability to see color changes.

Question 6 refers to the following information.

When more than one force acts on an object, their effects may cancel one another out. In that case, the object is said to be in equilibrium. For example, an airplane traveling horizontally at a constant speed is in equilibrium because the four forces acting on it are in balance.

FORCES ON AN AIRPLANE

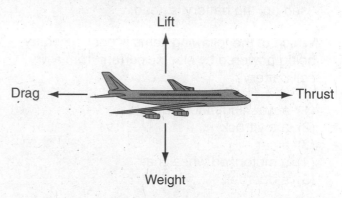

6. If the pilot wished to descend gradually, which of the following would he or she do?

   (1) increase lift
   (2) increase thrust
   (3) decrease lift
   (4) decrease weight
   (5) decrease drag

7. Brittany wants to test the effect of light on plant growth. She gets three geraniums of the same size, in similar pots. She places them in the same sunny window. Brittany gives them the same amount of water. She allows Plant A to stay on the windowsill for 12 hours a day; Plant B for 6 hours a day, and Plant C for 3 hours a day. The remaining hours they spend in a dark closet. Every week Brittany measures the height of the plants. At the end of four weeks, Plant A is the tallest. She concludes that the more light a plant gets, the more it grows.

Which of the following would be the most valid criticism of Brittany's conclusion about the relationship between light and plant growth?

(1) The geraniums were given different amounts of light each day.
(2) The geraniums spent varying amounts of time in the closet each day.
(3) The geraniums were given the same amount of water.
(4) Three geraniums are too small a sample on which to base such a broad conclusion.
(5) Geraniums are not likely to react to water in the same way as other green plants.

8. Dry cell batteries produce small amounts of electric current by means of a chemical reaction. When the supply of chemicals is used up, the battery is dead.

Which of the following items is best suited for being powered by electric current from a dry cell battery?

(1) a washing machine
(2) a toy truck
(3) a car
(4) a motorized wheelchair
(5) a doorbell

Question 9 refers to the following information and diagram.

A pedigree is a type of chart used to show how a trait is inherited in one family over several generations.

PEDIGREE FOR RED-GREEN COLORBLINDNESS IN THE PHILLIPS FAMILY

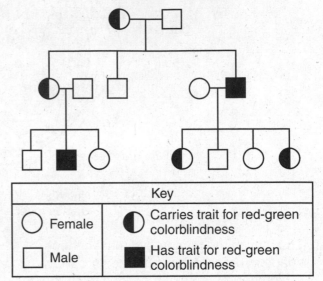

Key		
◯ Female	◑	Carries trait for red-green colorblindness
☐ Male	■	Has trait for red-green colorblindness

9. How many people in the third generation of the Phillips family have red-green colorblindness?

(1) none
(2) one
(3) two
(4) three
(5) four

Questions 10 through 13 refer to the following information and graph.

An ecosystem consists of a community of organisms and the environment in which they live. A regional ecosystem with distinctive forms of life and specific ranges of temperature and rainfall is called a biome. Information about six major biomes is shown on the graph below. The data for each biome were collected from a number of different locations in the biome.

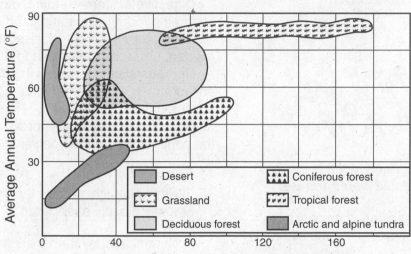

TEMPERATURE AND RAINFALL IN SOME BIOMES

10. Approximately what is the range of average annual temperatures in a tropical forest biome?

   (1) 89°F to 95°F
   (2) 77°F to 88°F
   (3) 72°F to 82°F
   (4) 63°F to 75°F
   (5) 50°F to 85°F

11. According to the graph, what is the major difference between a deciduous forest biome and a coniferous forest biome?

   (1) The deciduous forest biome generally has a higher average annual temperature.
   (2) The deciduous forest biome covers a much larger area of Earth.
   (3) On average, the deciduous forest biome gets more precipitation each year.
   (4) The deciduous forest biome is much more diverse.
   (5) The deciduous forest biome has a much smaller average annual temperature range.

12. On the graph, some biomes overlap. What does this overlapping mean?

   (1) Plants in each biome are different.
   (2) The biomes are located near each other.
   (3) Some of the biomes have similar average temperatures and rainfall.
   (4) Some of the biomes have similar plant and animal life.
   (5) The biomes are spreading outward and one type will prevail.

13. Which of the following conclusions is supported by the information given?

   (1) It is usually hotter in a desert biome than in a grasslands biome.
   (2) A tropical forest biome has annual precipitation of at least 180 inches.
   (3) More people live in deciduous forest biomes than arctic and alpine tundra biomes.
   (4) Some arctic and alpine tundra biomes get as little precipitation as desert biomes.
   (5) Desert biomes are characterized by an average annual precipitation of 30 inches.

Question 14 refers to the following diagrams.

COMPARISON OF AN EQUAL MASS OF LIQUID WATER AND ICE

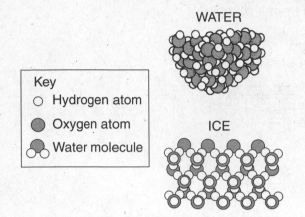

WATER

ICE

Key
○ Hydrogen atom
● Oxygen atom
Water molecule

14. According to the diagrams, what is the main difference between liquid water and ice?

(1) Liquid water molecules consist solely of hydrogen atoms, and ice molecules consist solely of oxygen atoms.
(2) Liquid water is made up of more molecules than the same mass of ice.
(3) Liquid water contains more oxygen atoms than the same mass of ice.
(4) Liquid water contains more hydrogen atoms than the same mass of ice.
(5) Liquid water molecules are closely packed in an irregular arrangement, and ice molecules form a regular lattice with large spaces.

Question 15 refers to the following information.

The human body contains many types of tissues and organs that work together in various systems. Following are brief descriptions of some of these systems and their functions.

Muscular system—moving skeletal and body parts such as the stomach and heart
Digestive system—eating, digesting, and absorbing foods; eliminating some wastes
Circulatory system—transporting nutrients, oxygen, hormones, waste, and other substances
Nervous system—receiving data from the environment, interpreting data, controlling actions of body parts
Reproductive system—producing sex cells for the continuation of the species

15. With which system are the eyes and ears mostly closely associated?

(1) muscular system
(2) digestive system
(3) circulatory system
(4) nervous system
(5) reproductive system

16. A survey of 460 ninth- and tenth-grade girls indicated that active girls who drink cola are five times more likely to fracture bones than active girls who do not drink cola. Some doctors think the phosphoric acid in cola drinks may affect bone mass, weakening it. Others think that girls who drink cola are more susceptible to fractures because the cola replaces milk in their diet. Milk is high in calcium and helps develop strong bones.

    Based on this information, which of the following is an opinion rather than a fact?

    (1) Four hundred sixty girls were surveyed for a study on cola drinking and fractures.
    (2) The girls were all active ninth and tenth graders.
    (3) Girls who drank cola had five times the number of fractures as girls who did not.
    (4) Phosphoric acid in cola affects bone mass, weakening it.
    (5) Milk is high in calcium and helps develop strong bones.

17. Alfred Nobel was a Swedish chemist who invented many explosives, including nitroglycerin and dynamite. As a result, he became very wealthy. Dismayed that his explosives were used in war, Nobel established a fund in his will to give annual awards for outstanding work promoting peace, as well as awards in the fields of literature, physics, chemistry, and physiology or medicine. The Nobel prize in the field of economics was added in 1969.

    Which of the following would be eligible for a Nobel Prize?

    (1) discovery of new reserves of petroleum
    (2) discovery of new subatomic particles that convey fundamental forces
    (3) discovery of several new species of birds
    (4) development of a new breed of sheep with silky wool
    (5) production of a play on the topic of eliminating world hunger

Question 18 refers to the following graph.

SOLUBILITY OF SELECTED SOLIDS IN WATER

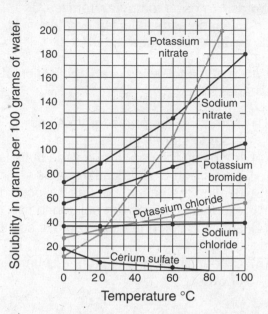

18. Many people think that increasing the temperature of the water will increase the solubility of any solid. Which line on the graph proves that this idea is wrong?

    (1) potassium nitrate
    (2) sodium nitrate
    (3) potassium bromide
    (4) potassium chloride
    (5) cerium sulfate

19. Charles's law states that the volume of a gas at constant pressure is directly proportional to its temperature. In other words, if a gas's temperature rises, its volume increases; if its temperature falls, its volume decreases.

Which of the following is an application of Charles's law?

(1) increasing the pressure on a gas in order to store it in less space
(2) removing the cap from a soda bottle so the carbon dioxide gas escapes
(3) heating the gas in a hot air balloon so it expands, causing the balloon to rise
(4) spraying cologne into a room to scent the air
(5) condensing fog to capture a source of water

20. In vitro fertilization is a procedure for fertilizing eggs outside a woman's reproductive system. The egg and sperm are usually taken from the parents, and the resulting child is genetically related to the parents. Treatment can take months or years, costs a great deal of money, and has a success rate of about 10 percent.

Which of the following would explain why a couple might choose in vitro fertilization over adoption?

(1) Adopting a child can take a long time.
(2) Adopting a child can be expensive.
(3) The parents want a child who is genetically their own.
(4) The parents want to ensure they have a healthy child.
(5) The parents want to ensure they have a girl.

21. Heat is a form of energy associated with the constant vibration of atoms and molecules. Heat energy can be transferred in three ways. In convection, heat is transferred by the flow of currents through gases and liquids. In conduction, heat is transferred from molecule to molecule. In radiation, heat is transferred through space by electromagnetic waves.

Some houses have heating systems in which hot air is blown through vents near the floor. With this type of system, the house is principally warmed by which method or methods of heat transfer?

(1) convection and conduction
(2) conduction and radiation
(3) convection and radiation
(4) convection only
(5) conduction only

22. In electrical engineering, the liquid metallic element mercury is sometimes used as a switch. A small quantity is placed in a tube, and, when the tube is tilted, the mercury flows between two electrical contacts, completing an electric circuit. Another type of mercury switch consists of a tiny cup of mercury into which two contacts are dipped, completing the circuit.

Which of the following is an unstated assumption important for understanding the paragraph?

(1) Mercury is a metal.
(2) Mercury is an element.
(3) Mercury conducts electricity.
(4) Mercury is used in electrical switches.
(5) Like all liquids, mercury flows.

Question 23 refers to the following information and map.

Currents at the ocean surface, such as the Gulf Stream, are kept in motion by winds and by Earth's rotation. Other currents, however, exist deep below the ocean surface and are kept in motion by differences in temperature and salinity (degree of saltiness) among large masses of water. Cold, salty water is dense, and so it sinks and is replaced by the less dense, warm, fresher water from the tropics. This causes currents to flow deep below the ocean surface, transferring heat between the tropics and the polar regions.

DEEP OCEAN CURRENTS

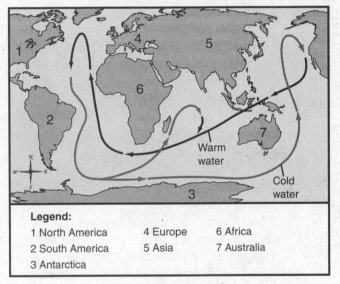

Legend:
1 North America   4 Europe   6 Africa
2 South America   5 Asia   7 Australia
3 Antarctica

23. Which of the following conclusions about the effects of the deep ocean currents is supported by the information given?

(1) The southward flow of tropical water warms the climate of Antarctica.
(2) The northward flow of tropical water warms the climate of Europe.
(3) The northward flow of tropical water warms the climate of Northeastern Asia.
(4) Warm tropical water is denser than the cold, salty water of the north and south latitudes.
(5) Warm tropical water flows from Africa toward Australia.

24. A stereomicroscope is a type of light microscope with two eyepieces. It magnifies objects only from 4 to 80 times, unlike more powerful light microscopes, which can magnify up to 1,500 times. However, the two eyepieces provide a three-dimensional view. Thus a stereomicroscope is suitable for examining larger objects, such as the veins on an insect's wing.

Which of the following would be best examined using a stereomicroscope?

(1) an atom of oxygen
(2) a protein molecule
(3) a blood cell
(4) a leaf
(5) a bird

Questions 25 through 27 refer to the following diagram and information.

The Doppler effect describes the apparent changes that take place in waves, such as sound waves, as a result of the movement of the source or observer of the waves. If the source of a sound is moving, the sound waves are pushed closer together in the direction of motion, as shown in the diagram. Their frequency increases and the pitch of the sound seems higher to the observer. If the sound is moving away from the observer, the sound waves are farther apart. Their frequency decreases and the pitch of the sound seems lower to the observer.

THE DOPPLER EFFECT

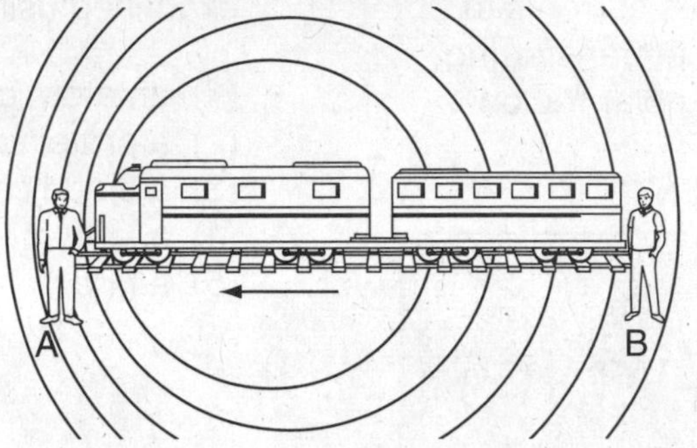

Observer A hears a higher pitch than Observer B.

25. If the source of a sound were moving toward you, then passed you and moved away, at what point would the sound seem the highest?

    (1) as it approached
    (2) when it was closest
    (3) as it moved away
    (4) when the sound was the loudest
    (5) when the sound reflected off an object

26. Which of the following best describes the sound heard by observer A in the diagram?

    (1) increasing pitch
    (2) decreasing pitch
    (3) increasing, then decreasing pitch
    (4) decreasing, then increasing pitch
    (5) no change in pitch

27. Which of the following conclusions can be supported by the information given?

    (1) The Doppler effect works only with sound waves.
    (2) The Doppler effect can be used to determine whether a sound source is moving away from or toward someone.
    (3) The Doppler effect works only within about 50 feet of the source of the sound.
    (4) As it moves in relation to the observer, the source of the sound waves actually changes the frequency of the waves it emits.
    (5) The Doppler effect is used to mask other sources of sound.

28. A lack of vitamin C in the diet weakens some body tissues and can result in a disease called scurvy. Many foods contain little or no vitamin C. However, large amounts of vitamin C are found in citrus fruits, tomatoes, many dark green vegetables, and members of the mustard family, which includes mustard greens, cabbage, broccoli, cauliflower, and kohlrabi. When food containing vitamin C is stored for a long time, cooked, or dried, much of the vitamin is destroyed.

A person concerned with getting as much vitamin C as possible should eat which of the following foods?

(1) iceberg lettuce
(2) a few slices of dried fruit
(3) boiled mustard greens
(4) a banana
(5) a fresh orange

29. One type of biological control of insect pests is to release males that have been exposed to radiation. The radiation causes deadly genetic defects, or mutations, in many of the sex cells of the male insects.

Which of the following would be likely to happen to a population of insect pests if a farmer used this form of biological control each year?

(1) The population would die out in one generation because none of the females' eggs would be fertilized.
(2) The population would die out completely after several generations because most of the females' eggs would not be fertilized.
(3) The population would remain very low over the generations because many fertilized eggs would be defective and die.
(4) The population would increase for several generations because more eggs would be fertilized.
(5) The population would remain about the same because the females would continue to mate.

Question 30 refers to the following graph.

NUMBER OF ANIMAL SPECIES

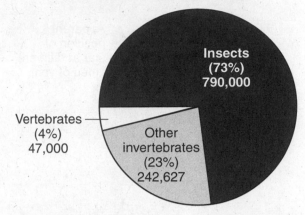

30. How does the number of invertebrate species (insects and other animals without backbones) compare with the number of vertebrate species?

(1) There are about one-fourth as many invertebrate species as vertebrate species.
(2) There are about 3 times as many invertebrate species as vertebrate species.
(3) There are about 4 times as many invertebrate species as vertebrate species.
(4) There are about 10 times as many invertebrate species as vertebrate species.
(5) There are about 24 times as many invertebrate species as vertebrate species.

Question 31 refers to the following diagram.

PARALLAX

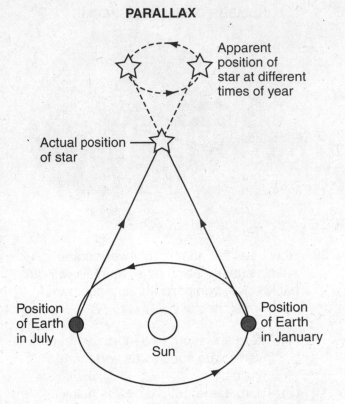

31. Stars appear in slightly different positions in the night sky at different times of year. Based on the diagram, what causes this phenomenon?

   (1) The stars have a distant orbit.
   (2) Earth's position changes relative to the stars.
   (3) The sun's position changes relative to the stars.
   (4) People mistake three stars for one star.
   (5) Earth rotates, producing day and night.

32. Scientists use models to help them understand things that are difficult to observe directly, such as things that are very large or very small. For example, scientists might use models to study the flow of energy on Earth or the structure of an atom. Some models are physical models—drawings, charts, or three-dimensional structures. Other models are mental, such as mathematical equations. Still others are computer models that show what might happen under certain conditions.

For which of the following areas of study would it be most helpful to use a model?

   (1) the short-term effect of aerobic exercise on stress
   (2) the relationship between a diet high in fat and heart disease
   (3) the social interactions of a group of chimpanzees
   (4) the growth and development of the Pacific salmon
   (5) the conditions necessary to create a self-contained ecosystem for astronauts

33. Selective breeding is the process of choosing a few organisms with desired traits and having them serve as parents of the next generation. For thousands of years, humans have been selectively breeding plants such as corn and wheat, and animals such as cows and horses.

What has generally been the purpose of selectively breeding a particular type of plant or animal?

   (1) satisfying scientific curiosity about the plant or animal
   (2) increasing the plant or animal's usefulness and value
   (3) experimenting with the plant or animal species on a large scale
   (4) creating a completely new plant or animal species
   (5) saving the plant or animal from possible extinction

34. Scientists have been debating whether Yucca Mountain is a safe place to bury radioactive waste. Some scientists believe that the calcite crystals found underground indicate that hot water circulated recently under the mountain. If this happened again, the hot water could corrode the storage containers and release dangerous radioactivity. Other scientists think that the crystals formed millions of years ago when Yucca Mountain was built from volcanic ash. They think that hot water is unlikely to seep through the site again. According to these scientists, the mountain is a safe place to store radioactive waste.

Which of the following is an opinion held by scientists who favor burying radioactive waste at Yucca Mountain?

(1) Yucca Mountain has been proposed as a radioactive waste burial site.
(2) Calcite crystals have been found underground at Yucca Mountain.
(3) Hot groundwater is able to corrode metal containers used for storing radioactive wastes.
(4) Hot groundwater is unlikely to seep through Yucca Mountain again.
(5) Yucca Mountain was originally formed from volcanic ash.

Question 35 refers to the following diagram.

WATER TABLE

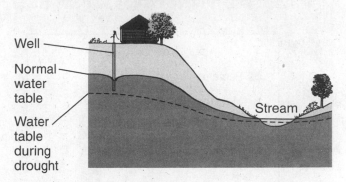

35. Which of the following statements is implied by the diagram?

(1) During long periods of drought, the well will run dry.
(2) During a heavy rain, water from the stream will flood the house.
(3) The level of water in the stream is usually higher than that of the water table.
(4) For trees to survive, they need to grow roots down to the water table.
(5) Well water is as safe to drink as water from a municipal water system.

Question 36 refers to the following graph.

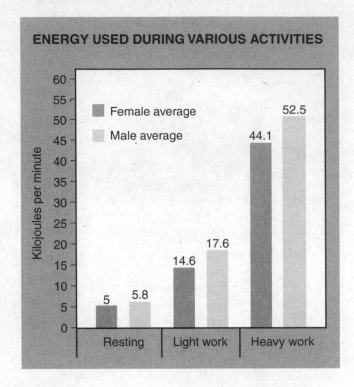

ENERGY USED DURING VARIOUS ACTIVITIES

y-axis: Kilojoules per minute

Female average
Male average

Resting: 5, 5.8
Light work: 14.6, 17.6
Heavy work: 44.1, 52.5

36. How does the amount of energy used per minute when a woman does heavy work compare with the amount of energy used when she rests?

   (1) She uses one-third the energy doing heavy work as resting.
   (2) She uses three times the energy doing heavy work as resting.
   (3) She uses nine times the energy doing heavy work as resting.
   (4) She uses ten times the energy doing heavy work as resting.
   (5) She uses forty-four times the energy doing heavy work as resting.

37. A magnetometer is a device used to measure magnetic fields. As the magnetometer passes through a magnetic field, it records the strength of the field as an electric voltage. Magnetometers are sometimes towed behind airplanes to measure Earth's magnetic field. Changes in the magnetic field help locate iron and other deposits.

   Which of the following is an unstated assumption important for understanding this paragraph?

   (1) A magnetometer measures magnetic fields.
   (2) The strength of a magnetic field is indicated by voltage.
   (3) Magnetometers can be towed behind airplanes.
   (4) Earth has a magnetic field.
   (5) Iron deposits are magnetic.

38. A population is a group of individuals of the same species. Occasionally a small group of isolated individuals establishes a new population. After generations of isolation, the new population may develop different characteristics than the population from which its founders originally came, even becoming a separate species.

   Under which of the following circumstances is this type of speciation most likely to occur?

   (1) whenever a useful genetic mutation is passed on to offspring
   (2) when a group of individuals colonize an island in the ocean
   (3) when a group of individuals colonize a new area readily accessible to their former home
   (4) when a group of individuals migrates frequently from one population to another
   (5) when a group of individuals settles in a new location but eventually dies out

Question 39 refers to the following information and diagram.

In 1953, scientist Stanley Miller set up a complex model to demonstrate that organic molecules, the basis of living organisms, might have formed in the conditions present on Earth when the planet was young. He kept the mixture of gases and water recirculating in his model for a week. By week's end there were organic molecules in the system.

MILLER'S ORIGINS OF LIFE EXPERIMENT

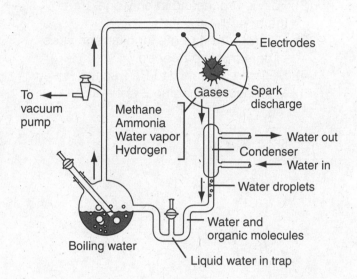

39. In Miller's model, the electrodes provided the energy needed for organic molecules to form from other substances. Which of the substances or processes on the early Earth did the electrodes simulate?

(1) the atmosphere
(2) the oceans
(3) heavy rainfall
(4) lightning
(5) bombardment by meteors

40. Wind can transport sand great distances. When the wind speed drops, the sand is deposited. Windbreak fences are sometimes built along beaches to slow the wind, causing the sand particles to fall along the fences.

Which of the following uses the same principle as the windbreak fences?

(1) Stone walls are built by farmers from rocks cleared from their fields.
(2) Electrified fences are used to keep livestock in and predators out.
(3) Snow fences are built along the sides of roads so snow will drift there and not on the roads.
(4) Levees are built along rivers to prevent flooding when the rivers rise.
(5) Dams are built across rivers to control the flow of water.

41. The faster a vehicle is traveling, the greater the distance it requires to come to a full stop. A car traveling 30 miles per hour needs about 75 feet to come to a stop. The same car going 50 miles per hour needs about 174 feet to come to a stop. This is because a moving vehicle has momentum, which depends on both the vehicle's mass and velocity. A large truck has more momentum than a car traveling at the same speed.

A person drives a large sport utility vehicle (SUV) and feels safe tailgating cars on the highway. What factor is the SUV driver failing to take into consideration?

(1) An SUV requires more space to stop than a car traveling the same speed.
(2) An SUV requires less stopping space than a car traveling the same speed.
(3) If the car ahead stops suddenly, the SUV will have plenty of room to stop.
(4) The higher the SUV's speed, the less space needed between the SUV and the car in front of it.
(5) An SUV is sturdier than a car, so SUV drivers and passengers will not be hurt in an accident.

Questions 42 and 43 refer to the following chart.

FORMATION OF SEDIMENTARY ROCKS		
Agent of Formation	Type of Material in the Rock	Type of Rock Produced
Streams, winds, glaciers	Boulders, pebbles Sand Silt, clay	Conglomerate Sandstone Shale
Chemical reaction in seawater, evaporation	Dissolved minerals	Rock salt, gypsum, some limestone
Organisms	Vegetation Remains of marine animals including shells	Peat and coal Most limestone

42. Which of the following sedimentary rocks was formed by the deposition and compaction of organic material?

(1) coal
(2) conglomerate
(3) rock salt
(4) sandstone
(5) shale

43. In areas of the southwestern United States, large deposits of gypsum are very common. What might this region have been like millions of years ago when the mineral began forming?

(1) a rolling plain drained by large rivers
(2) a mountain range dotted with glaciers
(3) a marshy freshwater area covered by lush plants
(4) a vast ocean
(5) a huge, hot desert

44. Until recently, scientists studying pain have had to rely on what people communicated, from words to winces to screams. However, the development of imaging technology such as MRI and PET scans has allowed scientists to pinpoint the areas of the brain that are activated by pain. As a result, scientists have found that different parts of the brain register pain from different causes.

What is implied by the new pain research?

(1) Objective studies of pain are impossible.
(2) Pain is processed in only one area of the brain.
(3) Different treatments for different types of pain may be needed.
(4) MRIs are superior to PET scans.
(5) Most pain is imagined, not real.

Question 45 refers to the following diagram.

EVAPORATION AND CONDENSATION

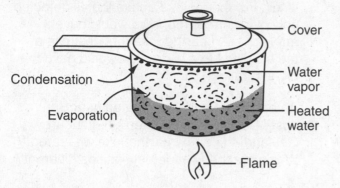

45. Which of the following best summarizes what is shown in the diagram?

   (1) In a closed container, liquid water evaporates and becomes water vapor.
   (2) In a closed container, water vapor condenses and becomes liquid water.
   (3) In a closed container, evaporation occurs from the surface of liquid water.
   (4) In a closed container, liquid water evaporates into water vapor, then condenses into liquid water.
   (5) Liquid water evaporates into water vapor, condenses into liquid water, and then freezes into ice crystals.

Question 46 refers to the following chart.

DURATION OF PREGNANCY IN SOME ANIMALS

Animal	Length of Pregnancy	Number of Young
Virginia opossum	12 days	8–14
Golden hamster	15 days	6–8
Lion	105–108 days	3–4
Human being	267 days	1
Indian elephant	660 days	1

46. Which of the following is a conclusion based on the data in the chart rather than a detail from the chart?

   (1) The Virginia opossum gives birth to 8 to 14 young in one litter.
   (2) The pregnancy of a golden hamster lasts 15 days.
   (3) Human beings usually give birth to one baby per pregnancy.
   (4) The pregnancy of an Indian elephant lasts 660 days.
   (5) The longer the pregnancy in a species, the fewer the young.

Question 47 refers to the following information and diagram.

When waves pass through the boundary between two types of matter, the waves bend. This phenomenon is known as refraction.

LIGHT REFRACTION IN WATER

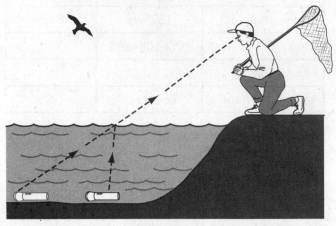

47. Which of the following conclusions is supported by the information given?
    (1) Knowing that light waves are refracted, the person should aim the net for the spot where he sees the flashlight.
    (2) Knowing that light waves are refracted, the person should aim for a spot closer than the one where the flashlight appears to be.
    (3) When the person sees a flying bird, the bird is really in a different place because of the refraction of light waves.
    (4) The only type of waves that is refracted is light waves.
    (5) Refraction occurs only at the boundary between air and water.

48. The Mercalli scale uses Roman numerals to rate earthquakes according to their effects on a particular place where the earthquake is felt. For example, a quake that is detected only by scientific monitors would have a rating of I. An earthquake that destroys all the buildings in a wide area would have the highest rating, XII.

An earthquake that originated near San Jose, California, was rated VII. In nearby Oakland, the same earthquake was rated V. Why were the two Mercalli ratings different?

    (1) The Mercalli scale measures the size of the earthquake waves at the site of the earthquake.
    (2) The Mercalli scale measures the size of the earthquake waves at various sites affected by the earthquake.
    (3) All earthquakes have at least two Mercalli ratings.
    (4) The earthquake caused more damage in Oakland than in San Jose, so the Mercalli rating in Oakland was lower.
    (5) The earthquake caused less damage in Oakland than in San Jose, so the Mercalli rating in Oakland was lower.

Question 49 refers to the following information and diagram.

Heartburn is a mild to severe burning pain, that results from stomach acid reflux. The diagram shows why heartburn occurs.

HEARTBURN

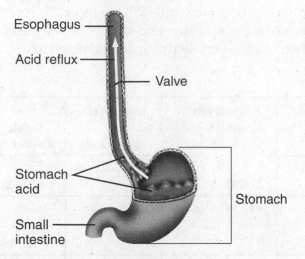

49. A young child complains of a stomachache. Does the child have heartburn?

   (1) Yes. Heartburn is caused by stomach acid.
   (2) Yes. Heartburn can cause an achy feeling as well as burning pain.
   (3) No. Heartburn usually causes pain in the chest, above the stomach.
   (4) No. Heartburn usually causes pain in the lower abdomen, below the stomach.
   (5) No. Heartburn is not related to stomach pain but to heart pain.

50. Methane hydrate consists of a shell of ice molecules surrounding molecules of methane, also known as natural gas. It is found under the polar permafrost and deep in ocean sediments. When it melts, one volume of methane hydrate yields about 160 volumes of methane. Scientists estimate that there is at least twice as much carbon in methane hydrate deposits as there is in deposits of all the known fossil fuels on Earth.

Which of the following countries is most likely to be involved in studies on the potential use of methane hydrate as a source of energy?

   (1) Saudi Arabia, which has huge reservoirs of petroleum and natural gas
   (2) Russia, a country with large areas of permafrost in its northern regions
   (3) Nepal, a landlocked, mountainous country in south central Asia
   (4) Botswana, a landlocked, largely desert country in southern Africa
   (5) Switzerland, a landlocked, mountainous country in central Europe

Answers start on page 315.

Posttest Performance Analysis Chart
Science

This chart can help you determine your strengths and weaknesses on the content and reading skill areas of the GED Science Posttest. Use the Answers and Explanations starting on page 315 to check your answers to the test. Then circle on the chart the numbers of the test questions you answered correctly. Put the total number correct for each content area and skill area in each row and column. Look at the total questions correct in each column and row and decide which areas are difficult for you. Use the lesson references to study those areas. Use the Study Planner on page 31 to guide your review.

Thinking Skill / Content Area	Comprehension (Lessons 1, 2, 6, 9, 13)	Application (Lessons 8, 15)	Analysis (Lessons 3, 4, 7, 10, 14, 17, 19)	Evaluation (Lessons 5, 11, 12, 16, 18, 20)	Total Correct
Life Science (Pages 32–107)	**9, 10, 12**, 44	15, 24, 28, 32, 38, **39, 49**	**4, 5, 11**, 16, 29, **30, 36, 46**	7, **13**, 20, 33	____/23
Earth and Space Science (Pages 108–155)	**35, 42**	40, **43**, 50	**31**, 34, 48	**3, 23**	____/10
Physical Science (Pages 156–218)	1, **25, 45**	2, 8, 17, 19, 21	**6, 14**, 22, **26**, 37	**18, 27**, 41, **47**	____/17
Total Correct	____/9	____/15	____/16	____/10	____/50

1–40 → Use the Study Planner on page 31 to organize your review.
41–50 → Congratulations! You're ready for the GED! You can get more practice with the Simulated Test on pages 239–259.

Boldfaced numbers indicate questions based on charts, graphs, diagrams, and drawings.

For additional help, see the *Steck-Vaughn GED Science Exercise Book.*

SCIENCE

Directions

The Science Simulated Test consists of multiple-choice questions intended to measure your understanding of general concepts in science. The questions are based on short readings or on graphs, charts, or diagrams. Study the information given, and then answer the questions that follow. Refer to the information as often as necessary in answering the questions.

You should spend no more than 80 minutes answering the 50 questions on the Science Simulated Test. Work carefully, but do not spend too much time on any one question. Do not skip any items. Make a reasonable guess when you are not sure of an answer. You will not be penalized for incorrect answers.

When time is up, mark the last item you finished. This will tell you whether you can finish the real GED Test in the time allowed. Then complete the test.

Record your answers to the questions on a copy of the answer sheet on page 340. Be sure that all required information is properly recorded on the answer sheet.

To record your answers, mark the numbered space on the answer sheet that corresponds to the answer you choose for each question on the test.

Example:

Which of the following is the smallest unit in a living thing?

(1) tissue
(2) organ
(3) cell
(4) muscle
(5) capillary   ① ② ● ④ ⑤

The correct answer is "cell"; therefore, answer space 3 should be marked on the answer sheet.

Do not rest the point of your pencil on the answer sheet while you are considering your answer. Make no stray or unnecessary marks. If you change an answer, erase your first mark completely. Mark only one answer space for each question; multiple answers will be scored as incorrect. Do not fold or crease your answer sheet.

When you finish the test, use the Performance Analysis Chart on page 259 to determine whether you are ready to take the real GED Test, and, if not, which skill areas need additional review.

Directions: Choose the one best answer to each question.

Questions 1 and 2 refer to the following chart.

RADIOACTIVE SUBSTANCES AND THEIR USES	
Substance	**Use**
Carbon 14	Estimating age of material that was once living
Arsenic 74	Finding brain tumors
Cobalt 60	Radiation treatment for cancer Tracing leaks or blockages in pipelines
Iodine 131	Treatment of thyroid gland problems
Radium	Radiation treatment for cancer
Uranium 235	Estimating the age of nonliving materials Production of energy in nuclear reactors Atomic weapons

1. If a scientist were interested in dating a human bone from an ancient civilization, which radioactive substance would he or she use?

   (1) carbon 14
   (2) arsenic 74
   (3) cobalt 60
   (4) radium
   (5) uranium 235

2. Which of the following conclusions can be supported by the information in the chart?

   (1) All radioactive substances are very expensive.
   (2) Uranium 235 is used only for the production of weapons.
   (3) Radioactive substances are always beneficial to humans.
   (4) Radioactive substances have many different uses.
   (5) Radioactive substances can be produced by humans.

Question 3 refers to the following information.

From observing the seismic waves produced by earthquakes whose epicenter (the place on Earth's surface directly above the point where the earthquake occurred) and time were known, scientists have determined the speeds at which different types of seismic waves travel.

COMPARISON OF DISTANCES DIFFERENT SEISMIC WAVES TRAVEL OVER TIME

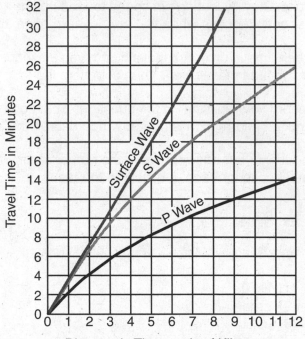

3. How can the information in this graph be used by scientists who make seismic recordings?

   (1) to assess the damage done by an earthquake
   (2) to find the distance to an earthquake's epicenter
   (3) to predict an earthquake in advance
   (4) to predict volcanic eruptions
   (5) to identify potential earthquake zones

Question 4 refers to the following information and diagrams.

The newest rock layer is at the top; the oldest rock layer is at the bottom.

LIFE CYCLE OF FAULT-BLOCK MOUNTAINS

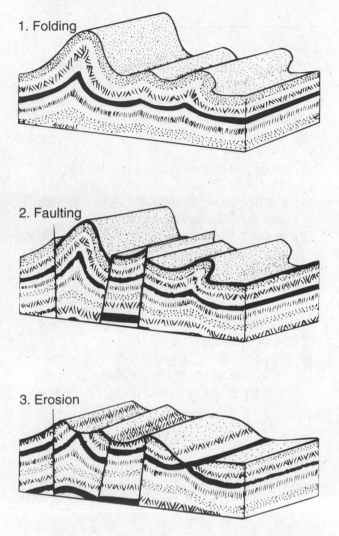

1. Folding

2. Faulting

3. Erosion

4. Older buried rock layers become exposed during which life cycle phase or phases?

    (1) folding only
    (2) faulting only
    (3) erosion only
    (4) folding and faulting
    (5) faulting and erosion

5. Microbiology is the study of microorganisms, especially single-celled life forms such as bacteria, protists, and fungi. The development of the microscope in the 1600s enabled scientists to see microorganisms for the first time. Today the field of microbiology makes great contributions to medicine and to the food industry.

Which of the following helped establish microbiology as a field in the life sciences?

    (1) the classification of bacteria, protists, and fungi
    (2) the invention of the microscope
    (3) its applications to the field of medicine
    (4) its applications to the food industry
    (5) its applications to the computer industry

6. Carbon monoxide is a gas produced as a byproduct of combustion in coal stoves, furnaces, and gas appliances when they do not get enough oxygen from the air. It is present in the exhaust of internal combustion engines, such as the ones in cars and lawn mowers.

Carbon monoxide is a deadly poison. Since it is colorless, odorless, and tasteless, it is very difficult to detect. Victims of carbon monoxide poisoning become drowsy and then unconscious. Death can occur in minutes.

Which of the following actions carries a high risk of carbon monoxide poisoning?

    (1) operating a well-vented coal furnace
    (2) mowing the lawn
    (3) using a properly installed gas stove
    (4) running a car engine in a closed garage
    (5) using a barbecue grill outdoors

Question 7 refers to the following information and diagrams.

Every cell carries out hundreds of chemical processes. These are controlled and speeded up by enzymes in the cell.

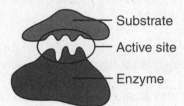

An enzyme is about to bind with its reacting molecule (substrate).

The enzyme holds the substrate in the active site and lowers the amount of energy needed to start the chemical reaction.

The enzyme releases the products of the reaction and returns to its original shape, ready to bind with another substrate molecule.

7. What is the best title for this information?

   (1) The Cell
   (2) Chemical Processes in the Cell
   (3) The Molecular Structure of an Enzyme
   (4) How an Enzyme Works
   (5) An Enzyme's Active Site

---

8. A parasite is an organism that lives in or on another organism, called the host. The parasite depends on the host for its survival, and the host is often harmed by the relationship.

Which of the following is a parasite?

   (1) the millipede, which lives in woodlands and eats decaying vegetation
   (2) the red-tailed hawk, which lives in rural or urban areas and preys on small rodents
   (3) the flea, which lives on the skin of birds and mammals and feeds on their blood
   (4) the barnacle, which attaches itself to rocks or boats and filters food particles from the water
   (5) the acacia ant, which feeds on nectar from acacia plants and attacks animals that try to eat the host plant

9. About 8 percent of men and 0.5 percent of women are colorblind; that is, they have trouble distinguishing colors. Most colorblind people cannot tell red from green. Completely colorblind people see only black, white, and shades of gray. However, complete colorblindness is extremely rare.

What is implied by the fact that many more men than women are colorblind?

(1) Color is less important to men than to women.
(2) The inheritability rate of colorblindness is related to gender.
(3) Colorblindness is an illness that cannot be treated.
(4) Colorblindness is associated with poor vision.
(5) Colorblindness is a harmless defect of vision.

10. A clone is an organism that develops from one parent through asexual reproduction, inheriting all the genetic material from that parent. Dolly the sheep was the first animal clone produced by scientists.

Which of the following organisms is a clone?

(1) a baby born to a mother who was artificially inseminated
(2) a colt born to a mare who mated with a racing stallion
(3) a coleus plant grown from a stem cutting buried in rooting mixture
(4) a pea plant grown from a seed that developed after pollination by another plant
(5) a spider hatched from an egg fertilized by the sperm of a male spider

Question 11 refers to the following diagram.

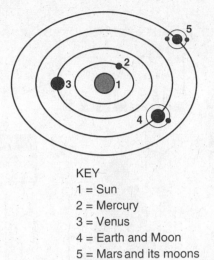

KEY
1 = Sun
2 = Mercury
3 = Venus
4 = Earth and Moon
5 = Mars and its moons

11. Which of the following statements is supported by the information in the diagram?

(1) Mars travels around the sun in less time than Earth does.
(2) The rotation of the planets causes day and night.
(3) Venus is the planet second closest to the sun.
(4) Earth is the only planet with significant amounts of water.
(5) Earth's moon is always farther from the sun than Earth is.

Questions 12 and 13 refer to the following diagram.

AIR POLLUTANTS FROM SMOKESTACKS

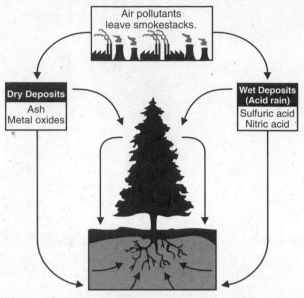

Acidified soil and water leach plant nutrients out of the soil. Heavy metals accumulate in harmful quantities.

12. What causes the air pollutants emitted by smokestacks to become wet deposits?

    (1) incomplete industrial processes
    (2) malfunctioning antipollution devices
    (3) the use of petroleum-based fuels
    (4) action of ocean water
    (5) water vapor in the air

13. What is the eventual effect of dry deposits and acid rain on plant life?

    (1) The plants thrive on the heavy metals building up in the soil.
    (2) The root systems are strengthened because of extra nutrients in the soil.
    (3) The leaves and stems are harmed, but root systems are unaffected.
    (4) The plants are weakened by lack of nutrients and harmed by the heavy metals.
    (5) There is no long-term effect on plant life.

14. Atoms are extremely small. However, even before advanced microscopes gave us images of atoms, scientists working many decades ago found evidence that atoms exist. For example, a small piece of dust suspended in a liquid moves in a random, irregular path. This motion, called Brownian motion, is the result of the dust being continuously hit by atoms or molecules of the liquid.

Another type of evidence for the existence of atoms is x-ray diffraction. x rays are high energy electromagnetic waves. When matter is exposed to x rays, most of the x rays pass right through it. However, some x rays bounce off the dense nuclei of atoms. If the atoms were not there, all the x rays would travel in a straight path.

As evidence for the existence of atoms, what do Brownian motion and x-ray diffraction have in common?

    (1) They both provide clear photographs of atoms.
    (2) They both involve types of electromagnetic waves.
    (3) They both provide indirect evidence of atoms.
    (4) They both involve liquid suspensions.
    (5) They both involve bombarding the atoms.

15. Light waves differ from sound waves in that light waves can travel through the emptiness of outer space as well as through matter. Sound waves can travel only through matter. Light waves travel faster than sound waves. The speed of sound waves in air at 32°F is 1,085 feet per second. The speed of light through air at any temperature is 186,282 miles per second.

Which of the following situations demonstrates that light waves and sound waves travel at different speeds?

(1) seeing lightning before hearing thunder
(2) watching a light show at a night club
(3) looking at neon signs
(4) flying faster than sound in a supersonic jet
(5) calculating the time it takes for sunlight to reach Earth

16. Carbon dioxide gas absorbs the infrared, or heat, radiation given off by Earth's surface, preventing it from escaping into space. The amount of carbon dioxide in the atmosphere varies from place to place and over time. For example, there is more carbon dioxide near cities and industrial areas. The amount of carbon dioxide in the atmosphere has been increasing for the past hundred years.

Which of the following is a conclusion about carbon dioxide in the atmosphere rather than a detail?

(1) Carbon dioxide is a gas in the atmosphere that absorbs infrared radiation given off by Earth.
(2) Different regions have different amounts of carbon dioxide in the local atmosphere.
(3) For at least a century, the amount of carbon dioxide in the atmosphere has been rising.
(4) The concentration of carbon dioxide is greater near cities and industrial areas.
(5) Increasing levels of carbon dioxide in the atmosphere may contribute to global warming.

Question 17 refers to the following information and graph.

Humidity is the concentration of water vapor in the atmosphere at a given time. The graph shows the maximum amount of water vapor the air can hold at various temperatures.

MAXIMUM AMOUNT OF WATER VAPOR IN AIR AT DIFFERENT TEMPERATURES

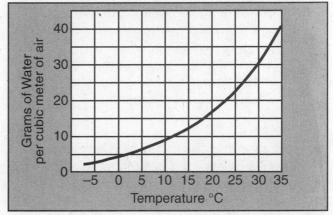

17. Which of the following is likely to happen if the amount of water vapor in the air at 35°C exceeds 41 grams per cubic meter?

(1) The humidity will decrease.
(2) The humidity will increase.
(3) The temperature will drop.
(4) Extra water will evaporate.
(5) It will rain.

18. Tides are the alternate rise and fall of the waters of the oceans. High tide occurs twice a day. Tides are caused primarily by the moon's gravitational pull on Earth. The sun also contributes to the tides, with its gravitational pull.

When would high tide be the highest?

(1) when the sun and moon are positioned in a straight line with Earth
(2) when the sun and moon are positioned at right angles to each other
(3) when there is a waxing crescent moon
(4) when there is a waning crescent moon
(5) when the sun has sunspots

19. Every moving object has kinetic energy, which is determined by both the object's mass and its speed. A moving object can transfer kinetic energy to a stationary object, which then moves.

Which of the following is implied by this information?

(1) The more mass and speed an object has, the less kinetic energy it has.
(2) The kinetic energy of a moving object cannot be measured.
(3) A moving object does not have kinetic energy.
(4) A stationary object does not have kinetic energy.
(5) A stationary object has more kinetic energy than a moving object.

Question 20 refers to the following diagram.

HOW A FISH BREATHES

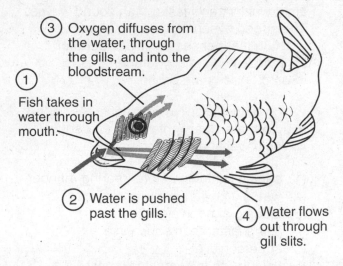

20. The function of a fish's gills is most similar to that of which human body part?

(1) the trachea, down which air travels from the mouth and nose to the lungs
(2) the lungs, which take oxygen from the air and transfer it to the bloodstream
(3) the diaphragm, which expands and contracts to move air in and out of the lungs
(4) the tongue, which aids in swallowing and speaking
(5) the intestines, which absorb water from digested food

21. Charles Darwin hypothesized that species evolve because of natural selection. Since individuals vary, some individuals will have traits that make them well suited for their environment. These individuals are more likely to survive, reproduce, and pass on these traits than individuals that do not possess these traits. Since individuals without these traits are not as well adapted to their environments, they die or have fewer offspring. For example, light-colored peppered moths were well adapted to live on clean trees; they were camouflaged from predatory birds. After the Industrial Revolution, the darker peppered moths were better adapted to live on the dark, sooty trees.

Which of the following experiments would best provide evidence about natural selection?

(1) Release equal numbers of light- and dark-colored moths in two areas, one clean and one sooty, and later count the survivors.
(2) Release a specific number of dark-colored moths in several sooty areas and later count the survivors.
(3) Release a specific number of dark-colored moths in several clean areas and later count the survivors.
(4) Release a specific number of light-colored moths in several sooty areas and later count the survivors.
(5) Release a specific number of light-colored moths in several clean areas and later count the survivors.

Questions 22 and 23 refer to the following chart.

PULSE RATE AFTER ONE MINUTE OF EXERCISE			
Subject's Physical Condition	Pulse Rate (per minute)		
	Light Exercise	Moderate Exercise	Heavy Exercise
Excellent	66	73	82
Very good	78	85	96
Average	90	98	111
Below average	102	107	126
Poor	114	120	142

22. Which of the following is an unstated assumption important for understanding the chart?

(1) The exercise done was either light, moderate, or heavy.
(2) The pulse rate is the number of heartbeats per minute.
(3) The subjects' physical condition varied from excellent to poor.
(4) Subjects in poor physical condition were unable to do the exercise.
(5) Very few people are in excellent physical condition.

23. Which of the following statements is supported by the information in the chart?

(1) The pulse rate continues to increase with additional minutes of exercise.
(2) People in poor physical condition should not do heavy exercise.
(3) The number of breaths per minute rises during exercise.
(4) When exercising, you should stop if you feel dizzy or short of breath.
(5) The greatest jump in the pulse rate comes between moderate and heavy exercise.

Question 24 refers to the following information and diagrams.

All magnets have two poles. Unlike poles attract each other, and like poles repel.

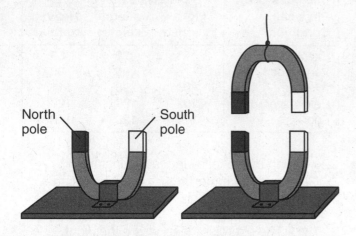

North pole   South pole

24. In the second diagram, a horseshoe magnet suspended on a string has been lowered near the magnet fixed to the table. What is likely to happen next?

(1) The top magnet will turn for about five minutes and then stop.
(2) The top magnet will turn until its north and south poles have exchanged places.
(3) The bottom magnet will turn until its north and south poles have exchanged places.
(4) Both magnets will turn until their north and south poles have exchanged places.
(5) Both magnets will remain stationary.

25. Human embryonic stem cells are cells in a very early stage of development. These cells have not yet begun to differentiate into various types of tissue, such as muscles and skin, but they have the capacity to do so. Some scientists are conducting research on human embryonic stem cells, hoping to use these cells to treat injury or disease. They are experimenting with methods of making the stem cells differentiate in particular ways.

Which of the following is a goal these scientists might have for their new stem cell technology?

(1) to develop new kinds of cell parts for our cells
(2) to make new kinds of body organs to give people new capabilities
(3) to develop skin of different colors and thicknesses
(4) to make new bone marrow cells for patients with leukemia
(5) to make new types of immune system cells to increase our ability to combat disease

Questions 26 and 27 refer to the following information and diagram.

In 1919, Robert H. Goddard proposed a type of rocket that would fly high above the atmosphere in space. People reacted skeptically, saying that a rocket's gases needed to push against the atmosphere in order for the rocket to move. To show the skeptics they were wrong, Goddard made a model and demonstrated that an atmosphere is not necessary for rocket flight.

GODDARD'S PISTOL DEMONSTRATION

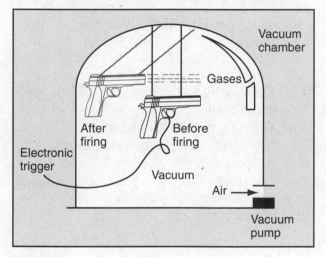

26. Which of the following best summarizes what is shown in the diagram?

    (1) Before the pistol was fired, the air was pumped out of the vacuum chamber.
    (2) A pistol's trigger was electrically fired in a vacuum.
    (3) A pistol hung by suspension wires in a vacuum swung back and forth after the pistol was fired.
    (4) When a pistol was fired in a vacuum, gases were ejected from the barrel and the pistol moved in the opposite direction.
    (5) When a pistol was fired, the bell jar was damaged and the vacuum could not be maintained.

27. Which of the following data from the demonstration support the conclusion that a rocket will move in the vacuum of outer space?

    (1) A vacuum pump was used to empty the chamber of air.
    (2) Two pistols were hung in a vacuum chamber and fired.
    (3) Electricity was used to fire the pistol in the vacuum chamber.
    (4) When the pistol was fired, gases were ejected out the barrel.
    (5) The ejected gases pushed the pistol backward in the vacuum chamber.

Question 28 refers to the following graph.

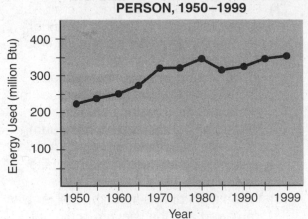

U.S. ENERGY CONSUMPTION PER PERSON, 1950–1999

28. Which of the following is a conclusion based on the graph rather than a detail?

    (1) Energy consumption is measured in British thermal units.
    (2) Per person energy consumption was about 225 million Btu in 1950.
    (3) In the early 1970s, per person consumption of energy leveled off.
    (4) Between 1950 and 1999, per person energy consumption increased.
    (5) Per person energy consumption was the same in 1980 and 1995.

29. The idea that life arises regularly from nonlife is called spontaneous generation. In the 1700s, a scientist claimed that spontaneous generation can occur under the right conditions. He designed one of the first experiments to test whether this was true. First he sealed gravy in a bottle and heated the bottle to kill any living things in it. After a few days he looked at the gravy under a microscope and found it swarming with microorganisms. He incorrectly concluded that "these little animals can only have come from the juice of the gravy."

    What was probably wrong with the experiment?

    (1) Gravy was not a suitable subject.
    (2) There were living things on the outside of the bottle.
    (3) The heat did not kill all the microorganisms in the gravy and the bottle.
    (4) The gravy was left in the bottle too long.
    (5) The microorganisms came from the microscope.

30. Ecological succession occurs when a community of interacting organisms is gradually replaced by a different community of interacting organisms.

    Which of the following is the best example of ecological succession?

    (1) Farmland is abandoned, grasses and shrubs move in, and eventually the area becomes forested.
    (2) A tundra ecosystem is inhabited by mosses, lichens, and grasses, and animals migrate in and out seasonally.
    (3) Tropical grasslands alternate between a rainy season and a dry season each year.
    (4) Intertidal zones undergo radical changes each day as the tides go in and out.
    (5) Forests are bulldozed to make way for a suburban development of houses and strip malls.

Question 31 refers to the following information and diagrams.

A camera has an adjustable hole, called an aperture, behind the lens.

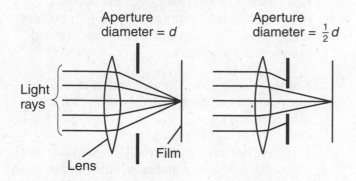

Aperture diameter = d   Aperture diameter = ½d

Light rays

Lens   Film

31. Based on the diagram, what is the effect of reducing the diameter of a camera's aperture?

(1) snapping a photograph
(2) focusing on the subject of the photograph
(3) setting a flash to go off automatically
(4) decreasing the amount of light that reaches the film
(5) spreading out the light rays that reach the film

Questions 32 and 33 refer to the following map.

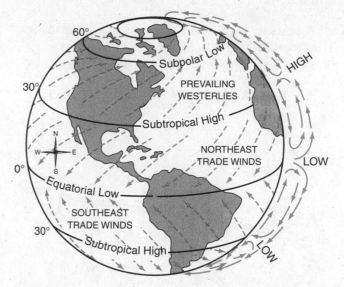

32. Which of the following would be the best title for this map?

(1) The Prevailing Westerlies
(2) High and Low Pressure Systems
(3) The Trade Winds
(4) The Western Hemisphere
(5) Global Wind Patterns

33. Which of the following people would find the information on this map most useful?

(1) a polar explorer planning an expedition
(2) a sailor making preliminary plans for an around-the-world trip
(3) an astronaut orbiting Earth in the space shuttle
(4) a meteorologist forecasting today's wind speed
(5) a paleoclimatologist studying ancient climates

Question 34 refers to the following information and diagram.

A seesaw is an example of a first-class lever. The fulcrum, or pivot, is between the effort (the boy's weight) and the load (his mother).

HOW A SEESAW WORKS AS A LEVER

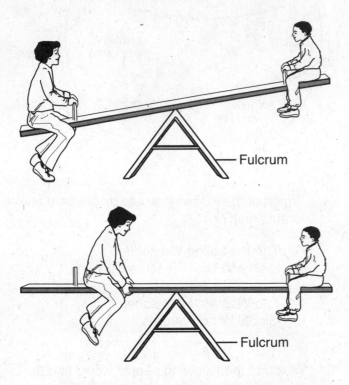

34. Under which circumstances would the boy be able to lift his mother higher into the air?

(1) if the boy moved closer to the fulcrum
(2) if the boy got off the seesaw and pushed down
(3) if the mother moved away from the fulcrum
(4) if the mother moved closer to the fulcrum
(5) if both mother and boy moved closer to the fulcrum

35. Electric current from a battery always flows in one direction and is called direct current (DC). In contrast, household current reverses direction at regular intervals and is called alternating current (AC). Since U.S. household current completes 60 cycles of reversal per second and European current completes 50 cycles of reversal per second, they are not compatible.

Sarah, who lives in Denver, wants to take an alarm clock on her trip to Germany. Which of the following should she do?

(1) Take her plug-in alarm clock since it runs on DC, which is standard worldwide.
(2) Take her plug-in alarm clock since it runs on AC, which is standard worldwide.
(3) Take an alarm clock that runs on AC batteries and contains its own power source.
(4) Take a battery-operated alarm clock, which runs on DC and contains its own power source.
(5) Rely on wake-up calls from her hotel operator, since American-made clocks will not operate in Europe.

36. Nerve impulses can move along the membrane of a neuron, or nerve cell, at about 1 meter per second. However, some neurons are coated with a substance called myelin. Myelin-coated neurons can transmit nerve impulses much faster—200 meters per second. The impulses jump between gaps in the myelin instead of traveling along the membrane. Myelin-coated neurons are common in vertebrates and much less common in invertebrates.

Which of the following animals is most likely to have large numbers of myelin-coated neurons?

(1) a badger
(2) a bumble bee
(3) a lobster
(4) a spider
(5) a starfish

Question 37 refers to the following information and graph.

The resources of an ecosystem can support a maximum number of individuals of a particular species. When this number, called the carrying capacity, is exceeded, the population falls. The graph shows how carrying capacity affects the population of water fleas in an ecosystem.

WATER FLEA POPULATION OVER TIME

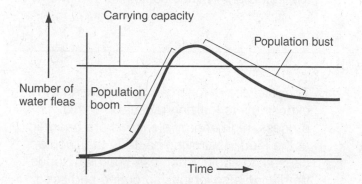

37. Which of the following best summarizes the information and the graph?

(1) The population of a species, such as water fleas, increases until the carrying capacity of the ecosystem is exceeded, and then it falls.
(2) The population of water fleas increases sharply, peaks, and then decreases gradually over time.
(3) The population of water fleas remains stable in a given ecosystem for long periods of time.
(4) The carrying capacity of the ecosystem rises sharply, then falls as resources of the ecosystem are used up.
(5) The carrying capacity of the ecosystem depends on the changing population of water fleas.

38. Convergence is the tendency of unrelated species to develop similar structures in order to adapt to similar environments. For example, the wings of a bat (a mammal) and those of an eagle (a bird) are similar, even though the bat and eagle are not closely related. Both evolved to adapt to life in the air.

Which of the following is an unstated assumption important for understanding this paragraph?

(1) Convergence is the tendency of unrelated species to develop similar structures.
(2) The structures are adaptations to life in similar environments.
(3) The development of convergent structures occurs gradually, over millions of years.
(4) Both bats and eagles have wings, even though the two species are not closely related.
(5) The wings of bats and eagles evolved as adaptations to life in the air.

Question 39 refers to the following diagram.

THREE WAYS TO REPRESENT WATER

39. Which of the following best restates what is shown above?

(1) A water molecule consists of two atoms of hydrogen and one atom of oxygen.
(2) Water consists of three atoms combined into a molecule.
(3) An oxygen atom is larger than a hydrogen atom.
(4) H is the chemical symbol for hydrogen, and O is the chemical symbol for oxygen.
(5) Water is a liquid resulting from the combination of two gases, hydrogen and oxygen.

Question 40 refers to the following diagrams.

SOUND WAVE PATTERNS RELATED TO AIRPLANE FLIGHT AT DIFFERENT SPEEDS

At the speed
of sound

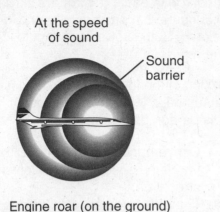

Sound
barrier

Engine roar (on the ground)

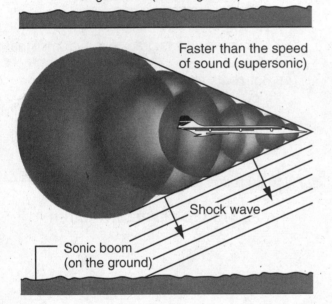

Faster than the speed
of sound (supersonic)

Shock wave

Sonic boom
(on the ground)

40. In which of the following situations would the information in the diagrams have to be taken into account?

(1) planning aircraft flight paths over populated areas
(2) recording the miles flown by supersonic aircraft
(3) learning how to fly an airplane
(4) learning emergency maneuvers in an airplane
(5) establishing price scales for airplane tickets

41. The shelf life of food can be increased by exposing it to ionizing radiation. In this process, high energy electrons are beamed at the food, destroying bacteria that would cause it to spoil. When used on plant foods, irradiation also inhibits sprouting and seed germination. Some people fear that eating irradiated food is harmful.

Which of the following is an opinion about irradiation rather than a fact?

(1) The shelf life of food can be increased by exposing it to ionizing radiation.
(2) High energy electrons are beamed at the food.
(3) Irradiation destroys bacteria that would cause food to spoil.
(4) Irradiation inhibits sprouting and seed germination in plants.
(5) Eating irradiated foods can be harmful to people's health.

Question 42 refers to the following diagram.

LEVELS OF ORGANIZATION IN THE HUMAN BODY

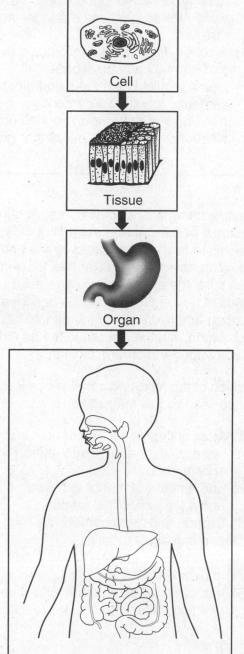

Cell

Tissue

Organ

Organ System

42. Which is the most complex level of organization shown in the diagram?

(1) the cell nucleus
(2) the cell
(3) tissue
(4) the stomach
(5) the organ system

43. Photosynthesis stores energy; cellular respiration releases energy. The products of photosynthesis (glucose and oxygen) are the raw materials of cellular respiration. The products of cellular respiration (energy, carbon dioxide, and water) are the raw materials of photosynthesis.

What is the relationship between photosynthesis and cellular respiration?

(1) They are essentially similar processes.
(2) They are opposite processes.
(3) Respiration is a type of photosynthesis.
(4) Photosynthesis is a type of respiration.
(5) Energy is a product of both processes.

Questions 44 and 45 refer to the following information and chart.

Blood alcohol content (BAC) is a measure of the percentage of alcohol in the bloodstream.

EFFECT OF ALCOHOL ON THE HUMAN BRAIN	
Blood Alcohol Content	Behavior
0.05%	Lack of judgment, lack of inhibition
0.1%	Reduced reaction time, difficulty walking and driving
0.2%	Sadness, weeping, abnormal behavior
0.3%	Double vision, inadequate hearing
0.45%	Loss of consciousness
0.65%	Death

44. A woman weighing 115 pounds and a man weighing 185 pounds each drink two shots of bourbon whiskey. How would their blood alcohol content compare?

   (1) Their blood alcohol content would be the same.
   (2) The man's blood alcohol content would be higher than the woman's.
   (3) The woman's blood alcohol content would be higher than the man's.
   (4) They both would have a blood alcohol content of zero.
   (5) They both would have a blood alcohol content of 0.1 percent.

45. Which of the following conclusions is supported by the information given?

   (1) Alcoholism is a disease in which people become addicted to alcohol.
   (2) Long-term alcohol use damages cells in the liver.
   (3) Alcohol affects both conscious behavior and normal body functions.
   (4) Death results when the blood alcohol content exceeds 0.3 percent.
   (5) It is illegal to drive when your blood alcohol content is 0.1 percent or greater.

46. In an experiment, a small candle is burned inside a bell jar. Although most of the candle seems to have disappeared by the end of the experiment, the bell jar has the same weight at the end of the experiment as it does at the beginning. This is because the carbon and hydrogen in the candle have combined with the oxygen in the air to form water vapor and carbon dioxide.

Which of the following conclusions is supported by this information?

   (1) Most of the matter in a candle melts rather than changing into other substances.
   (2) The amount of matter is the same before and after a chemical reaction.
   (3) Carbon and hydrogen always form water and carbon dioxide.
   (4) A burning candle will cause a bell jar to explode.
   (5) It is easier to experiment with chemical reactions than with nuclear reactions.

Question 47 refers to the following information and diagram.

Fractional distillation is based on the principle that different gases condense at different temperatures.

FRACTIONAL DISTILLATION OF CRUDE OIL

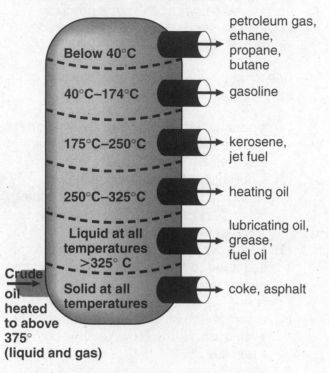

Below 40°C → petroleum gas, ethane, propane, butane

40°C–174°C → gasoline

175°C–250°C → kerosene, jet fuel

250°C–325°C → heating oil

Liquid at all temperatures >325° C → lubricating oil, grease, fuel oil

Solid at all temperatures → coke, asphalt

Crude oil heated to above 375° (liquid and gas)

47. Which of the following statements is supported by the information given?

   (1) The substances with the lowest condensing points rise to the top of the tower.
   (2) Gasoline condenses at a higher temperature than heating oil.
   (3) Crude oil enters the distillation tower at the top and various products separate out.
   (4) Kerosene separates out at about 300°C.
   (5) Crude oil is the end product of fractional distillation.

48. In 1957, the Soviet Union launched the first orbiting satellite in space. In response, the United States stepped up its space effort. During the 1960s, the United States spent $115.3 billion on NASA's Apollo program, whose goal was to land human astronauts on the moon. The Apollo program was supported by most of the U.S. public. Which of the following was the most likely reason for this?

   (1) It was the best use of federal tax dollars.
   (2) It provided employment for engineers.
   (3) It tapped into patriotic feelings about beating the Soviet Union in space exploration.
   (4) It provided an opportunity to do research in astronomy for research's sake.
   (5) It led to many products and technologies useful on Earth.

49. A phenotype is an observable trait, such as leaf shape, that is controlled by genes. In some cases, the genes responsible for a trait can produce different phenotypes under different environmental conditions. For example, the water buttercup is a plant that grows in shallow ponds. Some of its leaves grow above water, and some grow underwater. Above-water leaves are broad and well-developed—with lots of surface area to catch a lot of sunlight. Underwater leaves are finely divided and small.

Which of the following statements presents a conclusion rather than a supporting detail?

(1) Leaf shape is an example of a phenotype controlled by genes.
(2) The water buttercup grows in shallow ponds both above and under the water.
(3) Some of the water buttercup's leaves grow above the surface of the water and are large and broad.
(4) Some of the water buttercup's leaves grow underwater and are thin and finely divided.
(5) The genes responsible for some traits can produce different phenotypes under different environmental conditions.

50. Annuals are plants that grow from seed, flowering, producing seeds, and dying in the course of one growing season. Biennials also sprout from seeds; they grow roots, stems, and leaves during their first season. The leaves and stems die back to the ground in winter, but the roots remain alive. The following growing season, new stems and leaves grow and the plant produces flowers and seeds. Once biennials produce seeds, they die.

Based on the information above, which of the following is a biennial?

(1) a petunia, which grows in spring, flowers in summer, produces seeds in fall, and then dies
(2) a hollyhock, which grows leaves in spring and summer, dies back in winter, flowers and sets seed the following summer, and dies in the fall
(3) a tulip, which grows from a bulb and can be forced to flower indoors in the winter or can survive outdoors, blooming every spring
(4) a cactus that blooms every spring, after it rains, and turns brown every summer, when it is dry
(5) a tree that produces flowers and seeds early every spring and loses its leaves every fall

Answers start on page 321.

Simulated Test Performance Analysis Chart
Science

This chart can help you determine your strengths and weaknesses on the content and reading skill areas of the Simulated GED Science Test. Use the Answers and Explanations starting on page 321 to check your answers to the test. Then circle on the chart the numbers of the test questions you answered correctly. Put the total number correct for each content area and skill area in each row and column. Look at the total questions correct in each column and row and decide which areas are difficult for you. Use the lesson references to study those areas.

Thinking Skill / Content Area	Comprehension (Lessons 1, 2, 6, 9, 13)	Application (Lessons 8, 15)	Analysis (Lessons 3, 4, 7, 10, 14, 17, 19)	Evaluation (Lessons 5, 11, 12, 16, 18, 20)	Total Correct
Life Science (Pages 32–107)	**7**, 9, **37**, **42**	8, 10, **20**, 25, 29, 30, 50	5, **13**, **22**, 38, 41, 43, **44**, 49	21, **23**, 36, **45**	____/23
Earth and Space Science (Pages 108–155)	**4**, 32	**3**, 18, **33**	**12**, 16, **28**	**11**, 48	____/10
Physical Science (Pages 156–218)	19, **26**, **39**	**1**, 6, 15, 35, **40**	14, **17**, **24**, **31**, 34	**2**, **27**, 46, **47**	____/17
Total Correct	____/9	____/15	____/16	____/10	____/50

1–40 → You need more review.
41–50 → Congratulations! You're ready for the GED!

Boldfaced numbers indicate questions based on charts, graphs, diagrams, and drawings.

For additional help, see the *Steck-Vaughn GED Science Exercise Book.*

Answers and Explanations

1. **(1) 0–1 year** (Comprehension) According to the graph, children gain about 13 pounds between birth and 1 year. This is the largest gain shown on the graph. You can tell it's the largest because the slope of the lines between age 0 and age 1 is the steepest. You can also tell it's the largest weight gain by figuring out the weight gains during other years. Between ages 1 and 2 (option 2), children gain about 6 pounds. Between 2 and 3 (option 3), they gain about 4 pounds. Between 3 and 4 (option 4), they gain about 4 pounds. Between 4 and 5 (option 5), they gain about 5 pounds.

2. **(2) Billy's weight is above average for his age and sex.** (Analysis) According to the graph, at age 4 the average boy weighs about 36 pounds. Thus Billy, at 39 pounds, weighs more than the average 4-year-old boy. Option (1) is incorrect because Billy weighs more than average. Option (3) is incorrect because the average 5-year-old boy weighs about 41 pounds, and Billy weighs only 39 pounds. Option (4) is incorrect because the average 4-year-old girl weighs about 35 pounds, and Billy weighs more than that. Option (5) is incorrect because the average 3-year-old boy weighs about 33 pounds, and Billy weighs more than that.

3. **(1) A river flows from a higher elevation to a lower elevation.** (Analysis) Although the diagram shows the river flowing through the mountain valley, nothing in the diagram indicates the direction of flow. The artist takes for granted that you know that water flows downhill because of the force of gravity. Options (2), (3), and (4) are all incorrect because the diagram clearly shows these things; so they are not unstated, nor are they assumptions. Option (5) is incorrect because nothing in the diagram indicates that alluvial fans form only near volcanoes (they don't).

4. **(5) The majority of tomatoes fell in the middle of the weight range.** (Analysis) By examining the bar graph, you can see that most of the tomatoes weigh between 10 and 14 ounces, in the middle of the range of weights. Since a conclusion is a generalization based on many details, this is the only statement that is broad enough to serve as a conclusion. The remaining options are incorrect because they are all supporting details from the graph.

5. **(4) to store a great deal of oxygen in a small space** (Analysis) According to Boyle's Law, the volume of a gas becomes smaller as the pressure increases. This means that more oxygen can be stored in a cylinder if the oxygen is under pressure. Option (1) is not correct because if the oxygen is simply contained in a cylinder, it will be prevented from mixing with air; it does not need to be stored under pressure to prevent this mixing. Option (2) is incorrect because, although the oxygen gas will initially heat up when compressed, it is not stored under pressure for the purpose of heating it up. Option (3) is incorrect because oxygen is pressurized when stored for practical reasons, not to illustrate a law of nature. Option (5) is incorrect because the oxygen is already a gas.

6. **(5) The Development of the Cell Theory** (Comprehension) The passage traces a few highlights in the history of discoveries about cells, resulting in the formulation of the cell theory. Option (1) is incorrect because the focus of the passage is on cells, not on microscopes. Option (2) is incorrect because the passage does not give a detailed description of the appearance of the cells. Option (3) is not a good choice because the passage doesn't indicate whether these scientists were the first life scientists. Option (4) is incorrect because the information about Robert Hooke is a detail rather than an idea general enough to work as a title.

7. **(3) Leave the storm protection measures in place because the rain and winds will start again soon.** (Application) The family is experiencing the lull in the storm caused by the passage of the eye overhead. Once the eye passes, the rain and winds resume, with the winds blowing from the opposite direction, the west. Option (1) is incorrect because the hurricane has not passed; if the winds had been from the west, they could have concluded that the hurricane was over when the storm ended. Option (2) is based on an assumption that may not be true, so removing the storm protection measures does not make sense. Option (4) is incorrect because hurricanes are storms of such vast size that two of them would probably not occur within a space of two days. Option (5) is incorrect because the hurricane is not over, and taking a walk at this point might be dangerous.

8. **(4) coat it lightly with oil so that air and water will not reach the surface** (Application) Oiling the cookware provides an air- and water-resistant barrier to protect the iron from rusting. Option (1) is incorrect because water will cause the iron to rust. Options (2) and (3) offer only partial protection to the iron, and they are not practical when using cookware.

Option (5) is wrong because it does not involve a way to keep air and water away from the cookware surface.

9. **(2) fruit peels and coffee grounds** (Application) Fruit peels and coffee grounds are types of kitchen waste that were once living and that do not have a high-protein content, so they are ideal ingredients for a compost pile. Option (1) is incorrect because the gardener is producing a natural fertilizer by making compost; he or she would not need to add fertilizer or soil to the pile, although soil can be mixed with compost. Option (3) is incorrect because, although egg shells make good compost, eggs are a high-protein food and thus not good for a compost pile. Option (4) is incorrect because dead branches, although yard waste, take a very long time to decompose, and meat bones are a high-protein kitchen waste and so not good for compost. Option (5) is incorrect because the microscopic organisms come into the compost pile on their own; they are not added by the gardener.

10. **(1) chloroform** (Analysis) According to the chart, chloroform has the lowest boiling point of the liquids, 61.7 degrees Centigrade. Therefore, it would be the first to come to a boil. Options (2) through (4) are incorrect because it would take longer to heat these liquids to the boiling point than it would take to heat chloroform. Option (5) is not true since the liquids have different boiling points. Therefore, when heated at the same rate, they will start to boil at different times.

11. **(1) carnivores** (Application) Since cats eat mice they are meat-eaters and thus members of the group of mammals called carnivores. Option (2), cetaceans, is incorrect because cats are not ocean-dwellers. Option (3), marsupials, is incorrect because the female cat does not have a pouch. Option (4) is incorrect because cats are meat-eaters and rodents eat mostly plants. They are not primates, option (5), because they do not have specialized limbs for grasping (such as thumbs) or complex brains.

12. **(4) a pouch where the young stay after birth** (Evaluation) The pouch is listed as the key characteristic that makes marsupials different from other groups of mammals. Option (1) is incorrect because powerful hind legs are not a general characteristic of marsupials, but a specific characteristic of kangaroos. Option (2) is incorrect because long feet are not a key characteristic of marsupials. Option (3) is incorrect because grasping paws are generally characteristic of primates, not of marsupials. Option (5) is incorrect because all mother mammals produce milk for their young; thus this cannot be used as a distinguishing characteristic of marsupials from among other groups of mammals.

13. **(5) primates** (Application) Humans, with their complex brains, grasping thumbs, and depth perception, are members of the primate group of mammals. Thus a scientist who studies the evolution of humans over the years would probably be most interested in other primates, the closest evolutionary relatives of humans. Options (1) through (4) are incorrect because humans are not members of these groups. Carnivores include animals like lions and wolves. Cetaceans include whales and dolphins. Marsupials include opossums and kangaroos. Rodents include mice, squirrels, and rats.

14. **(4) The steel and air in a ship are less dense than water.** (Evaluation) The diagram shows that a hollow steel cube is less dense than water and so it floats. Steel ships float because they are not made of solid steel, but of steel and air—like the floating cube in the diagram, they are hollow. Thus they are less dense than an equal volume of solid steel, which would sink, and also less dense than water. Option (1) is incorrect because it does not explain why steel ships float; it simply restates that fact in another way, an example of circular reasoning. Option (2) is true of solid steel, but this fact doesn't explain why steel ships float (steel ships are not solid steel, but hollow). Option (3) is not true; if it were true, then solid steel would float, which does not happen, as the diagram shows. Option (5) is also not true, as the diagram indicates; if the steel and air were denser than water, then the ship would sink.

15. **(1) Place identical containers holding different materials in a sunny spot, and record their temperatures just before sundown and at regular intervals after sundown.** (Evaluation) To determine which is the best passive solar material, the materials must be tested under the same conditions—the same type of container and the same sunny location. In addition, temperature readings just before sundown, when the materials have absorbed the most heat, tell you which heat up the most. Then periodic temperature readings after sundown tell you which material takes the longest to give off its heat. Option (2) is incorrect because recording the temperature just twice, at sunrise and sundown, will not tell you how long each material took to radiate its heat energy. Option (3) is incorrect because it involves testing only one type of material, so no comparisons with other materials will be possible; checking how different amounts of a material absorb and radiate heat, although possibly useful, is not the

purpose of the experiment. Option (4) is incorrect because using different kinds of containers as well as different materials will not allow you to determine whether the container or the material is causing any difference noted in temperature; also feeling the containers, rather than taking temperature measurements, is not an accurate enough measure of their ability to radiate heat. Option (5) is incorrect because placing the materials in a shaded spot will not test their ability to absorb energy from the sun.

16. **(5) one north pole and one south pole** (Comprehension) According to the information given, every magnet has two poles, a north pole and a south pole. Therefore it follows that each of the two magnets that results when you cut a magnet in half will also have two poles, a north pole and a south pole. Option (1) is incorrect because a magnet has only one north pole. Option (2) is incorrect because a magnet has only one south pole. Options (3) and (4) are incorrect because a magnet has two poles, north and south.

17. **(1) Males do not live long and only a few are required to fertilize a queen.** (Evaluation) The role of the winged males is to fertilize a queen, so only a few males are needed to perform this function when there is one queen. Option (2) is not supported by information in the passage. Based on the information given, option (3) is not true; male ants hatch from unfertilized eggs. Option (4) is true, but it does not explain why there are fewer males than workers. Option (5) is not true; according to the information given, protecting the colony is a task done by the female workers, not by the winged males.

18. **(2) Scientists, like other people, sometimes have trouble changing long-held beliefs.** (Analysis) The writer assumes that the scientists are reluctant to credit the new findings because they are having trouble dealing with change, a characteristic common to many people. Options (1), (3), (4), and (5) are incorrect because they are all statements actually made in the paragraph.

19. **(5) Using electricity to clean up industrial solvents should be cheaper than using traditional methods.** (Analysis) Since this method is still in the testing stage, the researchers' belief that using electricity will be cheaper than traditional decontamination methods is an opinion. It cannot be proved true or false until the costs have been compared with those of the traditional methods. Options (1) through (4) are all facts stated in the passage, not opinions.

20. **(3) to release energy** (Comprehension) According to the information given, cellular respiration breaks down food molecules, giving off energy for the organism. Options (1) and (5) are incorrect because they describe parts of the process of cellular respiration, not its larger purpose. Option (2) is incorrect because proteins are broken down, not built, during cellular respiration. Option (4) is incorrect because the digestive system carries out the processes that take in food molecules. Cellular respiration takes place after the food molecules are in the cell.

21. **(5) static, rolling, and sliding friction** (Application) To start the file cabinet moving, the office workers need to overcome static friction; they encounter sliding friction as they push the cabinet across the floor and as they load it onto the dolly. As they push the dolly across the floor, they encounter rolling friction. The other options do not list all of the types of friction that occur in the situation.

22. **(2) The oil will probably spread farther south and west.** (Evaluation) If the oil spreads a couple of hundred miles to the south and west in the first two months, it will probably spread farther in this direction over the next two months. Option (1) is incorrect because the map indicates that most of the oil—72 percent—remained after the first two months. Option (3) is incorrect because if only 27 percent of the oil was cleaned up in the first two months, and if the pace of the cleanup continues, it is not likely that all the oil will be gone by the end of the next two months. Option (4) is incorrect because the oil spreads along the ocean's surface; it is not absorbed. Option (5) is incorrect because if only 20 percent of the oil evaporated in the first two months, it is not likely that all of it will evaporate completely in the next two months.

23. **(4) reluctance to spend profits on cleaning up accidents** (Evaluation) By placing the burden of paying for oil spill cleanups on the oil companies, Congress gave them a strong motivation to prevent accidents in the future. Options (1) and (2) are incorrect because although oil companies have environmental and ecological concerns, those are not their primary concerns; they are in business to recover and sell an environmental resource, oil. Option (3) is incorrect because the oil companies don't have much of an interest in particular local fisheries since their tankers operate worldwide.

Option (5) is incorrect because none of the given information supports any conclusion about employee morale.

24. **(3) seven** (Comprehension) The atoms of fluorine are shown to the left of the arrow in the electron dot diagram. If you count the dots, you will find that each atom has seven dots, or electrons. When the two atoms combine into a molecule (on the right side of the arrow), each atom has eight electrons in the outer shell because they share two of them.

25. **(1) a stretched rubber band** (Application) According to the information given, an object that has changed shape or moved its position has potential energy. Thus a stretched rubber band, since it has changed shape, has potential energy. Options (2), (3), (4), and (5) are incorrect because these items are not described with reference to their ability to move or to change shape. Thus, as described, they have no potential energy.

26. **(2) The return signals would become unbalanced.** (Analysis) According to the labels in the diagram, when the target is above or below or to one side or the other, the returning radar signals are unbalanced. Thus if the target, which was dead ahead, dives downward, the returning radar signals would become unbalanced. Option (1) is incorrect because the signals would stop being balanced as soon as the target started its dive. Option (3) is incorrect because this would occur only if the target were moving away, not toward, the fighter plane. Option (4) is incorrect because the return signals would not stop suddenly; that would happen only if the target disappeared. Option (5) is incorrect because the fighter plane would continue to pick up returning signals from the target, which is diving a relatively short distance.

27. **(3) the increase in the prey population between time *a* and time *c*** (Analysis) To answer this question, you must first locate the line representing the increasing population of predators between time *b* and time *d*. Then look for a cause—something that happened earlier that might be related to the increase in predator population. What happened was that an increase in prey preceded the increase in predators. When the predators had more to eat, their population increased. Option (1) is incorrect because the prey population increased between time *a* and time *b*. Options (2) and (4) are incorrect because anything that happened after time *d* cannot be a cause of events before time *d*. Option (5) is incorrect because it does not explain why the predator population increased; it simply describes the interval between the growth of one population and the growth of the other.

28. **(2) the carbon-oxygen cycle, in which carbon and oxygen are cycled through the environment** (Application) Through photosynthesis, green plants take carbon out of the environment in the form of carbon dioxide gas, and incorporate it in the food they make. They release oxygen into the environment. Thus photosynthesis plays a large role in cycling carbon and oxygen through the environment. Option (1) is incorrect because photosynthesis does not involve nitrogen or most types of bacteria. Option (3) is incorrect because photosynthesis is not directly involved in the development of organisms that undergo metamorphosis. Option (4) is incorrect because the cell cycle goes on in almost all cells and is not directly involved with photosynthesis. Option (5) is incorrect because the solar cycle is not affected by photosynthesis.

29. **(4) Members of the same species need the same resources.** (Evaluation) Members of the same species need the same resources, and so competition for these resources is likely to be more intense than when two species, with at least slightly different needs, are competing. Options (1) and (2) are both true, but neither supports the conclusion that competition within a species is more intense than competition between species. Option (3) is incorrect because members of a species take a mate from within their own species; they do not compete with other species for mates. Option (5) is incorrect because members of different species usually need at least slightly different resources.

30. **(3) An Electric Circuit** (Comprehension) The paragraph explains what an electric circuit is, and the drawing and schematic show an electric circuit, so this is a good title. Options (1) and (4) are incorrect because they focus on details, not on an idea general enough to serve as a title. Option (2) is too general to be a good title for this paragraph and illustration. Option (5) is incorrect because, although there is a light bulb in the circuit, the paragraph and illustration do not explain how a light bulb works.

31. **(5) The electric current would stop flowing, and the light bulb would not light up.** (Analysis) According to the paragraph, an electric circuit is a continuous path for the flow of current. When the path is interrupted, as by the cutting of the wire, then current stops flowing and the ammeter would register 0 current and the light bulb would not light up. Option (1) is incorrect because cutting the wires in a circuit would not affect the rate at which the chemicals in the battery get used up. Option (2) is incorrect because the ammeter would register a sudden drop in current if the wire were cut. Options (3)

and (4) are incorrect because the electric current would stop flowing if the wire were cut; the ammeter would work, but register 0 current; the light bulb would not light up.

32. **(3) installing the wiring for a new apartment building** (Application) A schematic would serve as a road map for installing the wiring in a new building. Option (1) is incorrect because if you were checking for electrical safety hazards, you would want to examine the actual wiring and appliances, not a diagram. Option (2) is incorrect because explaining how to operate a washing machine does not involve knowledge of its electrical circuits. Option (4) is incorrect because you can check the item to see which battery size is appropriate. Option (5) is incorrect because a schematic is a representation; to measure the actual current in a circuit, you would need an ammeter.

33. **(3) A geyser erupts when hot underground rocks heat water to boiling.** (Comprehension) This option covers all the main points of the diagram. The diagram shows hot rocks heating underground reservoirs of water. When the water gets hot enough, it boils and erupts through a vent on the surface. Option (1) is true, but it is just one detail shown in the diagram; it does not provide a good summary of the whole diagram. Option (2) is incorrect because a geyser's water has its source underground, not in surface lakes or rivers. Option (4) is incorrect because the diagram does not indicate any movement of rock. Option (5) is also true, but it does not summarize the diagram, which shows "any" geyser, not a particular geyser like Old Faithful, and does not indicate whether eruptions are regular.

34. **(2) in a hot-water heating system** (Application) The water in a geyser is boiling hot, so it works well in a hot-water heating system. The water would be too hot to be used in the applications given in the other options. It also might contain harmful dissolved minerals or other substances, which could also make it unfit for use for drinking, bathing, recreation, or irrigation.

35. **(5) Capillaries transport substances in the blood to and from the body's tissues.** (Analysis) This statement is a generalization, or conclusion, that can be drawn from the various details in the diagram. These details, including options (1), (2), (3), and (4), show various substances that enter and leave the blood.

36. **(4) Water flows from high elevations, such as mountains, to sea level.** (Analysis) The map shows that the watershed areas are bounded by mountainous areas, which are higher than sea level. Water flows downward. Options (1) and (2) are true but do not tell why rivers flow toward oceans. Option (3) is incorrect because the map shows at least one river, the Columbia, flowing west rather than south. Option (5) is incorrect because it is true only under flood conditions; it does not explain why rivers normally flow to sea level.

37. **(2) They saw that the Columbia River was flowing to the west.** (Application) After they crossed the Rocky Mountains, explorers saw that water was flowing to the west rather than to the southeast as it had been. This suggested that water was flowing to a western ocean, the Pacific. Options (1) and (4) are incorrect because they have nothing to do with confirming where the explorers were. Option (3) is incorrect because simply finding the source of the river would not indicate the general direction in which the river system flows. Option (5) is incorrect because a river's height and whether it is a major watershed are not related.

38. **(5) developing early warning detectors for forest fires** (Application) Since the fire beetles excel at long-distance detection of burning trees, understanding how they accomplish this may yield practical application in fire detection technology. Option (1) is incorrect because the beetles' ability to detect fires has nothing to do with reducing smoke. Option (2) is incorrect because if the fires were planned and controlled, as a part of a fire management program, there would not be a need for fire detection, which is what the beetles can do. Option (3) is incorrect because the beetles' ability to detect fire is not related to the development of chemicals to kill insects. Option (4) is incorrect because the uses to which beetles put their antennas is different from the uses to which cellular phone antennas are put.

39. **(2) in plastic wrap used to protect food from contamination or moisture** (Application) The information indicates that phthalates from flexible plastics might be harmful if these chemicals are taken into the bloodstream. These chemicals might enter the bloodstream via the digestive system, should the chemicals have contact with food people eat. So phthalates in plastic wrap used for food have the most potential to harm for people. Option (1) is incorrect because most medical labs throw away tissue samples after they have been tested; the tested samples do not come in contact with patients. Options (3), (4), and (5) are incorrect because they do not include uses in which the phthalates could easily enter the user's bloodstream.

Answers and Explanations

40. (1) Cell division takes about one-twentieth the time that interphase takes. (Analysis) If you examine the outer part of the circle graph you will see that interphase takes about 21 hours and cell division takes only 1 hour in the human liver cell. Thus cell division is much shorter than interphase—it takes about one twentieth the time that interphase takes. Option (2) is incorrect because cell division takes much less than half the time that interphase takes. Option (3) is incorrect because cell division takes less time than interphase, not more time. Option (4) is incorrect because interphase is divided into three, not eight, phases. Option (5) is incorrect because the circle graph shows that human liver cells undergo both interphase and cell division.

41. (1) a cardiologist (Application) Chest pain indicates a possible problem with the heart, located in the chest. In addition, high cholesterol is associated with blockages of the arteries. Thus the family doctor is likely to refer the patient to a cardiologist, who treats problems of the heart and arteries. Option (2), an endocrinologist, is incorrect because this specialist deals with diseases involving hormones. Option (3) is incorrect because the patient's problem is not with the blood itself but with the circulatory system—heart and arteries. The blood test is an indicator that something may be wrong with the circulatory system. Option (4) is incorrect because the patient shows no signs of growths or tumors. Option (5) is incorrect because the information does not indicate that the patient has problems with bones, joints, and muscles.

42. (4) good health (Evaluation) Since storing nuclear waste always involves the risk of radioactivity escaping into the environment, people who live near proposed sites and oppose them usually value their own health over any overall benefit to the larger community. Option (1) is incorrect because people generally organize into groups to oppose such sites; they do not work as individuals. Option (2), ambition, is not relevant to the siting of a nuclear waste disposal facility. Option (3) is incorrect because people who oppose a nuclear disposal site are not likely to benefit monetarily. Option (5) is a value they may hold, especially as they work as a group with their neighbors, but the purpose of working together is to safeguard the health of the neighborhood's residents, not to improve neighborhood relations.

43. (3) A more energetic shake will produce a wave of greater amplitude. (Evaluation) By comparing the two diagrams, you can see that when the hand moves up and down with a more energetic motion (in the second diagram), the rope carries a wave with more energy, or greater amplitude. Option (1) is incorrect because although some of the energy from the hand movement may be transferred into the air, nothing in the diagrams indicate that most of the energy is transferred into the air. Option (2) is incorrect because the energy produced by one shake will move down the rope, and eventually the wave will stop when the energy from the one shake is used up. Option (4) is incorrect because the diagrams show that amplitude is the distance between the top of a wave and the center line (rest position) of the wave. Option (5) is incorrect because, in both diagrams, the wave motion will move Point A and Point B up and down, so sometimes Point B will be above Point A.

44. (3) length of day (Analysis) If you read across each row, comparing the characteristics of Earth and Mars, you will find that in most cases the two planets are quite different. However, the length of their days is almost the same—about 24 hours. Option (1) is incorrect because Mars is much farther from the sun than Earth is. Option (2) is incorrect because the Martian year is almost twice as long as Earth's year. Option (4) is incorrect because Mars' surface gravity is about one-third that of Earth. Option (5) is incorrect because Earth's diameter is almost twice that of Mars.

45. (2) Camouflage protects organisms by making them difficult to detect. (Analysis) The writer assumes that you understand the purpose of camouflage and does not explain what camouflage is or what it is for. Options (1), (3), (4), and (5) are all facts stated in the paragraph and therefore are not unstated assumptions.

46. (5) an ax used to split wood (Application) The blade of an ax is a wedge. When you move the ax blade into something, like a log, it exerts a sideways force to split the log. Option (1) is incorrect because a steering wheel is not a wedge; it involves circular motion. Option (2) is incorrect because a balance scale is not a wedge; it is a type of lever in which effort force and resulting force work in the same direction, downward. Option (3) is incorrect because a handcart does not exert sideways force. Option (4) is incorrect because faucet handles involve circular motion.

47. (1) decrease calorie intake (Analysis) The results of this experiment indicated that total calorie intake affected weight gain or loss, not the percent of fat in the diet. Therefore, eating a diet with fewer calories will result in weight loss. Options (2) and (5) would result in weight gain, not loss, because of increased calories.

Options (3) and (4) are incorrect because the study showed that the critical factor in weight gain or loss is calories, not fat content.

48. **(3) Offspring of sexual reproduction differ genetically from each parent.** (Comprehension) Since sexual reproduction involves getting a mix of genetic material from two parents, then it follows that the offspring has a new set of genetic material and is not identical to either parent. Options (1) and (2) are incorrect because nothing in the paragraph indicates that either sexual or asexual reproduction occurs only among one type of organism. Option (4) is incorrect because offspring of asexual reproduction are identical genetically to their parents. Option (5) is incorrect because nothing in the paragraph compares the number of species that reproduce sexually and asexually.

49. **(4) Synthetic motor oil has a lower freezing point than natural motor oil.** (Evaluation) Since temperatures in cold climates are low, the lower freezing point of synthetic motor oil would enable people to keep their vehicles running at lower temperatures than would be possible if they used natural motor oil, which has a freezing point 10 to 15 degrees higher. Option (1), (2), and (3) are all true statements about natural motor oil, but they do not explain why people in colder climates should use synthetic motor oil. Option (5) is also true, but it does not explain why synthetic motor oil is superior to natural motor oil in colder climates.

50. **(4) Water evaporates and rises into the air, where it cools, forming clouds and then rain.** (Comprehension) This option touches on all the important points of the diagram—water on land and in the ocean, evaporation, and condensation into clouds and rain. All the remaining options are incorrect because they describe only small portions of the diagram, not all its main points.

UNIT 1: LIFE SCIENCE
Lesson 1
GED Skill Focus (Page 35)
1. **b.** Epithelial tissue forms protective surfaces for the body. Note that this main idea must be inferred from reading the first two sentences of the first paragraph; it is an unstated main idea.

2. Your answers may include the following: epithelial tissue is flat and broad; the cells of epithelial tissue are close together; the tissue can control which substances pass through it; the skin is formed of epithelial tissue; the lining of organs such as the stomach is made of epithelial tissue.

3. **b.** Connective tissue supports and holds together parts of the body.

4. Your answers may include the following: connective tissue is strong; bone and cartilage are types of connective tissue; calcium fills the spaces in connective tissue and gives it strength.

5. **a.** the skin

6. **a.** The cells are very close together.

GED Content Focus (Page 37)
1. **(2) All organisms are made up of cells, which carry out the basic life processes.** (Comprehension) This is the main idea of the paragraph, which is about cells and their functions. Option (1) is true, but the living processes of cells, rather than their death, is the focus of the paragraph. Options (3), (4), and (5) are also all true, but they are too specific to be the main idea of the paragraph. They are details that support the main idea.

2. **(5) The nucleus is one of the cell's most complex structures.** (Comprehension) The second paragraph is about the nucleus of the cell. Option (5) is the correct answer because it is a general statement that covers all the points made in the paragraph. Option (1) is incorrect because the paragraph focuses on the nucleus, not on the structures in the cytoplasm. Options (2) and (4) are incorrect because these are details not mentioned in the paragraph. Option (3) is a detail that supports the main idea.

3. **(4) The nucleus is the control center of the cell.** (Comprehension) Option (4) is correct because the nucleus directs all the complex activity of the cell. Options (1), (2), (3), and (5) are incorrect because they are details about the cell that do not relate to the importance of the nucleus.

4. **(2) to show and describe various cell structures** (Comprehension) Option (2) is correct because it gives the topic, or general idea, of the diagram of the cell and its structures. Options (1), (3), and (4) are incorrect because they are details, not the main idea. Option (5) is incorrect because the diagram does not show how materials pass through the cell membrane.

5. **(1) Ribosomes make proteins, the endoplasmic reticulum transports them, and the Golgi apparatus sends them where they are needed.** (Comprehension) To answer this question, you must look at the details of the diagram, and read the labels that describe the functions of the different organelles. Option (1) correctly describes the organelles that make, transport, and direct proteins. Options (2), (3), (4), and (5) are incorrect because they do not

describe all the organelles involved in making and processing proteins, or because they give incorrect details about organelle functions.

6. **(1) Organisms are made of cells that have specialized structures to carry out life processes.** (Comprehension) This sentence covers the main ideas of the passage and diagram: that living things are made of cells, that cells carry out life processes, and that cells have specific structures that carry out the functions relating to the life processes. Option (2) is too specific; it deals only with one-celled and many-celled organisms. Option (3) is also too specific; it only covers the life processes. Option (4) does not explain the basic importance of cells. Option (5) is too specific.

GED Practice (Pages 38–39)

1. **(1) Plant Cell Structures and Their Functions** (Comprehension) The diagram shows the structures of a plant cell, and the passage describes their functions. Option (2) is incorrect because the diagram and passage do not cover cellular reproduction. Option (3) is incorrect because the passage does not mention similarities between plant and animal cells. Option (4) is incorrect because it is a detail, not the main idea, of the passage and diagram. Option (5) is incorrect because only plant cells, not parts of plants, are discussed and shown.

2. **(4) chromoplasts** (Application) Chromoplasts contain yellow, orange, and red pigments that give daffodil and rose petals their color. Options (1), (2), (3), and (5) are incorrect because they are structures not involved with color in plants.

3. **(2) The vacuoles shrank as their water was used up.** (Analysis) Vacuoles help support the plant when they are full of water, so when they empty out, that support decreases and the plants wilt. Options (1), (3), (4), and (5) are incorrect because they are consequences that do not involve water.

4. **(2) Bacteria that enter your nose will be killed.** (Analysis) By destroying the cell wall, the protein kills the bacteria. Option (1) is incorrect because the protein cannot prevent bacteria from entering the nose when you breathe. Option (3) is incorrect because the protein cannot affect bacteria outside the nose. Option (4) is incorrect because if the cell wall is destroyed, the bacteria is destroyed and cannot reproduce. Option (5) is incorrect because the bacteria will change shape when the cell wall is broken down.

5. **(4) Cell biologists have succeeded in growing blood vessels from living cells.** (Comprehension) The passage and diagram describe growing blood vessels using other types of cells. Option (1) is incorrect because it is too general. Option (2) is not true. Option (3) is not mentioned in the passage or diagrams, and whether true or not, it is a detail. Option (5) also is a detail.

6. **(2) Scientists may someday be able to form replacement body parts from living cells.** (Analysis) Scientists are pursuing research of this type because they may someday be able to use the blood vessels to repair damage to the human circulatory system. Option (1) is incorrect because if artificial parts were superior, people would not bother to try to make parts from living cells. Option (3) is incorrect because it is only recently that scientists have succeeded in doing this. Option (4) is incorrect because the diagram gives the amount of time for blood vessel formation (eight weeks) without making a judgment about this length of time. Option (5) is incorrect because it is a fact stated in the diagram.

7. **(3) to provide a physical support for the growing nerve cells** (Application) The plastic would be likely to serve the same purpose in growing nerve cells as it does in growing blood vessels. Option (1) is incorrect because the plastic is placed between the cut nerves. Option (2) is incorrect because the plastic cannot provide living nerve cells. Option (4) is incorrect because the plastic does not function to take away wastes. Option (5) is incorrect because no muscle cells are present with the nerve cells and the plastic does not cause the nerve cells to grow.

GED Mini-Test (Pages 40–41)

1. **(3) The Process of Mitosis** (Comprehension) This title describes the main topic of the passage. Options (1), (2), and (4) are incorrect because they focus on details relating to interphase or mitosis. Option (5) is incorrect because the passage does not explain why cell division is important.

2. **(1) The nuclear membrane dissolves during prophase.** (Evaluation) Option (1) is correct because the second frame of the diagram shows the nuclear membrane disappearing during prophase. Option (2) is incorrect because the diagram does not show the spindle fibers as they form during prophase. Option (3) is incorrect because the diagram does not indicate what happens if spindle fibers are cut. Option (4) is incorrect because the diagram does not indicate anything about the protein content of the cell. Option (5) is incorrect because the diagram does not indicate the duration of each phase.

3. **(3) 6** (Comprehension) According to the passage, each daughter cell will have the same number of chromosomes as the parent cell after cell division. So if the parent cell has 6 chromosomes at the beginning of interphase (before cell division begins to take place), each daughter cell it eventually produces will also have 6 chromosomes.

4. **(4) Bacterial cells have genetic material but no nucleus.** (Evaluation) According to the paragraph, bacterial cells have no nucleus, but the diagram shows the genetic material of a bacterial cell suspended in the cytoplasm. Option (1) is incorrect because the paragraph states that bacterial cells are smaller. Options (2), (3), and (5) are incorrect because the diagram shows that bacterial cells have ribosomes, a cell wall and a cell membrane, and cytoplasm.

5. **(3) by combining its reproductive cell with that of another organism of the same species** (Analysis) Since each of the reproductive cells has half the normal number of chromosomes, combining two reproductive cells—one each from a male and a female—produces an offspring with the normal number of chromosomes. Option (1) is incorrect because this manner of reproduction does not require reproductive cells. Option (2) is incorrect because the resulting offspring would have only half the chromosomes it needed. Option (4) is incorrect because the result would be twice the number of chromosomes as needed. Option (5) is incorrect because organisms that reproduce sexually do so by means of their reproductive cells, not by combining nonreproductive cells.

6. **(2) The tips of the chromosomes may play a role in the rate of cell division.** (Comprehension) Since the tips of the chromosomes differ in healthy (normal cell division) and cancerous (rapid cell division) cells, the tips of the chromosomes are involved in the rate of cell division. This expresses the main idea of the paragraph. Options (1) and (4) are incorrect because they are details of the paragraph, not the main idea. Option (3) is incorrect because the structure of the chromosome does affect the rate of cell division. Option (5) is not true; according to the paragraph, cancer cells multiply faster than normal cells.

7. **(2) B** (Comprehension) Of the cells shown here, only those in Option (2) have hair-like structures (cilia) that can filter out dust. Options (1), (3), (4), and (5) show (1) white blood cells, (3) nerve cells, (4) red blood cells, and (5) cells in connective tissue, none of which have cilia.

Lesson 2
GED Skill Focus (Page 43)

1. **b.** Producing bread involves a natural process called alcoholic fermentation.

2. Your answer may be similar to the following: A product of fermentation, carbon dioxide gas, makes dough and batter rise.

3. **a.** Dough rises because of the bubbles that are formed by carbon dioxide gas.

4. **a.** Alcohol, carbon dioxide bubbles, and small amounts of energy are produced.

GED Content Focus (Page 45)

1. **(2) Plants make their own food through photosynthesis.** (Comprehension) This is the only option that states the main point of the passage. Options (1), (3), (4), and (5) are details mentioned in the passage.

2. **(1) sugar** (Comprehension) According to the passage and diagram, the plant produces sugar to use as food. Options (2) and (3) are byproducts of photosynthesis. Option (4) is an ingredient used in photosynthesis. Option (5) is a substance needed for photosynthesis to occur.

3. **(5) Water plus carbon dioxide, in the presence of light and chlorophyll, yields sugar, oxygen, and water.** (Comprehension) This is the only option that correctly restates all the elements of the photosynthesis equation. Option (1) omits chlorophyll. Option (2) omits light. Option (3) states incorrectly that hydrogen is a product. Option (4) says that oxygen is an ingredient and carbon dioxide a product, both of which are wrong.

4. **(3) In the light reactions, chemical energy splits water into hydrogen and oxygen.** (Comprehension) According to the passage, chlorophyll changes light energy into chemical energy, which then splits molecules of water. Option (1) is incorrect because only oxygen, not water, is a byproduct of both the light reactions and the dark reactions. Option (2) is incorrect because water is broken down in the light reactions and carbon dioxide is broken down in the dark reactions. Option (4) is incorrect because carbon dioxide is used in the dark reactions, not the light reactions. Option (5) is incorrect because the color of the products has nothing to do with the difference between the light and dark reactions.

5. **(5) water** (Comprehension) The diagram shows water on both sides of the equation, both entering and leaving the leaf; the passage states that water is split in the light reactions and it is

produced as a product of the dark reactions. Options (1) and (3) are incorrect because carbon dioxide and sunlight are shown in the diagram entering, but not leaving, the leaf and are mentioned in the passage as ingredients, but not as products. Option (2) is incorrect because the passage states that light energy is changed into chemical energy during photosynthesis, and the diagram does not show chemical energy either entering or during photosynthesis leaving the leaf. Option (4) is incorrect because the diagram indicates that sugar is manufactured within the leaf; it does not show sugar either entering or leaving the leaf.

6. **(1) Green plants capture the sun's light energy and change it to chemical energy that plants and animals can use.** (Evaluation) This is the only statement that is supported by the details in the passage and the diagram. Option (2) is incorrect because the ultimate source of energy is sunlight. Option (3) is incorrect because in most plants, photosynthesis takes place mainly in the leaves. Option (4) is incorrect because photosynthesis is only a minor source of water on Earth. Option (5) is incorrect because photosynthesis can take place in artificial light.

GED Practice (Pages 46–47)

1. **(2) the sum of all the chemical processes carried out by a cell** (Comprehension) As defined in the first sentence of the passage, metabolism is the total of all chemical processes in a cell. Option (1) is the definition of photosynthesis, not of metabolism. Option (3) is the definition of cellular respiration, not of metabolism. Option (4) is incorrect because it is only a partial definition of metabolism. Option (5) is incorrect because metabolism is related to cell processes, not to the amount of raw material.

2. **(5) sunburst** (Comprehension) The arrows, option (1), represent processes. Option (2), the circles, represent amino acids. Option (3), the chained circles, represent protein chains. Option (4), the hexagons, represent glucose.

3. **(4) There are fewer catabolic reactions.** (Analysis) Since glucose is a raw material of the catabolic reactions, less glucose means less catabolism. Option (1) is incorrect because light energy is not affected by the amount of glucose entering a cell. Option (2) is incorrect because the amount of glucose entering a cell would not affect the amount of amino acids that enter. Option (3) is incorrect because less glucose would mean less energy to make proteins. Option (5) is incorrect because the cell would produce less (not more) energy with less glucose.

4. **(2) increased catabolic reactions** (Application) More exercise means more energy will be needed, and catabolism will increase. Options (1) and (4) are incorrect because photosynthesis takes place only in green plants, not in the human body. Option (3) is incorrect because increased use of energy would not necessarily affect the rate of anabolism. Option (5) is the opposite of what would have happened.

5. **(4) The rate of cellular respiration goes up during exercise to give additional energy to the body.** (Analysis) Options (1) and (2) are incorrect because they do not pertain to Jason's experiment. Option (3) is incorrect because more energy is needed for exercise, not less. Option (5) is incorrect because the amount of carbon dioxide in exhaled breath is not directly related to lung capacity.

6. **(2) a dropper** (Analysis) A dropper would be useful for adding drops of sodium hydroxide solution to the water. Option (1) is incorrect because no heating is involved. Option (3) is incorrect because nothing needs to be measured with a spoon. Options (4) and (5) are also unnecessary for this procedure.

7. **(3) Jason did not measure the level of carbon dioxide in his breath when at rest, so he did not have enough data to draw a conclusion.** (Evaluation) Since he only measured the carbon dioxide after five minutes of exercise, he had nothing to compare this amount to. Options (1) and (5) are incorrect because five minutes of exercise (running) is enough to affect the rate of cellular respiration. Option (2) is incorrect because resting means he would be testing carbon dioxide under the wrong circumstances. Option (4) is incorrect because the passage indicates that both chemicals are used to measure exhaled carbon dioxide.

8. **(2) broad, flat shape** (Analysis) The shape of a leaf gives it a large surface area, so it can absorb lots of light energy. Option (1) is incorrect because the pores allow substances like carbon dioxide or water vapor to flow in and out. Option (3) is incorrect because the stalk provides support. Option (4) is incorrect because the veins allow transport of water and minerals. Option (5) is incorrect because the root system of the plant is not a characteristic of the leaf.

GED Mini-Test (Pages 48–49)

1. **(4) mitochondrion** (Comprehension) According to the passage, the bulk of the energy is released in the mitochondrion, not in the other cell structures listed in options (1), (2), (3), and (5).

2. **(5) Glucose and oxygen combine to yield carbon dioxide, water, and energy.** (Comprehension) Option (5) correctly restates the chemical formula for cellular respiration. Option (1) is incorrect because it is a restatement of the chemical formula for photosynthesis. Option (2) is incorrect because water and oxygen have been reversed as an ingredient and a product of respiration. Option (3) is incorrect because carbon dioxide is a product and oxygen an ingredient of respiration. Option (4) is incorrect because energy is released as a product, not absorbed as an ingredient, of respiration.

3. **(1) Less energy is released.** (Analysis) Both the diagram and the passage show that oxygen is one of the ingredients for cellular respiration; when the supply of oxygen is reduced, cellular respiration slows, and less energy will be released. Option (2) is incorrect because it is the opposite of what would happen. Option (3) is incorrect because with less oxygen, respiration slows down. Option (4) is incorrect because less cellular respiration means less, not more, of its product, carbon dioxide, is released. Option (5) is incorrect because the supply of oxygen does affect cellular respiration.

4. **(2) More green plants means more oxygen in the air.** (Evaluation) Since oxygen is a product of photosynthesis, more green plants means more oxygen released into the atmosphere. Option (1) is incorrect because it is the opposite of what is true. Option (3) is incorrect because with less photosynthesis taking place, carbon dioxide in the air would increase, not decrease. Fewer green plants making glucose means less glucose is produced, and so less energy is stored in glucose, not more, as stated in option (4). Option (5) may or may not be true, but the passage does not provide enough information to support it.

5. **(1) Carbohydrates are excellent sources of energy.** (Comprehension) The passage indicates that both sugars and starches are carbohydrates and are used by the body to release energy. Option (2) is incorrect because the passage does not compare the relative amounts of energy contained in sugars and starches. (Note that they both contain the same amount of energy per unit weight.) Option (3) is not true and is not suggested by the passage. Option (4) is incorrect because the passage does not deal with the relative amounts of sugars and starches in various foods. Although option (5) is true, it is not suggested by the passage.

6. **(3) Bread begins to taste sweet after it is chewed for several seconds.** (Evaluation) Sweetness is an indication of the presence of sugar, which is a breakdown product of starch. Options (1), (2), (4), and (5) are true, but they do not support the statement.

7. **(3) its reflectivity** (Analysis) Reflective plastic will cast more light on the plants, increasing the rate of photosynthesis. The other properties of the plastic will not affect the rate of photosynthesis.

8. **(2) Cellular respiration using oxygen is a more efficient way to release energy than lactic acid fermentation.** (Evaluation) Option (2) is supported by the statement that cellular respiration with oxygen yields 19 times as many ATP molecules as does lactic acid fermentation. Options (1) and (3) are not true, according to the information given. Options (4) and (5) are true, but they are not supported by the information given.

Lesson 3
GED Skill Focus (Page 51)

1. **a.** Genetics is the study of traits and how they are passed from parent to offspring.

2. Your answer may be similar to the following: Statement *a* is a fact because it can be proved true by confirming the definition of the word *genetics* by looking it up in a dictionary, a textbook, or the glossary of this book.

3. **b.** Gregor Mendel should have used animals rather than plants in his genetics experiments.

4. *Option b* is an opinion because it expresses a belief that Mendel should have done his work differently; there is no way to prove that it is correct. Option *a* can be proved true.

5. **a.** In the diagram, one pea has many more wrinkles than the other pea.
   b. Mendel had to judge whether offspring plants had wrinkled or round peas.

GED Content Focus (Page 53)

1. **(3) in all offspring that have a gene for it** (Comprehension) According to the passage and the diagram, a dominant trait will appear in any organism that has inherited it from at least one parent. Option (1) is wrong because the parent that shows the dominant trait may also have, and pass along, the recessive version of the trait. Option (2) is incorrect because an organism can have one parent that shows the recessive trait, but if the other parent shows the dominant trait, the offspring can inherit the dominant gene from that parent and so show the dominant trait. Option (4) is incorrect because an organism needs to have received a dominant gene from only one of its parents to show the dominant trait. Option (5) is incorrect because a dominant trait may appear in any generation.

2. **(3) Some of the F_2 generation plants showed the recessive trait.** (Evaluation) The recessive trait skipped a generation, but it was still there, ready to reappear. Option (1) is incorrect because all of the F_1 generation plants were hybrids and had received the recessive trait from one parent, although this trait did not show up in the F_1 generation. Option (2) is true, but it is not evidence that the recessive trait is hidden in that generation. Option (4) is true but does not support the idea that the recessive traits were hidden in the F_1 generation. Option (5) is not true and thus cannot support the conclusion; only about one-fourth of the F_2 generation plants showed the recessive trait.

3. **(2) A Punnett square is easier to read than sketches showing traits passing from parents to offspring.** (Analysis) Whether a chart or a drawing is easier to read is a matter of opinion. Options (1), (3), (4), and (5) are facts.

4. **(1) purebred plants** (Comprehension) According to the passage, Mendel first bred pea plants so certain characteristics consistently appeared. Such plants are purebred. He then used these as the parents. Option (2) is incorrect because Mendel's accuracy was based on breeding two different purebreds with one another. Option (3) is incorrect because Mendel focused on one type of trait at a time. Options (4) and (5) are incorrect because Mendel used both short and tall purebred plants.

5. **(2) From patterns of inheritance, he reasoned that traits must be transmitted on physical units.** (Analysis) Mendel kept track of the results of his breeding experiments, and soon he realized there were patterns in the passing of traits from one generation to the next. He thus hypothesized that there must be a physical unit that passes traits from parent to offspring. Option (1) is incorrect because nothing in the passage indicates that Mendel was working with anything other than the whole organism, the plants themselves. Option (3) is incorrect, because the cause-effect relationship that is stated neither makes sense nor answers the question. Option (4) is incorrect because plants have many traits; Mendel chose to study one trait at a time. Option (5) is true, but it does not explain how Mendel posited the existence of genes.

6. **(1) no chance** (Comprehension) All of the offspring are tall, because each one inherited the dominant trait, T. Therefore, there is no chance an offspring will be short.

GED Practice (Pages 54–55)

1. **(2) 1** (Comprehension) All the people represented in the Punnett square have cleft chins, because each has at least one copy of the dominant gene.

2. **(1) the phenotype of her chin** (Evaluation) All you can tell with any accuracy is the girl's appearance, or phenotype. Options (2) and (3) are incorrect because you can't tell whether the girl has a recessive gene or not simply by looking at her. Options (4) and (5) are incorrect because you cannot tell by looking at the girl whether one or both parents have a cleft chin, and if only one parent has a cleft chin, which one it is.

3. **(5) 4 out of 4** (Analysis) According to the information, the red plant has the genotype RR and the white plant has the genotype rr. So all the offspring would inherit the genotype Rr, which results in pink flowers. The Punnett square, below, shows how this works.

	R	R
r	Rr	Rr
r	Rr	Rr

RR = red
rr = white
Rr = pink

4. **(3) to map and sequence human DNA** (Comprehension) As stated in the second paragraph of the passage and also described in the third paragraph of the passage, the purpose of the research on the human genome is to map and sequence human DNA. Options (1), (2), (4), and (5) do not state the main purpose of this research.

5. **(5) The results of the private company's sequencing and mapping are of poor quality.** (Analysis) Based on the passage, that is the opinion of some scientists. The clue here is the phrase *poor quality*, since assessments of quality generally involve opinion, and are not strictly related to fact. Options (1), (2), (3), and (4) are incorrect because they are facts stated in or implied by the passage.

6. **(3) preventing and treating hereditary diseases** (Analysis) The more that is known about the human genome, the better medical scientists will be able to understand hereditary diseases and develop treatments for them. Option (1) is incorrect because the fast and efficient sequencers were designed before the genome was "read." Option (2) is not directly related to knowledge of the human genome. Options (4) and (5) are incorrect because they would involve study of the genomes of other species (bacteria or plants).

7. **(1) identifying criminals** (Application) By matching a DNA "fingerprint" taken from a

suspect's blood or other tissue to blood or tissue found at a crime scene, investigators can identify possible criminals. Option (2) is incorrect because blood typing does not require identifying DNA. Option (3) is incorrect because it does not refer to human DNA at all. Option (4) is incorrect because DNA is not needed to do laser surgery. Option (5) is incorrect because DNA fingerprints are not needed for treating disease.

GED Mini-Test (Pages 56–57)

1. **(1) controlling the production of proteins in the cell** (Comprehension) According to the passage, this is a function of DNA. Options (2) and (3) are incorrect because different cell structures perform these functions. Options (4) and (5) are not functions of DNA but of other chemicals in the cell.

2. **(4) TACAGTCG** (Comprehension) Since A always pairs with T and G always pairs with C, the match for ATGTCAGC is TACAGTCG.

3. **(5) The sidepieces of DNA are formed of alternating units of sugar and phosphate.** (Evaluation) The diagram clearly shows option (5) to be correct. Option (1) is incorrect because, as the diagram shows, the crosspieces are made of nitrogen bases not of sugar and phosphates. Option (2) is incorrect because both sidepieces of DNA contain both sugars and phosphates. Option (3) is incorrect because in the diagram thymine is always paired with adenine, not with guanine. Option (4) is incorrect because the diagram shows all four of the nucleotide bases attaching to the two sidepieces.

4. **(3) The Formation of Messenger RNA** (Comprehension) The diagram shows the three main steps in the process of the formation of messenger RNA, as described in the first paragraph of the passage. Options (1) and (4) are mentioned in the passage, but they are not shown in the diagram. Option (2) is the necessary first step in the process of messenger RNA formation, but it is not the main idea of the diagram. Option (5) is incorrect, because, although amino acids are mentioned in the passage, they are not formed in the nucleus and they are not shown in the diagram.

5. **(1) a change in the sequence of amino acids in a protein** (Analysis) Since the base sequence of DNA codes for protein synthesis, a mutation that changes one base in the DNA is likely to cause a change in the sequence of amino acids in a protein. Options (2), (3), (4), and (5) are all possibilities, depending on the nature of the protein affected by the mutation, but they are much less likely to occur.

6. **(5) The DNA database violates Icelanders' right to privacy.** (Analysis) This is an opinion because people's beliefs about what constitutes privacy vary. Options (1), (2), (3), and (4) are facts, since they can be proved true.

7. **(4) screening for genetic diseases** (Application) The DNA profiles of Icelanders would be very useful in conducting tests for genetic diseases. Options (1) and (2) are incorrect because HIV/AIDS and bacterial infections are infectious diseases that are not related to genetics. Option (3) is incorrect because diet is not related to genetics. Option (5) is incorrect because DNA profiles have nothing to do with infant vaccinations.

Lesson 4

GED Skill Focus (Page 59)

1. **a.** Air is pulled into and pushed out of the lungs by the diaphragm.
   c. Carbon dioxide and oxygen are gases in the air.

2. **b.** Capillary walls are thin enough to allow gas molecules to pass through.

3. **b.** The alveoli are enlarged to show detail; they are much smaller than the lungs.

GED Content Focus (Page 61)

1. **(2) to break down food into substances the body can use** (Comprehension) The purpose of the digestive system is explained in the second paragraph of the passage. Option (1) is true but is only a part of the digestive system's function. Option (3) is not true. Option (4) is the function of the immune system, not the digestive system. Option (5) is the function of the respiratory system, not the digestive system.

2. **(1) from the pancreas and the liver to the small intestine** (Comprehension) According to the passage, substances from the pancreas and liver enter the small intestine by means of small tubes, or ducts. Option (2) is incorrect because substances do not move from the pancreas to the liver. Options (3), (4), and (5) are incorrect because the esophagus, stomach, and small and large intestine are all connected so that substances pass directly from one to the next.

3. **(5) Stomach acid is strong enough to damage the stomach lining.** (Analysis) The writer assumes that you know that stomach acid is extremely strong. Options (1) through (4) are all true, but they are facts stated explicitly in the passage. They are not unstated assumptions.

4. **(4) to the large intestine** (Comprehension) According to the passage, the food leaves the small intestine and enters the large intestine. Options (1) and (2) are incorrect because food

passes through them before it reaches the small intestine. Options (3) and (5) are incorrect because food never actually enters the liver and the pancreas, although these organs contribute substances that aid digestion.

5. **(3) Saliva is a liquid.** (Analysis) This fact is assumed, but never stated, by the writer. Options (1), (2), (4), and (5) are all true, but they are facts stated explicitly in the passage; they are not unstated assumptions.

6. **(4) Fats would not be digested properly.** (Analysis) Bile from the liver breaks down fats into small droplets. This process would be disrupted if anything were wrong with the liver. Options (1), (2), (3), and (5) are not functions of the liver.

7. **(2) The salivary glands in the mouth produce saliva, which begins the breakdown of starches.** (Evaluation) This is a fact supported by the information about saliva in the passage and the diagram's label showing the salivary glands in the mouth. Option (1) is not the function of the digestive system; it is the function of the urinary system. Option (3) is incorrect because protein breakdown occurs in the small intestine, and bile from the liver breaks down fats, not protein. Option (4) is incorrect because solid waste passes out through the large intestine. Option (5) is not true because bile is an enzyme, not a nutrient, and it is released, not absorbed, by the liver.

GED Practice (Pages 62–63)

1. **(3) the left ventricle** (Comprehension) The left ventricle forces blood through the aorta, which leads to blood vessels throughout the body. Option (1), the right ventricle, sends oxygen-poor blood to the lungs. Option (2), the right atrium, collects oxygen-poor blood from the body. Option (4), the left atrium, receives oxygen-rich blood from the lungs. Option (5) is a pair of blood vessels, not a chamber of the heart.

2. **(4) The body would not get enough oxygen-rich blood.** (Analysis) Since the aorta sends oxygen-rich blood throughout the body, if it were partially blocked, the flow of this blood would be reduced. Option (1) is incorrect because blood doesn't enter the left ventricle through the aorta. Option (2) is incorrect because oxygen-poor blood enters the heart through the venae cavae, not through the aorta. Option (3) is incorrect because the oxygen-poor blood passes to the lungs through the pulmonary arteries, not through the aorta. Option (5) is incorrect because oxygen-rich blood does not enter the venae cavae.

3. **(1) The arteries and veins are blood vessels, and they are part of the circulatory system.** (Analysis) The writer gives information about veins and arteries and their functions, but does not state explicitly that they are blood vessels and part of the circulatory system. Options (2) through (5) are all true, but they are stated in the passage or shown in the diagram.

4. **(1) a woman who lives in a wooded area of the Upper Midwest** (Application) According to the map and passage, people living in the Upper Midwest have a high risk of contracting Lyme disease if they live, work, or play in wooded areas. Option (2) is incorrect because people who live and work in large cities like Chicago are not likely to come into contact with deer ticks. Option (3) is incorrect because the map shows that the Great Plains is a low-risk area. Option (4) is incorrect because a man who works at sea is not likely to come into contact with deer ticks. Option (5) is incorrect because the vaccine is not approved for use with children.

5. **(5) The vaccine stimulates the immune system to make bacteria-killing antibodies.** (Evaluation) This statement is supported by the description of how the vaccine works. Options (1), (2), (3), and (4) are incorrect because the information in the passage contradicts them.

GED Mini-Test (Pages 64–65)

1. **(3) They are at right angles so head movement in any direction can be detected.** (Comprehension) The diagram shows that the semicircular canals are interconnected and positioned at right angles to each other. Options (1), (2), (4), and (5) do not correctly describe how the semicircular canals are arranged, so these options are all incorrect.

2. **(2) Less blood would circulate in the body.** (Analysis) Clogged blood vessels become narrower, allowing less blood to flow throughout the body. Option (1) is incorrect because it is the opposite of what actually would happen. Option (3) is not true because blood vessels do not change in type. Option (4) is not true because all blood would still remain within the circulatory system. Option (5) is not true because clogged blood vessels do affect the manufacture of blood cells.

3. **(2) Wearing sneakers may reduce the chance of developing arthritis in the knees.** (Evaluation) Sneakers, since they are flat, do not produce the same stress on the knees as high heels do, and so they may help prevent osteoarthritis in the knees. There is no information in the passage to support options (1), (3), (4), and (5).

4. **(4) Healthy sections of a man's intestine are used to replace diseased sections.** (Application) Of the choices given, this one involves the greatest compatibility between donor and recipient, since they are the same person. The closer the compatibility, the greater the chance of a successful transplant. Options (1), (2), (3), and (5) are incorrect because they involve donors and recipients who are more distantly, if at all, related than the man described in option (4). Therefore, these transplants are less likely to be compatible and less likely to succeed.

5. **(1) adrenal** (Analysis) According to the chart, adrenaline secreted by the adrenal glands prepares the body for emergencies. The reactions stated in the question are reactions to emergency situations and are caused by adrenaline. Options (2), (3), (4), and (5) are incorrect because they name other endocrine glands with other functions.

6. **(2) oxytocin** (Comprehension) According to the chart, oxytocin is the hormone that causes uterine contractions during labor, or childbirth. Option (1) is not mentioned in the chart. Options (3) and (4) are sex hormones, produced by the ovaries and the testes respectively. Option (5) is the hormone secreted in emergencies.

7. **(3) by the blood** (Analysis) The function of the blood is to carry substances throughout the body. Options (1), (2), (4), and (5) are incorrect because they list systems or substances that do not transport substances throughout the body; they each have other functions.

8. **(3) insulin** (Comprehension) According to the chart, insulin secreted by the pancreas lowers the level of sugar in the blood. Therefore, a high level of sugar may indicate inadequate amounts of the hormone insulin. Options (1), (2), (4), and (5) are incorrect because these hormones do not affect blood sugar levels.

Lesson 5
GED Skill Focus (Page 67)

1. **a.** language   L
   b. visual cues   R
   c. logic   L
   d. emotions   R
   e. spatial cues   R
   f. sequence   L

2. **a.** People are either right-brained or left-brained, depending on whether they are logical or artistic.

3. **a.** Messages can travel between the two hemispheres of the brain across the corpus callosum.

c. When you read a story, the right side of the brain processes visual and emotional cues and the left side processes language.

GED Content Focus (Page 69)

1. **(1) the axons of interneurons or other motor neurons** (Comprehension) According to the passage, motor neurons receive information from interneurons. The diagram shows that impulses are transmitted from the axons of neurons. Thus a motor neuron receives impulses from the axons of interneurons. Option (2) is incorrect because motor neurons do not receive impulses directly from sensory neurons. Options (3) and (4) are incorrect because the dendrites receive information. Option (5) is incorrect because motor neurons receive impulses from interneurons, not sensory neurons, and because the cell body of a neuron does not transmit impulses.

2. **(5) the fingertips** (Application) Of all the body parts listed, the fingertips are the most sensitive, so it is likely they have more sensory neurons than options (1), (2), (3), or (4).

3. **(2) Neurotransmitters carry the signal from one neuron to another.** (Evaluation) Neurotransmitters are chemical messengers between neurons. Option (1) is incorrect because signals travel within a neuron by electrical impulses; however, as the question text implies, neurotransmitters transmit signals from one neuron to another. Option (3) is an example of faulty logic; in fact, a neuron has both a dendrite and an axon as well as other parts. Option (4) is incorrect because motor neurons pass information to muscle fibers. Option (5) is incorrect because all neurons produce neurotransmitters.

4. **(2) Messages from the brain would not reach the legs and the pelvis.** (Analysis) A break in the spinal cord at waist level would cut the lower portion of the body off from communication with the brain and vice versa. Option (1) is incorrect because the spinal cord would continue to function. Options (3), (4), and (5) are incorrect because messages would continue to travel between the brain and body parts above the waist.

5. **(3) Information is transmitted to and from all parts of the body via the brain and spinal cord.** (Comprehension) Like a communications network, the nerves, spinal cord, and brain send and receive information throughout the body. Options (1), (2), (4), and (5) are all true, but none of them explains how the nervous system functions as a communications network.

6. (3) The spinal cord controls some activities of the nervous system. (Evaluation) The statement that the brain controls the activities of the nervous system is an example of oversimplification. According to the passage, both the brain and the spinal cord control the activities of the nervous system. Options (1), (2), and (4) are true, but they do not explain why the statement is an example of faulty logic. Option (5) is not true.

GED Practice (Page 70)

1. (5) Information is also passed by interneurons in the spinal cord. (Evaluation) According to the diagram, interneurons, as well as sensory and motor neurons, are involved in simple reflexes. Options (1), (2), (3), and (4) are untrue. Simple reflexes involve all three types of neurons and involve the spinal cord, not the brain.

2. (3) A child learns to say "please" because she then gets what she asked for. (Application) Saying "please" (a learned behavior) gets the child what she wants (a reward). Options (1) and (2) are incorrect because the behavior is followed by something that is not a reward. Option (4) is an example of a simple reflex, not a learned behavior. Option (5) is an example of learning by observing.

3. (2) A simple reflex involves the spinal cord, and learned behavior involves the brain. (Analysis) A simple reflex is automatically processed in the spinal cord, but learned behavior is processed in the brain. Option (1) is the opposite of what occurs. Option (3) is incorrect because simple reflexes do not involve the brain. Options (4) and (5) are incorrect because sensory and motor neurons can be involved in both reflexes and learning.

4. (3) The dog learned to link the tone with food. (Comprehension) According to the passage and diagram, after a few trials in which the tone and the food were presented together, the dog learned that the tone signaled food. Therefore, it salivated when it heard the tone because it expected to receive food. Option (1) is incorrect because nothing in the passage or diagram indicates that the dog was extremely hungry. Option (2) is not relevant. Option (4) is incorrect because the tone was linked with food, not punishment. Option (5) is incorrect because dogs salivate at a tone only if they are taught to do so.

5. (3) eventually stop salivating at the sound of the tone (Analysis) The dog would eventually learn that the tone did not mean that food was coming, and so the dog would stop salivating at its sound. Option (1) is incorrect because the learning, described above, would probably take place. Option (2) is incorrect because it is not the same situation; the question states that the food is no longer being paired with the tone, so the dog would learn to stop making the association between the food and the tone, as described above. Option (4) is incorrect because salivation at food is a simple reflex and will not stop. Option (5) is incorrect because the dog's behavior would eventually become consistent, and he would always salivate at the food.

6. (1) A dog learns to hide from a child who frequently pulled its tail. (Application) If the approach of the child were paired with a painful experience, the dog would associate the two, just as Pavlov's dog associated the tone with the food. Options (2) and (3) are incorrect because they are not examples of learning a response as a result of associating two events. Options (4) and (5) are examples of learning a behavior because it is rewarded.

GED Mini-Test (Pages 72–73)

1. (3) Multiple intelligences cannot be measured by standard intelligence tests. (Comprehension) A standard intelligence test would measure only linguistic and logical-mathematical ability. Options (1) and (2) are incorrect because both of these ideas contradict the theory of multiple intelligences. Options (4) and (5) are generalizations that do not follow from the theory of multiple intelligences.

2. (1) linguistic and logical-mathematical (Comprehension) Studying this book involves language and reasoning, the abilities involved in linguistic and logical-mathematical intelligence. Options (2), (3), (4), and (5) are incorrect because they do not involve language and reasoning ability.

3. (2) an elementary school teacher (Application) A teacher can use this theory to tailor lessons to the specific abilities of each student. Options (1), (3), (4), and (5) involve work that does not necessarily involve helping other people learn, and so would not require a person to use the theory of multiple intelligences. However, a person doing the kind of work listed in each of these options might employ different intelligences on the job.

4. (1) Specific brain areas specialize in different functions. (Evaluation) This tends to support the theory of multiple intelligences, because in different people different areas of the brain might work better. Options (2) and (3) would support the theory that intelligence is a single general ability. Options (4) and (5) do not provide evidence for multiple intelligences.

5. **(3) Both the cerebellum and the cerebrum control movement.** (Evaluation) The sentence given in the question stem is an oversimplification, as more than one part of the brain is involved in controlling movement. Options (1), (2), and (4) are not true. Option (5) is true, but it has nothing to do with the function of the cerebellum.

6. **(2) vision** (Analysis) Since the perception of vision is located in the occipital lobe, a blow to the back of the head is likely to affect it. Options (1) and (4) are located at the side of the head. Option (3) is controlled by the brain stem at the base of the brain. Option (5) is controlled in the upper part of the cerebrum.

7. **(2) The Human Brain** (Comprehension) The passage and diagram focus on the structure of the human brain. The passage does not describe the entire nervous system, making options (1) and (5) incorrect. It describes more than just the cerebrum, making option (3) incorrect. It describes the human brain, not brains in general, making option (4) incorrect.

8. **(5) while listening to one person's voice at a crowded party** (Application) In this situation, you are picking out one voice from a babble of voices, an example of selective attention. The other situations involve one main stimulus and thus do not involve picking out one stimulus from many.

Lesson 6
GED Skill Focus (Page 75)
1. **b.** Head lice have developed resistance to the insecticide permethrin.

2. **b.** Permethrin is no longer effective in treating head lice. A mutation that made the lice resistant to the insecticide has been passed down through generations, and now most lice are resistant.

3. **a.** Head lice that were resistant to permethrin survived treatment. They reproduced and their offspring inherited this resistance.

4. **a.** Permethrin is no longer effective in treating head lice. A mutation gave some lice resistance, and they passed the resistance to their offspring.

GED Content Focus (Page 77)
1. **(5) the process by which living things change over time** (Comprehension) According to the passage, evolution involves change over time (many generations). Option (1) is incorrect because evolution is not a quick change. Option (2) does not mention change. Options (3) and (4) refer to natural selection.

2. **(3) Soot darkened the tree trunks, better camouflaging the dark moths.**

(Comprehension) According to the passage, soot from increased smoke darkened tree trunks, providing camouflage for the dark peppered moths, which previously had been visible against the light tree trunks. Option (1) is true but does not explain why soot favored the dark peppered moths. Option (2) is not true. Options (4) and (5) also are not true, as they were not effects of the soot.

3. **(3) variation** (Application) The steps of natural selection can be found in the chart. Variation refers to differences between individuals of a species. Options (1), (2), (4), and (5) refer to other steps in natural selection.

4. **(4) survival** (Application) The steps of natural selection are shown in the chart. Because cactus plants store their own water, they have a trait that enables them to survive in their environment. Option (1) refers to the fact that there are too many organisms for an environment's resources. Option (2) refers to the competition among those organisms. Option (3) refers to the different traits that individuals have. Option (5) refers to the production of the next generation.

5. **(3) Weak die, leaving well-adapted individuals to reproduce and pass on their traits.** (Comprehension) This sentence touches on all the important points regarding natural selection. Option (1) is incorrect because it refers to evolution rather than to natural selection. The remaining options are incomplete descriptions of natural selection; they each describe only one step in the process: option (2) described survival, option (4), competition, and option (5), variation.

6. **(1) Plant and animal species will continue to evolve.** (Analysis) Evolution is change over time, not just change in the past. Options (2) and (3) are incorrect because both plants and animals will continue to evolve. Options (4) and (5) are incorrect because evolution by natural selection will continue, causing plant and animal species to change.

GED Practice (Pages 78–79)
1. **(3) They are positioned side by side below the humerus.** (Analysis) Although the shapes of these bones differ in the different species, in all cases they are positioned side be side below the humerus. Options (1) and (2) are incorrect because they describe the phalanges. Option (4) is incorrect, as the diagram shows. Option (5) is not true; according to the diagram, these bones are parts of limbs.

2. **(1) Homologous structures are evidence supporting the theory of evolution.**

(Comprehension) This sentence is broad enough to cover the important points of the passage. Option (2) is true but incomplete. Options (3) and (4) describe details, not main points. Option (5) is not true.

3. **(3) Whales, humans, dogs, and birds had a common ancestor.** (Evaluation) The information in the passage and diagram supports this statement. Option (1) is not true because homologous structures are not common to all animals but rather are found only in related species. Option (2) is incorrect because neither the passage nor the diagram discusses how closely or distantly related are the animals whose forelimbs are shown. Option (4) is not true because phalanges are bones in human's fingers, not in the wrist, and in the dog's foot, not in the leg. Option (5) is incorrect because the forelimbs of mammals are not necessarily arms.

4. **(4) fungi** (Comprehension) On the branching tree, animals and fungi originate from one offshoot and are closer to one another than to the other types of organisms. The diagram indicates that the remaining options are organisms more distantly related to animals than fungi.

5. **(1) determining if two people are related** (Application) Just as comparative DNA sequencing can be used to determine whether two species are related, so can it be used to determine whether two individuals are related. Note that the word comparative in the question is a clue: the answer should refer to a comparison of the DNA of two different individuals or species. Option (2) is incorrect because extracting DNA from fossils is a separate process. Options (3) and (5) are incorrect because comparative gene sequencing does not reveal age. Option (4) is incorrect because the general structure of the DNA molecule was discovered decades ago, in the 1950s, and comparative sequencing could not be done without a previous understanding of DNA's general structure.

6. **(1) DNA sequencing provides evidence for evolutionary relationships, sometimes overturning previously held views.** (Comprehension) This provides an overall summary of the passage and diagram. Options (2), (3), (4), and (5), while true, are details, not important points, of the passage and diagram.

GED Mini-Test (Pages 80–81)

1. **(1) environmental changes** (Comprehension) According to the passage, environmental changes are a cause of speciation. Option (2) is incorrect because environmental stability would promote species stability. Option (3) is incorrect because

the entire species would continue to evolve as a group. Option (4) is incorrect because when a species stops reproducing it dies out. Option (5) is incorrect because a large food supply suggests a stable environment, which is not likely to lead to speciation.

2. **(3) They became less alike.** (Analysis) As the honeycreepers were dispersed into different environments, they adapted differently to fit their different habitats. Options (1) and (4) are not true. Option (2) is incorrect because species cannot reproduce with one another. Option (5) is incorrect because evolutionary change among animals such as birds does not generally happen within such a short period.

3. **(5) It would not be able to eat enough to live.** (Analysis) Since its beak is not suited for catching insects, it is likely the honeycreeper would starve. Options (1) and (2) are incorrect because adaptations are inherited traits that occur from one generation to the next, not in a single individual. Options (3) and (4) are not likely to happen since different species do not usually share their resources.

4. **(2) created more variety** (Comprehension) Speciation leads to more diversity, or variety, in plant and animal life. Option (1) is the opposite of what speciation does. Options (3) and (5) are incorrect because speciation increases variety. Option (4) is incorrect because speciation does not affect the rate of formation of new varieties.

5. **(5) Fish, bird, and human embryos have similarities at an early stage of development.** (Comprehension) The diagram shows that fish, birds, and humans look similar at the early embryo stage. Options (1), (2), and (4) include points taken from the paragraph, not the diagram. Option (3) is commonly accepted as fact but is a detail suggested by neither the paragraph nor the diagram.

6. **(5) The common ancestor of fish, birds, and humans was probably a water animal.** (Evaluation) The statement is supported by the existence of gill slits in early stages of the three embryos. Options (1), (2), and (4) may or may not be true, but there is not enough information given to tell. The diagram contradicts option (3).

7. **(1) Bluebirds and butterflies have wings.** (Application) The wings are adaptations to life in the air, but bluebirds are birds and butterflies are insects, so they are not closely related. In the remaining options, the adaptations belong to closely related species and so are not examples of convergence.

8. **(1) white coloring** (Application) White coloring is camouflage in a snowy polar region. The remaining traits would not be useful in a polar environment.

9. **(2) plotting the evolutionary relationships among extinct organisms** (Evaluation) By studying fossils, scientists can figure out evolutionary relationships. Options (1) and (5) are incorrect because fossils tell about the past, not the present or the future. Option (3) is incorrect because fossils are of ancient, not modern organisms. Option (4) is incorrect because the fossil record does not go back as far as the formation of Earth.

Lesson 7
GED Skill Focus (Page 83)
1. **b.** All green plants, such as grasses and seaweeds, are producers.

2. Answers will vary. Sample details: Consumers get energy by eating producers. Rabbits and sea urchins are primary consumers. Foxes and seals are secondary consumers. Foxes and seals eat primary consumers. Owls and killer whales are tertiary consumers.

3. Answers will vary. Sample details: The sun provides energy for the grass. Rabbits get energy by eating grass. Foxes get energy by eating rabbits. Foxes are secondary consumers.

4. **a.** In a food chain, energy flows from the sun to producers and then to consumers.

5. Answers will vary. Sample details: Energy from the sun is used by the grass to produce food. Rabbits eat grass, and foxes eat rabbits.

GED Content Focus (Page 85)
1. **(1) the energy relationships among organisms in an ecosystem** (Comprehension) A food web shows which organisms eat which others, and those relationships involve the transfer of energy. Option (2) is incorrect because a food web shows plants as well as animals. Option (3) is too general. Option (4) is incorrect because a food web shows energy relationships and can be constructed for a city area as well as a wilderness area. Option (5) is incorrect because a food web shows food and energy relationships that exist in an ecosystem.

2. **(4) the tawny owl** (Analysis) By examining the arrows that indicate the flow of energy, you can see that the owl is one of the highest level consumers because there is no organism that preys on it. Options (1), (2), (3), and (5) are incorrect because there are organisms that feed on them in the food web.

3. **(5) rabbits** (Analysis) Rabbits feed on plants, so if plants disappeared, rabbits would immediately

be out of food. Options (1), (2), (3), and (4) are incorrect because they are secondary or tertiary consumers and the effect on them would not be immediate.

4. **(4) Weasels get energy by eating mice.** (Analysis) This is a supporting detail that is shown in the food web. Options (1), (2), (3), and (5) are conclusions based on the passage and the diagram.

5. **(5) omnivore** (Application) Most people are omnivores in daily life, and under the circumstances described in the question, people would be likely to eat anything because they would be extremely hungry. Option (1) is incorrect because only the sun is the energy source. Option (2) is incorrect because only green plants are producers. Option (3) is incorrect because decomposers break down decaying matter. Option (4) is incorrect because the hiker is likely to eat anything to ease his hunger, not just meat.

6. **(1) Energy is constantly flowing through the woodland ecosystem.** (Analysis) This is a conclusion. Options (2), (3), (4), and (5) are details that support this conclusion.

GED Practice (Pages 86–87)
1. **(4) as biomass** (Comprehension) As stated in the first paragraph of the passage, energy is stored as organic matter, or biomass, in a food chain. Option (1) is incorrect because a trophic level is a concept defined by feeding level, not an energy storage medium. Option (2) is incorrect because sunlight is the source of energy, not a place to store it, for a food chain. Option (3) is incorrect because energy in a food chain is lost, not stored, as heat. Option (5) is only partially correct, since animals are also part of the food chain and they store energy in their tissues.

2. **(3) A food chain can support more primary consumers than secondary consumers.** (Analysis) This is a conclusion supported by the information in the passage and diagram. Options (1), (2), (4), and (5) are all details from the passage and diagram.

3. **(2) The most biomass is at the base of the energy pyramid.** (Evaluation) As indicated in the second paragraph and by the energy pyramid diagram, the section at the base of the pyramid is the largest, representing the amount of biomass at that level. Option (1) is incorrect because the illustration and passage indicate that the higher in an energy pyramid you go, the less biomass there is. Option (3) is incorrect because, according to the illustration, there are more voles than weasels in the energy pyramid. Option (4) is incorrect because, as indicated by the illustration, weasels do not eat tawny owls. Option (5) is

incorrect because, according to the passage, the higher you go in the energy pyramid, the less energy is available.

4. **(5) seals** (Application) Since the seals are at the top of the energy pyramid, you would expect to find the fewest seals. Options (1), (2), (3), and (4) are incorrect because, as the question text indicates, they are organisms lower in the energy pyramid.

5. **(1) In many regions, coyotes now have no natural enemies.** (Comprehension) Wolves prey on coyotes, so after wolves were killed off in many areas, the coyotes had no predator. Options (2), (3), (4), and (5) are all true, but they do not explain why the absence of wolves has helped coyotes thrive.

6. **(5) The coyote's adaptability in feeding and other behaviors has helped it enlarge its range.** (Analysis) This is a conclusion. Options (1), (2), (3), and (4) are details that support the conclusion that coyotes are adaptable in feeding and other behaviors.

7. **(2) Coyotes can live in many types of ecosystems and climates.** (Evaluation) Since their range is so extensive, as indicated by the map and the passage, you can infer that coyotes can adapt to hot, temperate, and cold climates and various types of terrain among various types of animals. Option (1) is incorrect because the map shows that coyotes live in all types of areas. Option (3) is incorrect because it's likely the coyote population is much higher now, since their range is so much bigger. Option (4) is incorrect because the passage states that coyotes are comfortable living among humans. Option (5) is incorrect because the passage states coyotes spread not from the eastern forests, but from the western plains to other areas of the continent.

GED Mini-Test (Pages 88–89)

1. **(5) the rapid reproduction of rabbits and lack of predators** (Analysis) The rapid reproduction of rabbits unchecked by predators led to the overpopulation of rabbits in Australia. Option (1) is incorrect since it is likely to be a solution to overpopulation. Option (2) is incorrect because continued imports would not, if predators were available, result in overpopulation. Option (3) is a result of overpopulation. Option (4) would result in the opposite of what actually happened.

2. **(3) Prevent the introduction of new organisms.** (Comprehension) According to the passage, preventing the interjection of new species is the best solution. Option (1) is a solution, but not the best one. Options (2) and (5) would increase, not solve, the problem.

Option (4) is generally not controllable by humans and overall, may have a harmful effect on the ecosystem.

3. **(3) In stable ecosystems, one consumer usually checks another's population growth.** (Evaluation) Application of this principle leads to the conclusion that introducing a predator may control the organism that is overrunning its new environment. Option (1) is true, but it does not support the conclusion in the question stem. Option (2) is not true. Option (4) is incorrect because there is nothing to indicate that time will eventually solve the overpopulation problem. Option (5) may be true in the long run, but it does not support the conclusion stated in the question stem.

4. **(2) It has food that rabbits eat.** (Analysis) Since rabbits thrived in Australia, you can assume they found plenty to eat. Options (1) and (3) are incorrect because without food, rabbits would have starved. Option (4) is incorrect because if there were many meat-eating animals, it is likely that the rabbits would have been eaten. Option (5) cannot be true, because if the ecosystem were similar to Europe's, the rabbit population would not have gotten out of control.

5. **(3) ecosystem** (Application) Dr. Tilman is working with a community of plants plus its surroundings, the soil and air—that is, an ecosystem. Option (1) is incorrect because the plots described contain more than one population. Option (2) is incorrect because the plots include the surrounding nonliving elements in the environment, not just the living organisms. Options (4) and (5) are incorrect because the plots are too small and do not include all the organisms contained in a biome or the biosphere.

6. **(5) biosphere** (Application) A large, self-sustaining environment that includes organisms and their physical surroundings is a biosphere. The key here is the word "self-sustaining," that is, containing everything needed to sustain life, like Earth. Options (1) to (4) are incorrect because the level of complexity is too low in each of them.

7. **(3) There are more herons and egrets because clean water means more fish to eat.** (Evaluation) As the water got cleaner, fish populations increased, which meant more food for water birds. The information in the passage and graphs does not support options (1), (2), (4), and (5).

8. **(1) Cowbirds lay their eggs in the nests of songbirds, which incubate and raise cowbird chicks.** (Application) In this case, cowbirds benefit by not having to use up energy

hatching and feeding offspring, and songbirds use up energy they could otherwise use to hatch and raise their own chicks. Options (2), (3), (4), and (5) are incorrect because they are all symbiotic relationships — relationships in which both species benefit.

Lesson 8

GED Skill Focus (Page 91)

1. **b.** It takes place in animals and plants.
   c. Oxygen is used.
   d. Carbon dioxide is released.

2. **a.** Respiration uses up oxygen from the air and releases carbon dioxide into the air.

3. **a.** It takes place only in plants.
   c. The sun's energy is needed for it to take place.
   d. Carbon dioxide is used.
   e. Oxygen is released.

4. **a.** Photosynthesis uses up carbon dioxide from the air and releases oxygen into the air.

GED Content Focus (Page 93)

1. **(4) from the soil** (Comprehension) It is stated in the second paragraph that plants get nitrogen from the soil. Therefore, options (1), (2), (3), and (5) are incorrect because they are sources other than soil.

2. **(5) in the soil and in the roots of legumes** (Comprehension) The diagram shows that nitrogen fixation takes place in the soil and in nodules on roots of legumes. Options (1), (2), (3), and (4) are incorrect because they include locations other than the two mentioned in the information.

3. **(4) nitrification** (Comprehension) Nitrification is the process by which nitrogen is made available to plants by the breakdown of decaying organisms. Options (1) and (2) name other nitrogen conversion processes. Options (3) and (5) are processes that are not involved with the nitrogen cycle.

4. **(1) The amount of nitrogen processed will decrease.** (Application) With the death of many plants, including legumes, less nitrogen will be fixed. The heat of the fire will also kill off nitrogen-fixing bacteria in the soil, also causing a reduction in nitrogen in the ecosystem. Finally, animals are less likely to be present in a burned region, because of the reduction in plant food, so animal wastes and remains will be reduced, releasing less nitrogen through decomposition. Option (2) is incorrect because there are fewer organisms to take part in the nitrogen cycle, so it is not likely to speed up. Options (3) and (4) are incorrect because plants and animals do not get nitrogen from the air. Option (5) is incorrect because the vegetation (including legumes) in

the area has been burned and it will take a while for plant populations (including legumes that may colonize the burned region) to grow or regenerate to their pre-fire numbers.

5. **(2) from nitrogen-fixing bacteria on their roots** (Comprehension) Since soybeans are legumes, and since legumes have nitrogen-fixing bacteria in nodules on their roots, it follows that soybeans will get most of their nitrogen from that source. Option (1) is incorrect because lightning strikes are relatively rare in any given area, so they do not provide much nitrogen. Options (3) and (4) are incorrect because plants do not get nitrogen from the air. Option (5) is a source of nitrogen for soybeans, but not the primary source.

6. **(1) from legumes** (Application) Since the goats are in the soybean fields, they will eat soybeans, which as legumes are a good source of nitrogen. Options (2) and (3) are incorrect because there are not likely to be significant lightning strikes or a lot of grass growing in the soybean fields. Option (4) is incorrect because goats eat plants, not animals. Option (5) is incorrect because goats do not eat soil and the nitrogen that nitrifying bacteria produce is used by plants, not animals.

7. **(4) protein synthesis** (Analysis) According to the passage, nitrogen is used in protein synthesis. Therefore, if the nitrogen cycle were stopped, protein synthesis is likely to be affected first. Options (1), (2), (3), and (5) are incorrect because they would not be immediately affected by an interruption in the nitrogen cycle. They would eventually be affected as the supply of proteins available to support life processes was reduced.

GED Practice (Pages 94–95)

1. **(1) Water vapor in the air condenses into droplets.** (Analysis) The second paragraph describes what causes clouds to form. Option (2) is incorrect because heavy droplets in clouds result in some form of precipitation. Option (3) does not relate to cloud formation and incorrectly states that droplets in the air, rather than surface water, evaporate to form water vapor. Option (4) is not related to cloud formation. Option (5) is incorrect because although a similar process is related to cloud formation, warm air, not cool air, comes from the surface of Earth and cool air is above Earth's surface.

2. **(2) water running down the bathroom walls after someone takes a hot bath** (Application) Steam (water vapor) from the hot shower water condenses on the cooler walls, and heavy drops of water start running down the walls. Option (1) is only a small part of the water cycle. Options (3) and (4) do not have anything to do with the water cycle. Option (5) involves

turning water from a solid to a liquid and then to a solid again, which is not a key part of the water cycle.

3. **(2) by comparing the amount of water dripping off redwoods to the amount collected in deforested areas.** (Comprehension) To prove that one quantity is greater than another, both must be measured, which is what the scientists did. Option (1) does not yield enough information for comparison. Option (3) is not directly related to measuring the amount of water collected from fog. Option (4) is not directly related to measuring the amount of water collected from fog and also is not something that scientists are likely to be able to do. Option (5) is incorrect because it involves comparing the wrong factors.

4. **(4) using fog collectors in dry coastal regions to collect water** (Application) Like the redwood trees, fog collectors capture water from fog. Options (1), (2), and (5) are incorrect because they involve rainwater, not fog. Option (3) is incorrect because it involves removing a dissolved substance from water.

5. **(3) Water from fog drips down the needles, branches, and trunks of redwoods into the soil.** (Evaluation) The water drips from the tree into the soil, where it is available to other plants and animals of the habitat. Option (1) is incorrect because it does not explain how redwoods contribute water to their habitats. Option (2) is incorrect because it does not explain how the water gets from the redwoods to the rest of the habitat. Option (4) is incorrect because it restates the conclusion. Option (5) is incorrect because the amount of forested land is not relevant to whether redwoods provide water to the habitats that still exist.

6. **(5) Deforestation contributes to the drying of local wells and springs.** (Evaluation) Since people often act in their own interests, when their personal water supply is threatened, they are more likely to support redwood conservation measures. Option (1) deals with past practices that cannot be changed and is not, in itself, a motivation for stopping logging. Options (2), (3), and (4) give motivation to log, not to conserve.

GED Mini-Test (Pages 96–97)

1. **(1) emissions from factories, power plants, and cars** (Comprehension) According to the passage and the diagram, waste gases from industrial and vehicular sources mix with water vapor in the air, making the resulting rain acidic. Option (2) describes the usual formation of rain without indicating the source of the acid.

Options (3), (4), and (5) are incorrect because they reflect pollution problems in water on Earth, not in rain.

2. **(4) The emissions that cause acid rain in the state probably originate some other place.** (Evaluation) Since the waste gases from emissions often travel great distances before mixing with water vapor and causing acid rain, controlling emissions within the state is not likely to help that state reduce its acid rainfall. Option (1) may be true, but it is not the reason that the officials' plan is faulty. Option (2) is incorrect because the state can enforce controls if it chooses to. Options (3) and (5) are not true.

3. **(1) damage to aquatic organisms** (Analysis) Since acid rain causes the water in streams and lakes to become acidic, the most likely effect is damage to organisms that live in them. Option (2) would be a cause of pollution, not an effect. Option (3) is incorrect because acid rain pollution of a stream or lake is not likely to move upstream. Options (4) and (5) are not results of acid rain pollution.

4. **(4) digestion** (Application) Like decomposition, digestion is a process in which large complex substances are broken down in stages into simple substances. Options (1), (2), (3), and (5) are incorrect because they have nothing to do with the breakdown of complex substances into simpler, more usable components.

5. **(5) lightning** (Comprehension) According to the passage and diagram, lightning may have provided the energy for early chemical reactions. Options (1), (2), (3), and (4) are incorrect because they are compounds involved in the chemical reactions and do not provide energy for reactions. (Note: methane is a simple organic molecule.)

6. **(1) combined to form living things** (Analysis) According to the passage, organic molecules are the building blocks of all living things. Therefore, organic molecules had to exist before living things could evolve. Option (2) is incorrect because organic molecules do not give rise to carbon; carbon is part of any organic molecule. Option (3) is incorrect because energy was obtained from other sources before life emerged. Option (4) is incorrect because organic molecules do not make up most of the atmosphere; most gases in the atmosphere are formed from inorganic molecules. Option (5) is not true, since organic molecules do not produce rain.

7. **(1) The composition of the atmosphere has changed through constant interaction with living things.** (Comprehension) Since today's atmosphere differs considerably from the atmosphere when life arose, you can infer that

interaction with living things helped cause the changes. Option (2) is not true; today's atmosphere has more oxygen than was present in early Earth's atmosphere. Option (3) is not true; the first cells were not animal cells and as the passage states, they gave off oxygen, not carbon dioxide. Option (4) is incorrect because, according to the passage, life came into being about 3.5 billion years ago, not 5 billion years ago, and life probably first evolved in oceans, not in the atmosphere and the oceans. Option (5) is not correct because, according to the passage, these gases formed Earth's early atmosphere, not the first living things.

Unit 1 Cumulative Review (Pages 98–106)

1. **(1) The use of herbicide-resistant crops is controversial.** (Comprehension) This statement is general enough to cover the main idea of the passage; the first paragraph explains what herbicide-resistant crops are and the second paragraph discusses the pros and cons of their use. Option (2) is an opinion related to the topic but one that is not directly stated in the passage, nor is it the implied main idea of the passage. Options (3), (4), and (5) are details from the passage that are too specific to be the main idea.

2. **(1) herbicides** (Comprehension) This is explained in the first paragraph of the passage. Options (2), (3), (4), and (5) describe crops that are resistant to other types of agricultural problems.

3. **(4) Improved cultivation techniques are preferable to herbicide use.** (Analysis) This statement reflects the opinion of some environmental groups. The clue word here is *preferable*. Not everyone shares this point of view. Options (1), (2), (3), and (5) are statements of fact presented in the passage.

4. **(3) Weeds are a problem in large farming areas.** (Analysis) The passage gives both pro-herbicide and anti-herbicide points of view. Both sides agree that weeds must be controlled; they differ as to how. Option (1) is incorrect because the author includes the environmentalists' view that herbicides are not safe. Option (2) is incorrect because the passage describes some practices that do not require the use of herbicides to grow crops. Options (4) and (5) are not true.

5. **(3) Vestigial structures are the remains of well-developed and functional structures.** (Analysis) This is the conclusion to which scientists came after examining the evidence for vestigial structures. Options (1), (2), (4), and (5) are details, stated in the paragraph or shown in the diagram, that support the conclusion.

6. **(1) During the winter, a hibernating bear lives on the energy stored as fat.** (Application) The hibernating bear is an example of the later use of energy stored in lipids in the bear's body. Options (2) and (4) do not involve lipids. Option (3) involves eating something for quick, not stored, energy. Option (5) is true but it discusses the composition of lipids, not their use.

7. **(1) Water molecules pass through the cell membrane until a balance between the inside and outside of the cell has been reached.** (Comprehension) Option (2) is incorrect, because water molecules move both into and out of the cell and osmosis does not cause water to become more concentrated inside the cell membrane, but is a process that results in a balance of water molecules inside and out of the cell. Option (3) is incorrect because osmosis does not involve the movement of air molecules, but of water molecules. Options (4) and (5) are incorrect because osmosis occurs in all cells, not exclusively in plant cells or in one-celled organisms.

8. **(2) The cells of plant roots absorb water from the surrounding soil.** (Application) Water flows across the cell membrane of root cells into the plant when there is more water in the soil than in the root cells. Option (1) describes cell division, not osmosis. Option (3) involves diffusion of oxygen and carbon dioxide, not water, across a membrane. Option (4) describes the movement of water through a pore (a small hole) out of a leaf, not across any membrane. Option (5) describes a method by which proteins, not water, enter cells.

9. **(1) Different types of joints allow for different types of movement.** (Comprehension) The diagram shows how four different joints allow different movements. Option (2) gives some details. Option (3) is much too general to be a good summary of the diagram; the skeleton is not even shown or discussed in the diagram. Option (4) is mentioned in the passage, not the diagram. Option (5) is not true, since the diagram shows specific movements for specific joints.

10. **(2) One function of the skeleton is to allow the body to move through movement of bones.** (Analysis) The author does not mention the skeleton at all; he or she assumes you are aware that the skeleton is the system that supports the body and allows it to move. Options (1), (3), and (5) are shown in the diagram. Option (4) is mentioned in the passage.

11. **(1) the hip** (Application) A ball-and-socket joint allows a rotating movement. Of the joints listed, only the hip permits a rotating movement.

Answers and Explanations

Option (2) is incorrect because the thumb is a saddle joint, as shown in the diagram. Option (3), the elbow, includes both a hinge and a pivot joint. Option (4), the knuckles, and option (5), the knee, are hinge joints.

12. **(5) It is primarily inborn.** (Comprehension) Options (1), (2), and (3) are incorrect because the passage does not assess the cuckoo's behavior in terms of ethics or other subjective standards. Option (4) is incorrect because the passage indicates that most of the cuckoo's behaviors are instinctive; the cuckoo chick does not learn to act like its foster parents and never sees its cuckoo parents to learn from them.

13. **(3) 10** (Comprehension) The population density in 1700 was 11 people per square mile, and the population density in 1999 was 115 people per square mile; 115 divided by 11 is about 10.

14. **(3) Increasing the amount of inhabitable land is one way to reduce population density.** (Analysis) This conclusion is based on the information about how population density is calculated. Options (1), (2), (4), and (5) are all details related to the world's population density rather than general conclusions.

15. **(1) quadrupled** (Comprehension) In the 99 years between 1900 and 1999, the population density quadrupled (27 times 4 is 108, close to the 1999 figure of 115). Therefore, if this rate of growth continues, the population density in 2098 is likely to be four times what it was in 1999.

16. **(3) A virus is genetic material that appears lifeless until it takes over a cell to reproduce.** (Comprehension) This sentence restates the points of the paragraph. Options (1) and (2) are incorrect because they restate only portions of the information. Options (4) and (5) are incorrect because there is no discussion of the common cold or of treating viral diseases in the information given.

17. **(2) the process by which an immature form changes into a different adult form** (Comprehension) Option (2) restates the process of metamorphosis as described in the passage. Option (1) is incorrect because metamorphosis does not refer to reproduction. Option (3) is incorrect because metamorphosis is not merely growth; it applies only to organisms whose form changes at different stages of development. Option (4) describes aging, not metamorphosis. Option (5) refers to respiration through gills, not metamorphosis.

18. **(4) the development of a caterpillar into a butterfly** (Application) The development of a caterpillar into a butterfly, like the tadpole and frog, involves a change of form during growth.

Options (1), (2), (3), and (5) involve only growth; there is no complete change of the form of the organism from one stage to another.

19. **(3) Different body structures are suitable for different environments.** (Analysis) The diagram shows the tadpole's structures, suitable for underwater swimming, and the frog's structures, suitable for land dwelling. The passage mentions lungs and gills and also mentions that tadpoles live in water and adult frogs live on land. But the author assumes you know that different structures are adapted to different environments. Options (1) and (2) are incorrect since few animals and no plants undergo metamorphosis. Options (4) and (5) are not true and are not closely related to the subject of the passage.

20. **(2) There are almost as many women as men with colon cancer.** (Evaluation) The graph shows that women get colon cancer at almost the same rate as men. For example, at age 70, about 250 out of 100,000 women get colon cancer, and about 350 out of 100,000 men get colon cancer. Therefore, saying colon cancer is a man's disease is a generalization that is not true. Option (1) is true, but it does not explain what is wrong with the statement. Options (3) and (4) are not true, as indicated by the graph. No information about option (5) is included in the graph and this information, whether true or not, does not directly explain why the statement is illogical.

21. **(4) give blood to anyone** (Comprehension) According to the chart on the left, a person with type O blood can give blood to those with types A, B, AB, and O, in other words, everyone. Options (1), (2), and (3) are incorrect because someone with type O blood can get blood only from those who also have type O blood. Option (5) is incorrect because a person with type O blood can give blood to anyone.

22. **(1) Blood Type Frequency in Selected Populations** (Comprehension) The chart provides information on the percentage of people who have each blood type in several population groups. Option (2) is too general. Options (3) and (4) have nothing to do with the subject of the chart on the right. Option (5) is too specific, since groups other than Americans are represented.

23. **(3) About three-tenths** (Comprehension) The chart on the right shows that 30 percent of the Chinese have type O blood; 30% is three-tenths. Option (1) states the incidence of blood type AB, not type O, among the Chinese. Option (2) restates the incidence of blood type A, not type O, among the Chinese. Option (4) does not

accurately restate the incidence of type O or any of the other blood types. Option (5) is not true, as the chart shows.

24. **(4) age 70–90 after one introduction** (Comprehension) According to the graph, the group that did most poorly was the oldest group after just one introduction; they recalled only about 12 percent of the names. Options (1), (2), (3), and (5) are incorrect because they show percentages greater than 12%.

25. **(3) The 50–59 age group recalled about 66 percent; other age groups did better or worse.** (Evaluation) The statement is an oversimplification. When you examine the graph you see that people of various ages did better or worse than recalling 66 percent. Options (1) and (2) are incorrect, based on the passage, and so do not correctly address the lack of logic of the statement. Options (4) and (5) are true, but do not relate to the statement and so do not address why it is illogical.

26. **(5) The ability to recall names declines with age, but repetition improves recall at all ages.** (Comprehension) This statement covers the main points of the passage and diagram. Option (1) is too general and doesn't relate to the experiment. Options (2) and (3) are details. Option (4) is not true.

27. **(4) in a greenhouse** (Application) In a greenhouse full of plants, evidence of transpiration can be found in the humid air and condensation on the inner glass. Options (1) and (2) are incorrect because there are few plants and little transpiration in either type of environment. Option (3) is incorrect because ocean plants do not transpire since they are underwater. Option (5) is incorrect because the water vapor from the plants in the field would disperse into the air and would be difficult to detect.

28. **(2) Montana** (Comprehension) The map shows that the state of Montana includes portions of all three ranges in different parts of the state. Option (1) is incorrect because Idaho includes only one of the populations. Options (3) and (4) are incorrect because no wolf population is shown in either of these states. Option (5) is incorrect because Wyoming has only one wolf population—in and around Yellowstone.

29. **(4) The Range of the Gray Wolf** (Comprehension) The subject of the map is the locations where gray wolves can be found today. Option (1) is incorrect because the map shows far more than Yellowstone National Park. Option (2) is incorrect because the map shows more than these three states; it also shows portions of Nevada, Utah, and Canada. Option (3) is incorrect because the map's primary purpose is

not to show national parks but to show where wolves live. Option (5) is incorrect because the map shows that wolves live outside national parks as well as inside them.

30. **(5) The gray wolf should no longer be considered endangered.** (Analysis) This is an opinion because it is a belief held by some people, but not others. The key word is *should*. Options (1), (2), (3), and (4) are facts stated in or implied by the passage.

31. **(3) restoring tallgrass varieties to small portions of the Great Plains** (Application) Restoring once-native plant species to an ecosystem is similar to restoring an animal species to its former ecosystem. Options (1), (2), (4), and (5) are incorrect because they do not involve the restoration of a species to its former ecosystem. Option (1) is incorrect, because it involves changing an altered ecosystem so it is more like its natural state, not returning a once native species to its ecosystem. Options (2) and (5) are ways of protecting native species, not returning them to their ecosystem. Option (4) deals with the introduction of a nonnative species, not the return of a native species.

32. **(3) microorganisms grown in a sterile food medium** (Comprehension) This definition of culture appears in the chart. Options (1), (2), (4), and (5) do not define a culture.

33. **(4) Koch's experiments with anthrax bacteria** (Analysis) The experimental method that Koch used in his anthrax investigations was primarily responsible for this idea becoming accepted as fact. Option (1) was not involved with the acceptance of this idea as a fact. Options (2) and (5) predated Koch by more than 200 years and so could not have caused the idea's acceptance. Option (3) did contribute, but it was not a direct cause of the idea becoming accepted as fact.

34. **(5) If a disease is not caused by a particular type of bacterium, it must be caused by a virus.** (Evaluation) In fact, bacteria, viruses, fungi, other microorganisms, or a combination of factors can cause disease. Therefore, option (5) is an example of faulty logic based on an either-or error. Options (1), (2), and (3) all accurately describe steps in Koch's method. Option (4) is a valid conclusion that can be drawn based on the passage.

35. **(2) eating too little of foods high in iodine** (Comprehension) According to the question text, goiter is caused by a lack of iodine in the diet. Option (1) is incorrect because, as indicated by the question text, fish contains iodine, which prevents goiter. Option (4) is incorrect because fertilizing the soil with iodine, if it does

anything, would prevent goiter in people who eat food grown in the soil. Options (3) and (5) are incorrect because goiter is caused by a diet deficiency, not by a germ or a gene.

UNIT 2: EARTH AND SPACE SCIENCE

Lesson 9

GED Skill Focus (Page 111)

1. **a.** The crust is the only layer of Earth that people can see.

2. **b.** The crust beneath Africa is about 40 kilometers thick.

3. The crust is about 40 kilometers deep under continents. Since Africa is a continent, the crust is probably about 40 kilometers deep beneath it.

4. **a.** Earth has a magnetic field.

5. Since Earth's core is made of iron, which is magnetic, it follows that Earth has a magnetic field just as a magnet does.

GED Content Focus (Page 113)

1. **(2) The locations of the continents in relation to one another are constantly changing.** (Comprehension) The fact that the continents have moved in the past and that the plates are still moving today implies that the locations of the continents are changing relative to one another. Option (1) is incorrect because the continents have drifted for millions of years and continue to drift. Option (3) is incorrect because the accumulated movement of millions of years is noticeable. Option (4) is not true; according to the passage, the continents are embedded in the plates, which are formed by the crust and upper mantle. Option (5) is incorrect because the passage states that the continents have broken up, implying that once there was a single large continent composed of at least several, if not all, of our present-day continents.

2. **(1) Materials circulate between the mantle and crust at ridges and trenches.** (Comprehension) The diagram shows portions of the crust moving into the mantle at a trench, and mantle rising up into the crust at a ridge, implying that materials are moving between crust and mantle. Option (2) is the opposite of what happens as shown by the diagram. Option (3) is not true; as the diagram shows, the mantle is thicker than the crust everywhere. Option (4) is not true because the mantle covers thousands of miles, and as the diagram shows, the convection currents occur throughout the mantle. Option (5) is not true; the diagram shows that convection currents occur throughout the mantle, not just under the continents.

3. **(4) Plates are pulling apart mostly under the oceans.** (Evaluation) According to the map, most areas with plates moving apart are located under the oceans. Option (1) is incorrect because the map shows that the Indo-Australian plate is moving away from the Antarctic plate. Option (2) cannot be true, since, as the map shows, the Antarctic plate is now as far south as it could possibly be. Option (3) is incorrect because, as the map shows, the North American plate is moving away from the Eurasian plate. Option (5) is incorrect because the map shows that most boundaries involve plates moving toward each other or away from each other.

4. **(5) the Andes, formed by the collision of the Nazca and South American plates** (Application) According to the passage, the Himalayas were formed by the collision of the Indo-Australian and Eurasian plates. This is most similar to the formation of the Andes, which, as the map shows, were also caused by plates colliding. Options (1), (3), and (4) are incorrect because these formations are the result of two plates moving apart. Option (2) is incorrect because the passage and map indicate that the San Andreas fault is caused by two plates sliding past one another, not colliding.

5. **(1) The plates would no longer move and the continents no longer drift.** (Analysis) To answer this question, you must look at the convection diagram, which explains that heat currents in the mantle cause the plates to move. If Earth's interior were cold, these currents would stop and so, presumably, would continental drift. Options (2), (3), (4), and (5) are incorrect because they all involve continued movement of the plates.

6. **(2) The theory of plate tectonics explains how the continents drift.** (Analysis) According to the second paragraph, the theory of plate tectonics explains how the continents drift. Option (1) is the opposite of the correct answer. Options (3) and (4) are not true; plate tectonics helps explain both the movement of the continents and the development of oceans, not exclusively one or the other. Option (5) is incorrect because only the theory of plate tectonics explains how rocks in the mantle move.

GED Practice (Pages 114–115)

1. **(5) South America and Africa would be farther apart.** (Comprehension) The maps show that South America is moving away from Africa, widening the Atlantic. This implies that South America and Africa will continue to move farther apart. Option (1) is incorrect because, since the world has always changed, it is likely

that it will continue to change over the next hundred million years. Options (2) and (3) are unlikely to occur, given that the relative areas of the oceans and of the continents has stayed stable over time. Option (4) is the opposite of what the map would show—the map series shows the continents on either side of the Atlantic increasingly drifting apart and thus this ocean widening.

2. **(2) The animals might have crossed the oceans on driftwood.** (Evaluation) Before the idea of continental drift was widely accepted, this was one of the explanations proposed for the presence of the same fossils on widely separated continents. Option (1) is incorrect because it does not explain why the same fossils are found on both continents. Option (3) is highly unlikely because species of land animals could not swim thousands of miles across the ocean and survive. Since fossils are imbedded in rock, option (4) is not likely. Option (5) has nothing to do with fossils.

3. **(4) He did not have a strong explanation for how the continents moved.** (Comprehension) Without a good explanation for what caused the continents to move, Wegener's idea was quite weak, and it was with this that his critics found most fault. Options (1) and (2) were also sources of criticism, but not as important as Wegener's inability to explain how the continents moved. Option (3) is not true— there is evidence that the continents were once joined. Option (5) is incorrect, because Pangaea was not imaginary, but part of the hypothesis. However, as with options (1) and (2), Wegener's critics did not debate smaller details of Wegener's theories but whether he could explain what he proposed.

4. **(5) The continents originally formed one large land mass and then moved apart.** (Analysis) This was the conclusion Wegener drew. Options (1), (2), (3), and (4) are all supporting details that he cited to support this conclusion.

5. **(5) the occurrence of earthquakes along plate boundaries** (Application) Because plate boundaries are areas where a lot of geologic activity occurs, it follows that earthquakes would occur along plate boundaries. Options (1), (2), and (4) have nothing to do with plate tectonics. Option (3) is a result of erosion and the deposition of sediment on the ocean floor, not plate tectonics.

GED Mini-Test (Pages 116–117)

1. **(2) heat currents in the mantle** (Comprehension) According to the diagram and the passage, heated rock circulates in the mantle, pushing up through the crust and causing the sea floor to spread. Option (1) is incorrect because the diagram shows that the heat currents are in the mantle, not in the crust. Option (3) is incorrect because the aging of the sea floor occurs with the passage of time and is not a cause of sea floor spreading. Options (4) and (5) each results from sea floor spreading, as shown in the diagram and/or explained in previous passages.

2. **(2) The farther from the ridge, the older the sea floor.** (Comprehension) New crust formed at the ridge pushes the older sea floor crust outward. It follows that the farther from the ridge, the older the sea floor. Option (1) is incorrect because it is the opposite of what the diagram implies. Options (3) and (4) are incorrect because the diagram does not label a specific ocean and because sea floor spreading occurs in all the oceans. Option (5) is not implied by the diagram and in fact is not true.

3. **(1) It collides with a plate and dips below it.** (Analysis) As shown in the diagram, when the sea floor meets another plate, the sea floor dips beneath this plate, forming a trench. Option (2) is incorrect because if the sea floor were lighter than the continental plates, it would rise above them or push them up from below, but not form a deep trench where it meets them. Option (3) is incorrect because the mantle does not collapse; the material in it circulates due to convection currents. Option (4), earthquake action, is a result, not a cause, of the plate movement, including the sea floor dipping below a continental plate. Option (5) is incorrect because the sea floor is descending, not rising, at this point.

4. **(3) The Atlantic Ocean will widen.** (Evaluation) Since scientists have estimated the actual rate of spreading, this supports the conclusion that the ocean is getting wider. Options (1) and (2) are incorrect because the depth of the ocean depends on factors other than sea floor spreading. Option (4) is the opposite of what will happen, because spreading implies widening of the ocean. Option (5) is incorrect because the spreading of the sea floor indicates that the width of the ocean is changing.

5. **(3) Types of Plate Boundaries** (Comprehension) The information is about the three types of plate boundaries. Options (1) and (5) are too general. Options (2) and (4) do not describe the information in the passage and diagram.

6. **(1) The Juan de Fuca plate is descending below the North American plate.** (Application) The key fact here is that one plate is descending below another, which is

characteristic of a convergent boundary. Option (2) is an example of a break within a plate rather than at a boundary. Options (3) and (5) are examples of divergent boundaries. Option (4) is an example of a transform fault boundary.

7. **(1) The continental plates and the upper mantle move together rather than independently.** (Evaluation) This conclusion is supported by the fact that the continental plates are attached to the upper mantle by deep keels of rock. Options (2) is incorrect because, according to the passage, the keels, which reach into the upper mantle, are solid rock and because the information implies that there is solid rock in the mantle below the partially molten layer. Option (3) is incorrect because the keels attach the plates to the upper mantle. If the plates slid and the upper mantle did not, the keels would rip off. Option (4) is incorrect because the passage does not indicate that the oceanic plates have keels as the continental plates do; nor does it indicate that the oceanic plates are anchored to the upper mantle in any other way. Option (5) is not supported by the information and, in fact, it is incorrect; the keels of the continental plates make these plates much deeper than the oceanic plates.

8. **(5) The world's deepest trenches are in the Pacific Ocean.** (Evaluation) As the passage indicates, the table shows the deepest trenches in each ocean. Thus, the world's deepest trenches are in the Pacific, because they are the deepest trenches in the table. Options (1), (3), and (4) contradict the information given in the table. Option (2) is incorrect because trenches are depressions, not spreading.

Lesson 10
GED Skill Focus (Page 119)

1. **b.** Steam and magma create great pressure, eventually causing a forceful eruption.

2. **b.** "... the pressure becomes great enough to cause a violent explosion."

3. **a.** deposits of two types of materials, ash and cinder

4. **a.** Cinder and ash explode into the air.
   c. Cinder and ash form a cone-shaped mountain.

GED Content (Page 121)

1. **(2) Movements along faults cause earthquakes.** (Comprehension) The main idea of the paragraph is that earthquakes are caused by movements along different types of faults. Option (1) does not mention faults. Options (3) and (4) are details from the paragraph. Option (5) is a detail that is not mentioned in the paragraph.

2. **(2) A steep face of rock is exposed.** (Analysis) According to the diagram, in both the normal and reverse faults the result is the exposure of a vertical rock face where previously the land had been flat. Option (1) is incorrect because rocks move up or down, not sideways, in these types of fault. Option (3) is incorrect because according to the passage, rocks are pulled apart only in normal faults. Option (4) is incorrect because the diagram shows the layers are no longer lined up. Option (5) is incorrect because according to the passage, rocks are pushed together only in reverse faults.

3. **(3) mountains** (Analysis) According to the diagram, reverse and normal faults thrust rock layers up or down, resulting in steep rock faces. Eventually mountains would form from this type of activity. Options (1), (2), and (4) do not result from faulting. Option (5) is incorrect because it refers to the climate of an area, not the landscape features.

4. **(1) Surface waves are the most destructive type of seismic wave.** (Evaluation) According to the passage, surface waves cause the ground to bend and twist, sometimes causing buildings to collapse. The passage gives no comparable information on the destructiveness of primary and secondary seismic waves. So options (2), (3), (4), and (5) are not supported by the information given in the passage.

5. **(5) the amount of energy released from the focus** (Comprehension) The second to last paragraph of the passage states that the more energy released by an earthquake, the stronger an earthquake is. Options (1), (2), and (3) are incorrect because, while they may be important in other ways, they do not determine the strength of an earthquake. Option (4) may be related to the strength of an earthquake, but it is not mentioned in the passage.

6. **(1) are unstable due to the movements of the tectonic plates** (Analysis) The boundaries are the areas where plates are pushing together, pulling apart, or sliding past one another, so these areas are very unstable, making earthquakes likely. Option (2) is not true; plate boundaries are not solid rock; they are areas where there are cracks or faults. Option (3) is true of some, but not all, boundaries and does not explain the relationship of boundaries to earthquake activity. Option (4) is not true; areas around plate boundaries change as a result of plate movement. Option (5) describes locations of earthquakes, not why earthquakes are likely to occur along plate boundaries.

1. **(4) A jackhammer breaks apart a roadway surface.** (Application) According to the passage, mechanical weathering involves a physical breaking down of rock. This is the only example of a physical breakdown among the choices. Option (1) is incorrect because weathering involves physical breakdown, not physical movement. Options (2), (3), and (5) are all examples or results of chemical weathering.

2. **(1) Acid rain wears away marble.** (Application) According to the passage, chemical weathering involves changes in the weathered substance through reaction with substances in the environment. Options (2) and (3) are examples of mechanical weathering. Options (4) and (5) have nothing to do with the weathering of rock.

3. **(2) wearing away and transporting** (Comprehension) According to the first sentence of the passage, erosion consists of two processes, the wearing away of rock and soil and its transport elsewhere. Option (1) is incorrect because transporting is necessary for erosion to take place. Option (3) is incorrect because erosion involves wearing away material, not depositing it. Options (4) and (5) are incorrect, because both involve an inappropriate use of the verb *load* and because, for option (5), erosion does not involve things diverging.

4. **(3) Erosion would increase along the bluff.** (Analysis) With more water in the river exerting more force on its channel, erosion would increase. Option (1) is unlikely; the river will rise and the bluff would be exposed to less, not more, air. Option (2) is incorrect because more water means more erosion, not less. Option (4) is incorrect because there would be more eroded material in the river during a surge. Option (5) is not true; erosion would continue and, in fact, increase.

5. **(3) analyzing historical data and measuring seismic activity and movement along faults** (Comprehension) According to the passage, these are the two main methods. Option (1) is incorrect because climatic data are not relevant to earthquake prediction. Option (2) is a monitoring technique, not a main method of predicting earthquakes. Option (4) is incorrect because although GPS data can be used to infer seismic activity, the GPS satellites actually record location, not seismic activity. Option (5) is incorrect because waiting for a mainshock is not a prediction method.

6. **(4) Local officials practiced emergency responses and so were better prepared for the earthquake.** (Analysis) Even though the prediction was wrong about the timing of the mainshock, it did prompt government officials to run emergency drills. Thus when the mainshock occurred, they were better prepared to respond. Options (1), (2), and (3) are not mentioned in the passage and also are not true; each method had been used prior to the Loma Prieta earthquake. Option (5) is an indicator of failure, not success.

7. **(5) reduced loss of life and property damage from future earthquakes** (Evaluation) Government funding is often awarded when there is a possible benefit to society as a result of the research. Options (1), (2), and (3) are scientific or technical benefits, which play a lesser role in decision making about funding research. Option (4) is not a likely result of earthquake research.

GED Mini-Test (Pages 124–125)

1. **(5) Causes and Effects of Glaciers** (Comprehension) The passage explains how mountain glaciers are formed (causes) and the changes they make on the landscape (effects). Option (1) is incorrect because the passage does not discuss the history of glaciers. Option (2) is too general. Options (3) and (4) are too specific.

2. **(3) The edges of the glacier would melt, making it smaller.** (Analysis) Since glaciers form from excess snow and ice that do not melt from season to season, it follows that unusually warm weather would cause more melting. This would make the glacier smaller. Options (1), (2), and (4) describe what happens when glaciers build up. Option (5) occurs irrespective of the summer weather.

3. **(4) an eruption from a side vent** (Analysis) The diagram shows several paths on the sides as well as the center of the volcano that the magma takes through the volcano. This implies that a shield volcano may erupt from a side vent. Options (1), (2), (3), and (5) are contrary to the details of the information in the paragraph and diagram.

4. **(5) Kilauea Iki, whose lava spread over Hawaii during several months** (Application) This is the only volcano that fits the description of a shield volcano, with slow, relatively gentle lava flows. Options (1), (2), (3), and (4) have characteristics that are opposite to those of a shield volcano.

5. **(1) Because of its weight, most sand is blown near the ground.** (Analysis) The diagram shows wind-blown sand bouncing along near the ground, wearing away the base of the rock. Nothing in the information given suggests that option (2), (3), or (4) is true. Option (5) may

happen eventually, but it does not explain the low-to-the-ground action of sand and wind.

6. **(5) Rocks of volcanic origin are igneous rocks.** (Evaluation) Since volcanoes occur where magma reaches the surface and eventually cools, it follows that rocks resulting from volcanic activity are igneous rocks. Options (1), (2), (3), and (4) make no mention of magma being involved in the formation. In fact, options (1) and (3) describe the formation of sedimentary rocks, and options (2) and (4) describe the conditions under which metamorphic rocks form.

7. **(3) south central California** (Comprehension) By consulting the key and looking for a cluster of earthquakes that occurred in the last day, you can see that the earthquakes in the last day occurred mostly in south central California. Options (1), (2), (4), and (5) are areas that do not show large numbers of earthquakes within the last day.

8. **(4) Earthquakes are an everyday occurrence in California.** (Evaluation) With so many minor quakes occurring during a one-week period, you can conclude that earthquake activity is frequent in California. Option (1) is not true since the map shows a week in February with lots of earthquake activity. Option (2) is incorrect because none of the earthquakes had a magnitude as great as 6 that week. Option (3) may or may not be true, but there is no way to tell from the map. Option (5) is incorrect because most of the earthquakes were of very low magnitude and probably went unnoticed by most people.

Lesson 11
GED Skill Focus (Page 127)

1. **a.** It takes one full year for Earth to revolve around the sun.

2. The dates shown in the diagram indicate that Earth revolves around the sun in one year. The diagram does not show the tilt of Earth's axis changing direction; in fact, the axis points in the same direction on all four of the dates shown.

3. **b.** On March 21 and September 21, neither hemisphere leans toward the sun.

4. On those two dates, the angle of Earth's axis with respect to the sun is the same and neither hemisphere is tilted toward the sun, so the number of hours of daylight will be the same. Information about the southern hemisphere on June 21 is irrelevant to the conclusion stated in question 3.

GED Content Focus (Page 129)

1. **(3) dry air** (Comprehension) According to the chart, both types of continental air masses contain dry air. Options (1), (2), (4), and (5) are incorrect because maritime, not continental, air masses contain moist air.

2. **(1) maritime polar** (Comprehension) Snow implies that the air mass has moist air, so it must be maritime. Snow also implies that it is a cold air mass, so it must be polar. Options (2), (3), (4), and (5) are incorrect because they involve tropical (warm) air masses or continental (dry) air masses.

3. **(3) A maritime tropical air mass brings hot, humid weather to the southern United States.** (Evaluation) This event supports the generalization that maritime air masses bring damp weather to the United States. Option (1) is incorrect because it does not relate directly to weather in the United States. Options (2) and (4) are incorrect because facts about where the air masses originate do not support conclusions about the specific type of weather they bring to a specific place. Option (5) is incorrect because it relates to continental air masses, not to maritime air masses.

4. **(2) time of year** (Evaluation) The diagram of the warm front shows precipitation where the warm air mass (the maritime tropical air mass) rises over the cold air mass (the continental polar air mass). To decide whether the forecast for snow is likely to be correct, you would need to know the time of year. If it were spring, summer, or autumn, it would be more likely to rain than to snow. In winter, it would be more likely to snow. Option (1), the time of day, is not as likely to affect the type of precipitation as the time of year. Options (3), (4), and (5) are not relevant to the type of precipitation that is likely to fall.

5. **(4) The weather would be about the same for a few days.** (Analysis) According to the passage, air masses have similar temperature and moisture conditions and cover thousands of square miles. Therefore if an air mass is stalled over a place, it's likely the weather will remain about the same while the air mass is still there. Option (1) describes a characteristic of air masses, not a result of an air mass stalling. Option (2) is not likely, since a characteristic of an air mass is fairly uniform temperature and moisture conditions. Option (3) describes weather along quickly passing fronts, not within air masses. Option (5) is incorrect because nothing indicates that conditions would change so drastically.

6. **(2) Rainy weather is associated with the passing of a front.** (Evaluation) According to the passage and diagrams, precipitation is

associated with fronts. Option (1) is incorrect because continental polar air masses are dry. Option (3) is true, but there is no information in the passage or diagram to support it. Option (4) is incorrect because the relative amount of rain caused by warm and cold fronts is not discussed. Option (5) is incorrect because both types of front occur year round, and this is not discussed in the passage or indicated in the diagram.

GED Practice (Pages 130–131)

1. **(2) Weather patterns result from differences in moist sea air and dry land air.** (Comprehension) This general idea is stated in the topic sentence of the passage. Options (1), (3), (4), and (5) are details from the passage or diagram.

2. **(4) Warm air rises over the land during the day and over the sea during the night.** (Evaluation) The diagram shows this to be the case. Although options (1), (2), (3), and (5) are factually correct statements, none alone explains why the wind shifts direction after sunset.

3. **(1) March** (Application) The Center tracks storms from May through November, which implies that storms are not as much of a problem during the rest of the year. The only month listed that is not in this hurricane season is March. Options (2), (3), (4), and (5) are incorrect because those months are in the prime hurricane season during which the Center does track storms, as stated in the passage.

4. **(3) public skepticism about later hurricane warnings** (Analysis) A warning that results in an evacuation that turns out to be unnecessary is likely to make people think that warnings in the future will also turn out to be wrong. Options (1) and (2) are incorrect because damage and deaths are likely to be reduced as a result of the warning in areas the hurricane did hit, and would not occur in areas where it didn't. Option (4) is not likely to result, because, as the passage states, for safety reasons, the Tropical Prediction Center prefers to issue wide-area warnings even if they turn out to be inaccurate. Option (5) is not a likely result of such an error.

5. **(3) In short-term forecasts, the current data are very similar to the projected data, increasing accuracy.** (Evaluation) When the time frame is very short, conditions are not likely to change too much, so predictions can be more accurate. Options (1) and (2) are incorrect because historical data are equally applicable to short- and long-term forecasts, and so they do not explain why short-term forecasts tend to be more accurate. Option (4) is incorrect because it is the opposite of what actually happens. Option (5) is true of both short- and long-term forecasts, so it does not explain why short-term forecasts are more accurate than long-term forecasts.

GED Mini-Test (Pages 132–133)

1. **(3) the weather conditions of a region over a long time** (Comprehension) The difference between weather and climate is explained in the first sentence of the passage. Option (1) describes weather, not climate. Option (2) is too specific. Options (4) and (5) are aspects of climate, but do not explain what climate is.

2. **(3) Europe** (Application) A person who liked moderate weather and four seasons would most enjoy living in Europe, the only place listed that has a temperate climate. Options (1), (2), (4), and (5) have primarily a tropical rainy climate which does not result in four distinct seasons.

3. **(2) The sun's rays are more concentrated near the equator than near the poles.** (Evaluation) More concentrated rays means that the area near the equator gets more of the sun's energy, making the climate warmer. Options (1), (3), (4), and (5) are not supported by the information in the passage or the diagram.

4. **(5) fewer and weaker El Niño events** (Analysis) If warm water temperatures in the eastern tropical Pacific caused more frequent, stronger El Niño events, then cooler temperatures in that same zone would likely have the opposite effect. Option (1) is not true; the information shows that ocean temperatures have a major effect on atmospheric conditions. Options (2) and (4) describe the opposite of what would occur. Nothing in the information supports option (3).

5. **(2) There are variations in sunspot activity.** (Analysis) This is the only fact among the options given. Option (1) is false, because the passage states that there are times of both low and high sunspot activity, meaning there are fewer sunspots sometimes and more other times. Options (3) and (5) are opinions or hypotheses, and the passage gives no solid proof for either. Option (4) is not likely to be true because the effect of sunspots on North America is given as an example in the passage; if sunspots affect North America, they are likely to affect the rest of the world, too.

6. **(4) the specific way in which sunspots affect weather** (Evaluation) Unless you can explain the exact mechanism by which sunspot activity results in drought in North America, you cannot show a cause-and-effect relationship between the two events. The remaining options all involve data that would be useful to know

Answers and Explanations

but are not directly relevant to demonstrating a cause-and-effect relationship between sunspot activity and drought.

7. **(2) move toward the equator** (Application) Since ice is moving south from the North Pole, residents of North America would tend to move south, toward the equator. Option (1) would not help since ice would be spreading north in the Southern Hemisphere. Option (3) is incorrect because the ice sheets in the northern part of the continent would make the region difficult to live in. Option (4) is not likely because human beings are very adaptable and have survived previous ice ages. Option (5) is the opposite of what happens during an ice age.

Lesson 12
GED Skill Focus (Page 135)
1. **b.** a process that uses solar energy stored in ocean water to produce electricity

2. **a.** Other relatively inexpensive sources of energy are still available.

3. **a.** island nations near the equator

4. **a.** political and economic independence
   d. a cleaner environment

GED Content Focus (Page 137)
1. **(3) formed underground from the remains of plants and animals** (Comprehension) According to the second paragraph, fossil fuels formed from compacted organic remains. Options (1), (2), and (5) are incorrect because fossil fuels were formed naturally on Earth. Option (4) is incorrect because fossil fuels are formed from organic remains, not inorganic materials such as magma. (Since magma is molten rock, it is inorganic.)

2. **(4) Fossil fuels have been important to industry for more than a century and continue to be of great importance.** (Evaluation) The passage clearly refers to the importance of fossil fuels to industry for the last 150 years and into the present. Options (1), (2), (3), and (5) are incorrect because they each contradict the information in the passage.

3. **(4) Africa** (Comprehension) The key shows which symbol is used for coal, and a look at the map indicates that Africa is the continent with the least coal (because it has the fewer coal symbols). Options (1), (2), (3), and (5) are incorrect because the map indicates that these locations have more coal than Africa.

4. **(2) using windmills instead of coal-burning power plants to generate electricity** (Application) In this example, oil, a nonrenewable resource, is replaced by the energy of wind, which is a renewable resource.

Options (1), (3), and (4) are ways to conserve energy resources, not to replace a nonrenewable resource with a renewable one. Option (5) involves substituting a nonrenewable resource (gasoline) for a renewable resource (the energy you use when walking), which is the opposite of what the question asks.

5. **(4) Oil is available and relatively cheap.** (Evaluation) The fact that oil is still plentiful and fairly inexpensive would be unlikely to impress a person who values the conservation of natural resources. Options (1), (2), and (3) are strong positive aspects of solar energy. Option (5) is a strong negative aspect of energy from fossil fuels.

6. **(1) Some of the current resources would no longer be indicated, and some new ones would appear on the map.** (Analysis) Some resources will be used up in the next hundred years, so they will not be on the future map. As the passage indicates, new resources will be discovered during the next hundred years, so they will be added to the map. Option (2) is not likely, as we will continue to use up resources. Nothing in the passage or the map indicates that there will be more coal than oil resources, so option (3) is incorrect. Option (4) is incorrect because the passage implies that new resources will continue to be searched for and found. Option (5) is incorrect because the passage implies that it's unlikely all resources will be used up in the next hundred years.

GED Practice (Pages 138–139)
1. **(3) a wilderness research station** (Application) Of the options given, the research station is the only one distant enough not to be served by a power plant, so it is the most likely to use wind power as a source of energy. Options (1), (2), (4), and (5) are all likely to be connected to power plants.

2. **(2) Having a wind generator means having power if the main source of electricity fails.** (Evaluation) Having a backup power source would be a good reason to have a wind generator on a modern farm. Option (1) is incorrect because having to maintain your own equipment is more work than simply plugging into the power grid. Option (3) is incorrect because in most locations, wind is not as reliable as a power plant. Option (4) is incorrect, because; as the passage indicates, wind energy is still relatively expensive compared with getting power from a power plant. Option (5) is not true and, in any case, would bestow no benefit to the farmer.

3. **(5) Water power is not available in that location.** (Evaluation) According to the graph, water is the cheapest source of power. A person

considering cost over other factors would choose water if it were available. Option (1) is not true; water is cheaper than wind. Options (2), (3), and (4) are all true but they are not reasons for choosing wind over an even cheaper alternative.

4. **(5) was eight times greater** (Comprehension) According to the graph, in 1900, about 500 cubic kilometers were used and in 2000, about 4,000 cubic kilometers were used. That is an eightfold increase ($500 \times 8 = 4{,}000$).

5. **(3) The percentage of fresh water would decline as ice caps melted into the ocean.** (Analysis) As the ice caps melted, fresh water would flow into the oceans, increasing the amount of salty water and decreasing the amount of fresh water. Option (1) is incorrect because 97.5 is the percentage of salt water, not fresh water. Option (2) is incorrect because more water would be salty. Option (4) is incorrect because the fresh water would run off into the ocean and become salty water. Option (5) is incorrect because there would be an effect on the amount of fresh water on Earth.

6. **(2) improve water management, including water treatment, distribution, and conservation** (Evaluation) Better use of water, especially better water treatment for people without clean drinking water, may help us with water in the future. Option (1) is incorrect because increasing water use for any purpose will not help us meet future needs. Option (3) is incorrect because taking water away from agriculture will affect the food supply. Options (4) and (5) are only partial solutions to water problems.

GED Mini-Test (Pages 140–141)

1. **(2) About half the volume of soil consists of space, through which water and air circulate.** (Comprehension) The spaces in soil make the soil less dense than rock. Options (1), (3), (4), and (5) are true, but they do not explain the difference in density between soil and rock.

2. **(1) The soil would be unable to support much plant and animal life.** (Analysis) The top two layers of soil contain the bulk of soil's plant and animal life. Once that is gone, the remaining layer is not suitable to sustain much life. Option (2) is incorrect because the diagram shows that C horizon soil is coarser, not finer. Option (3) is incorrect because the passage indicates that C horizon soil does not contain much organic matter. Option (4) is incorrect because C Horizon soil is not rich. Option (5) is incorrect because the bedrock is below the remaining C horizon layer.

3. **(3) plant fewer, more drought-resistant crops** (Application) A farmer who values soil conservation highly would most likely try to protect the soil while still growing crops. Option (1) is incorrect because the drought would require the farmer to make some changes to protect the soil from drying up and blowing away. Options (2) and (4) would both result in further loss of water in the A horizon, which would increase the amount of soil that would dry up and blow away. Option (5) is not likely, since the farmer must grow some crops to make a living.

4. **(4) Some Imported Minerals and Their Uses** (Comprehension) This title covers the information in the passage and chart. Options (1) and (2) are too general since the chart covers only imported minerals. Option (3) is incorrect because the chart shows five imported minerals, not the five most important minerals. Option (5) is incorrect because the chart lists minerals that are not resources of the United States.

5. **(5) sheet mica and thallium** (Comprehension) According to the chart, these two minerals are used in the electronics industry. Options (1), (2), (3), and (4) are incorrect because the chart indicates that one or both of the minerals listed are used mainly for purposes other than electronics.

6. **(4) The United States would reduce its dependence on foreign nations.** (Evaluation) Nations usually wish to be as self-sufficient as possible so that politics does not interrupt the supply of a critical resource. Thus they may be willing to spend more on extracting the resource than on importing it. Options (1), (2), and (3) are all true but do not explain why a nation would spend more to develop its own supply of thallium. Option (5) is not true.

7. **(2) decreased agricultural production** (Analysis) With reduced photosynthesis caused by haze from air pollution, agricultural crops will not grow as well, reducing output. Option (1) is incorrect because there is no indication that the air pollution affects wind speeds. Options (3) and (5) are the opposite of what would occur, based on the information in the passage. Option (4) is incorrect because the haze from the air pollution is likely to reduce the number of sunny days, not increase them.

8. **(3) About one-fifth of the watersheds had serious quality problems.** (Evaluation) According to the circle graph, 21%, or about one-fifth, of the watersheds had serious quality problems. Options (1) and (2) are incorrect because more than half the watersheds had some degree of water quality problems. Option (4)

is incorrect because only 21% had serious quality problems. Option (5) is not true because the graph does not show the percentage of watersheds not tested, and only 27%, or about one-quarter, had insufficient data.

Lesson 13
GED Skill Focus (Page 143)

1. **a.** Scientists are located in the Milky Way, so they do not have a distant view of the entire galaxy.

2. **a.** The star is likely to take longer than 225 million years to make one turn around the center of the galaxy.

3. **b.** Its appearance will have changed.

4. **b.** a relatively flat disk of stars seen from the edge

Content Focus (Page 145)

1. **(2) the sun and all the objects that revolve around it** (Comprehension) According to the first paragraph, this is the definition of the solar system. Option (1) is incorrect because it omits the larger bodies, such as planets, revolving around the sun. Option (3) omits the smaller bodies, such as asteroids, comets, and dust. Options (4) and (5) omit the sun.

2. **(3) The solar system will continue to develop and change.** (Comprehension) The fact that the solar system evolved into its present form suggests that it will continue to change. Options (1), (2), and (4) restate the information that is given in either the passage or the diagram; they are not implications of it. Option (5) is not implied by the development of the solar system.

3. **(5) Pluto** (Comprehension) The diagram shows that Pluto is tiny compared to the other outer planets, the gas giants, and the passage states that it is rocky, unlike the gas giants. Options (1), (2), (3), and (4) are gas giants with rings.

4. **(3) The location and physical nature of Mars make its exploration feasible.** (Comprehension) Mars is relatively close to Earth and has a solid surface, unlike the gas giants, making an exploratory landing on the planet possible. Option (1) is not true; scientists are studying these planets with great interest. Nothing in the information, passage, or diagram supports the statements made in options (2), (4), or (5).

5. **(3) The inner planets will be destroyed.** (Analysis) Since the diameter of the sun is likely to increase to 10 to 100 times its present size, the sun is likely to destroy the inner planets by engulfing them. Options (1) and (2) are incorrect because the expansion of the sun means that both the inner and outer planets would be more likely to heat up than to become cooler.

Option (4) is incorrect because planet formation occurs when the solar system is young and is not likely to occur at other times. Option (5) is incorrect because the solar system will change if the sun changes.

6. **(4) The U.S. wanted to perform experiments concerning the effects of weightlessness.** (Evaluation) The United States has the technology for crewed space travel, but has decided to concentrate on learning the effects of weightlessness rather than continue manned missions to the moon. Option (1) is true, but it is not the reason for abandoning exploration of the moon. Options (2), (3), and (5) are not true because, as the passage states, U.S. astronauts successfully landed on the moon several times, beginning in 1969.

GED Practice (Pages 146–147)

1. **(5) The sun is likely to end up a white dwarf.** (Comprehension) The facts that the sun is a low-mass star and that low-mass stars evolve into white dwarfs imply that the sun will eventually become a white dwarf. Options (1), (2), and (3) are all true for both low- and high-mass stars and, so, do not follow from the fact that the sun is a low-mass star. Option (4) is incorrect because, according to the passage, the sun is in the main sequence phase.

2. **(4) a supernova** (Comprehension) The passage describes and the diagram shows that the supernova is an explosion, the most spectacular of the options listed.

3. **(4) Eventually, stars run out of "fuel" and collapse.** (Evaluation) According to the passage and diagram, all stars eventually run out of fuel, end their fusion reactions, and collapse. Options (1) and (2) are incorrect because there is no information regarding planets in the passage or diagram. Option (3) is not true; both low-mass and high-mass stars become giants. Option (5) is not true; according to the passage, a star in the white dwarf stage gives off very little radiation.

4. **(2) Fireworks explode, sending sparks, ashes, and smoke in all directions.** (Application) This is the only option that describes an instantaneous explosion that results in material flying in all directions similar to the Big Bang. Option (1) is incorrect because it does not describe an explosive event with material flying off in all directions. Option (3) is incorrect because the Big Bang was not the result of a collision. Options (4) and (5) are incorrect because neither describes an instantaneous explosion.

5. **(2) The universe would collapse in on itself.** (Analysis) The graph shows that if the

universe has too much mass, it will begin to contract, eventually collapsing in on itself. Scientists have named this scenario the "Big Crunch." According to the graph, option (1) is the opposite of what would happen. Options (3) and (5) are incorrect because the graph gives no evidence that a contracting universe would cause a parallel universe to exist or that another Big Bang would occur. According to the graph, option (4) describes a universe that is neither expanding nor contracting.

6. **(3) They have observed its gravitational effects on visible objects.** (Evaluation) The evidence for dark matter is indirect. The existence of dark matter is inferred from the behavior of the visible objects around it. Options (1) and (2) are incorrect because dark matter is not visible. Options (4) and (5) are evidence for the Big Bang theory, not dark matter.

GED Mini-Test (Pages 148–149)

1. **(3) It is farther from the sun than Earth is.** (Comprehension) Since the distance from Earth to the sun is one astronomical unit, it follows that a planet more than one astronomical unit from the sun will be farther from the sun than Earth is. Options (1) and (2) are therefore incorrect. Option (4) is incorrect because a planet farther from the sun than Earth is likely to receive less solar energy than Earth does. Option (5) has nothing to do with distance from the sun.

2. **(5) 240 minutes** (Application) It takes the sun's light 8 minutes to travel one astronomical unit. Therefore it would take 30×8, or 240 minutes, to travel 30 astronomical units—the distance from the sun to Neptune.

3. **(2) Optical telescopes magnify images of distant objects.** (Analysis) It is assumed that you understand that optical telescopes magnify images. Options (1), (3), (4), and (5) are stated directly in the passage.

4. **(3) Optical Telescopes** (Comprehension) The passage covers optical telescopes, from the land-based telescope used by Galileo to the Hubble Space Telescope. Options (1) and (4) are too specific. Option (2) is too general because the passage discusses only optical telescopes, not other types of telescopes. Option (5) is incorrect because radio telescopes are not discussed.

5. **(4) debris thrown out of the large crater by the meteorite's impact** (Analysis) If you examine the diagram, you will see that the secondary craters are formed as a result of debris being blasted out of the large crater by the meteor's impact. Options (1) and (2) are incorrect because the diagram indicates there is only one

meteorite and not several of them. Option (3) is incorrect because the diagram labels indicate that a meteorite, not a comet, formed the crater. Option (5) is incorrect because the diagram shows the holes being punched from above; it indicates nothing about the ground settling after impact.

6. **(3) Earth has fewer craters than the moon, which has no atmosphere.** (Evaluation) The fact that Earth, with a thick atmosphere, has few craters, and the moon, with no atmosphere, has many, supports the conclusion that many objects burn up in the atmosphere and so never reach the surface of Earth. Options (1) and (2) are true, but they have nothing to do with crater formation on Earth. Options (4) and (5) are true, but they do not concern the formation of craters by objects from space.

7. **(2) an amateur astronomer** (Application) The diagram shows a situation in which an amateur astronomer would find himself or herself. Option (1) is incorrect because planetary scientists study the planets, not the stars. Option (3) has nothing to do with astronomy. Option (4) is incorrect because a manufacturer is more interested in the object manufactured than in what can be seen with it and because it is not possible to make a telescope that can avoid this type of optical illusion. Option (5) is incorrect because such a scientist would be interested in the sun, not in optical double stars.

8. **(1) data from a space probe to Pluto** (Evaluation) A space probe that actually got close to Pluto would be able to get better information about the mass of Pluto and Charon than we can from telescopes on Earth or above Earth. Options (2) and (3) are incorrect because, as the question text states, telescopes cannot get good enough images to determine the relative mass of Pluto and Charon. Options (4) and (5) would provide general data about the two types of systems. However, these data would not specifically be applicable to Pluto and Charon.

Unit 2 Cumulative Review (Pages 150–154)

1. **(3) The mesosphere ends.** (Comprehension) The diagram shows that at 50 miles above Earth's surface the mesosphere ends and the thermosphere begins. Options (1), (2), and (4) occur at other altitudes. Option (5) is incorrect because it is not true and because no information about air molecules is given in the diagram.

2. **(5) decreases, then increases, then decreases and increases again** (Comprehension) This is correct because the temperature decreases from 20°C to −55°C at the border between the troposphere and

stratosphere; then it increases to 0°C at the border between the stratosphere and mesosphere; then it decreases to –100°C near the top of the mesosphere; finally it reaches 2,000°C near the top of the thermosphere. Options (1), (2), (3), and (4) are incorrect because they do not correctly or completely describe the changes in temperature that occur as altitude increases.

3. **(1) A runner from Boston, which is at sea level, has trouble breathing while jogging in the Rocky Mountains.** (Evaluation) A runner from a sea-level location gets less oxygen per breath than he or she is accustomed to when running at a higher altitude. Thus, the runner has trouble breathing. Options (2) and (3) may be true, but they do not provide evidence that less oxygen is available at higher altitudes. Option (4) makes no sense; a mountain climber needs to re-create atmospheric conditions at a high altitude, not at sea level. Option (5) is true; but it has nothing to do with the amount of oxygen in the air.

4. **(5) SETI projects are based on dreams rather than realistic possibilities about space.** (Analysis) The scientific value of SETI projects is debated in the scientific community. Some think looking for aliens is an activity best left for science fiction; others think it is a worthwhile scientific endeavor. Options (1), (2), (3), and (4) are facts about radio waves and SETI.

5. **(1) Overview of the Rock Cycle** (Comprehension) The paragraph and the diagram give general information about the steps in the processes through which one type of rock turns into another, which is called the rock cycle. Options (2), (4), and (5) are too specific. Option (3) is not related to the topic of the diagram.

6. **(4) Weathering and erosion can affect all kinds of rocks on Earth's surface.** (Evaluation) The diagram shows that when igneous, sedimentary, and metamorphic rocks are exposed, they are all subject to weathering and erosion. Option (1) is incorrect because metamorphic rocks are also formed from sedimentary rocks. Option (2) is incorrect because sedimentary rocks are formed by pressure. Option (3) is incorrect because igneous rocks are formed from magma. Option (5) is incorrect because heat and pressure cause sedimentary rocks to form metamorphic rocks.

7. **(2) sedimentary** (Application) Sedimentary rocks are the most likely to have layers. The stripes indicate layers of sediments. Option (1) is a form of sediment, not rock. Options (3), (4), and (5) are incorrect, because magma and igneous rocks, including granite, are unlikely to have stripes of different colors.

8. **(1) igneous** (Analysis) A volcano would have magma in, on, and around it. So igneous rock is most likely to be found in the area. Options (2), (3), (4), and (5) are incorrect because metamorphic rock, which includes slate, and sedimentary rock, which includes limestone, are less likely to be found in the area than igneous rock is.

9. **(4) Humans did not exist for most of geologic time.** (Analysis) This statement is a conclusion reached by comparing the amount of time humans have existed with all the geologic time preceding our development. Options (1), (2), (3), and (5) are all details regarding the era during which humans appeared, the Cenozoic.

10. **(3) fish, land plants, and dinosaurs** (Comprehension) By the Mesozoic, fish and land plants had already evolved. Dinosaurs first appeared during the Mesozoic. Since these organisms existed at that time, it follows that their fossils could occur in rocks of the Mesozoic Era. Option (1) is incorrect since many other organisms besides simple ocean organisms had appeared by the Mesozoic Era. Options (2), (4), and (5) are incorrect because horses, primates, and humans did not appear until after the Mesozoic Era, and so they would not be found in Mesozoic fossils.

11. **(2) 160 million years** (Comprehension) The time line is measured in millions of years. Dinosaurs appeared slightly less than 225 million years ago and died out about 65 million years ago. Subtracting 65 million from 225 million gives 160 million years. Option (1) gives the time when dinosaurs died out. Option (3) gives the time when dinosaurs first appeared. Options (4) and (5) are longer than the period that dinosaurs existed.

12. **(2) sea-living invertebrates** (Analysis) Options (1), (3), and (4) are incorrect because the time line shows that these organisms appeared after the first fish. Option (5) is incorrect for the same reason, and even if land plants had existed, the fish would not have been able to leave the water to eat them.

13. **(3) global climate change** (Analysis) The time line shows an ice age before the dying out of sea invertebrates, so this climate change may have contributed to their demise. Options (1) and (2) occurred well after the sea invertebrates died out. Options (4) and (5) occurred very much earlier than the dying out of sea invertebrates, so were not likely to be causes.

14. **(3) The Great Lakes are younger than the Rocky Mountains.** (Evaluation) The time line shows that the Rocky Mountains appeared before the Great Lakes. Option (1) is incorrect because

according to the time line, air-breathing animals appeared in the early Paleozoic and amphibians did not appear until the late Paleozoic. Option (2) is incorrect because the time line shows that dinosaurs lived during the Mesozoic Era. Option (4) is incorrect because the time line shows that dinosaurs died out about 65 million years ago. Option (5) is incorrect because the time line shows that the first life forms developed in the oceans.

15. **(4) Australia** (Comprehension) According to the map, earthquake zones pass to the north of Australia but do not cross the continent itself. Options (1), (2), and (3) have earthquake zones. Option (5) is not shown on the map.

16. **(4) an island in the northern Pacific** (Application) Of the locations listed, only the northern Pacific has many volcanoes. In fact, Dante explored a volcano on one of Alaska's Aleutian Islands in the northern Pacific.

17. **(3) There are different types of granite, each made of different minerals.** (Evaluation) One of the characteristics of a mineral is that it is made of particular, that is, specific elements. The fact that there are different types of granite, each formed from different minerals, supports the idea that granite is not made of particular elements but can be made of an assortment of different elements. Thus, granite is not a mineral; it is a rock made of different and varying minerals. It is not itself a mineral. Options (1), (2), (4), and (5) are true, but options (1) and (5), as characteristics of minerals, could be used to contradict the conclusion; options (2) and (4) are irrelevant to the conclusion.

18. **(3) The minerals removed from ores are valuable resources.** (Analysis) The writer assumes you know that the minerals removed from ores are valuable; otherwise people would not take the trouble to mine and smelt them. Options (1), (2), (4), and (5) are details that are stated in the passage.

19. **(3) the mouth of the Annapolis River, Nova Scotia, with large variation in high and low tides** (Application) One requirement for a tidal power station is a great difference in the water level at high and low tide, so this location is the best of those listed. Options (1), (4), and (5) are incorrect because to take advantage of the tides, tidal power stations must be at the mouth of a river, where it meets the sea, not inland. Option (2) is not a good location because the tidal difference is too low and a dam would block shipping in a busy harbor like New York's.

20. **(2) rising and falling tides** (Comprehension) The flow of water caused by rising and falling tides powers a tidal power plant. Options (1) and (4) are other types of water power. Option (3) is a machine that uses water power. Option (5) occurs in a tidal power station but is not the source of energy for the station.

21. **(2) environmental protection** (Evaluation) One of the problems associated with a tidal power plant is that it constitutes an artificial barrier that disrupts the ecosystem. Normally organisms and water would move freely in and out of the river, but constructing a dam for a power plant would make that impossible. Therefore people who are concerned about protecting the environment are likely to oppose building the power plant. Options (1), (3), (4), and (5) are values that are not likely to be associated with opposition to the tidal power plant.

22. **(1) The position of the moon is also a factor in the occurrence of a lunar eclipse.** (Evaluation) The position of all three bodies— sun, Earth, and moon—is critical in determining when a lunar eclipse occurs. Option (2) is incorrect because the season does not affect whether a lunar eclipse occurs. Option (3) is not true; Earth is always revolving around the sun. Option (4) is true but it does not explain why considering only the positions of the sun and Earth is an oversimplification. Option (5) is not true; Earth's position is one factor in determining the occurrence of a lunar eclipse.

UNIT 3: PHYSICAL SCIENCE
Lesson 14
GED Skill Focus (Page 159)
1. **a.** Both are made up of different substances that keep their properties.

2. **a.** In a solution, the substances are distributed evenly throughout, and in other mixtures they may be distributed unevenly.

3. **b.** (Substances are) solids.
   d. (Substances) keep their own properties.
   e. (Substances) can be separated by mechanical means.
   g. (Substances are) distributed evenly.
   h. (Substances are) a solid and a liquid.

GED Content Focus (Page 161)
1. **(1) definite shape; definite volume** (Comprehension) According to the passage, definite shape and volume are two properties of solids. Option (2) is incorrect because solids have definite volume. Option (3) is incorrect because it is the opposite of what is true. Option (4) is incorrect because solids have definite shape.

Option (5) is incorrect because the molecules in solids do move; they vibrate.

2. **(1) Both have molecules that move randomly.** (Analysis) The diagram shows that the molecules in gases and liquids move, and the passage indicates that they move randomly. Options (2) and (3) are characteristics of solids, not liquids and gases. Option (4) is incorrect because it is true only of liquids and solids; gases cannot evaporate, since they are already in vapor form. Option (5) is incorrect because only a solid can melt.

3. **(4) A liquid has no definite shape; it takes the shape of its container.** (Application) Because a liquid has no definite shape, it can assume the shape of its container when poured. Thus the batter will fill the heart-shaped baking pan. Options (1) and (2) are incorrect because they do not relate to the pouring of the cake batter; additionally they are not true because solids have definite volumes and definite shapes and do not take the shape of the container in which they are placed. Option (3) is incorrect because liquids do not have a definite shape. Option (5) is incorrect because it does not relate to the pouring of the cake batter, and because it is not true; a gas does not have a definite shape or a definite volume.

4. **(2) leaving ice cream on a hot stove** (Application) According to the passage, the addition of heat to a solid will make it melt, changing it to a liquid state. Option (1) is incorrect because the substance would still remain a liquid; no change of state will take place. Option (3) is incorrect because pricking a balloon will allow the gas to escape, but the gas does not change its state. Options (4) and (5) are incorrect because in each case, the material does not change state but remains a solid.

5. **(3) a gas changes to a liquid** (Analysis) Condensation and vaporization are opposite processes: condensation involves the changing of a gas to a liquid; vaporization involves the changing of a liquid to a gas. Options (1), (4), and (5) are incorrect because condensation does not involve a change to a solid. Option (2) is the opposite of the correct answer.

6. **(3) at its boiling point** (Comprehension) The definition of the boiling point is the temperature at which a liquid changes to a gas. Options (1) and (2) refer to the temperature at which a solid changes to a liquid and vice versa. Option (4) refers to the temperature at which a gas changes to a liquid. Option (5) is also the wrong term for this temperature, although it correctly describes what occurs at this temperature.

7. **(4) Molecules in gases move faster than molecules in liquids.** (Evaluation) According to the diagram, the molecules in gases move faster than those in liquids as indicated by the "tails" of motion on the gas molecules compared to the "jiggling" of molecules of a liquid. Option (1) is the opposite of what actually occurs. Options (2) and (3) are not supported by the diagram and, in fact, are not true. Option (5) is true for a gas, not a solid.

GED Practice (Pages 162–163)

1. **(5) gold** (Comprehension) According to the graph, the density of lead is 11.3 grams per cubic centimeter. Of the options listed, only gold has a higher density—19.3 grams per cubic centimeter. All the other substances offered as options (1), (2), (3), and (4) are less dense than lead.

2. **(1) Its density increases.** (Analysis) When ice melts, it becomes liquid water. According to the graph, the density of ice is 0.9 grams per cubic centimeter and the density of water is 1.0 gram per cubic centimeter. Therefore the density of ice increases when it melts. Note that water is unusual in this respect. When most solids melt, their densities decrease.

3. **(5) Density alone cannot be used to identify a particular substance.** (Application) Although iron, option (2), has a density of about 7.9 grams per cubic centimeter, more information about the unknown substance is needed to definitively identify it. Options (1), (2), (3), and (4) are incorrect because their densities are 4.5, 11.3, and 13.6 grams per cubic centimeter, respectively—all different from 7.9.

4. **(2) the effect of molecules as they hit the sides of their container** (Comprehension) According to the passage, pressure is the force with which the molecules of gas hit the sides of the container. Option (1) is related to the pressure of a gas, but it is not the definition of pressure. Option (3) is incorrect because pressure is related to molecular motion, not to the product of volume and temperature. Option (4) refers to the amount of heat held by a gas, not the pressure it exerts. Option (5) is incorrect, because it does not relate to pressure but to volume of a gas; it is nonsensical, as well, because gases always quickly come to fill the volume of their container, so the volume of the gas and of the container (its "size") are the same.

5. **(4) low temperature, large volume** (Analysis) According to the passage and diagrams, pressure increases when temperature increases or volume decreases. Therefore pressure would decrease when temperature was low and the volume was large. Option (1) is incorrect

UNIT 3

because high temperature would increase pressure. Option (2) is incorrect because high temperature and small volume would increase pressure. Option (3) is incorrect because the pressure would not be least under "medium" conditions. Option (5) is incorrect because the small volume would increase pressure.

6. **(3) Pressure increases when volume decreases and temperature remains the same.** (Evaluation) This statement is supported by diagram B which shows pressure increasing as volume decreases and temperature remains constant. Option (1) is not shown in the diagrams and it is incorrect because pressure would remain constant (not change) if temperature and volume remained the same (constant). Option (2) is incorrect because the pressure would increase when temperature increases and volume remains the same, as shown in A. Option (4) is incorrect because the pressure would remain the same if temperature and volume both doubled, as shown in C. Option (5) is not shown in the diagrams, and it is incorrect because pressure would increase if temperature increased and volume decreased since each change alone causes pressure to increase.

GED Mini-Test (Pages 164–165)

1. **(5) Methods of Separating Mixtures** (Comprehension) The table lists, describes, and gives examples of different ways to separate mixtures, so this title covers the content. Options (1) and (4) are incorrect because the table covers separation methods, not types or ingredients of mixtures. Options (2) and (3) are incorrect because they are too specific.

2. **(1) They both involve solutions.** (Analysis) In distillation, a solution is boiled to separate out ingredients; in extraction, a solvent is used to create a solution of one of the mixture's ingredients. Options (2), (3), and (4) are incorrect because neither distillation nor extraction involve magnetism, density, or appearance. Option (5) is incorrect because only distillation would be used to remove salt from seawater.

3. **(4) extraction** (Application) The trichloroethylene is a solvent that dissolved the stain and removed it, a process known as extraction. Option (1) is incorrect because you cannot sort a stain from a fabric. Option (2) is incorrect because salad dressing stains are not magnetic. Option (3) is incorrect because the tablecloth was not boiled. Option (5) is incorrect since using a chemical solvent does not involve differences in density.

4. **(3) distillation** (Application) Boiling crude petroleum yields different products as various

ingredients reach their boiling points, boil off, and then condense, in a process called distillation. Options (1) and (2) are incorrect because the ingredients of petroleum cannot be separated by sorting or by using magnetism. Option (4) is incorrect because boiling and condensing are not part of the extraction process. Option (5) is incorrect because density is not used to separate petroleum.

5. **(3) The molecules in solutions are smaller than the particles in colloids.** (Comprehension) The first sentence of the second paragraph highlights the key difference between colloids and solutions: the particles of colloids are much bigger than the molecules of solutions. Option (1) is not true; some colloids are liquids and some solutions are gases. Option (2) may or may not be true, depending on the specific colloid and solution involved, but the passage and diagram do not discuss the freezing points of colloids and solutions. Option (4) is contradicted by the passage and diagram, which shows that particles of a colloid cannot pass through the semipermeable membrane. Option (5) is incorrect because the passage and the diagram do not support it; the passage gives examples of gases and liquids that are colloids, not solids; the passage doesn't list examples of solutions, but it doesn't say that solutions are always liquids (they aren't).

6. **(3) Both the colloid particles and the solute molecules would flow through.** (Analysis) A wire mesh has much larger, visible openings through which both the particles of a colloid and the molecules of a solution would be able to pass. Option (1) is incorrect since the molecules of a solution could flow through the semipermeable membrane, with its tiny openings, then they could also flow through a wire mesh, with much larger openings. Option (2) is incorrect because the wire mesh openings would be large enough for the colloid particles to pass through. Option (4) is incorrect because the wire mesh would let more pass than the semipermeable membrane would. Option (5) is incorrect because all the particles would be able to flow through the wire mesh, not just water molecules.

7. **(1) The particles of a suspension are larger than the molecules of a solution.** (Comprehension) Since the particles of suspensions are larger than those of colloids and the particles of colloids are larger than the molecules of solutions, it follows that the particles of suspensions are larger than the molecules of solutions. Option (2) is incorrect because the particles of a suspension, being larger than those of a colloid, will not flow through something that a colloid could not flow through.

Option (3) does not follow from the information given; a suspension could be a gas. Option (4) also does not follow from the information in the passage and diagram, which do not discuss color as a property of colloids and suspensions. Option (5) is not true; by definition, any type of mixture can be separated into its ingredients.

8. **(1) When it snows, calcium chloride is applied to roads to prevent the formation of ice.** (Evaluation) According to the passage, adding a solute (like calcium chloride) to a solvent (snow or water), lowers the freezing point; that's the purpose of salting icy roads. Option (2) is incorrect because it does not involve a solute. Option (3) is incorrect because it focuses on the expansion of water when it freezes, not on changes in the freezing point. Options (4) and (5) are both true, but they do not describe the effect of a solute.

Lesson 15

GED Skill Focus (Page 167)

1. **a.** a substance that cannot be broken down into simpler substances by chemical means

2. **a.** helium, which can be broken down only into helium atoms by chemical means
   c. copper, which is made up of copper atoms
   f. mercury, which can be broken down only into mercury atoms by chemical means

3. **a.** in the nucleus

GED Content Focus (Page 169)

1. **(3) potassium (K)** (Comprehension) According to the passage, in the horizontal rows, or periods, elements are arranged in order of increasing atomic number—the number of protons in the nucleus of an atom of the element. The table shows that of all the options, potassium has the lowest atomic number—19.

2. **(2) neon (Ne), argon (Ar), krypton (Kr)** (Comprehension) This is correct because these elements are all in the same family (or column), group VIIIB. The elements in Options (1), (3), (4), and (5) are not all members of the same family. If you selected either option (4) or option (5), you confused elements in the same period (row) with elements in the same group (column).

3. **(3) atomic number and properties** (Comprehension) According to the second paragraph, elements are arranged in the periodic table according to atomic number (number of protons) and similar physical and chemical properties. Options (1) and (4) are incorrect because atomic mass is not the basis of the periodic table. Option (2) is incorrect because it does not mention the factor of properties. Option (5) is incorrect because, although metals and nonmetals appear in different areas of the

table, these factors are too general to form the basis of the periodic table.

4. **(4) group VII** (Application) This element forms an acid with hydrogen, which is the definition of Group VII. Options (1), (2), (3), and (5) are incorrect because the groups in these options are not described as forming acids.

5. **(1) group I** (Application) This element is silvery, like most metals. It causes an explosion when it is dropped into water. This is a violent reaction, which is typical of elements in group I. Option (2) is incorrect because there is no mention of a salt. Option (3) is incorrect because there is no description of oxygen-containing compounds. Option (4) is incorrect because there is no mention of acids. Option (5) is incorrect because group VIII elements are nonreactive gases and the element in the question is a solid.

GED Practice (Pages 170–171)

1. **(3) calcium giving up two electrons to two fluorine atoms** (Application) As the passage states, ionic bonds involve the transfer of electrons between two or more atoms. Calcium gives up, or transfers, two of its electrons to two fluorine atoms, forming ionic bonds. The result is the ionic compound, CaF_2. Option (1) is an example of covalent bonding, since the electrons are shared among the hydrogen and oxygen atoms; this results in the covalent compound H_2O—or water. Options (2), (4), and (5) are each examples of mixtures, not ionic compounds.

2. **(1) Compounds form from atoms of different elements.** (Analysis) The first paragraph of the passage states that ionic bonds form only between two different elements, resulting in ionic compounds. The third paragraph of the passage states that covalent compounds form from atoms of two or more different elements bonding covalently. Since both ionic and covalent compounds involve the joining of atoms of two or more different elements, the passage assumes but does not state that all compounds form from atoms of two or more elements; it differentiates compounds from molecules, which can be formed from atoms of a single element or atoms of different elements. Options (2), (3), and (4) are stated directly in the passage. Option (5) is contradicted by the passage; molecules, by definition, have covalent, not ionic, bonds.

3. **(4) The chemical formula for propane is C_3H_8.** (Evaluation) The structural formula for propane shows that a propane molecule is made up of three atoms of carbon and eight atoms of hydrogen. Option (1) is incorrect because propane has no nitrogen atoms. Option (2) is incorrect because propane has eight atoms of

UNIT 3

hydrogen, not three. Option (3) is incorrect because propane has no oxygen atoms. Option (5) is incorrect because propane has eight hydrogen atoms, not six.

4. **(2) quarks** (Comprehension) According to the passage, protons and neutrons are made up of subatomic particles called quarks. Option (1) is incorrect; cosmic rays are not subatomic particles, but they contain many types of subatomic particles. Options (3) and (4) are incorrect because bosons are force-carrying particles, and the passage does not say that they are found in protons and neutrons. Option (5) is incorrect because electrons are negatively charged particles different from protons and neutrons.

5. **(3) boson** (Application) According to the passage, bosons are force-carrying particles. If the gluon, a force-carrying particle, is produced by a collision in an accelerator, then it is likely to be a boson. None of the other options is a force-carrying particle.

6. **(5) Understanding subatomic particles may lead to advances in technology.** (Evaluation) Advances in technology are valued by many Americans, because such advances often lead to economic growth. Thus the potential for technological applications would be an argument that could be used in favor of the building of a new accelerator. All the other options are arguments that people would use if they opposed the building of a new accelerator.

GED Mini-Test (Pages 172–173)

1. **(2) They are both organic compounds and hydrocarbons.** (Comprehension) The passage describes the alkane series as the most abundant of the hydrocarbons. Since a hydrocarbon is a special kind of organic compound, the members of the alkane series must be organic compounds also. Option (1) is incorrect because members of the alkane series are organic compounds, not living things. The term organic means carbon-based. All living things on Earth contain organic compounds, but organic compounds themselves are not living. Option (3) is incorrect because the chart lists members that are gases and a solid at room temperature. Option (4) is incorrect because the chart lists formulas for members having different numbers of carbon atoms. Option (5) is incorrect because members of the alkane series are made up of only carbon and hydrogen, not helium.

2. **(1) C_3H_8** (Application) The fuel that escapes from the container is a gas, and propane, C_3H_8, is a gas at room temperature. Options (2), (3), (4), and (5) are incorrect because these compounds are not gases at room temperature.

3. **(2) Butane boils at a higher temperature than ethane.** (Evaluation) The chart lists boiling points in order from lowest to highest temperature. The boiling point of butane (–1°C) is higher than that of ethane (–89°C). Option (1) is incorrect because heptane boils at a higher temperature than hexane. Option (3) is incorrect because melting points are not provided. Option (4) is incorrect because, of the series members listed, eicosane contains the most carbon atoms. Option (5) is incorrect because pentane contains five carbon atoms and twelve hydrogen atoms, as compared to four carbon atoms and ten hydrogen atoms for butane.

4. **(1) repetitive** (Comprehension) According to the passage and diagram, monomers are repeating units that make up polymers. Option (2) is incorrect because the passage indicates that monomers are small. Option (3) is incorrect because monomers are joined by covalent bonds, not ionic bonds. Options (4) and (5) are not true; none of the examples cited in the passage are metals or gases.

5. **(4) cross-linked polymer** (Application) In the DNA molecule, the sugar phosphates form two chains and the nitrogen bases form the cross-links. Thus DNA can be classified as a cross-linked polymer. Option (1) is incorrect because DNA consists of millions of monomers, not just one. Option (2) is incorrect because DNA does not have a simple linear structure. Option (3) is incorrect because DNA does not have a branched structure. Option (5) is incorrect because DNA is an acid, not a sugar.

6. **(2) the absence or presence of links between the chains** (Analysis) Both types of plastics are polymers, but they have different structures. It is likely that the cross-linked structure of the Bakelite™ is the reason Bakelite does not melt; the structure is so rigid that heat cannot rearrange the molecules. In the linear polymer plastics, nothing connects adjacent chains, so when they are heated, the chains can slip past one another as they liquefy. Option (1) is incorrect because all plastics are polymers, not monomers. Option (3) describes a property of linear polymer plastics, but it doesn't explain the difference between the two types of polymers. Option (4) is incorrect because cellulose is another polymer, not a component of Bakelite. Option (5) is incorrect because, as the passage states, polyethylene is a linear, or straight, chain polymer, not a branching one.

7. **(4) eight** (Application) The question text states that the two hydrogen atoms and the oxygen atom bond covalently to form a water molecule. The diagram shows the covalent bonds: the two

hydrogen atoms and the oxygen atom are sharing two pairs of electrons. Since covalent bonding involves each atom contributing one electron to form the bond, each unbonded hydrogen atom must have had a single electron. The oxygen atom also must have contributed one atom to each of the two bonds. So, before the bonding occurred, the oxygen atom must have had the two electrons in the inner shell, plus the four free electrons in the outer shell, plus two of the electrons (out of four) now being shared in the two covalent bonds. This adds up to a total of eight electrons. Option (1) is incorrect; only the hydrogen atoms have one electron. Option (2) is incorrect; there are two electrons in the oxygen atom's inner shell, but that is not the total number. Option (3) is incorrect because there are six electrons in an oxygen atom's outer shell, but that is not the total number. Option (5) is incorrect because ten is the total number of electrons the oxygen atom and the two hydrogen atoms have altogether.

Lesson 16
GED Skill Focus (Page 175)
1. **a.** Chemical reactions involve substances changing into other substances.

2. The atoms of substances are rearranged to produce new substances with different chemical and physical properties.

3. **b.** the format of a typical chemical equation: reactants → products
   c. a specific chemical equation: $C + O_2 \rightarrow CO_2$

4. **b.** CO_2 is a product of the chemical reaction

5. Carbon dioxide is shown on the right side of the arrow; therefore it is a product of the reaction.

GED Content Focus (Page 177)
1. **(5) Atoms combine or rearrange to form molecules.** (Comprehension) As the passage states, during a chemical reaction atoms can combine to form molecules. Options (1) and (2) are incorrect, because, as the passage states, atoms are neither created nor destroyed in chemical reactions. Option (3) is not true, because changing state is a physical change, not a chemical change; the substances changing state retain their chemical properties. Option (4) is incorrect; atoms do not change into other atoms in a chemical reaction.

2. **(3) One molecule of methane combines with two molecules of oxygen to yield one molecule of carbon dioxide and two molecules of water.** (Comprehension) CH_4 stands for one molecule of methane; the plus sign means "combines"; $2O_2$ stands for two molecules of oxygen; the arrow means "yields"; CO_2 stands for one molecule of carbon dioxide;

and $2H_2O$ stands for two molecules of water. Option (1) is true, but it is too general to be the best restatement of the equation; it has no quantities. Option (2) does not accurately describe the reactants or the products of this reaction. Option (4) is incorrect because it does not accurately describe the number of molecules that are reactants or products. Option (5) is incorrect because it describes what each compound is made of, not what the chemical equation represents.

3. **(3) 4Fe** (Analysis) On the right side of the equation are four atoms of iron ($2Fe_2$). To balance the equation, there must be four atoms of Fe on the left side as well. None of the other options yields four atoms of iron.

4. **(1) During the process of rusting, small amounts of heat energy are released.** (Evaluation) Since the release of energy characterizes an exothermic reaction, if rusting is an exothermic reaction (which it is and which is the conclusion to be supported), energy would be released. Option (2) is incorrect because activation energy refers to the energy needed to get a reaction started. Options (3) and (5) are true but do not support the conclusion. Option (4) would support the conclusion that rusting is the opposite kind of reaction, an endothermic reaction.

5. **(4) Some exothermic reactions are more useful for the energy they release than for their products.** (Evaluation) The burning of methane or wood is an example of exothermic reactions that are valued for the heat released, not for the products. Option (1) is not true, and neither electricity nor magnetism is discussed in this passage. Option (2) is not true, and covalent bonds and ionic bonds are not discussed in the passage. Option (3) is not true; boiling water is an endothermic process as implied although not stated in the passage. Option (5) is not true; according to the last paragraph, activation energy is necessary for starting many chemical reactions.

6. **(3) It provides activation energy.** (Application) The spark provides the energy that is needed to start the reaction; without energy from the spark, the natural gas the burner releases would not start to burn. Options (1) and (2) are incorrect because the spark is not among the reactants (the natural gas and oxygen) and products (carbon dioxide and water) described in the question. There is no information given to support options (4) and (5), and they are not true.

GED Practice (Pages 178–179)
1. **(1) to provide an acid for sodium bicarbonate to react with** (Comprehension)

According to the passage, sodium bicarbonate reacts with an acid to produce the gas carbon dioxide, and that baking powder contains a compound, such as tartrate, that produces the acid. This implies that the purpose of this acid-producing substance is to ensure that the acid needed for the sodium bicarbonate to work is present. Option (2) is incorrect because sodium bicarbonate breaks down to form carbon dioxide. Option (3) is incorrect because the passage gives no indication that the tartrate reacts with carbon dioxide. Option (4) is incorrect because the passage gives no indication that the tartrate forms salt. Option (5) is incorrect because sodium bicarbonate is one of the substances in baking powder to begin with.

2. **4) It reacts with sodium bicarbonate to produce CO_2 and H_2O.** (Evaluation) The passage states that sodium bicarbonate reacts with an acid to produce carbon dioxide and water. Since the question implies that the reactions of sodium bicarbonate and sour milk result in these products, this is evidence that sour milk contains an acid. Option (1) is contradicted by the passage, which lists sodium bicarbonate and substances that release acid when combined with water, but not sour milk, as the components of baking powder; it also doesn't support the idea that sour milk contains an acid. Options (2) and (3) are true but are not related to whether a substance is an acid or not. Option (5) is not true of sour milk but of sodium bicarbonate; as with options (1), (2), and (3), this option also gives no evidence either way of whether or not sour milk is an acid.

3. **(5) carbon dioxide gas** (Analysis) It is gas bubbles that cause the cake to rise, and the passage states that carbon dioxide gas, not oxygen, is produced. Options (1), (3), and (4) are incorrect because they are not gases, and options (1) and (4) are not produced when sodium bicarbonate reacts. Option (2) is a gas, but there is no mention of oxygen in the passage.

4. **(3) Moisture in the air reacts with the tartrate.** (Analysis) This is correct because, as the passage states, tartrate reacts with water to produce acid. The acid in turn will react with the sodium bicarbonate in baking powder to release carbon dioxide gas, thus leaving only sodium carbonate, which will have no effect on cake batter. Option (1) is incorrect because heat, not moisture, causes sodium bicarbonate to break down. Options (2), (4), and (5) are incorrect because no mention is made in the passage of reactions involving baking powder and oxygen.

5. **(2) Methane provides the most heat.** (Evaluation) According to the table, methane provides the most heat per gram combusted: 13.3 kilocalories. Option (1) is incorrect because natural gas releases more heat than oil. Option (3) is incorrect because wood gives off less than half the heat of oil. Option (4) is incorrect because wood gives off less heat than coal. Option (5) is incorrect because coal gives off less heat than oil.

6. **(3) It is more precise.** (Analysis) The significance of the laser method of controlling reactions is that it allows scientists to control reactions more precisely, to the point that particular molecular bonds can be targeted. Options (1) and (2) are both differences from earlier techniques, but they are not significant differences. Option (4) is true of earlier techniques as well. Option (5) is a description of two earlier techniques.

7. **(3) to provide activation energy** (Application) Laser beams supply targeted activation energy to start a reaction. Laser beams are light and cannot function in the manners listed in the other options.

8. **(2) Laser control of reactions allows scientists to break specific bonds between atoms.** (Evaluation) The fact that lasers can target particular molecular bonds is evidence that some chemical reactions can be controlled at the molecular level. Option (1) describes imprecise forms of control that do not target molecules. Options (3), (4), and (5) are true, but they do not provide evidence that some chemical reactions can be controlled at the molecular level.

GED Mini-Test (Pages 180–181)

1. **(4) sulfuric acid, citric acid, pure water, magnesium hydroxide, sodium hydroxide** (Comprehension) This is correct because the pH scale starts low with strong acids, has neutral substances in the middle, and ends high with the strong bases. The substances in option (4) have been identified in the passage as a strong acid, a weak acid, a neutral substance, a weak base, and a strong base, following the order of the pH scale from lowest to highest. Options (1), (2), and (3) are not in order. In option (5) the correct order is exactly reversed and reads from highest to lowest.

2. **(3) a base** (Analysis) This is correct because bases neutralize acids and thus would relieve an acid stomach. Option (1) is incorrect because a salt does not neutralize an acid. Option (2) is incorrect because adding an acid to an acid stomach would increase indigestion. Option (4) is incorrect since H^+ ions are characteristic of acids. Adding them to an upset stomach would increase the upset. Option (5) is incorrect because water is not a base, it is neutral.

3. **(3) a salt** (Application) The passage states that the reaction between an acid and a base produces water and a salt. Options (1), (2), (4), and (5) are incorrect because such a reaction would not produce either an acid or a base.

4. **(3) 7** (Comprehension) This is correct because the passage states that salts and water are neutral substances and neutral is pH 7.0. Options (1) and (2) are incorrect because they are pH values of acids, and options (4) and (5) are incorrect because they are pH values of bases.

5. **(5) hydrogen** (Comprehension) According to the passage and diagram, hydrogen is the element added during an addition reaction. Options (1), (2), (3), and (4) are incorrect because these elements are not mentioned in connection with addition reactions.

6. **(4) double (or triple) bonds** (Comprehension) The passage states that unsaturated molecules contain bonds other than single bonds and saturated molecules contain only single bonds. Option (1) is incorrect because both kinds of molecules can contain hydrogen atoms. Option (2) is only true of saturated molecules. Option (3) is not true because both kinds of molecules contain shared electrons. Option (5) is incorrect because both kinds of molecules can contain carbon atoms.

7. **(2) Single bonding occurs between its carbon atoms.** (Comprehension) The passage states that ethane is a saturated hydrocarbon, in which only one electron of each carbon atom is paired with one electron of another carbon atom to form a single bond; the other electrons are shared with hydrogen atoms. Option (1) is incorrect because ethane is saturated. Option (3) is incorrect because according to the passage, double bonding does not occur between the carbon atoms of ethane. Option (4) is not stated in the passage and it is not true. Option (5) is incorrect because ethane's chemical formula is given in the passage as C_2H_6, which indicates that it has six hydrogen atoms.

8. **(5) The product is C_2H_6.** (Evaluation) The product contains two carbon atoms and six hydrogen atoms, so it can be restated as C_2H_6. Option (1) is incorrect since the only saturated hydrocarbon is the product. Option (2) is incorrect because the reactant H_2 is not a hydrocarbon. Option (3) is incorrect since C_2H_6 is the product, not a reactant. Option (4) is incorrect since the product only contains single bonds.

9. **(1) Saturated hydrocarbons can be produced from unsaturated hydrocarbons through addition reactions.** (Evaluation)

The chemical equation shows an addition reaction in which a saturated hydrocarbon is produced from an unsaturated hydrocarbon. Option (2) is incorrect because addition reactions yield saturated, not unsaturated, hydrocarbons. Option (3) is incorrect because the number of carbon atoms in the hydrocarbon remains the same after an addition reaction; it is the number of hydrogen atoms that increases. Option (4) is incorrect because ethane can be made from ethene by an addition reaction, not the other way around. Option (5) is true but is not supported by the information presented.

Lesson 17
GED Skill Focus (Page 183)
1. **b.** 240 miles

2. **a.** 80 miles per hour

3. **b.** The average speed of the train is not the same thing as the actual speed of the train.

4. **c.** The graphs show two aspects of the same trip.

GED Content Focus (Page 185)
1. **(2) A package on the seat of a car going 60 miles per hour slides forward when the car stops suddenly.** (Application) This is correct because the package keeps moving forward even though the car stops. The package stays in motion because no force was applied to it; the brakes acted on the car, not on the package. Option (1) is incorrect because it is related to Newton's second law, which is concerned with force, mass, and acceleration. Options (3), (4), and (5) are incorrect. While they describe types of motion, these options do not demonstrate an object remaining in motion or at rest (Newton's first law).

2. **(4) the force of gravity** (Analysis) Gravity from a star, planet, or moon is the most likely force to affect a spacecraft in outer space. Option (1) is incorrect because the spacecraft is not using fuel in outer space. Option (2) might warm the spacecraft, but will not cause a change of direction. Option (3) is incorrect because the force of friction is absent in outer space where there is no air. Option (5) is incorrect because acceleration is a change in direction or speed, but it is not a cause for such a change.

3. **(3) Large force and small mass yield rapid acceleration.** (Analysis) The engineer is assuming that a large engine will provide a large force, and knows that a lightweight body will provide small mass. Applying Newton's Second Law of Motion, she knows the resulting acceleration will be very rapid, a good characteristic for a racing car. Options (1) and (2) are incorrect because they involve Newton's

First Law of Motion, which is not the underlying assumption for the car's design. Options (4) and (5) are incorrect according to Newton's Second Law of Motion.

4. **(5) A car traveling at 40 miles per hour goes around a curve at the same speed.** (Application) This is correct because force is required to change the direction of motion. All the other options are incorrect because they describe either objects at rest or objects continuing in motion at a constant speed and in a straight line.

5. **(4) mass, force, and acceleration** (Comprehension) Newton's Second Law of Motion states that an object (mass) will accelerate in the direction of and in proportion to the size of the force that acts on it. Option (1) is incorrect because it omits force. Option (2) is incorrect because it omits mass and acceleration. Option (3) is incorrect because it omits mass. Option (5) is incorrect because it omits force.

6. **(1) Small players accelerate quickly, while large players apply force to stop opponents.** (Analysis) The football team is assigning positions to its players based on the assumption that Newton's second law of motion applies to people playing football. Option (2) is not necessarily true and doesn't explain the assignments. Options (3) and (4) may be true in some cases, but they do not explain the assignments. Option (5) is a true statement according to Newton's second law, but, like the other options, it does not explain the assignments.

GED Practice (Page 186–187)

1. **4) the backward "kick" of a fired rifle** (Application) When the bullet is fired out the barrel of a rifle, this action force causes a reaction that pushes the rifle back, causing a "kick." Because a person is so much larger than a bullet, the kick does not move the person very far. All of the other options describe an action force rather than a reaction force: hot air rushes out of a balloon, wind pushes against a kite, the force of the ball pushes against the wall, the swimmer's arm and hand push against the water.

2. **(3) the force exerted by gases escaping the rear of the engine** (Analysis) As the hot gases escape the rear of the engine, they exert a force against the engine, pushing it forward. Option (1) is incorrect because air flowing through the engine doesn't have anything to do with how a rocket moves or with Newton's Third Law; in fact, there is no air in space to flow through the rocket engine. Option (2) explains how lift works, the principle behind airplane flight, not rocket propulsion. Option (4) is incorrect because

gravity pulls the rocket downward, back to Earth, working against its forward acceleration. Option (5) is incorrect because air flow would exert friction, which would tend to slow the rocket, not move it forward and, in fact, there is no air in space to have any effect at all on the rocket.

3. **(1) The truck has a larger mass than the car does.** (Evaluation) Momentum is defined as mass times velocity. That the truck and the car are moving at the same speed, and thus have the same velocity, is given. Since the truck has more mass than the small car, option (1) supports the idea that the truck has more momentum than the car does. Option (2) is the opposite of what is true. Options (3) and (4) are incorrect, because the car and truck have the same velocity, as stated in the question text. Option (5) is true but irrelevant to determining momentum.

4. **(4) The less the impact force on the driver, the less serious his injuries are likely to be.** (Analysis) This is an assumption underlying the passage: that seatbelts reduce impact force and thus reduce injuries. Options (1), (2), and (5) are incorrect because they are actually stated in the passage. Option (3) is incorrect because nothing in the passage indicates that the writer assumes that air bags have serious drawbacks; the passage simply describes how air bags work.

5. **(2) by restraining forward motion and decreasing the impact force** (Comprehension) According to the passage and diagram, a seatbelt decreases the impact force in a collision. Options (1) and (4) are incorrect because seatbelts reduce the impact force, not increase it. Option (3) is incorrect because seatbelts restrain the forward motion. Option (5) is incorrect because that is not the principle by which seatbelts work, although seatbelts do indeed concentrate the impact force more than air bags, which spread it out.

6. **(5) snowshoes, which spread the weight of a person over a large area, allowing her to walk on the surface of the snow** (Application) Like an air bag distributing the impact force over a large area of the driver's body, reducing the pressure on any one point, snowshoes distribute a person's weight over a large area so that there is not enough pressure at any one point to break through the surface of the snow. Option (1) is incorrect because the rising of a hot air balloon has to do with differing densities, not with spreading force over a large area. Option (2) is incorrect because it is an application of Newton's Third Law of Motion, not of the idea of force, area, and pressure. Option (3) is incorrect because it does not

involve the spreading of force over a large area. Option (4) is incorrect because ball bearings actually work by concentrating the force of friction on a very small area.

GED Mini-Test (Pages 188–189)

1. **(3) The solid arrow shows the pull of Earth on the moon.** (Comprehension) The drawing goes along with the passage, indicating that Earth's gravity, as shown by the solid arrow, exerts a force pulling the moon toward Earth. The arrow described in option (1) shows how the moon would move if Earth's gravity did not exert a force on the moon. The arrow described in option (2) indicates how the moon moves due to the force of Earth's gravity. Option (4) is contradicted by the passage, which states that the moon is in orbit around Earth, not moving straight toward Earth. Option (5) is incorrect, because the passage indicates that gravity causes objects to be attracted to one another rather than repelled, or pushed apart.

2. **(2) Mass is the amount of matter in an object.** (Analysis) The passage does not include a definition of mass, although you need to know what mass is to understand the information presented. Option (1) is not true; mass is not the volume of an object. Option (3) is true, but it is stated directly in the passage and not assumed. Options (4) and (5) are not true; all objects have mass, and mass can be measured.

3. **(3) Speed involves distance divided by time, and velocity involves speed as well as direction.** (Comprehension) The difference between speed and velocity is that velocity takes account of the direction of motion and speed does not. Option (1) is incorrect because speed involves distance divided by time, not just distance, and velocity also involves direction. Option (2) is incorrect because velocity involves time and direction as well as distance. Option (4) is incorrect because the definition of speed is too general and because velocity is an indication of speed and direction, not just distance. Option (5) is incorrect because the definition of speed is too general and because velocity is not a measure of time.

4. **(5) 20 feet north at 5 feet per second** (Application) Velocity includes both direction and speed. It is the only option that mentions a direction, north. The remaining options are examples of speed; they give information about distance over time, but no information about direction.

5. **(4) He used a parachute with a larger surface area.** (Analysis) A larger surface area of the parachute would increase air resistance and thus decrease the terminal velocity. Option (1) is

incorrect because as long as the altitude is high enough for the sky diver to reach terminal velocity, it doesn't matter how high it is. Option (2) is incorrect because the sky diver's body mass is not likely to change significantly from one day to the next. Options (3) and (5) are incorrect because the landing site and the speed of the airplane are irrelevant to the terminal velocity of the sky diver.

6. **(1) her mass** (Evaluation) The body mass of the sky diver will affect the duration of the jump because it affects the point at which terminal velocity is reached. Options (2) and (3) are incorrect because the volume and height of the sky diver are not critical factors. Options (4) and (5) are incorrect because the speed and type of airplane do not affect the length of time the jump takes.

7. **(2) increased friction on the moving parts** (Analysis) An engine low on oil is not well-lubricated, and its moving parts will have increased friction and thus increased wear. Option (1) is incorrect because insufficient oil means increased, not decreased friction. Options (3) and (4) are incorrect because friction does not affect stationary parts. Option (5) is incorrect because low oil means more friction, which means more difficult movement of the engine's parts.

8. **(3) the pull of Earth's gravity on the Mir space station** (Application) The ball swung on a string is pulled to the center of the circle by centripetal force, and the Mir space station is held in its circular orbit because it is pulled toward Earth by the force of gravity. None of the remaining options describe circular motion, the key element here.

9. **(5) a car whose speedometer reads 65 miles per hour** (Application) A speedometer indicates the speed of a vehicle at any given moment. It is the only example of instantaneous speed among the options. Options (1) and (4) are examples in which the speed is changing. Options (2) and (3) are examples that allow you to calculate average, not instantaneous, speed.

Lesson 18
GED Skill Focus (Page 191)

1. **b.** Work is done when a force moves an object over a distance, and it can be expressed by the formula work = force × distance.

2. **a.** Moving a heavy object along a ramp to the top takes less effort than lifting it straight up.

3. **a.** The distance along the slope is greater than the distance straight up the side.

4. **a.** the force applied to the crate
   b. the distance the crate travels

GED Content Focus (Page 193)

1. **(2) a turning Ferris wheel** (Application) Since the Ferris wheel is in motion, it has kinetic energy. The other options are examples of things at rest, which have potential energy rather than kinetic energy.

2. **(3) a car parked on a hill** (Application) This is an example of potential energy because, if the brake were released, the car would roll down the hill. The other options are all examples of things in motion, which have kinetic energy rather than potential energy.

3. **(5) The book has kinetic energy during lifting; it has potential energy at rest on the table.** (Evaluation) Kinetic energy is the energy of motion, which the book—like the hammer in the first diagram—has while being lifted. Potential energy is the energy of position, which the book—like the hammer in the second diagram—has while motionless. Since all matter, whether moving or still, has energy, options (1) and (2) are not true. Option (3) is not true because the book gains potential energy when it is placed on the table. Option (4) is the reverse of what is true.

4. **(1) The cars gain potential energy gradually as they move higher.** (Analysis) The chain that lifts the roller coaster cars transfers energy steadily to the cars. The potential energy increases gradually, not just at the top of the hill, so option (2) is incorrect. Option (3) is incorrect because the cars are gaining potential, not kinetic, energy. (Their kinetic energy remains the same since the cars move at a slow, steady pace.) Option (4) is the opposite of what happens. Option (5) is incorrect because energy is transferred from the chain to the cars, not the other way around.

5. **(4) condensation from gas to liquid** (Application) In condensation, the molecules of a gas lose kinetic energy and slow down. Eventually they slow down enough to become a liquid. In options (1), (2), (3), and (5) the molecules of matter are moving faster and thus gaining kinetic energy, not losing it. Also, option (5) does not describe a change in state.

6. **(5) Energy is conserved in a system; it is neither created nor destroyed.** (Comprehension) The width of the base of the arrow in the diagram is equal to the width of the two arrows showing where the energy is transferred, indicating that no energy is created or destroyed; rather it is conserved, that is, the amount remains the same. Option (1) is incorrect because the arrows do not represent types of energy, but the amount of energy. Options (2), (3), and (4) are true, but they are not what the arrows in the diagram represent.

GED Practice Lesson 18 (Pages 194–195)

1. **(3) gasoline and the battery** (Comprehension) According to the passage and the diagram, chemical energy in a car comes from the gasoline, which is converted to heat energy, and from the chemicals in the battery, which is converted to electrical energy. Options (1) and (2) are incorrect because lubricating oil is not a source of energy in a car's engine; it reduces friction. Options (4) and (5) are incorrect because the engine and drive train are not sources of energy; they are means by which energy is converted from one form to another.

2. **(3) the miles it travels per gallon of gasoline** (Evaluation) The distance traveled per unit of chemical energy is a good indication of an engine's efficiency, or the amount of work it can do. The further the car goes on one gallon of gasoline, the better use the engine is making of the heat energy produced. Option (1) would give you only a partial indication of efficiency; unless you also knew the total amount of heat produced in the engine you would not be able to assess the engine's efficiency based on the amount of heat wasted. Option (2) is incorrect because the size of the gas tank only tells you how much fuel a car can hold; it does not tell you how efficiently the car uses the fuel. Option (4) is incorrect because it is an indication of tire wear, not engine efficiency. Option (5) is incorrect because the mix of air and gas does not provide a good indication of the car engine's efficiency.

3. **(2) a bicycle** (Application) A bicycle is powered by chemical energy in a person's leg muscles being converted to mechanical energy as the person pedals. Options (1) and (4) are incorrect; they are engines similar to a car's engine, powered by chemical energy of gasoline or other fuel. Option (3) is incorrect because an automatic garage door opener is powered by electrical energy. Option (5) is incorrect because clothes drier is powered by electrical or gas energy.

4. **(4) less energy available for plants** (Analysis) A decrease in photosynthesis means less chemical energy available in the food web for organisms including green plants and all others. (For a review of energy transfers in ecosystems, see Lesson 7.) Options (1), (2), and (3) are incorrect because the sun would continue to produce the same amount of energy regardless of what happened on Earth. Option (5) is incorrect because the amount of chemical energy available for plants would be less if there were less photosynthesis.

Answers and Explanations

5. **(3) either heat or electrical energy**
(Comprehension) According to the passage, both the gasoline engine, which gives off heat energy, and the electric motor, which gives off electrical energy, can power the drive train. Since both can power the drive train, options (1) and (2) are incorrect. Options (4) and (5), light energy and nuclear energy, are not used to power the drive train of a parallel gasoline-electric car.

6. **(1) They have a greater driving range and their batteries recharge automatically.**
(Analysis) All-electric cars cannot be driven more than 80 miles or so before they need recharging, which takes three to eight hours. Therefore, they are not practical vehicles for most people. In contrast, gasoline-electric hybrid vehicles are about as practical as conventional cars, with a much longer driving range and no need for battery recharging. Option (2) is not a viable comparison of practicality since all-electric cars don't use gasoline at all. Options (3) and (4) are not true; because the hybrid car uses gasoline, it gives off more heat and air pollution than an all-electric car. Option (5) is true but not related to the cars' practicality.

7. **(3) the convenience of a conventional car** (Evaluation) The low operating cost of an all-electric vehicle is apparently not enough to compensate for the inconvenience of the short driving range and the time needed for battery recharging. Consumers value convenience highly. Options (1), (2), (4), and (5) are incorrect because if consumers valued a cleaner environment, conservation of resources, low operating costs, or being trendsetters more than convenience, they would have bought more all-electric cars.

GED Mini-Test (Pages 196–197)

1. **(2) when the two objects are at the same temperature** (Comprehension) According to the third part of the diagram, the heat transfer stops when the hot object has transferred enough energy to the cold object so that their temperatures are equal. Option (1) is incorrect because molecules are always moving, even in cold objects. Option (3) is incorrect because the diagram does not show the two objects being pulled apart. Option (4) is incorrect because the cold object does not lose heat, it gains heat from the hot object. Option (5) is incorrect because it indicates when the heat transfer starts, not when it stops.

2. **(3) popcorn popping** (Application) As popcorn pops, the kernels move and collide with one another. This is most similar to the movement of molecules in a heated substance. Options (1), (2), and (4) are steady movements not typical of heated molecules. Option (5) is the opposite of what happens to a heated molecule.

3. **(2) Your hand's heat is absorbed by the ice.** (Evaluation) According to the passage and diagram, heat moves from a hot object to a cold object; in this case from your warm hand to the cold ice. Option (1) is incorrect because, according to the passage, cold is the absence of heat, not something that can flow. Option (3) is incorrect because the ice gains heat energy and then melts. Options (4) and (5) are incorrect because they state the opposite of what is actually happening—the molecules in your hand are losing energy to the molecules in the ice, which are gaining energy.

4. **(4) The hot object transfers heat to the air.** (Analysis) Not only are the two objects in contact with one another and thus transferring heat from the hot object to the cold object, they are also in contact with the air. Since the hot object is hotter than the air, as shown by the thermometer in the diagram, there will be heat transfer from the hot object to the air. Options (1) and (2) are incorrect because heat is transferred from hot to cold objects or substances, not the other way around. Option (3) is incorrect because the air absorbs heat from the hot object, since, as indicated in the diagram, it is cooler than the hot object. Option (5) is incorrect because the two objects are in contact with substances other than just one another, so other heat transfers among all these substances are taking place.

5. **(2) distance the rope is pulled** (Evaluation) According to the passage and diagram, the distance the rope is pulled is equal to the distance the load travels. Therefore, if you know the distance the rope is pulled, you can figure out the distance the load moves. Options (1), (3), and (4) are not needed in order to figure out the distance the load moved. Option (5), the total length of the rope, gives you the maximum distance the load can travel, but it is not adequate to figure out how far the load actually moved.

6. **(5) The friction from the pulley wheel must be overcome by the effort used in pulling the rope.** (Analysis) Although in theory the effort force equals the load in a single pulley system, in reality, the person pulling on the rope must expend a little extra force (effort) to overcome the friction of the pulley wheel. Option (1) is true but it does not explain why the person pulling on the rope must exert a little extra effort. Options (2) and (3) are incorrect because in a simple pulley system the distance pulled on the rope is equal to the distance the load moves. Option (4) is incorrect because the load does not change in weight as it moves up.

7. **(2) Heat released from many cars raises the temperature of heavily traveled streets.** (Analysis) Since car engines waste most of the heat they produce, it is absorbed by their surroundings. Thus the more traffic, the warmer the street from heat pollution of vehicles. Option (1) is incorrect because the heavily traveled streets and lightly traveled streets are likely to absorb about the same amount of sunlight, if shadiness and street orientation are the same. Option (3) may increase the friction of traveling on worn-away streets, but this is not as significant as waste heat from vehicle engines. Options (4) and (5) may or may not be true in specific instances; not enough information has been provided to evaluate their significance.

8. **(4) Your new job requires you to transport heavy supplies in your car.** (Application) Increasing the horsepower of the car's engine will help you carry a heavier load, such as the heavy supplies. Options (1) and (3) are not related to a car's horsepower. Options (2) and (5) would be good reasons to buy a car with a lower-horsepower engine, not a higher-horsepower engine, since the latter would burn more fuel and add more pollutants to the atmosphere.

Lesson 19
GED Skill Focus (Page 199)

1. **a.** It would have a negative charge.

2. **b.** The paper moves closer to the comb.

3. **a.** The negative and positive ions will attract each other.

GED Content Focus (Page 201)

1. **(5) an area of force** (Comprehension) According to the passage, an electric field is an area of force. Options (1), (3), and (4) are incorrect because they are examples of matter, not forces. Option (2) is incorrect because it relates to the strength of an electric field not to its definition.

2. **(4) increasing their force of attraction** (Analysis) According to the passage, the strength of an electric field decreases as distance increases. Thus the strength of the field must increase as distance decreases. Since the two particles are unlike, it is the force of attraction that is increased. Options (1) and (2) are incorrect because the particles' electric charges would not be affected. Option (3) is incorrect because electricity is not flowing in this situation. Option (5) is the opposite of the effect that would occur.

3. **(2) Both make possible the flow of something from one place to another.** (Analysis) Voltage pushes electrons through a wire just as water pressure pushes water through

a hose. Options (1), (3), and (4) are incorrect because they apply only to voltage. Option (5) is incorrect because water can't be used to power a chemical battery.

4. **(3) the flow of electrons or other charged particles** (Comprehension) This is the definition given in the passage. Options (1) and (2) are incorrect because they do not describe an electric current but describe the behavior of particles with opposite charges. Option (4) is incorrect because it defines resistance. Option (5) describes the unit used to measure electrical energy.

5. **(1) to open and close the circuit, controlling the flow of current** (Comprehension) A circuit is a closed, continuous pathway. Without a switch to stop and start the flow of current, a circuit would be operating all the time. Options (2) and (5) are incorrect because a switch does not provide energy for a circuit; in the diagram on page 200, a battery provides the circuit's energy. Options (3) and (4) are incorrect because a switch simply allows the current to flow; it does not affect the speed of the electrons.

6. **(3) It would double.** (Analysis) To find the new current, substitute the values for voltage and resistance in the formula $V = I \times R$: $V = 18$ volts, and $R = 9$ ohms (4 ohms plus 5 ohms = 9 ohms). Thus $18 = 2 \times 9$. The current would be 2 amps, double the amperes shown in the diagram (1 amp). You can also arrive at the correct answer by a process of elimination. Given the formula $V = I \times R$, if the voltage doubles and the resistance remains the same, the current must double to keep the equation in balance. Thus Options (1), (2), and (4) are wrong because they involve either nothing happening to the current or the current decreasing. You can eliminate option (5) because voltage would equal current only when resistance is 1 ohm ($V = I \times 1$). In this circuit, resistance is 9 ohms.

7. **(2) a decrease in current** (Analysis) This is correct because, as the formula $V = I \times R$ indicates, if voltage remains constant and resistance increases, current would decrease. Option (1) is the opposite of what would happen. Option (3) is incorrect, because increased resistance would not cause current to stop flowing; only interrupting the circuit would do that. Option (4) is incorrect, because increasing the resistance would have no effect on the switch. Option (5) describes what happens when current increases; so like option (1), it is the opposite of what would actually happen.

GED Practice (Pages 202–203)

1. **(4) An electric current produces a magnetic field.** (Comprehension) This

relationship is described in the first paragraph of the passage. Option (1) is true, but it does not answer the question because it does not say anything specific about electricity. Option (2) is true, but this passage discusses only the production of a magnetic field from electric current, not the reverse. Option (3) is not true, because it fails to specify that the wire must be conducting an electric current. Option (5) is true, but the passage discusses the relationship between electricity and magnetism, not just magnetism.

2. **(2) picking up pieces of metal on the site and depositing them elsewhere on the site** (Application) This is correct because the electromagnet will gain and lose its magnetism as the current is turned on and off. Thus it is ideal for picking up metal objects, and then dropping them again. Option (1) is incorrect because there is no way of knowing whether this machine is equipped to travel long distances. Options (3) and (4) are incorrect because the crane's electromagnet would not be able to do these things. Option (5) is incorrect because whatever the relative strength of other machines on the site, the electromagnet could be used only to lift objects that are magnetic.

3. **(3) The needle responds to the magnetic field produced by the current in the wire.** (Analysis) The current in the wire produces a magnetic field that is closer to the compass and thus stronger than the magnetic field of Earth, so the compass needle is deflected. Option (1) is incorrect because it is not true; after the electricity has been switched off, the compass will again point north. Option (1) also does not adequately relate cause and effect. Option (2) may or may not be true, but it does not explain why the compass needle deflects from north. Option (4) is true but does not explain the movement of the needle itself. Option (5) is incorrect because the magnetism of the compass needle is not produced by current in a wire, but by the compass needle itself being magnetic.

4. **(5) Magnetism is related to the movement of electrons.** (Evaluation) Option (5) is correct, because, the passage states and the diagram shows that electric current, which is the flowing movement of electrons, produces a magnetic field. Therefore the passage supports the hypothesis that magnetism is related to the movement of electrons. Options (1) and (2) are incorrect because neither is true and because neither the passage nor the diagram compares natural magnets and electromagnets in terms of strength or current use. Option (3) is true, but nothing in the passage or diagram indicates that magnets affect electric current. Option (4) is also

true, but the passage discusses only soft iron as a core material for an electromagnet.

5. **(1) An electric current flowing through a wire produces a magnetic field.** (Comprehension) Oersted discovered this when the electric current he had produced caused a nearby compass needle to move. Option (2) was known before Oersted's time, as indicated by the fact that Oersted had a compass. Option (3) is the opposite of what Oersted discovered. Option (4) is a discovery that the passage indicates Faraday made. Option (5) is incorrect because, as the passage indicates, electric motors were a later invention by people other than Oersted.

6. **(3) A compass needle is magnetic.** (Analysis) The author does not explain that the compass needle was magnetic; he assumes you know that this is why the compass needle moved when the nearby electric current produced a magnetic field. All the other options are actually stated in the passage.

7. **(4) the large-scale generation of electricity by means of moving magnetic fields** (Analysis) Once the principles of electromagnetism were understood, the large-scale generation of electricity using moving magnetic fields became possible. Options (1), (2), (3), and (5) are incorrect because an internal combustion engine, a locomotive engine, windmill powering a mechanical pump, and batteries do not involve electromagnetism.

8. **(5) Electromagnetism had many potentially valuable applications.** (Evaluation) The interest in magnetism increased once its relationship to electricity was better understood, because the interaction between electricity and magnetism could be put to practical uses. Option (1) is incorrect; nothing in the passage indicates that lodestones had many uses. Option (2) is true, but it is not the correct choice because compasses had been used in navigation since the 1200s. Option (3) is true, but it does not explain why the scientists should focus so much attention on magnetism rather than on other phenomena. Option (4) is not true as related to the understanding of magnetism, because as the question indicates it was the discoveries of the 19th-century scientists Oersted, Ampère, and Faraday that sparked new interest in magnetism, not a renewed interest in ancient civilizations.

GED Mini-Test (Pages 204–205)

1. **(4) rubber** (Comprehension) The paragraph indicates that rubber is a good insulator, so option (4) is correct. The paragraph also states that metals are good conductors and thus are the opposite of good insulators. Since options (1),

(2), (3), and (5) are metals, they would not be good insulators.

2. **(1) electrical wire for a lamp** (Application) Since a conductor allows electrical current to flow easily through it, it would make a good electrical wire. Options (2) and (3) are objects in which insulators are used to prevent electric shock. Options (4) and (5) are also objects for which insulators are more appropriate materials than conductors.

3. **(1) A silver pipe is likely to have a lower resistance than a plastic pipe.** (Evaluation) Since conductors allow electric current to flow easily through them, they would also tend to have low resistance. Also, since metals tend to be better conductors than nonmetals, silver would be likely to have a lower resistance than plastic. Although option (2) is true, it is an incorrect answer, because the paragraph does not mention the effect of temperature or how well a substance conducts electricity. Option (3) is incorrect because the paragraph indicates that porcelain (a nonmetal) is a better insulator than silver (a metal). Option (4) is incorrect because the paragraph indicates that glass has a higher resistance than copper. Option (5) is incorrect because the paragraph implies that electrons move more readily through metals than through nonmetals.

4. **(2) Bulb *B* also will not light.** (Analysis) Since bulb *A* is in a series circuit, when the circuit is broken because of burned-out bulb *A*, bulb *B* also will not light. Option (1) will not fix the circuit, since it is the burned-out bulb that has stopped the current flow in the circuit, not a defective wire. Option (3) is incorrect, because bulb *C* is in a parallel circuit, and when the current flow is interrupted by this burned out bulb (bulb *C*), current continues to flow through the other path, keeping bulb *D* lit. Option (4) is incorrect, because replacing bulb *C*, not rewiring the circuit, will restore current flow throughout the circuit. Option (5) is incorrect because the burning out of a single light bulb in each circuit does not indicate that the batteries need to be replaced.

5. **(3) The current continues in all but one path of the circuit.** (Evaluation) The fact that the other lights still work after the bulb burned out indicates that the circuit must be a parallel circuit. Options (1) and (4) are incorrect because power failures and circuit breakers would stop the flow of current in both parallel and series circuits. Option (2) is incorrect because it would occur only if the circuit were a series circuit. Option (5) contradicts the information given in the question, that the kitchen is on a single circuit.

6. **(2) the rotation of the coil** (Comprehension) According to the passage and the diagram, the turning coil turns the shaft of the motor. Option (1) is incorrect because the battery provides energy. Options (3), (4), and (5) are incorrect because the magnet is stationary and thus it cannot turn a shaft.

7. **(1) The coil would stop turning.** (Analysis) If the current flowed only in one direction, the coil would have a stationary magnetic field. Thus once the south pole of the moving coil was attracted to the north pole of the stationary magnet, the coil would stop turning. Option (2) would occur only if the current changed direction more frequently. Option (3) is incorrect because the magnet doesn't move and it is a natural magnet, not an electromagnet; therefore its magnetic field doesn't reverse. Option (4) is incorrect because the magnetic field of the coil reverses only when the current reverses. Option (5) is incorrect because the battery continues to provide electrical energy and thus would eventually run down, whether the current is flowing in one direction or two.

8. **(5) a generator, which uses a magnetic field to produce electricity** (Application) In a generator, a moving magnet produces current in a coil of wire, an application of the principle of electromagnetic induction. Option (1) is an example of a machine that uses electricity to produce magnetism, not the other way around. Options (2) and (3) do not involve electromagnetism. Option (4) is incorrect because a battery generates electric current by a chemical reaction, not by magnetism.

9. **(1) gravity** (Comprehension) According to the table, only gravity involves attraction between objects larger than atoms. Gravitational attraction causes such common occurrences as objects feeling heavy and objects falling. Option (2) is incorrect because static electricity is the only visible effect of the electromagnetic force that you see acting between objects and this is less common than the effects of gravity listed above. Even though the results of electromagnetic force can be seen, the force actually operates at the subatomic level—as do the forces listed in options (3) and (4). Option (5) is incorrect because not all of these forces are easily seen everyday.

Lesson 20
GED Skill Focus (Page 207)

1. **a.** a disturbance that travels through space or matter

2. **b.** Every wave has a wavelength that is at least twice its amplitude.

e. To accurately measure wavelength, you need at least two troughs.

3. **b.** Saying a wave has great amplitude is the same as saying it is high.

GED Content Focus (Page 209)

1. **(3) an accordion being played** (Application) This is correct because it represents a back-and-forth motion with compressions and rarifications (disturbances) generated in the same direction as the wave travels (the movement of the accordion). The other options are incorrect because they represent up-and-down disturbances moving perpendicular to the motion of travel of the waves; this is characteristic of transverse, not longitudinal waves.

2. **(5) a stereo and speaker system** (Application) This is correct because the sound from the speakers would not be able to travel on the moon, where there is no air. Option (1), a flashlight, would be useful because light waves do not need a medium through which to travel. Option (2), thermal underwear, would be useful to help keep warm. Option (3), oxygen, would be useful for breathing since the moon has no atmosphere and therefore no oxygen. You might at first conclude that Option (4), a space helmet with built-in CD player with earphones, would be useless but that would be a hasty generalization. In fact, sound would travel to your ears through the wires that attach the CD player to the earphones and then through the air in the helmet to your ears.

3. **(4) a mix of all the colors of visible light** (Comprehension) According to the passage and the diagram, white light is made of light of varying wavelengths, or colors. Option (1) is incorrect because white light is a blend of all the colors, not just one. Option (2) is incorrect because a prism is a clear piece of glass, and it doesn't form white light or any other kind of light. Option (3) is incorrect because it simply describes what white light is, not what forms white light; this option gives an example of a circular reasoning. Option (5) is incorrect because all light is a form of transverse, not longitudinal, waves.

4. **(3) Red light is bent the least.** (Evaluation) Since red light is at the opposite end of the visible spectrum from violet light, as described in the text and shown in the diagram, red light must be the least bent of all the colors of light. As a result, Options (1) and (5) are incorrect. Neither the passage nor the diagram mentions the speed of light, so option (2) is incorrect; the diagram shows and the passage indicates that it is not true. Option (4) is incorrect, since, as the passage states, different colors of light bend at different angles in the prism.

5. **(2) Water waves require water through which to travel.** (Evaluation) Water waves are transverse waves that clearly require a medium—water—through which to travel. Therefore concluding that all transverse waves can travel through empty space is a hasty generalization based on the characteristics of light waves, another type of transverse wave. Options (1) and (4) are incorrect because they support the conclusion; they do not provide evidence to disprove it. Option (3) is incorrect because the characteristics of sound waves are irrelevant: sound waves are longitudinal waves, not transverse waves. Option (5) is incorrect because it is not relevant to the conclusion being drawn.

6. **(5) The sound becomes softer.** (Analysis) Decreased energy in a sound wave results in a softer sound. The farther from the source of a sound you are, the less audible it is. Options (1) and (2) are incorrect because only the medium the sound waves travel in, not the distance, affects the speed of sound waves. Option (3) is a general characteristic of sound waves traveling in a particular medium at a uniform temperature, not a result of a decrease in energy. Option (4) is the opposite of what would result.

GED Practice (Pages 210–211)

1. **(4) electric and magnetic fields that oscillate in a wave** (Comprehension) This is a restatement of the definition given in the passage. Option (1) is incorrect because it is circular reasoning: it is simply another way of describing electromagnetic radiation. Option (2) is incorrect because the disturbances in electromagnetic radiation are in two directions. Option (3) is incorrect because electromagnetic radiation consists of transverse, not longitudinal, waves. Option (5) is incorrect because visible light is a form of electromagnetic radiation, not the other way around.

2. **(2) at right angles to the direction of motion** (Comprehension) According to the diagram and the passage, the electric and magnetic fields oscillate perpendicular to the direction of motion. Options (1) and (4) are incorrect because they describe the disturbance in a longitudinal wave, not in a transverse wave such as an electromagnetic wave. Option (3) is incorrect because the angles are 90° angles, not 45° angles. Option (5) is incorrect because the motion is perpendicular to the direction of motion, not circular.

3. **(3) Light waves have shorter wavelengths.** (Analysis) According to the diagram of the electromagnetic spectrum, visible light waves have shorter wavelengths than radio waves. Options (1) and (2) are incorrect because both the diagram and the passage indicate that all

UNIT 3

types of electromagnetic waves consist of both magnetic and electric fields. Option (4) is incorrect because the passage states that electromagnetic waves can travel through a vacuum, so neither needs a medium through which to travel. Option (5) is incorrect because the diagram indicates and the passage states that radio waves are part of the electromagnetic spectrum; they are not sound waves.

4. **(2) They travel through a vacuum at 186,282 miles per second.** (Evaluation) According to the diagram of the electromagnetic spectrum, infrared waves are electromagnetic waves. According to the passage, all electromagnetic waves travel at the same speed through a vacuum, at 186,282 miles per second. Option (1) is incorrect because X-ray machines produce X rays, not infrared waves. Option (3) is incorrect because all electromagnetic waves travel at the same speed through space, which is a vacuum. Option (4) is incorrect because infrared waves have wavelengths from about 10^{-4} to about 10^{-6} meters. Option (5) is incorrect because the diagram shows that infrared waves are a type of electromagnetic wave.

5. **(1) Cell phones emit microwaves near the head.** (Comprehension) According to the passage, cell phone use has become a matter of concern because the phones emit this type of electromagnetic radiation right near the brain. People are concerned because the phones may pose a health risk to users. Options (2) and (4) are incorrect because they focus on aspects of cell phones not relevant to the risk of developing brain cancer. Option (3) is incorrect; the mice were exposed to similar radiation but not specifically to cell phones, and the type of cancer they developed is not specified. Option (5) is incorrect because the fact that cell phones are wireless does not make people suspect them of possibly causing increased risk for brain cancer.

6. **(2) Use a cell phone with a remote antenna to lessen microwave intensity near the head.** (Application) Increasing the distance between the source of microwave emissions (the antenna) and the user's head will reduce the bombardment of microwaves on the brain, thereby decreasing whatever risk, if any, exists. Option (1) is incorrect because using the cell phone outdoors does not affect the distance between the cell phone's antenna and the person's head. Option (3) is incorrect because even if the user alternates sides of the head, the brain is still being hit by microwaves. Options (4) and (5) are incorrect because the antenna is in use whether the calls are incoming or outgoing.

7. **(4) No definitive link has been found between cell phone use and brain cancer.** (Evaluation) According to the passage, neither the animal studies nor the human studies has offered conclusive evidence that cell phones are associated with higher than normal risks of developing brain cancer. Options (1), (2), and (5) are incorrect because they are hasty generalizations that are not supported by the information presented in the passage; to date, there is not enough evidence to reach any of these conclusions. Option (3) is incorrect because the passage states that high levels of microwaves are needed to heat food in microwave ovens, not low levels.

GED Mini-Test (Pages 212–213)

1. **(4) number of cycles that pass a given point and time** (Comprehension) Frequency is defined in the first sentence of the passage as the number of waves that pass a given point in a specific unit of time. Options (1), (2), and (3) are incorrect because neither height (another word for amplitude) nor distance between crests or troughs is directly related to frequency. Option (5) is incorrect because calculating frequency does not involve distance.

2. **(1) decreased speed** (Analysis) If both wavelength and frequency decrease, it follows that when you multiply them, the resulting speed will also decrease. Option (2) is incorrect because speed is calculated by multiplying wavelength times frequency. If you decrease both, the speed will change. Option (3) is incorrect, because if both wavelength and frequency are decreased, speed cannot increase. Options (4) and (5) are incorrect because wavelength and frequency alone do not determine the distance a wave travels; you need to know travel times to determine if the distance the wave travels has increased or decreased.

3. **(2) The Effect of Microwaves on Water Molecules** (Comprehension) The diagram shows how microwaves twist water molecules, which produces heat energy to warm food. Option (1) is too general. Option (3) is a detail about a part of a microwave oven that is not shown in the diagram. Option (4) is incorrect, because the diagram shows the water molecules not the microwaves changing. Option (5) is not the topic of the diagram, which focuses on the action of the microwaves, not the design of the oven.

4. **(4) Food with a high water content heats more rapidly in a microwave oven than dry food does.** (Evaluation) Since microwaves act on water molecules, causing them to twist back and forth, producing heat, you can conclude that food with a high water content

will heat up more rapidly than dry food. Option (1) is incorrect because nothing in the passage or diagram indicates that other types of electromagnetic radiation have that effect on water molecules. Option (2) is incorrect because a microwave oven converts electromagnetic energy to heat energy, not the other way around. Option (3) is incorrect because a conventional oven does not use microwaves; it conducts heat from a heat source to cook food. Option (5) may or may not be true, but nothing in the passage or diagram provides information to support this conclusion.

5. **(2) Its molecules are too far apart.** (Analysis) According to the passage, solids are the most effective transmitters of sound waves because their molecules are packed close together. Liquids, whose molecules are less close together, are rated in the middle for sound transmission; therefore the reason gases are least effective at sound transmission must be because their molecules are far apart. Option (1) is incorrect because the molecules of gases are far apart, not close together. Similarly, option (3) is incorrect, because gas molecules are far apart, and therefore gases are not dense. Option (4) is incorrect because gases are not described as elastic in the passage. Option (5) is incorrect because it's a circular argument. Saying that gas is the least effective transmitter of sound waves is another way of saying that sound waves travel more slowly through it.

6. **(4) Put your ear to the ground.** (Application) Since sound waves travel faster through solid ground than they do through air, putting your ear to the ground means you will hear a distant sound sooner. The other options all have to do with sound and hearing, but not with the fact that sound waves travel fastest through solids.

7. **(5) Sound waves travel more slowly than light waves do.** (Evaluation) There is a time lag between seeing the ball hit and hearing the sound because sound waves travel much more slowly than light waves do. Options (1) and (4) would not affect the timing at which a person would hear the sound. Options (2) and (3) would not affect the speed at which the sound traveled.

8. **(3) its electromagnetic fields** (Analysis) Since infrared waves are a form of electromagnetic radiation, they produce electric and magnetic fields that affect the ability of the sensor to conduct electricity. Options (1) and (2) are incorrect because these are properties of matter, not of waves. Options (4) and (5) are wave properties, but they are not the cause of changes in conductivity in the thermometer's sensor.

9. **(4) The probe is not pointed directly at the eardrum.** (Analysis) If the probe is not pointing at the eardrum, it will not pick up the proper infrared radiation and thus will cause an inaccurate reading. Option (1) is incorrect because saying that the thermometer gives an incorrect temperature reading is the same as saying that the thermometer is sometimes inaccurate. This is circular reasoning. Option (2) is incorrect because infrared radiation is characterized by wavelengths in a small range of the electromagnetic spectrum; if the wavelengths change dramatically (which they don't), the eardrum is producing another type of radiation; (it doesn't). Option (3) is contradicted by information in the passage and the diagram. Option (5) is incorrect because only conventional thermometers use mercury; ear thermometers do not use mercury; if they did, this would be shown in the diagram.

Unit 3 Cumulative Review (Pages 214–217)

1. **(3) C_4H_{10}** (Comprehension) If you count the number of carbon (C) and hydrogen (H) atoms in the structural formulas of straight chain butane and branched chain butane, you will see that each structural formula contains 4 carbon and 10 hydrogen atoms. Thus the chemical formula for both types of butane is C_4H_{10}. You can eliminate Options (1) and (5) because they have an incorrect number of carbon atoms. Option (2) has an incorrect number of hydrogen atoms. Option (4) is incorrect because butane does not have any oxygen (O) atoms.

2. **(5) Decane has more isomers.** (Analysis) The passage states that the more carbon atoms in a hydrocarbon molecule, the more isomers it can form. Decane has more carbon atoms than pentane does, so it will form more isomers. In fact, decane has 75 isomers compared to pentane's 3 isomers. Therefore, options (2), (3), and (4) are incorrect. Option (1) is incorrect because, as the chemical formula shows, decane has more hydrogen atoms than pentane.

3. **(1) Oxygen more easily reaches the parts of a straight-chain molecule.** (Evaluation) The only factor that can account for a difference in the way the isomers burn is their only physical difference, a difference in atomic arrangement. Since the isomers do not differ in chemical composition, options (2), (3), (4), and (5) are incorrect.

4. **(3) Pull a few coils of a loose spring toward you and then quickly release them.** (Application) The key characteristic of a longitudinal wave is that the direction of the wave's motion and the direction of the disturbance the wave causes are the same. This

can be modeled by plucking and releasing the coils of a loose spring. Option (1) is incorrect because the up-and-down motion of the rope is perpendicular to the motion of the wave; this pattern of motion is characteristic of a transverse rather than a longitudinal wave. Option (2) is incorrect because the rotation of a jump rope does not model the linear disturbance of a longitudinal wave. Options (4) and (5) are incorrect because skipping a stone and throwing a bounce pass are more similar to the motion caused by a transverse wave than a longitudinal wave, since the up-and-down motion is perpendicular to the direction both the stone and the ball travel.

5. **(4) an unstable nucleus** (Comprehension) According to the passage, with atoms of different sizes, certain proportions of protons to neutrons in the nucleus of an atom results in nuclear instability, and thus radioactive decay. Option (1) is incorrect because the number of electrons in an atom does not determine whether or not an atom is radioactive. Option (2) is incorrect because all atoms have a single nucleus; no atom has multiple nuclei. Option (3) is a property of radioactive atoms, not a cause of radioactivity. Option (5) is incorrect because it simply restates what radioactivity is, rather than explaining what causes it (an example of circular reasoning).

6. **(5) a geologist interested in estimating the age of rock samples** (Application) By finding out the amount of radioactive material compared to the amount of stable material in a rock sample, geologists can estimate the age of the rock. The remaining options are incorrect because information about the half-life of radioactive substances would not be useful to scientists engaging in the activities described in options (1), (2), (3), and (4).

7. **(3) After 22,920 years, $\frac{1}{16}$ gram of carbon-14 will remain of the original 1 gram.** (Evaluation) The diagram shows that every 5,730 years, half of the carbon-14 has decayed. At 17,190 years, $\frac{1}{8}$ gram is left. After another 5,730 years, or 22,920 years altogether, half of $\frac{1}{8}$, or $\frac{1}{16}$, gram would be left. Option (1) is incorrect because $\frac{1}{16}$ gram would be left. Option (2) is incorrect because $\frac{1}{8}$ gram remains after 17,190 years. Option (4) is incorrect because it is a hasty generalization. The passage gives only one example of a half-life, not enough to conclude how long a typical half-life is. Option (5) is incorrect because with a half-life of 5,730 years, carbon-14 decays to unmeasurable amounts in thousands, rather than millions of years.

8. **(2) A fluid is a liquid or a gas.** (Analysis) The writer assumes that you understand that a fluid is either a liquid or a gas—any substance whose molecules can move freely and randomly. The other options are incorrect because they are all stated in the passage.

9. **(1) decreased speed** (Analysis) Since drag slows down moving objects, increasing drag would decrease an object's speed. Option (2) is the opposite of what would occur. Option (3) is incorrect because, as the paragraph implies and the diagrams show, streamlining causes decreased drag and smoother airflow, so increased drag means rougher airflow. Option (4) is incorrect because increasing the drag means the rate at which air flows over the object decreases. Option (5) is incorrect because drag is a kind of friction, so increasing drag means increasing friction.

10. **(2) taper the hood and fenders to streamline the design** (Analysis) If the automobile were streamlined, it would experience less drag. This means that it would take less force (and thus less fuel) to move at a particular speed or go a certain distance. Options (1), (4), and (5) would have no effect or airflow or fuel efficiency. Option (3) would create more drag, making the car less fuel efficient.

11. **(3) A material's opposition to the flow of electric current is known as its resistance.** (Comprehension) The main focus of the passage is to explain what resistance is, and this sentence does that. Options (1), (4), and (5) are all details too specific to be the main idea. Option (2) is true, but it is not discussed in the paragraph.

12. **(5) Replace a thin steel wire with a thick copper wire.** (Application) If the voltage remains the same, any change that decreases the resistance increases the current. A thicker wire has a lower resistance than a thinner wire, and copper has a lower resistance than steel, so replacing a thin steel wire with a thick copper wire decreases the resistance, which increases the current. Options (1), (2), (3), and (4) all are changes that would increase the resistance, which would decrease the current.

13. **(2) Two nuclei and several neutrons are released when a nucleus is hit by a neutron.** (Comprehension) This summarizes what is shown in the diagram of nuclear fission. Option (1) is incorrect because electrons are not released, according to the diagram. Option (3) is incorrect because according to the diagram, protons are not released by nuclear fission, neutrons are, and because the nucleus lengthens only in the process of splitting in two. Options (4) and (5) may be true, but they do not summarize what is shown in the diagram.

14. **(5) It was morally wrong for scientists to develop nuclear weapons.** (Analysis) To this day, there is still debate over whether it was morally acceptable for scientists to develop the nuclear weapons that were, soon after their development, dropped on two Japanese cities near the end of World War II. The other options are incorrect because they are all statements of fact from the passage, not opinions.

15. **(3) scientific and technical challenge** (Evaluation) To go from the first controlled nuclear fission in 1942 to a working bomb in three years was a great scientific and technological challenge, the sort of challenge likely to motivate the physicists. Option (1) is not likely to be correct because developing the bomb, as the passage indicates, was a team effort. Option (2) is unlikely because developing weapons of mass destruction is the opposite of developing nonviolent means of conflict resolution. Option (4) is incorrect because nothing in the passage indicates that the physicists were expecting a large monetary reward. Option (5) is incorrect because the passage indicates that after the war, many of the scientists came to regret the destruction caused by their work and tried to stop the spread of nuclear weapons.

16. **(2) A rough surface reflects parallel light rays at different angles.** (Evaluation) The right diagram shows that when parallel rays hit a rough surface, light is reflected (as shown by the blue lines), but the reflected rays bounce off at different angles. Option (1) is incorrect, because the diagram shows that parallel incoming rays can be reflected. Option (3) is incorrect, because the law of reflection does hold for rough surfaces: the angle of incidence is always equal to the angle of reflection. The parallel light rays are reflected off a rough surface at different angles because they hit the rough surface at different angles. Options (4) and (5) are incorrect because they are based on a misunderstanding of the word *normal,* which in the diagrams refers to the line perpendicular to the surface.

POSTTEST (Pages 219–237)

1. **(3) a chemical reaction in which heat energy is absorbed** (Comprehension) The last two sentences of the paragraph explain that an endothermic reaction is one in which heat is absorbed. Option (1) is not true; in chemical reactions, the properties of matter change. Option (2) is incorrect because it describes an exothermic reaction. Option (4) is incorrect because it describes activation energy. Option (5) is incorrect because chemical reactions need activation energy in order to start.

2. **(5) the source of activation energy** (Application) In this case, the flame provides heat energy to start the coals burning. Option (1) is incorrect because the flaming lighter is not a property, it is a form of matter. Option (2) is incorrect because the burning of the fuel in the lighter is itself an exothermic reaction releasing heat. Option (3) is incorrect because the flaming lighter is part of a chemical reaction, not a physical change. Option (4) is incorrect because the results of this chemical reaction are ashes, gases, and heat.

3. **(1) Earth's interior is composed of material much denser than the material in the crust.** (Evaluation) The diagram indicates that the density of Earth increases as you go from the crust toward the core. Averaging the greater density of Earth's interior with the lower density of the crust gives Earth's average density. Option (2) is true, but it is incorrect because it does not help explain how Earth's average density can be greater than the density of the crust. Option (3) is not true; according to the diagram, the crust contains silicon and oxygen, and the interior, iron and nickel. Option (4) is true since density is the relationship between mass and volume; but this fact alone doesn't explain why Earth's average density is greater than that of the crust, so option (4) is incorrect. Option (5) is incorrect because even if the density of the oceans was figured into the average density of Earth's crust, a lower density added to the calculation would reduce the density for the crust, not increase it.

4. **(3) the ciliary muscles** (Analysis) According to the diagram, these muscles are in a position to pull the lens as needed to alter its shape. Options (1), (2), (4), and (5) are incorrect because the superior and inferior rectus muscles, cornea, and optic nerve are not connected to the lens and so could not control its shape.

5. **(3) The amount of light entering the eye varies.** (Analysis) The smaller the pupil, the less light enters the eye; the larger the pupil, the more light enters the eye. Option (1) is incorrect because the iris, not the pupil, is the colored portion of the eye. Option (2) is incorrect because the eye's blind spot does not change position; it is the region at the back of the retina where the optic nerve enters, and there are no light receptor cells on the retina there. Option (4) is incorrect; the cornea does bulge, but this is not caused by the adjustment of the iris. Option (5) is incorrect because the iris is not related to seeing colors.

6. **(3) decrease lift** (Analysis) To descend gradually, the pilot needs to decrease lift so that

the weight of the plane will be greater than the lift. This can be done by altering the air flow over the wings. Option (1) is incorrect because increasing lift will result in increased altitude. Option (2) is incorrect because increased thrust would result in greater forward speed, not descent. Option (4) is incorrect, because decreasing weight will cause the plane to ascend or become steady in course, rather than descend. Option (5) is incorrect because decreasing drag would increase the plane's forward speed; it would not cause the plane to descend slowly.

7. **(4) Three geraniums are too small a sample on which to base such a broad conclusion.** (Evaluation) Brittany's conclusion on the basis of one experiment with three geraniums is a hasty generalization. A researcher must test many more plants, of different types, before he or she would be justified in drawing such a broad conclusion. Options (1) and (2) are incorrect because giving the geraniums different amounts of light each day was part of the experiment; it was the independent variable. Option (3) is incorrect because giving the geraniums the same amount of water means that water cannot be the cause of extra growth; it was a constant in the experiment. Option (5) is incorrect because the reaction of geraniums to water is not relevant to the conclusion regarding their reaction to light, and because based on this experiment, no conclusion can be drawn regarding a comparison of geraniums and other green plants and how they react to watering.

8. **(2) a toy truck** (Application) Dry cell batteries are used to power small, portable objects that are not used all the time and whose continued use is not essential. A toy truck is small, needs very little electric current, and if it stops running when the battery runs out, that's not a matter of great concern. Option (1) is incorrect because a washing machine is a large, fixed appliance that requires household level current; a dry cell battery would not be suitable. Options (3) and (4) are incorrect because cars and motorized wheelchairs need large amounts of current that dry cell batteries cannot provide. Option (5) is incorrect because a doorbell is a fixed item in a household, so it is practical to run it off the household current, not on a battery.

9. **(2) one** (Comprehension) To answer this question, first locate the third generation, which is the bottom row of males and females. Look along that row for anyone who shows the trait of red-green colorblindness, indicated by complete shading. There is only one person, a male, who has red-green colorblindness. (Note that the half-shaded circles represent females who carry the trait, but do not have it themselves.)

10. **(2) 77°F to 88°F** (Comprehension) First locate the area that represents the tropical forest biome, in the upper right portion of the graph. Then check the vertical axis for the temperature range of this biome. (Note that each interval represents 15° so the interval mark between 60 and 90 represents 75.) According to the graph, the tropical forest biome has an average annual temperature between 77°F and 88°F. Option (1) is incorrect because the graph shows the tropical forest biome has an average annual temperature below 90°F. Options (3), (4), and (5) are all average annual temperatures too low for the tropical forest biome.

11. **(1) The deciduous forest biome generally has a higher average annual temperature.** (Analysis) The average annual temperature for a deciduous forest biome ranges from about 50°F to about 80°F; and the average annual temperature for a coniferous forest biome ranges from about 35°F to 65°F. Therefore, on average, the deciduous forest biome is warmer than the coniferous forest biome. Option (2) is incorrect because this graph does not indicate how much area is covered by either type of biome. Option (3) is incorrect because, on average, the coniferous and deciduous forest get close to the same range of precipitation annually. Option (4) may be true, but diversity is not an issue addressed by the information given. Option (5) is not true; both biomes have annual temperature ranges of about 30°F.

12. **(3) Some of the biomes have similar average temperature and rainfall.** (Comprehension) Where two biomes overlap on the graph, they do so because average temperature and rainfall conditions are similar. Option (1) is true, but it is not the correct answer because overlapping areas on the graph indicate overlapping average temperature and rainfall data. Options (2) and (5) are incorrect because no location data is given on the graph. Option (4) is incorrect because, by definition, different biomes are characterized by different plants and animals.

13. **(4) Some arctic and alpine tundra biomes get as little precipitation as desert biomes.** (Evaluation) If you look at the precipitation axis of the graph, you will see that desert biomes get less than about 15 inches of precipitation per year. Some arctic and alpine tundra biomes also get less than 15 inches of precipitation per year. Option (1) is incorrect because the grasslands biome may have a hotter annual temperature than a desert biome. Option (2) is incorrect because 180 inches is the top of the annual precipitation range, not the bottom. Option (3) is true, but the paragraph and graph do not provide evidence to support it. Option (5) is not

true; desert biomes get up to about 15 inches of precipitation per year.

14. **(5) Liquid water molecules are closely packed in an irregular arrangement, and ice molecules form a regular lattice with large spaces.** (Analysis) In the liquid water diagram, there is no space between the tightly jumbled water molecules, but the ice diagram shows a regular arrangement of molecules in a lattice formation with large spaces between the molecules. That is why water expands when it freezes. Option (1) is incorrect because the diagram shows that both liquid water and ice have both hydrogen and oxygen atoms. Options (2), (3), and (4) are incorrect because the same mass of water and ice have the same number of atoms; the ice just takes up more space.

15. **(4) nervous system** (Application) The eyes and ears receive sensory data and pass it on to the brain, which interprets what we see and hear. Options (1), (2), (3), and (5) are incorrect because these systems do not involve collecting sensory information—the main function of the eyes and ears.

16. **(4) Phosphoric acid in cola affects bone mass, weakening it.** (Analysis) According to the information, scientists disagree about the reason for the association between cola drinking and bone fractures, and this is one of the opinions they hold. Note that this statement does not contain any of the usual opinion clue words, so you cannot tell that this is an opinion from the statement itself. You must look at the context of the statement in the passage to determine that it is an opinion. Options (1), (2), (3), and (5) are not opinions; they are facts stated in the information.

17. **(2) discovery of new subatomic particles that convey fundamental forces** (Application) This project would qualify for a Nobel Prize in physics. Option (1) is incorrect because there is no Nobel Prize given for the category of earth science. Option (3) is incorrect because there is no Nobel Prize given for the category of zoology. Option (4) is incorrect because there is no Nobel Prize given for the category of animal breeding. Option (5) is incorrect because there is no Nobel Prize given for the category of performing arts.

18. **(5) cerium sulfate** (Evaluation) Notice that the cerium sulfate line slopes downward. That indicates that the solubility of cerium sulfate decreases as the temperature increases. Therefore the behavior of cerium sulfate in solution proves that increasing water temperature does not always increase solubility. Options (1), (2), (3),

and (4) are incorrect because the solubility of these substances does increase with increased water temperature.

19. **(3) heating the gas in a hot air balloon so it expands, causing the balloon to rise** (Application) When the gas in a hot air balloon is heated, its volume increases and the gas becomes less dense, causing the balloon to rise. This is an application of Charles's Law regarding gas temperature and volume. Options (1) and (2) are incorrect because they involve changes in pressure, not changes in temperature. Option (4) is incorrect because spraying the cologne does not involve a change in temperature and volume. Option (5) is incorrect because it involves changing a gas to a liquid. Charles's law applies only to gases.

20. **(3) The parents want a child who is genetically their own.** (Evaluation) When the egg and sperm come from the parents, the resulting child conceived by in vitro fertilization has their genetic heritage. Having a child who is a "blood relative" is important to many people. Options (1) and (2) are both true, but they are not reasons for preferring in vitro fertilization, which can also take a long time and cost a lot of money. Option (4) is incorrect because any child might develop health problems. Option (5) is incorrect because they are more likely to ensure they have a girl through adoption than through in vitro fertilization.

21. **(4) convection only** (Application) In a hot air heating system, hot air comes from vents on or near the floor and circulates in the house through convection. Options (1) and (5) are incorrect because conduction does not play a major role heating the house with this system. Options (2) and (3) are incorrect because radiation also does not play a major role in home heating with this system.

22. **(3) Mercury conducts electricity.** (Analysis) The purpose of a switch is to complete an electric circuit, allowing electric current to flow. In this paragraph, the writer takes for granted that mercury conducts electricity; this fact is not actually stated. All the other options are facts actually stated in the paragraph; they are not assumed.

23. **(2) The northward flow of tropical water warms the climate of Europe.** (Evaluation) According to the paragraph, the deep ocean currents move heat from the tropics. According to the map, warm water flows north from the tropics to Europe, warming the climate there. Options (1) and (3) are incorrect because cold currents flow near Antarctica and Northeastern Asia. Option (4) is incorrect; according to the

paragraph, cold salty water is denser than warm, fresher tropical water. Option (5) is incorrect because the map shows the warm current flowing in the opposite direction, from Australia toward Africa.

24. **(4) a leaf** (Application) Like an insect's wing, a leaf is thin but three-dimensional and the right size to be examined under a stereomicroscope. Options (1), (2), and (3) are all too small for a stereomicroscope. Option (5) is too big.

25. **(1) as it approached** (Comprehension) According to the paragraph and diagram, the sound waves are pushed together as the source of a sound approaches, so an approaching sound source has a high pitch. As the diagram shows, the sound waves are closest together during the approach of the source. Option (2) is incorrect because when the sound source is closest to you, you hear the sound waves at the side of the source, not in front; the sound waves at the side are not pushed closely together, so the sound is not high-pitched. Option (3) is incorrect because, as indicated by the paragraph and the diagram, the sound's pitch would be dropping as the sound moved away from you. Option (4) is incorrect because volume is independent of pitch change. Option (5) is incorrect because reflection would distort the sound but not change its frequency.

26. **(1) increasing pitch** (Analysis) According to the paragraph and the diagram, the sound waves are pushed together as the source of a sound approaches, so a sound's pitch increases as the source approaches. As the diagram shows, the source of the sound is approaching Observer A. Options (2), (3), (4), and (5) are contradicted by the text and diagram.

27. **(2) The Doppler effect can be used to determine whether a sound source is moving away from or toward someone.** (Evaluation) Since the pitch rises as a source of sound approaches and falls as it recedes, the changes in pitch can be used to place the moving source of sound. Option (1) is incorrect because the paragraph indicates that sound is an example of a type of wave that can be subject to the Doppler effect; in fact, the Doppler effect works with other types of waves, such as light waves. Option (3) is incorrect because many sounds can be heard more than 50 feet away and the Doppler effect is noticeable with any frequency and volume of sound that is audible or otherwise detectable. Option (4) is incorrect because the source of the sound is emitting waves of the same frequency; it is the changing relationship between source and listener that creates the Doppler effect. Option (5) is incorrect because nothing in the paragraph or diagram gives any information about sound waves interfering with one another.

28. **(5) a fresh orange** (Application) Fresh, uncooked foods are the best source of Vitamin C, and citrus fruits like oranges are an especially good source. Options (1) and (4) are not especially high in vitamin C, although both contain some vitamin C. Option (2) is not a good source of vitamin C because drying fruit generally destroys much of its vitamin C. Option (3) has some vitamin C, but because the greens were cooked, much of it has been destroyed.

29. **(3) The population would remain very low over the generations because many fertilized eggs would be defective and die.** (Analysis) Although the males could mate with the females, many of the resulting fertilized eggs would be defective. This would lower the number of healthy insects born each year. However, there would still be some healthy males to fertilize eggs; this would result in a few healthy offspring, so the population would not die out completely. Option (1) is incorrect because many of the females' eggs would be fertilized, and some of these would result in healthy insects. Option (2) is incorrect because although the population would remain low over the generations, enough healthy eggs would survive to produce some new offspring. Option (4) is incorrect because releasing irradiated males will result in fewer successful fertilizations, so the population will drop. Option (5) is incorrect because although mating would continue, the number of healthy insect offspring would decrease.

30. **(5) There are about 24 times as many invertebrate species as vertebrate species.** (Analysis) As you can see from the circle graph, invertebrates, including insects, far outnumber vertebrates. In fact, only 4 percent of animals are vertebrates, and 96 percent are invertebrates. Thus there are about 24 times (96 divided by 4) the number of invertebrate species as vertebrate species. All of the other options give numbers that are too low.

31. **(2) Earth's position changes relative to the stars.** (Analysis) According to the diagram, the stars appear in different locations at different times of year because of Earth's revolution around the sun. Option (1) is incorrect because the circle shown on the diagram is the path of the star as seen from Earth, not an orbit. Option (3) is incorrect because, according to the diagram, the relative position of the sun and the

Answers and Explanations

star remains the same. Option (4) is incorrect because the diagram shows only one star in different apparent positions at different times of year. Option (5) is incorrect because the diagram shows that it is Earth's revolution around the sun, not Earth's rotation, that is related to parallax.

32. **(5) the conditions necessary to create a self-contained ecosystem for astronauts** (Application) An ecosystem is a large, complex thing, and creating an ecosystem for astronauts would begin by modeling one here on Earth. Option (1) is incorrect because studying the effect on aerobic exercise on stress can be done by experimentation and surveys; a model is not needed. Option (2) is incorrect because the relationship between a high-fat diet and heart disease could be studied by surveying people regarding their diets and their health. Option (3), the social interactions of a group of chimpanzees, could be studied by observing the chimpanzees. Option (4), the growth and development of the Pacific salmon, could be studied by direct examination of fish.

33. **(2) increasing the plant or animal's usefulness and value** (Evaluation) The main purpose of selective breeding has always been to increase the value of the plant or animal to humans. The original domestication of grains and animals was the first use of selective breeding by humans, thousands of years ago. Option (1) might be a purpose of selective breeding, but only a minor one. Option (3) is incorrect because selective breeding is usually done on a small scale, and then used widely if it is successful. Option (4) is incorrect because the main purpose of selective breeding is to improve the plant or animal from our point of view; if it eventually becomes another species, that is a by-product of the process, not a goal. Option (5) is incorrect because selective breeding has been only rarely used for this purpose in recent years; its main purpose has always been economic.

34. **(4) Hot groundwater is unlikely to seep through Yucca Mountain again.** (Analysis) Those who favor storing radioactive waste at Yucca Mountain are of the opinion that hot groundwater is not a likely threat, and thus the storage containers will be safe. Options (1), (2), (3), and (5) are incorrect because they are all facts stated in the paragraph, not opinions.

35. **(1) During long periods of drought, the well will run dry.** (Comprehension) The diagram shows the normal position of the water table and its position during periods of drought. Since the water table falls below the bottom of the well during droughts, the diagram suggests

that the well will run dry. Option (2) is incorrect because the house is situated well above the stream, so it is unlikely to flood during a heavy rain. Option (3) is incorrect because the diagram shows that the level of water in the stream is the same as that of the water table. Option (4) is incorrect because the diagram does not show the roots of the trees, so no information about the trees' survival is implied. Option (5) is incorrect because the diagram does not include any information, either way, about water quality.

36. **(3) She uses nine times the energy doing heavy work as resting.** (Analysis) At rest, a woman uses an average of 5 kilojoules per minute of energy. Doing heavy work, she uses about 44 kilojoules, or about nine times as much. Option (1) is incorrect because heavy work requires more energy than resting, not less. Option (2) is incorrect because this is the amount of energy used in light, not heavy, work. Option (4) is incorrect because heavy work uses less than ten times the energy of resting. Option (5) is incorrect because 44.1 kilojoules is the average amount of energy a woman uses during heavy work, not the ratio of the amount of energy used during heavy work and resting.

37. **(5) Iron deposits are magnetic.** (Analysis) The paragraph does not state outright that iron is magnetic, although this information is important for understanding the paragraph. This fact is common knowledge. Options (1) through (4) are all incorrect because they are not assumptions; they are facts stated in the paragraph.

38. **(2) when a group of individuals colonize an island in the ocean** (Application) An island in the ocean is geographically isolated, so that a population inbreeds over generations. Under these circumstances the population sometimes evolves into a new species. Option (1) is incorrect because, although rare, a useful genetic mutation can happen in any population, but it would lead to speciation only if the population were isolated. Options (3) and (4) are incorrect because the populations are not isolated. Option (5) is incorrect because offspring are necessary for speciation to occur; without them, the group becomes extinct.

39. **(4) lightning** (Application) As the diagram shows, the electrodes provided sparks, or electrical energy, in Miller's model, just as lightning would have provided electrical energy on early Earth. This energy could have changed the substances on Earth into organic molecules. Option (1), the atmosphere, is simulated by the collection of gases in the model. Option (2), the oceans, is simulated by the water. Option (3), heavy rainfall, is not part of the model, although

the boiling water does provide water vapor that condenses near the bottom of the model. Option (5), bombardment by meteors, is also not replicated by Miller's model.

40. **(3) Snow fences are built along the sides of roads so snow will drift there and not on the roads.** (Application) Like sand, snow is blown by the wind and falls to the ground when the wind slows down. The snow fences along roads are designed to pile up drifting snow and keep the roads clear. Option (1) is incorrect because the stone walls are not designed to catch particles carried by the wind, although they may do this, but to mark the boundary of a farmer's field. Option (2) is incorrect because the electrified fences are meant to keep livestock in a specific area, not to slow wind movement. Options (4) and (5) are incorrect because these structures are barriers intended to stop the movement of water, not to cause the deposit of material in the water.

41. **(1) An SUV requires more space to stop than a car traveling at the same speed.** (Evaluation) Since a large SUV has much more mass than a typical car, it needs more space to stop than a car traveling at the same speed. Therefore, if the car in front of an SUV stops suddenly, the SUV will crash into the car because the SUV needs more room to stop. Options (2) and (3) are incorrect because an SUV requires more stopping space than a car. Option (4) is incorrect because the higher the speed of the SUV, the more space needed for stopping, and so the more space needed between the SUV and the car in front. Option (5) is incorrect because any accident at highway speeds can injure SUV drivers and passengers.

42. **(1) coal** (Comprehension) According to the chart, coal is a sedimentary rock formed from the remains of organisms. Options (2), (4), and (5) are incorrect because conglomerate, sandstone, and shale are formed by the action of streams, glaciers, and wind. Option (3) is incorrect because rock salt is formed through chemical reactions in seawater or through evaporation of seawater.

43. **(4) a vast ocean** (Application) The chart indicates that gypsum results from chemical reactions in or the evaporation of seawater; so, for gypsum to form, millions of years ago, the region must have been covered by an ocean. None of the other options lists a region in which gypsum is likely to form.

44. **(3) Different treatments for different types of pain may be needed.** (Comprehension) Since the MRIs and PET scans are showing that different areas of the brain are activated by pain with different causes, it follows that different types of pain may respond to different types of treatments. Option (1) is incorrect because the paragraph indicates that with brain imaging technology, objective studies of pain are now possible. Option (2) is incorrect because the paragraph indicates that the brain images show that many different areas of the brain are activated by pain. Option (4) is incorrect because nothing in the paragraph suggests that one type of imaging technology is superior to the other. Option (5) is incorrect because nothing in the paragraph suggests that pain is not real.

45. **(4) In a closed container, liquid water evaporates into water vapor, then condenses into liquid water.** (Comprehension) This statement covers all the main points of the diagram: water, evaporation, vapor, and condensation in a closed container. Option (1) is incorrect because it leaves out condensation. Option (2) is incorrect because it leaves out evaporation. Option (3) is incorrect because it is a detail, not a summary. Option (5) is incorrect because it omits the important fact that the container is closed and the diagram does not show the freezing process.

46. **(5) The longer the pregnancy in a species, the fewer the young.** (Analysis) The chart arranges the animals by length of pregnancy, from shortest to longest. The animals with the shortest pregnancies have the highest number of offspring, while the animals with the longest pregnancies have the fewest (one). This is a generalization based on the details in the chart. The remaining options are all too specific to be conclusions: they are details from the chart.

47. **(2) Knowing that light waves are refracted, the person should aim for a spot closer than the one where the flashlight appears to be.** (Evaluation) If the person aimed for the image of the flashlight, he would miss, so option (2) is incorrect. He compensates for the refraction of the light waves and aims closer to shore in order to pick up the flashlight. Option (1) is incorrect because the person is not aiming at the spot where he sees the flashlight. Option (3) is incorrect because a person sees a flying bird exactly where the bird is because the light waves from the bird are not refracted. They are not refracted because the waves are just traveling through air; they are not passing the boundary between two substances. Option (4) is incorrect because nothing in the paragraph or diagram indicates that only light waves are refracted. In fact, all electromagnetic waves and sound waves are also refracted. Option (5) is incorrect because, as the paragraph

Answers and Explanations

indicates, refraction can occur at the boundary between any two types of substances. For example, when light enters a prism or other thick glass, plastic, or lens, it bends.

48. **(5) The earthquake caused less damage in Oakland than in San Jose, so the Mercalli rating in Oakland was lower.** (Analysis) The Mercalli scale rates the effects of an earthquake in a particular place. Therefore, the same earthquake can have different ratings in the different areas it affects. Options (1) and (2) are incorrect because the Mercalli scale does not measure the size of earthquake waves. Option (3) is incorrect because some very slight earthquakes will have only one Mercalli reading, at the site of a scientific monitoring device. Option (4) is incorrect because the earthquake caused less damage in Oakland.

49. **(3) No. Heartburn usually causes pain in the chest, above the stomach.** (Application) The diagram shows that acid moving from the stomach into the esophagus (which is in the chest) causes heartburn. Option (1) is incorrect because, although heartburn is caused by stomach acid, it is not caused by stomach acid in the stomach but by stomach acid flowing upward into the esophagus, as the diagram indicates. Option (2) is incorrect, because the site of the pain is incorrect and because nothing in the paragraph or diagram indicates that heartburn can cause aching (it can't). Option (4) is incorrect because the site of the pain is incorrect. Option (5) is incorrect because heartburn is related neither to heart pain nor to stomach pain, but to pain in the esophagus.

50. **(2) Russia, a country with large areas of permafrost in its northern regions** (Application) According to the paragraph, methane hydrate is found under permafrost and deep in ocean sediments. Of the countries listed, Russia, with its large northern expanse, is most likely to have huge deposits of methane hydrate. Since methane hydrate has potential value as a fuel, Russia is among the countries actively doing research on the feasibility of mining and using it. Option (1) is incorrect; a nation with lots of petroleum and natural gas does not have the incentive to study an untried source of fuel. Options (3), (4), and (5) are incorrect because these nations have neither permafrost regions nor access to the ocean. Therefore they are not likely to be interested in studying how to mine and process methane hydrate for fuel.

SIMULATED TEST (Pages 239–258)

1. **(1) carbon 14** (Application) The chart indicates that carbon 14 is used to estimate the age of material that was once alive, such as a human bone. None of the other radioactive substances listed as options are used to estimate age of living materials.

2. **(4) Radioactive substances have many different uses.** (Evaluation) The chart lists five radioactive substances and describes some of their various uses, so this is a reasonable conclusion. Option (1) is incorrect because no information is given about the cost of the substances listed in the chart. Option (2) is incorrect because uranium 235 is also used as fuel in nuclear reactors. Option (3) is incorrect because radioactive substances are used in atomic weapons, which are harmful to people. Option (5), although true, is incorrect because the chart does not give any information about the origin of radioactive substances.

3. **(2) to find the distance to an earthquake's epicenter** (Application) By comparing the times at which the three different types of waves arrive at a seismic recording station, scientists can calculate how far they have traveled from the epicenter of the earthquake. Option (1) is incorrect because damage assessment must be done on site. Options (3) and (5) are incorrect because once the waves arrive, the earthquake has already happened. Option (4) is incorrect because although volcanoes and earthquakes are both related to stresses in Earth's plates, volcanic eruptions cannot be predicted by seismic wave arrival times.

4. **(5) faulting and erosion** (Comprehension) In the second diagram, faulting exposes older rock layers when a rock mass slips down past several layers of an adjacent rock mass. In the third diagram, erosion has exposed older rock layers as the layers above them have worn away. Options (1) and (4) are incorrect because at the folding stage the older rock layers are still at the bottom of the formation. Options (2) and (3) are incorrect because they are incomplete.

5. **(2) the invention of the microscope** (Analysis) Prior to the invention of the microscope, the existence of microorganisms was unknown because they could not be seen. The microscope helped make microorganisms objects of scientific study. Option (1) is incorrect because classification was made possible once microbiology was already a field of study. Options (3) and (4) are incorrect because these were later developments in microbiology. Option (5) is incorrect because this field is not mentioned in the passage and there are few if any applications to the computer industry at this point.

6. **(4) running a car engine in a closed garage** (Application) Since carbon monoxide is

in the exhaust of a car engine, the amount of carbon monoxide in the air builds up rapidly when a car engine is run without ventilation. Option (1) is incorrect because a well-vented coal furnace will direct the exhaust to the outside. Options (2) and (5) are incorrect because using a lawn mower and grill outdoors provides plenty of ventilation. Option (3) is incorrect because a properly installed stove has enough ventilation to prevent carbon monoxide poisoning.

7. **(4) How an Enzyme Works** (Comprehension) This title covers the main idea of the diagram, which is to show how an enzyme interacts with a reacting molecule (substrate) to speed up certain chemical reactions. Options (1) and (2) are too general to serve as a title for the information. Option (3) is incorrect because the information does not show the enzyme's molecular structure. Option (5) is too specific, focusing on only part of the diagram.

8. **(3) the flea, which lives on the skin of birds and mammals and eats their blood** (Application) The flea lives on or near its host, and it harms its host, two characteristics of a parasite. Option (1) is incorrect because the millipede does not live on or near a living host and feeds on matter that is already dead. Option (2) is incorrect because the red-tailed hawk doesn't live on or in another organism, and it kills its prey. Option (4) is incorrect because the barnacle does not live on or harm a host organism. Option (5) is incorrect because the ant is providing a benefit to the host organism.

9. **(2) The inheritability rate of colorblindness is related to gender.** (Comprehension) Colorblindness is an inherited trait that is linked to sex, which accounts for the much higher percentage of men with colorblindness. Option (1) is incorrect because perceiving color is equally important to men and women. Option (3) is incorrect because colorblindness is not an illness. Option (4) is incorrect because the statement is unrelated to the distribution of colorblindness between the sexes. Option (5) is true under most circumstances, but it is not related to the distribution of colorblindness between the sexes.

10. **(3) a coleus plant grown from a stem cutting buried in rooting mixture** (Application) A plant grown from a cutting is a clone of the parent plant; it inherits all the parent plant's genetic material. Option (1) is incorrect because a baby born through artificial insemination still receives genetic material from both the father and mother. Option (2) is incorrect because the colt is born as a result

of sexual reproduction, in which the genetic material of two parents is combined. Option (4) is incorrect because a plant that grows from a seed that developed after pollination by another plant inherits genetic material from two parent plants. Option (5) is incorrect because the newly hatched spider inherited genetic material from both parent spiders.

11. **(3) Venus is the planet second closest to the sun.** (Evaluation) In the diagram, Mercury is the first planet orbiting the sun and Venus is the planet second closest to the sun. (Note that the sun is labeled "1".) Option (1) is not true. Mars, being further from the sun, takes longer to revolve around the sun. The diagram does not contain enough information to support options (2) and (4). Option (5) is not true. Since the moon revolves around Earth, at times it is closer to the sun than Earth is.

12. **(5) water vapor in the air** (Analysis) The water vapor in the air combines with the solid pollutants to form sulfuric acid and nitric acid, which are components of acid rain. Options (1), (2), and (3) are involved in the production of air pollutants; they cannot affect pollutants that have been released. Option (4) is incorrect because although the oceans are polluted by dry deposits and by acid rain, they are not directly involved in the production of wet deposits.

13. **(4) The plants are weakened by lack of nutrients and harmed by the heavy metals.** (Analysis) The diagram shows how the tree is a victim of the action of acidified soil as nutrients are removed and harmful metals are concentrated. Option (1) is incorrect because the diagram indicates that heavy metals are harmful in concentration. Option (2) is incorrect because pollution does not cause extra nutrients to accumulate in the soil. Option (3) is incorrect because the entire plant is weakened, not just the upper part. Option (5) is incorrect because the acidified soil results in undernourished plants.

14. **(3) They both provide indirect evidence of atoms.** (Analysis) The movement of the dust particle is indirect evidence that atoms are present and moving, and the X rays provide indirect evidence that atoms are there because the rays bounce off something. Option (1) is incorrect because neither Brownian motion nor X-ray diffraction provides images of atoms. Option (2) is incorrect because Brownian motion does not involve electromagnetic waves. Option (4) is incorrect because X rays do not involve liquid suspensions. Option (5) is incorrect because only X-ray diffraction involves bombarding the atoms; in Brownian motion, the atoms are bombarding the dust particle.

15. **(1) seeing lightning before hearing thunder** (Application) Because light travels much faster than sound, you see lightning before you hear the thunder that accompanies it during a thunderstorm. Option (2) is incorrect because the distances in a night club are so small that· you perceive light and sound at the same time. Options (3), (4), and (5) are incorrect because they do not compare the perception of light and sound. They involve either light or sound.

16. **(5) Increasing levels of carbon dioxide in the atmosphere may contribute to global warming.** (Analysis) This is a generalization based on the details given in the paragraph, especially the first paragraph. All the remaining options are incorrect because they are specific details from the paragraph, not conclusions.

17. **(5) It will rain.** (Analysis) If there is more water vapor in the air than the air can hold at a particular temperature, then the extra water condenses and falls as rain. Option (1) is incorrect because humidity would decrease only if the amount of water vapor decreased. Option (2) is incorrect because the air is already holding the maximum amount of moisture; the humidity cannot increase. Option (3) is incorrect because the condensation of the extra water vapor causes the temperature to rise, not to fall. Option (4) is incorrect because the water in the air is already in vapor form; it cannot evaporate.

18. **(1) when the sun and moon are positioned in a straight line with Earth** (Application) When the sun and moon are positioned in a straight line with Earth, the sun's gravitational pull is added to that of the moon, increasing the total gravitational force exerted on Earth and thus increasing the height of the tides. Option (2) would cause the lowest high tides, because the gravitational pull of the moon and the gravitational pull of the sun would be at right angles to each other, reducing the total gravitational force exerted on Earth and thus reducing the height of the tides. Options (3) and (4) are incorrect, because when the moon is a crescent (either waxing or waning), the sun and the moon are not in a line. As a result the sun and the moon's gravitational pull on Earth would not be added to the maximum extent and the high tides could not be the highest. Option (5) is incorrect, because sunspots do not affect the sun's gravitational pull, and so have no effect on tides on Earth.

19. **(4) A stationary object does not have kinetic energy.** (Comprehension) According to the paragraph, moving objects have kinetic energy. Stationary objects can gain kinetic energy if kinetic energy is transferred from a moving object, which then causes the stationary objects to move. The paragraph establishes that kinetic energy is defined by motion and implies that stationary objects, therefore, do not have kinetic energy. Option (1) is incorrect because an object with more mass and speed has more kinetic energy, not less. In addition, the paragraph does not give enough information to deduce this. Option (2) is not true, and nothing in the paragraph indicates that measurement of kinetic energy is impossible. Option (3) is contradicted by the paragraph. Option (5) is not true because a stationary object does not have any kinetic energy.

20. **(2) the lungs, which take oxygen from the air and transfer it to the bloodstream** (Application) Just as a fish's gills remove oxygen from water and transfer it to the blood, a person's lungs remove oxygen from the air and transfer it to the blood. Option (1) is incorrect because the trachea serves as a passageway for air. Option (3) is incorrect because the function of the diaphragm is to act as a bellows, not to absorb oxygen. Option (4) is incorrect because the tongue does not play an active role in respiration. Option (5) is incorrect because the intestines absorb water, not oxygen.

21. **(1) Release equal numbers of light- and dark-colored moths in two areas, one clean and one sooty, and later count the survivors.** (Evaluation) If Darwin's hypothesis is correct, you would expect that fewer light-colored moths would remain in the sooty area, and fewer dark-colored moths would remain in the clean area. None of the other options will produce enough data for comparison. All the data will be about one type of moth in one environment, so there will be no way to judge which type survived better.

22. **(2) The pulse rate is the number of heartbeats per minute.** (Analysis) The chart does not define *pulse*; the definition is considered common knowledge. Options (1) and (3) are incorrect because this information is given in the chart. Option (4) is incorrect because the data in the chart indicate that the subjects in poor condition did all three types of exercise. Option (5) may be true, but nothing in the chart suggests that the author assumes that this is so; there is no information about the number of subjects in each category.

23. **(5) The greatest jump in the pulse rate comes between moderate and heavy exercise.** (Evaluation) If you examine the pulse rates, you will see that no matter the person's physical condition, the pulse rate jumped more between moderate and heavy exercise than

between light and moderate exercise. Option (1) is incorrect because there is no pulse data beyond one minute. Option (2) cannot be concluded from the data; people in poor physical condition participated successfully in the study. Option (3) is true, but it is not supported by the chart, which gives no information about breaths per minute. Option (4) is good advice, but nothing in the chart provides evidence for its soundness.

24. **(2) The top magnet will turn until its north and south poles have exchanged places.** (Analysis) In the second diagram, the like poles are close to one another and they repel one another. Because the top magnet is suspended and free to move, it will turn until its north pole is near the bottom magnet's south pole, and its south pole is near the bottom magnet's north pole. Option (1) is incorrect because once the opposite poles line up, the force of attraction is likely to slow and stop the top magnet's turning. Options (3) and (4) are incorrect because the bottom magnet is fixed to the table and cannot move. Option (5) is incorrect because the top magnet is suspended on a string and is free to move.

25. **(4) to make new bone marrow cells for patients with leukemia** (Application) The information states that stem cells are cells that have not yet begun to differentiate into various types of tissue, and that scientists are experimenting with stem cells to make them differentiate in particular ways to treat injury or disease. Option (4) is the only option related to causing stem cells to differentiate into a particular type of cell, bone marrow cells, useful for treating disease, leukemia. Options (1), (2), and (5) are incorrect because they relate to causing stem cells not to differentiate but to form new types of cell parts, organs, or cells; the information does not indicate whether this is possible. Option (3) is incorrect because it is a cosmetic application and does not relate directly to the treatment of disease.

26. **(4) When a pistol was fired in a vacuum, gases were ejected from the barrel and the pistol moved in the opposite direction.** (Comprehension) This sentence covers all the main points of the diagram, providing a good summary of what the diagram shows. Option (1) is incorrect because it doesn't explain what happened to the pistol after firing, the critical thing the demonstration showed. Option (2) is incorrect because it focuses on a minor detail related to the demonstration. Option (3) is incorrect; the diagram does not indicate that the pistol will swing back and forth, (although it will), and this fact is irrelevant to the demonstration. Option (5) is incorrect

because the diagram does not show any negative effect on the bell jar of the pistol firing.

27. **(5) The ejected gases pushed the pistol backward in the vacuum chamber.** (Evaluation) Goddard used the pistol in a vacuum chamber as a stand-in for a rocket in space. Just as the pistol moves when the ejected gas pushes on it, a rocket moves when its ejected gas pushes on the rocket. Options (1), (3), and (4) are all true, but they do not explain why a rocket moves in the vacuum of space. Option (2) is incorrect because only one pistol was hung in the vacuum chamber; the "second" pistol in the diagram is an image of the movement of the "first" pistol.

28. **(4) Between 1950 and 1999, per person energy consumption increased.** (Analysis) The graph's trend line was generally upward from 1950 to 1999, indicating that per person energy consumption generally increased during this period. Options (1), (2), (3), and (5) are all details from the graph, not general conclusions based on the graph.

29. **(3) The heat did not kill all the microorganisms in the gravy and the bottle.** (Evaluation) It is likely that the scientist did not apply enough heat long enough to kill all the microorganisms in the gravy and the bottle, and so they multiplied over the few days during which he left the gravy bottled. Option (1) is not true; gravy would provide lots of nutrients for microorganisms. Option (2) would have been true, but the answer is incorrect; scientist found the microorganisms in the gravy, not on the outside of the bottle. Option (4) is incorrect because the longer the gravy was left in the bottle, the more microorganisms there would probably be. Option (5) is incorrect because the gravy was swarming with microorganisms. Because there were so many, it is unlikely that the gravy was sterile before being placed under the microscope; it is highly unlikely that a large number of microorganisms would quickly drop from the surface of the microscope into the gravy.

30. **(1) Farmland is abandoned, grasses and shrubs move in, and eventually the area becomes forested.** (Application) This is an example of ecological succession that has taken place in large portions of the eastern United States over the last century or so. Options (2) and (3) are incorrect because they describe two stable ecosystems, the tundra and tropical grasslands. The changes in these ecosystems are regular and seasonal. Option (4) is incorrect because an intertidal zone is stable; the changes it experiences happen daily. Option (5) is not an

example of ecological succession because it is not a gradual change.

31. **(4) decreasing the amount of light that reaches the film** (Analysis) In the second diagram, the diameter of the aperture is half that of the first diagram. In the second diagram, fewer rays of light are entering the camera and hitting the film. Options (1), (2), and (3) are incorrect because they are the function of other parts of the camera, not of the aperture. Option (5) is incorrect because the light rays are concentrated; they are not spread out, and focusing the light rays is a function of the lens, not of the aperture.

32. **(5) Global Wind Patterns** (Comprehension) The map shows surface wind patterns that prevail over the globe, so this is a good, comprehensive title for the map. Options (1) and (3) are incorrect because they are too specific to be good titles: they focus on two of the prevailing winds. Although high and low pressure zones are shown, those are not the main focus of the map, so Option (2) is incorrect. Option (4) is too general to be a good title; even though the continents of the Western Hemisphere are shown on the map, the point of the map is to show wind patterns, not half the world.

33. **(2) a sailor making preliminary plans for an around-the-world trip** (Application) A person who is traveling around the world in a sailboat would want to take advantage of the prevailing wind patterns in planning his or her route. Option (1) is incorrect because polar explorers are concerned with local weather conditions, not prevailing winds. Option (3) is incorrect because an astronaut orbiting above the atmosphere is not concerned about surface wind patterns. Option (4) is incorrect because the map does not give wind speed, only wind direction; a meteorologist would have to use an anemometer to measure wind speed in a particular area on a given day to make an accurate prediction about wind speed. Option (5) is incorrect because prevailing wind patterns do not provide evidence for ancient climates.

34. **(4) if the mother moved closer to the fulcrum** (Analysis) The diagram shows that the boy is able to lift his mother only after she has moved a certain distance closer to the fulcrum. You can infer from this that, as the mother gets closer to the fulcrum, the boy will be able to lift the mother higher. Option (1) is incorrect because the boy's effort would have less effect the closer he is to the fulcrum and the mother would drop. Option (2) is incorrect because the boy's effort would be much less if he were not on the seesaw; when he sits on the seesaw, he pushes down with his body, instead of only his arms.

Option (3) is incorrect because more effort would be required to lift the mother if she moved away from the fulcrum. Option (5) is incorrect because the mother would drop if both moved toward the fulcrum.

35. **(4) Take a battery-operated alarm clock, which runs on DC and contains its own power source.** (Application) Option (1) is incorrect because her plug-in alarm clock operates on AC, not on DC. Option (2) is incorrect because America and Europe use different cycles of AC, as the paragraph indicates. Option (3) is incorrect because batteries produce DC, not AC. Option (5) is incorrect because battery-operated American-made clocks will operate anywhere.

36. **(1) a badger** (Application) Of all the animals listed, the badger is the only vertebrate, and myelin-coated neurons are most common in vertebrates. The remaining options are incorrect because these are invertebrates, which are less likely to have myelin-coated nerve cells.

37. **(1) The population of a species, such as water fleas, increases until the carrying capacity of the ecosystem is exceeded, and then it falls.** (Comprehension) Of all the options, this one covers the main points of the information in the paragraph and diagram comprehensively. Option (2) is incorrect because the idea of carrying capacity is omitted. Option (3) is not true; according to the graph, the population rises and falls. Option (4) is not true; the graph shows that the carrying capacity remains stable. Option (5) is not true; the population of water fleas is dependent on the carrying capacity of the ecosystem, not vice versa.

38. **(3) The development of convergent structures occurs gradually, over millions of years.** (Analysis) The author of the paragraph takes for granted that the reader knows that the evolution of convergent structures takes a long time. Options (1), (2), (4), and (5) are all incorrect because they are actually stated in the paragraph and thus are not unstated assumptions.

39. **(1) A water molecule consists of two atoms of hydrogen and one atom of oxygen.** (Comprehension) This option restates in words what is shown by the three symbolic representations of water. Option (2) is true, but it is incorrect because it is not specific; a water molecule is made up of specific types of atoms. Options (3) and (4) are true, but they are incorrect because they do not restate the information; they are details. Option (5) is incorrect because the diagram does not indicate anything about state of matter, and because water can exist in any of the three states, depending on temperature, as can hydrogen and oxygen.

40. **(1) planning aircraft flight paths over populated areas** (Application) The disturbance created by sonic booms, and the noise produced by aircraft engines, have to be taken into account when flight paths are mapped over areas that are populated. Option (2) is incorrect because distance traveled is unrelated to the sounds and sonic booms of aircraft. Options (3) and (4) are incorrect because sounds and sonic booms are not relevant to learning to operate a plane. Option (5) is incorrect because sound waves and sonic booms are not related to the price of airplane tickets.

41. **(5) Eating irradiated foods can be harmful to people's health.** (Analysis) According to the paragraph, this is a belief held by some people; it is not a fact. All of the remaining options are facts stated in the paragraph.

42. **(5) the organ system** (Comprehension) The organ system, the highest level of organization shown, is the most complex because it is made of cells, tissues, and organs. Option (1) is incorrect; the cell nucleus is part of the cell and not considered a separate level of organization. Options (2), (3), and (4) are incorrect because they are less complex levels of organization than the skeletal system.

43. **(2) They are opposite processes.** (Analysis) The products of photosynthesis are the raw materials of cellular respiration, and vice versa, so you can think of these two processes as being opposite of one another, helping to keep the biosphere in balance. Option (1) is not true; they are very different processes in their inputs and outputs. Options (3) and (4) are incorrect because neither photosynthesis nor cellular respiration is a category that includes the other. Option (5) is not true; while energy is a product of cellular respiration, it is a necessary input for photosynthesis.

44. **(3) The woman's blood alcohol level would be higher than the man's.** (Analysis) Because the woman weighs less than the man, her body is smaller and she has less blood. Therefore the concentration of alcohol in her blood would be higher than the concentration of alcohol in the man's blood, even though they have drunk the same amount. Options (1), (2), and (5) are incorrect because the woman weighs less than the man and therefore her blood alcohol level would be higher. Option (4) is incorrect because no one has a blood alcohol level of zero after two shots of bourbon whiskey.

45. **(3) Alcohol affects both conscious behavior and normal body functions.** (Evaluation) According to the chart, alcohol affects behavior that is under conscious control (such as judgment and inhibition), as well as normal body functions (like eyesight and hearing), and eventually the functions necessary for life—breathing and heartbeat. Options (1) and (2) are true, but they are not correct choices because no information is given about alcoholism as a disease or about the long-term effects of alcohol. Option (4) is incorrect because death results at 0.65 percent blood alcohol content. Option (5) is incorrect because no information is given about legal issues regarding alcohol use; (in some states this option may be true, but legal levels of blood alcohol vary from state to state).

46. **(2) The amount of matter is the same before and after a chemical reaction.** (Evaluation) This is a statement of the law of conservation of matter. It is proved by the fact that the bell jar weighs the same before and after the candle burned. Option (1) may be true of some candles, but it is not supported by the information in the passage. Option (3) is not true for two reasons: first, oxygen is also needed to form water and carbon dioxide; second, carbon and hydrogen can form many other compounds, such as methane and other hydrocarbons. Option (4) is not supported by the data from the experiment; the jar did not explode. Option (5) is true but not supported by the information given.

47. **(1) The substances with the lowest condensing points rise to the top of the tower.** (Evaluation) According to the diagram, the hot crude oil vapor enters near the base of the distillation tower and most of it then rises. As it rises it cools, and various products separate out at their condensation points. Option (2) is not true; gasoline condenses at a lower temperature than heating oil. Option (3) is incorrect because the crude oil enters near the base of the tower. Option (4) is incorrect because kerosene separates out below 250°C. Option (5) is incorrect because crude oil is the raw material of fractional distillation, not the end product.

48. **(3) It tapped into patriotic feelings about beating the Soviet Union in space exploration.** (Evaluation) The paragraph indicates that competition with the Soviet Union over space technologies spurred the United States to step up its efforts to explore space. The space race, as it was called, motivated Americans to develop the technology to land human astronauts on the moon in less than a decade. Options (1) and (2) are incorrect because the source of NASA's public support did not have to do with economic issues like efficiency of

government spending and employment for
engineers. Option (4) is incorrect because the
Apollo program was not "research for the sake
of research." It was a practical, goal-oriented
project. Option (5) is true, but this option is
incorrect because during the 1960s the public
did not anticipate that many new products and
technologies developed by the Apollo program
would have applications in ordinary life.

49. **(5) The genes responsible for some traits
can produce different phenotypes under
different environmental conditions.**
(Analysis) This is a conclusion, a generalization,
rather than a detail. All the remaining options
are details given in the paragraph; they are
elements of the example chosen to support
the generalization about the effect of the
environment on phenotypes for some traits.

50. **(2) A hollyhock, which grows leaves in
spring and summer, dies back in winter,
flowers and sets seed the following
summer, and dies in the fall.** (Application)
According to the information, biennials grow
without flowering the first season; the second
season, they flower, produce seeds, and then die.
The hollyhock, described in option (2), is the
only one of the plants that follows this pattern.
Option (1) is incorrect because the petunia
follows the pattern of an annual. Options (3), (4),
and (5) all describe plants that do not die after
the second growing season; they live for a
number of years and are neither annuals nor
biennials, but perennials.

Glossary

acceleration any change in the speed or direction of motion of an object

acid a substance with a pH less than 7.0 that releases hydrogen ions in a water solution; for example, vinegar

acid rain rain that is highly acidic because of sulfur oxides, nitrogen oxides, and other air pollutants dissolved in it; can damage plant and animal life

activation energy the energy that must be added to start a chemical reaction

adaptation a process that helps an organism survive and function in its environment

adequacy being satisfactory; being sufficient for the purpose

air mass a large body of air that has the same temperature and moisture throughout

alimentary canal the tube that makes up the digestive system

alveoli small air sacs in the lungs at the end of bronchioles where oxygen passes into the blood and carbon dioxide is released from the blood

amplitude the distance between the rest position and crest of a wave

antibodies substances produced by the body's immune system that fight disease

aorta a large artery that carries oxygen-rich blood from the heart to other parts of the body

applying ideas taking information learned in one set of circumstances and using it in another situation

artery a blood vessel that carries blood away from the heart

assess to determine the importance, adequacy, or significance of something

asteroid a small celestial body, sometimes called a minor planet, that revolves around the sun

atmosphere the layers of gases that surround Earth

atom the smallest particle of an element that has all the properties of that element

atomic mass the total number of protons and neutrons in the nucleus of an element

atomic number the number of protons in the nucleus of an element

atrium one of the upper chambers of the heart (plural, *atria*)

base a substance with a pH greater than 7.0 that releases hydroxide ions in a water solution; for example, milk of magnesia

big bang the explosion in which the universe began

biomass the total mass of the living organisms in a particular place

boiling point the temperature at which a liquid changes into a gas

bosons force-carrying subatomic particles

brain stem the part of the human brain that controls automatic functions such as breathing and heartbeat

bronchi the two tubes that lead from the trachea into each of the lungs

bronchioles tubes branching off the bronchi in the lungs and ending in alveoli

capillaries very small blood vessels

carbohydrate an organic compound of carbon, oxygen, and hydrogen that is part of many foods; for example, sugars and starch

carbon-oxygen cycle the continuous circulation of carbon and oxygen through the biosphere primarily through the processes of photosynthesis, respiration, and decomposition

carnivore an animal that eats only other animals

cause something that makes something else (an effect) happen

cause-and-effect relationship a situation in which one thing (a cause) results in another (an effect)

cell the smallest unit of life that can exist independently and that makes up all living organisms

cell membrane thin layer of matter enclosing a cell

cellular respiration the chemical process requiring oxygen by which living things convert food to energy

cerebellum the part of the human brain that controls movement, coordination, and balance; located below the cerebrum at the base of the skull

cerebrum the largest part of the human brain, which coordinates all higher functions such as perception, thinking, and conscious activity

chemical equation a grouping of formulas and symbols that shows what happens in a chemical reaction

chemical formula the representation of an element, ion, molecule, or compound by symbols (letters and numbers); for example: oxygen is written O_2, carbon dioxide is written CO_2, hydroxide is written OH^-

chemical reaction a change in which atoms of one or more substances form one or more new substances with different chemical and physical properties; may be exothermic or endothermic

chromatin the part of a cell's nucleus that contains genetic information

chromosome a part of a cell that contains genetic information, encoded in DNA

circular argument a form of faulty logic in which a conclusion is supported by reasons that simply restate the conclusion

circulatory system the system, consisting of the heart, blood vessels, and blood, that carries nutrients and oxygen to the body's tissues and removes carbon dioxide and waste products

climate average weather conditions in a particular region over a long period of time

coal a solid fossil fuel

colloid a mixture in which fine particles are spread out throughout a second substance; for example, foam

compare to identify how things are alike

compound a substance formed by the chemical combination of two or more elements in which each loses its identity and the new substance has properties different from these original elements; for example, water is a compound of hydrogen and oxygen

conclusion a logical result or generalization

condensation the change of a gas into a liquid

condense to change from a gas to a liquid; for example, from steam to water

conductor a substance through which electric current flows easily

consumers organisms in a food chain that get their food energy by eating other organisms

context the situation within which something is said or done

contrast to identify how things are different

convection current in Earth science, the flow of heated mantle rock upward into the crust and of cooled crust downward into the mantle

covalent bond a chemical combination of two or more atoms in which pairs of electrons are shared

crest the high point of a wave

crust the outer layer of Earth, including Earth's surface

cytoplasm in a cell, the jellylike matter that surrounds the nucleus and contains cell structures (called *organelles*) that carry out the cell's activities

daughter cells the cells produced as a result of cell division, each identical to the parent cell

decomposer in a food chain, an organism that breaks down dead plants and animals; for example, certain bacteria and fungi

denitrification the process by which certain bacteria in the soil change nitrates into gaseous nitrogen, returning it to the air

density a measure of mass in relation to volume

diffusion movement of a substance from a region of higher concentration to a region of lower concentration

digestive system the system of the body that breaks food down into nutrients the body can use and expels leftover wastes

DNA the molecule that contains hereditary information and controls the activities of each cell; found in chromosomes

dominant trait a trait that will appear in an offspring if one parent contributes it; dominant traits suppress recessive traits

drag the force slowing or stopping the movement of an object through a gas or liquid

earthquake the shaking and trembling that results from sudden movements of rock deep within Earth

ecology a field of life science that involves the study of the relationships of organisms to their environments and to one another

ecosystem a community of organisms in its physical environment; for example, a swamp

effect something that happens because something else happened (a cause)

effort a force applied to an object

egg cell the female reproductive cell; also called the *ovum*

either-or error a form of faulty logic in which only two choices are presented although other choices also exist

electric circuit a continuous pathway over which electric current can flow

electric current the flow of charged particles, often electrons

electric field the area of force that surrounds a charged particle

electromagnetic radiation the wave motion of alternating electric and magnetic fields

electromagnetic spectrum the entire range of electromagnetic waves from those with long wavelengths (radio waves) to those with short wavelengths (gamma waves)

electromagnetism the relationship between electricity and magnetism

electron a negatively charged particle that revolves around the nucleus of an atom

element a substance that cannot be broken down into simpler substances by chemical means; for example, carbon

endocrine system the body system made up of endocrine glands; these glands secrete hormones into the bloodstream to regulate body processes

endothermic reaction a chemical reaction that absorbs energy

energy the ability to do work

enzyme a protein that speeds up chemical reactions that take place in cells

epicenter the point on Earth's surface directly above the focus of an earthquake

erosion the gradual wearing away and moving of rock, soil, and sand along Earth's surface

evaluate to examine something in order to judge its significance

evaporate to change from a liquid to a gas; for example, from water to water vapor

evolution change over time; usually refers to the development of new species over time

exothermic reaction a chemical reaction that releases energy

fact something real that can be proved true

fault a break in Earth's crust

faulty logic errors in reasoning

fermentation a type of cellular respiration not requiring oxygen, in which food is broken down into carbon dioxide and alcohol, with the release of energy

focus in Earth science, the point beneath Earth's surface where rocks break and move to start an earthquake

food chain the transfer of energy from one organism to the next, each organism consuming the previous one

food web the complex pattern of energy transfer in an ecosystem; consists of many interrelated food chains

force a push or pull acting on an object; for example, friction

fossil the preserved remains or imprint of a once-living thing

fossil fuel a source of energy formed over long periods of time from the remains of plants and animals; coal, oil, and natural gas are all fossil fuels

freezing point the temperature at which a liquid changes to a solid

frequency the number of waves that pass a given point in a given amount of time

friction a force that slows down or prevents motion

front the boundary between two air masses

galaxy a group of millions or billions of stars; for example, the Milky Way

gas the state of matter that has no definite shape or volume; for example, the air

gene a part of the genetic molecule DNA that determines a particular trait

genetics the study of inherited characteristics

genome all the genetic information about a single individual or species as coded by the DNA that makes up its chromosomes

genotype the genetic makeup of an individual organism

glacier a large mass of moving ice

global warming the trend toward higher average temperatures on Earth's surface

gravity the force of attraction that exists between all objects in the universe

habitat the place in which an organism usually lives

half-life the time needed for half the nuclei in a sample of radioactive material to decay into another substance by giving off nuclear particles or energy

hasty generalization a form of faulty logic in which a conclusion is based on insufficient evidence

hemisphere half a sphere. In life science, usually refers to the right and left hemispheres, or halves, of the brain; in Earth science, usually refers to half a planet or moon

herbicide a chemical that kills plants

herbivore an animal that eats only plants

homologous structures body parts from different organisms with a common genetic heritage that have similar structure but perform different functions; for example, a bird's wing and a human's arm

hormone a substance that is secreted into the bloodstream by endocrine glands

hurricane a large tropical storm with average wind speeds of at least 74 miles per hour

hybrid an organism that carries both the dominant and recessive versions of a particular trait

hydrocarbon any organic compound that contains only the elements hydrogen and carbon

igneous rock a type of rock formed when hot liquid rock cools; for example, granite

immune system the body system that provides protection against disease

implication a fact or idea that is suggested by stated information

imply to suggest something without actually stating it

incomplete dominance a pattern of inheritance in which a trait appears as a blend when dominant and recessive versions of it are inherited

inertia the tendency of an object to keep moving or remain at rest

infer to figure out something that is suggested by stated information

inference a fact or idea that you figure out based on stated information

inner core the solid iron and nickel center of Earth

insulator a material that resists the flow of electric current

ion an atom that has taken on a negative or positive charge by gaining or losing electrons

ionic bond the bond between two or more ions (atoms in which one or more electrons have been gained or lost)

isomers compounds that have the same number and types of atoms (and thus the same chemical formula) but a different arrangement of atoms and different properties

joint the place where one bone meets another

kinetic energy the energy of an object in motion

lava magma, or molten rock, that breaks through Earth's surface in a volcanic eruption

liquid the state of matter that has definite volume but no definite shape; for example, water at room temperature

load an object to which force is being applied

longitudinal wave a wave that pushes and pulls molecules back and forth parallel to its direction of travel; for example, sound waves

magma hot liquid rock beneath Earth's surface

main idea the central topic of a paragraph, passage, or diagram

mantle a layer of Earth below the crust

mass the amount of matter an object contains

matter anything that has mass and takes up space

melting point the temperature at which a solid changes into a liquid

metabolism all the chemical processes taking place in a living organism

metamorphic rock a type of rock formed when rock is subject to extreme heat or pressure; for example, marble

metamorphosis the process by which the immature form of an organism turns into a very different adult form; for example, caterpillars metamorphose into moths or butterflies

Milky Way the spiral galaxy in which our sun is located

mitosis the process by which a cell nucleus divides during cell division to form two daughter nuclei identical to the parent nucleus

mixture a mechanical combination of substances in which each substance keeps its own properties; for example, gravel, air, and mayonnaise

molecule a group of atoms that are held together by covalent or ionic bonds

momentum an object's mass multiplied by its velocity, or speed in a straight line

mutation a change in an organism's DNA that causes a change in an inherited characteristic

natural gas a gaseous fossil fuel

natural selection the process by which individuals having characteristics that help them adapt to their environment are more likely to survive, reproduce, and pass these characteristics to their offspring

nervous system the communications and control system of an organism consisting of interconnecting nerve cells

neuron a nerve cell, the basic unit of the nervous system

neurotransmitter a chemical involved in communication between neurons or between a neuron and a muscle

neutron an uncharged particle that forms part of the nucleus of an atom

Newton's First Law of Motion a law developed by Newton stating that objects at rest tend to stay at rest, and objects in motion tend to stay in motion unless they are acted upon by an outside force

Newton's Second Law of Motion a law developed by Newton stating that objects will accelerate in the direction of the force that acts upon them; mass and force will affect the rate and direction of acceleration

Newton's Third Law of Motion a law developed by Newton stating that if one object exerts a force on another object, the second object exerts an equal and opposite force on the first object

nitrification the process by which bacteria convert nitrogen in the soil to ammonia, nitrite, and nitrate, a form of nitrogen that plants can use

nitrogen cycle the continuous circulation of nitrogen through the biosphere primarily through the action of bacteria, precipitation, and decomposition

nitrogen fixation a process by which certain bacteria take nitrogen from the atmosphere and combine it with other substances into a form plants can use

nonrenewable resource a resource that cannot be replaced once it is used up; for example, coal

nuclear fission the splitting of an atomic nucleus into two smaller nuclei and two or three neutrons, releasing large amounts of energy

nuclear membrane in a cell, the layer of matter that separates the nucleus from the cytoplasm

nuclear power plant a facility that generates electricity by using radioactive fuel, which explodes in a nuclear chain reaction

nucleus in life science, the part of a cell that controls the cell's activities; in physical science, an atom's small, dense core, which consists of protons and neutrons

nutrient a substance, found in food, that is necessary for the growth and health of an organism; for example, proteins, carbohydrates, fats, minerals, and vitamins

omnivore an animal that eats both plants and other animals

opinion a belief that may or may not be true

orbit the path taken by a planet or moon around the focus of the system to which it belongs; for example, Earth's orbit around the sun.

organ a group of different tissues that work together to perform a specific function or functions

organelle a structure within a cell that performs a specific function to keep the cell alive; for example, a mitochondrion

organic molecule a molecule that contains carbon combined with nitrogen, hydrogen, or oxygen; the building block of all living organisms

organism a living being

osmosis diffusion of a solvent, often water, through a semipermeable membrane until its concentration is equal on both sides of the membrane

outer core the layer of Earth between the mantle and the inner core

oversimplification a form of faulty logic in which something is simplified so much that it becomes incorrect

oxidation a reaction in which an element loses electrons; often in oxidation, the element reacts with oxygen; for example, iron reacts with oxygen to form iron oxide (rust)

parent cell the cell undergoing mitosis and cell division

particle accelerator a long, narrow tunnel, charged with electric and magnetic fields, used to accelerate and collide particles to release energy and create new particles

periodic table an arrangement of the elements according to their properties and atomic number

petroleum a liquid fossil fuel; also called *oil*

phenotype in genetics, the observable physical characteristics of an individual organism

photosynthesis the chemical process by which green plants convert water and carbon dioxide into food and oxygen using energy absorbed from sunlight or other light

pH scale range of numbers from 0 to 14 that indicates the relative acidic or basic character of a solution: 7 indicates a neutral solution; numbers lower than 7 indicate an acid; numbers higher than 7 indicate a base

planet a large celestial body that revolves around a star; for example, Earth and Jupiter

plate tectonics a theory that explains how Earth's crust is formed, changes over time, and is destroyed

population a group of organisms of the same species that live in the same area

population density the number of people who live in a specific area

potential energy energy stored in the position of an object at rest

predator an animal that gets its food by hunting and killing it

producers organisms in a food chain that produce their own food, usually through photosynthesis

product a substance formed as a result of a chemical reaction

proton a particle with a positive charge that forms part of the nucleus of an atom

purebred in genetics, an organism that when bred always produces the same trait in its offspring

quarks subatomic particles that make up protons and neutrons

radioactivity a property of some elements that involves giving off particles or energy from the nucleus until a more stable element is produced

reactant a substance that is an ingredient of a chemical reaction

recessive trait a trait that does not appear when combined with a dominant trait, and that must be contributed by both parents in order to appear in an offspring; that is, a trait that appears in the genotype but not in the phenotype

reflection the bouncing of light, or other waves, off a surface

reflex a rapid, automatic response to a condition in an organism's environment; for example, squinting in strong light

renewable resource a resource that can be replaced; for example, trees

resistance a force that opposes or slows motion; in reference to electricity, the opposition a material offers to the free flow of electric current

resources the things organisms need to live, such as water, food, and energy

respiratory system the system of the body involved in exchanging oxygen for carbon dioxide

restate information to say something in another way

revolve to move in a circular or elliptical path around a central object; for example, Earth revolves around the sun

ribosome a part of a cell that has a role in making proteins

Richter scale a measure of the amount of energy released by an earthquake; the Richter scale starts at 0 and although it has no upper limit, no earthquake recorded has measured stronger than 9

rotate to turn on its own central axis

salt a neutral compound with a pH of 7.0 that results from the chemical combination of an acid and a base; for example, sodium chloride (table salt)

sea floor spreading the movement of sea floor crust away from the mid-ocean ridges, where new crust is pushing up from the mantle

sedimentary rock a type of rock formed by the hardening of particles of sand, mud, clay, or other sediments; for example, sandstone

seismic waves vibrations caused by movement of rock during an earthquake

senses the means by which animals get information about their environment: sight, hearing, taste, touch, and smell

sexual reproduction a form of reproduction in which genetic material from two parents is combined in the offspring

solar system the sun and all the planets, moons, and other objects that orbit the sun

solid a form of matter that has definite shape and volume; for example, a brick

solute the substance being dissolved in a solution; for example, the salt in salt water

solution a mixture in which one or more substances are dissolved in another; for example, salt water

solvent the substance doing the dissolving in a solution; for example, the water in salt water

species a group of genetically similar organisms that can mate and produce fertile offspring; for example, dogs

static electricity an electrical discharge resulting from the build-up of charge on an insulated body

stimulus anything in the environment that influences the nervous system; for example, the sight of a snake or the smell of coffee

structural formula a diagram using symbols representing the arrangement of atoms in a molecule

subatomic particles particles smaller than protons, neutrons, and electrons; also called *elementary particles*

summarize to tell briefly the important points

supporting details observations, measurements, and other facts that back up a conclusion

synapse the space between two neurons or between a neuron and a muscle across which nerve impulses are transmitted

tectonic plates large fragments of Earth's crust and upper mantle that fit together like pieces of a puzzle

tissue a group of similar cells that have a similar function; for example, muscle tissue

trachea the tube through which air passes from the back of the mouth to the lungs; also called the *windpipe*

trait a characteristic of an organism, often inherited; for example, brown eyes

transverse wave a wave in which the disturbance is at right angles to the direction of the wave's travel; for example, light waves

trophic level in a food chain, the position occupied by each species

trough the low point of a wave

unstated assumption a fact or idea that is taken for granted and not actually stated

vaccine a substance given to produce immunity to a disease without producing the symptoms of the disease

value a belief that is prized as extremely important

vaporization the change of a liquid to a gas

vein a blood vessel that carries blood toward the heart

velocity the rate of motion of an object in a certain direction

ventricle one of the lower chambers of the heart

virus a single molecule of genetic material surrounded by a coat of protein

volcano a place where magma breaks through Earth's surface

volt unit of measure of the voltage of an electric current

voltage the energy needed to move an electron or other charged particle, measured in volts

volume the amount of space taken up by a substance or object

water cycle the continuous movement of water from Earth's surface to the air, and back to the surface again

wave a disturbance that travels through space or matter; for example, radio waves

wavelength the distance between the crests of two consecutive waves

weather the state of the atmosphere at any given time with respect to temperature, moisture, wind direction and velocity, and air pressure

weathering the process by which large rocks are broken down in place into smaller rocks; may be chemical or mechanical

wind moving air

work the result of a force moving an object over a distance

Index

Answer Sheet

GED Science Test

Name: _____ Class: _____ Date: _____

○ Pretest   ○ Posttest   ○ Simulated Test

1 ① ② ③ ④ ⑤	11 ① ② ③ ④ ⑤	21 ① ② ③ ④ ⑤	31 ① ② ③ ④ ⑤	41 ① ② ③ ④ ⑤
2 ① ② ③ ④ ⑤	12 ① ② ③ ④ ⑤	22 ① ② ③ ④ ⑤	32 ① ② ③ ④ ⑤	42 ① ② ③ ④ ⑤
3 ① ② ③ ④ ⑤	13 ① ② ③ ④ ⑤	23 ① ② ③ ④ ⑤	33 ① ② ③ ④ ⑤	43 ① ② ③ ④ ⑤
4 ① ② ③ ④ ⑤	14 ① ② ③ ④ ⑤	24 ① ② ③ ④ ⑤	34 ① ② ③ ④ ⑤	44 ① ② ③ ④ ⑤
5 ① ② ③ ④ ⑤	15 ① ② ③ ④ ⑤	25 ① ② ③ ④ ⑤	35 ① ② ③ ④ ⑤	45 ① ② ③ ④ ⑤
6 ① ② ③ ④ ⑤	16 ① ② ③ ④ ⑤	26 ① ② ③ ④ ⑤	36 ① ② ③ ④ ⑤	46 ① ② ③ ④ ⑤
7 ① ② ③ ④ ⑤	17 ① ② ③ ④ ⑤	27 ① ② ③ ④ ⑤	37 ① ② ③ ④ ⑤	47 ① ② ③ ④ ⑤
8 ① ② ③ ④ ⑤	18 ① ② ③ ④ ⑤	28 ① ② ③ ④ ⑤	38 ① ② ③ ④ ⑤	48 ① ② ③ ④ ⑤
9 ① ② ③ ④ ⑤	19 ① ② ③ ④ ⑤	29 ① ② ③ ④ ⑤	39 ① ② ③ ④ ⑤	49 ① ② ③ ④ ⑤
10 ① ② ③ ④ ⑤	20 ① ② ③ ④ ⑤	30 ① ② ③ ④ ⑤	40 ① ② ③ ④ ⑤	50 ① ② ③ ④ ⑤